RENEWAL OF RELIGIOUS THOUGHT

THEOLOGY OF RENEWAL

VOLUME 1

RENEWAL OF
RELIGIOUS THOUGHT

Proceedings of the Congress on the
Theology of the Renewal of the Church
Centenary of Canada, 1867–1967

Introduction by
PAUL-ÉMILE CARDINAL LÉGER

Edited by
L. K. SHOOK, C.S.B.

HERDER AND HERDER

1968
HERDER AND HERDER NEW YORK
232 Madison Avenue, New York 10016

Contents

Vatican City, February 27, 1967

His Excellency
The Most Reverend Philip F. Pocock, D.D.
Archbishop of Toronto
55 Gould Street
Toronto 2, Ontario
Canada

Your Excellency,

With cordial satisfaction has the sovereign pontiff learned that, from the 20th to the 25th of August next, there will be held in Toronto a great theological congress and institute, with the intent of studying some of the major religious problems of our time. Particularly deserving of the attention and approval of the Holy Father is the fact that the congress, taking inspiration from the decrees of the Second Vatican Ecumenical Council, has chosen as its theme "The Theology of the Renewal of the Church."

The prestige and interest which the timeliness and dignity of its subject confer on the congress are augmented even more by the purpose assigned to it, namely, that of exalting the Centenary of the Confederation of Canada, in such a way that the congress will have not merely a national, but also an international character.

This is, then, an event of exceptional religious and national importance, attracting the attention of all the citizens of Canada, and giving to all those who are willing and able a good occasion to deepen and extend their religious knowledge, while also acquiring, by the light of Christian faith, a more intimate and salutary experience of the mystery of salvation.

The Holy Father also obtained sincere pleasure from the knowledge that the initiative of holding this congress is due to the most reverend hierarchy of Canada. This is not only to their great credit; it is also a happy augury for a serene and fruitful discussion; and hopeful expectation derives also from the fact that its organization has been entrusted to the famed and meritorious Pontifical Institute of Mediaeval Studies, assisted by a national coordinating committee.

Even a rapid glance at the themes of the conference suffices to show at once the intimate connection deliberately established between its central theme, "Theology of the Renewal of the Church," and the acts of the Second Vatican Ecumenical Council. In fact, the renewal of the life of the Church will be studied in all its aspects—doctrine, structure, worship, apostolic activity, discipline, relationship with the modern world, and even the media of social communication which divine Providence and human progress have placed at the Church's disposal in our century, in order to render more rapid and efficacious the fulfilment of that mission of salvation which our Redeemer, before his ascension into heaven, entrusted to his apostles, and to their successors and collaborators.

It is well known that the history of the evangelization of the world, even though, by the power of the divine Spirit, it has renewed the spiritual face of the earth (See Ps. 103, 30), has not constituted a peaceful triumph. Even in recent years the Church, despite the marvellous proofs she has given of her unity, her holiness, her catholicity, and her apostolicity, has been deeply affected by the vicissitudes of world history, since in that world must all her children live. Changes and advances of every kind—social, economic, political, philosophical, scientific, and cultural—have undoubtedly conferred great benefits even on the People of God. Nevertheless, there have been and still are serious shadows and gaps in human civilization, and hence there have been deplorable influences and spiritual damage in the minds and customs of the faithful. It is not

8

strange, therefore, that the shepherds of Christ's flock, with the sovereign pontiffs at their head, adverted to the need for a general renewal and fitting adaptation of the Church's life to the spiritual needs of our era.

In the noble desire of making the Spouse of Christ more worthy of her divine Founder, and better equipped for her work of universal salvation, Popes Pius XI and Pius XII both considered the idea of a new ecumenical council, to complete the doctrinal programme of the First Vatican Council, and also to initiate the plan of pastoral reform which that assembly had been impeded from considering. The truly providential idea of a twenty-first ecumenical council, eagerly welcomed by Pope John XXIII, was put into effect by him in times more propitious for the life of the Church; he carefully prepared it and presided over its first session.

It may well be said that the conciliar assemblies were the most eloquent and far-reaching expression of that consciousness, always nourished by the Church, of the continual need of reform and renewal. Indeed, this necessity is, as it were, consubstantial to her, since, being a living organism—though in pilgrimage on this earth, and capable, with the grace of God, of development and progress—she is also subject, because of her human condition, aggravated by the consequences of original sin, to phenomena of change, weakening, and regress. Those same biblical images used in the dogmatic constitution *Lumen gentium* to describe the life of the Church, calling her the Fold, the Field, the Family, the Building of God composed of living stones, the Spouse, and Body of Christ, suggest ideas of life, flowering, and expansion. On the other hand, those very images remind us that snares and dangers of every kind, internal and external, threaten the intellectual and moral life of the People of God, and can provoke errors, moral deviations, damage to discipline, and dislocations in the social fabric.

The Gospel parables of the kingdom of God are, in reality, also a prophecy, and the history of the Church provides exhaustive proofs of the constant efforts of her pastors, of the Fathers and doctors of the Church, of her numerous saints, to

9

defend the spiritual integrity of the Spouse of Christ, and restore to her that flowering of holiness, beauty, and glory, which the divine Saviour merited for her by his bloody immolation (see Eph. 5, 25–26).

The work of reform and renewal, however, has not always been easy and harmonious. From her very beginnings, in fact, the Church has had to lament the rising up within her of various attempts of false reform and disturbing innovations, often induced under the specious pretext of conforming her more closely to the spirit and teaching of the Gospel, and enabling her more fully to perform her mission in the world. Our Lord himself foretold to his disciples the coming of many false prophets (see Mt. 24, 11); nor did the apostles fail to denounce their earliest appearance to the community of the believers (see Tit. 1, 10; 2 Jn. 1, 7). Numerous calls to vigilance against the propagators of harmful novelties have been issued by councils, popes, and bishops.

Since, however, the divine Redeemer instituted his Church as one and indefectible, since he promised to be with her until the consummation of the world, since he sent her from the Father the Holy Spirit of truth, the Consoler, she has ever continued with unshakeable confidence her work of spiritual renewal, reproving all those things which might alter her true physiognomy. In this way, "speaking the truth in love," she has grown up "in every way into him who is the Head, into Christ" (Eph. 4, 15).

Like the twenty ecumenical councils which preceded it but in a much vaster measure because of its predominantly pastoral character, the Second Vatican Council also intended to initiate a profound renewal in the Church of God in accordance with the aims and hopes of Pope John XXIII who, in his Allocution of December 8, 1962, at the end of the first session, declared in prophetic words: "The Ecumenical Council will truly be that new Pentecost . . . that will increase the Church's wealth of spiritual strength and extend her maternal influence and saving power to every sphere of human endeavour. Then will we see the extension of Christ's kingdom on earth, and throughout the world will re-echo more clearly, more eloquently, the good news of man's redemption; confirming the kingship of almighty God, strengthening the bonds of fraternal love among men, and establishing that peace which was promised in this world to men of good will" (*AAS*, LV 1963, pp. 39–40).

In these words of the late pontiff we see outlined, in its essential traits, the theology of the renewal which he so ardently desired. The Council marked indeed a new Pentecost for the Church insofar as its principal author was the Holy Spirit, of whom we read in the constitution *Lumen gentium:* "By the power of the Gospel, he makes the Church grow, perpetually renews her, and leads her to perfect union with her Spouse" (art. 4).

Thanks to the illuminating and stimulating guidance of the divine Paraclete, and to her assistance whom Pope John XXIII named patroness of the Council and Pope Paul VI, at the close of the third session, proclaimed Mother of the Church, there were issued constitutions, decrees, and declarations, the principal scope of which was the enrichment of the Mystical Body of Christ in truth and charity, according to the apostle's exhortation: "Be renewed in the spirit of your minds, and put on the new nature, created after the likeness of God in true righteousness and holiness" (Eph. 4, 23–24).

The work of *aggiornamento* of the Church, the programme of which was happily completed by the most imposing ecumenical assembly in the history of the Church, has been neither easy nor brief. Apart from the laborious discussions, there has been no lack of dangers and perils of doctrinal pronouncements, of reforms of cult and discipline, which would have constituted truly disquieting innovations. The new vicar of Christ, Pope Paul VI, was, however, no less desirous than his predecessor of a "new enthusiasm, a new joy and serenity of mind in the unreserved acceptance by all of the entire Christian faith," and of "the need to repudiate and guard against erroneous teaching and dangerous ideologies" (Pope John XXIII: Opening Discourse, October 11, 1962; *AAS,* LIV, 1962, pp. 791–792). In his first encyclical letter, *Ecclesiam Suam,* he had already re-

11

ferred to the Church's need of healthy renewal in order to avert the threat of "Modernism (which) is an error which is still making its appearance under various new guises, wholly inconsistent with any genuine religious expression," and to remove "the errors we see circulating in the Church itself, and to which people are exposed who have only a partial understanding of the Church and its mission, and who do not pay close enough attention to divine revelation and the Church's Christ-given authority to teach" (August 6, 1963: *AAS,* LVI, 1964, p. 618).

Under the ever more evident influence of the Spirit of truth, who was invoked each morning in the eucharistic sacrifice and in the moving prayer recited by the entire Council assembly, the sacred Synod searched "into the sacred tradition and doctrine of the Church—the treasury out of which the Church continually brings forth new things that are in harmony with the things that are old" (declaration on religious freedom *Dignitatis humanae,* art. 1). Hence the conciliar acts contain no lamentable novelties concerning doctrine, worship, discipline, the forms of apostolate, and of the Church's action in the world, such as would imply substantial reforms and innovations and give rise to the suspicion that she had fallen short in her mission of guarding faithfully the doctrine of the faith, which was entrusted to her as a divine deposit by her Founder; or that she had erred in explaining and applying it to the intellectual and moral needs of the human generation of our time (see First Vatican Council, dogmatic constitution *De fide catholica,* art. 4).

Neither can any doubt arise that the Holy Spirit, once the Council was over, has as it were diminished his assistance. No, he is present as the Soul of the Church in all her members to teach them all truth (see Jn. 16, 13). Therefore, he is present and he acts through the commissions which were set up in order that the interpretation and implementation of the documents of the Council should always and everywhere respect their spirit and their letter. He is particularly present to assist the pastors of the various communities of the faithful, since it is first of all their right and duty to promote the healthy renewal of the Christian life. Above all, he is present in the sovereign pontiff, and strengthens him with his light and the fire of his love.

In this respect, it is well to recall what the sacred Synod, confirming the clear teaching of the First Vatican Council (in its dogmatic constitution *De Ecclesia Christi,* art. 4) declared: "This religious submission of will and of mind (due to the bishops teaching in communion with the Roman pontiff) must be shown in a special way to the authentic teaching authority of the Roman pontiff, even when he is not speaking *ex cathedra.* That is, it must be shown in such a way that his supreme magisterium is acknowledged with reverence, the judgments made by him are sincerely adhered to, according to his manifest mind and will. His mind and will in the matter may be known chiefly either from the character of the documents, from his frequent repetition of the same doctrine, or from his manner of speaking" (dogmatic constitution *Lumen gentium,* art. 3).

Since, as visible head and supreme pastor of the Church, the Holy Father has more at heart than any other the re-flourishing of her life in every aspect, he nourishes the lively confidence that the theological congress and institute to be held in Toronto will also mark a glorious page in the religious history of Catholic Canada. It is indeed to be hoped that the lectures and papers to be delivered by outstanding prelates, illustrious theologians, and many other experts, will make a precious contribution to the proper understanding of the renewal of the Church, and to its prompt realization, in full concord of thought and action with the organizations named for that same purpose by the Holy See.

Everyone should, of course, be convinced that this concord of minds and hearts is of the highest importance for the progress of the Church. In order, however, that this be true progress, it is the duty of each and all to hear, even before the voice of one's own talents or of human opinions, "what the Spirit says to the Churches" (Apoc. 2, 7), through the voice of those who, enjoying "a secure charism of truth" (St. Irenaeus: *Adversus haereses,* IV, 26; *PG,* 7, 1058), preserve the Church, in the Holy Father's words, "from doctrinal, constitutional, liturgical, or disciplinary sacrifices which she cannot make without falling short of her fidelity to the truth of the Gospel and of the tradition which derives therefrom" (radio-television message to the participants in the Ecumenical Dialogue, April 13, 1966; *AAS,* LVIII, 1966, p. 390).

Let it, then, be clear to all that the theology of the renewal of the Church is not so much a light which rises from below, as rather a gift which descends "from the Father of lights, with whom there is no variation or shadow due to change" (Jas. 1, 17). That theology is a reflection of the theology of the Incarnation of the Word of God, of whom the Church is not a simple product, but the Body and the completion or "fulness of him" (Eph. 1, 23).

Wherefore the People of God also, like its Head and Prototype, must regard itself and live as a reality which is at the same time divine and human, visible and invisible, personal and communitary, institutional and free; clinging immovably to truths and laws which come from God himself, respecting those institutions of magisterium, government, and worship which have Jesus for their Author; but also taking pains to adapt the understanding, the expression, the observance, and the forms of these to the altered spiritual and social circumstances of modern times. Only in this way can a perennial springtime be promoted in that one irreplaceable tree which is the kingdom of God, born from the smallest of all seeds (see Mt. 13, 32), but today become in Christ "a kind of sacrament or sign of intimate union with God, and of the unity of all mankind" (dogmatic constitution *Lumen gentium,* art. 1).

In the consoling hope that in Canada, too, that nation so very dear to his heart, the Kingdom of God may bear ever more abundant fruits of truth and of goodness, the sovereign pontiff invokes with all his heart upon those participating in the theological congress and institute an effusion of heavenly charisms; and to all he lovingly imparts his apostolic blessing.

14

With the assurance of my personal esteem and high consideration, I remain

Devotedly yours in Christ,
A. G. Cicognani
Secretary of State

RENEWAL OF RELIGIOUS THOUGHT

INTRODUCTION

THEOLOGY OF THE RENEWAL
OF THE CHURCH

PAUL-ÉMILE CARDINAL LÉGER

THE subject of theology of renewal presents numerous difficulties. Not least among them is the continual risk of reversing the terms, and so yielding to the temptation of taking the easy way out by talking about the renewal of theology.

Well then, why do we make renewal one of the characteristics of the life of the Church? Is there not a great deal of good sense in the view the descendant of David put forward so many years ago: "I the Preacher have been king over Israel in Jerusalem. And I applied my mind to seek and to search out by wisdom all that is done under heaven; it is an unhappy business that God has given to the sons of men to be busy with."[1]

Happily, the exegetes will save the theologians once again by telling them not to take at face value this bantering malice, the product of the philosophy of a sceptical mind. We are faced here with a paradox of the Holy Spirit who uses such means to warn us never to accept the means for the end, and that in sum, our being men entails the courageous acceptance of the human condition in which God has placed us. And this condition demands that we turn our eyes with confidence towards that new heaven which was promised to us by the seer of the Apocalypse.[2] No, truthfully, when we ponder the matter we perceive that noth-

[1] Ecclesiastes 1, 12–13.
[2] See Apocalypse 21, 1.

19

ing is more foreign to the true vocation of the Church than stale custom and the debility of age. Notwithstanding the fact that it has been divinely established and that from it springs the promise of eternity, the Church can never be satisfied with its attempt to be ever more like Christ and to follow his Gospel given to mankind. To be truly faithful the Church must continually renew itself. Those who refuse to accept the renewal because they believe themselves to be faithful to the Church could endanger its real faithfulness.

Renewal is not easy to define. Not all change is renewal: a thing can change for better or for worse; one can even, in changing, alter the essentials or damage forms which have an abiding usefulness, which are, indeed, indispensable. Renewal demands that we respect what is unalterable and that we co-operate in the unfolding of the true tradition. Nonetheless, renewal is not simply a return to forms and customs of the past. It is rather what in French we call a *ressourcement,* a return to the sources in the sense that the life which gave birth to the Church must spring up ever more vigorously without endangering her own proper and unalterable nature.

Renewal tries to understand better God's revelation given once and for all to the Church, in order to put it into terms which are meaningful for the past and the present. It is a more faithful listening to the word in order that it may be proclaimed more effectively.

"In his gracious goodness," says the Council, "God has seen to it that what he has revealed for the salvation of all nations would abide perpetually in its full integrity and be handed on to all generations."[3] Renewal cannot change the word of God, nor allow any part of what has been revealed to be lost. Otherwise it could not be termed renewal, and far from revitalizing the Church, would cut it off from what is vital to its life. Renewal, in sum, must not only, under the leadership of the magisterium, respect Tradition and Scripture, it must be based upon them.

There is in the Church, more than in any other historical

[3] *Dogmatic Constitution on Divine Revelation,* art. 7.

community, a tension between fidelity to the unalterable and the necessary adaptation which life imposes. The magisterium, the servant of the word, must therefore remain in constant touch with Tradition and Scripture without ever divorcing itself from the present and the particular set of circumstances in which the Church exercises her mission. It is to witness to your attachment to this magisterium, much more than to ask me to display a competence which I do not possess in theological matters, that you have asked me to inaugurate, in my capacity as bishop, this international congress of theology. The magisterium is a guide in your reflection and a constant reminder of the ecclesial reality. It seeks to find, as do you, although in a different manner, the synthesis between what is permanent and what changes. It is its duty to maintain harmony between that which cannot change and that which must be renewed.

To fulfill this task properly, the magisterium needs you, and you need freedom. Your freedom is not only of importance, but is essential for your work. The fidelity of the theologian to the magisterium must not be interpreted as a passive obedience which excludes all initiative. Rather must it be understood in the light of different gifts bestowed by the Spirit on the Church for different functions and charisms.[4] The Council recognized that theologians had "a lawful freedom of inquiry and of thought, and the freedom to express their minds humbly and courageously about those matters in which they enjoy competence."[5] Such a freedom well understood and accompanied by sincere self-criticism will put your efforts at the service of a true renewal of the Church, and, in collaboration with the magisterium, ensure that the word of God is heard in a world which is changing constantly.

In order to clarify the sense of renewal in the Church and the practice of your essential freedom, let us seek together to discover why the Church must renew herself. I see three reasons which have provided me with three topics. The Church renews

[4] See Ephesians 4, 11 and *passim*.
[5] *Pastoral Constitution on the Church in the Modern World*, art. 62.

herself because renewal is: 1. a constant of her history; 2. a law of her life; and 3. a condition of her faithfulness.

1. God has entered into history; the Gospel is lived in time and the Church evolves in a world of change. Two thousand years of life is a relatively short time, but it is long enough to enable us to sketch an outline of the important changes which have occurred in the Church.

The Church has changed its ways of prayer many times without altering the essentials of its liturgical and sacramental life. The Latin Church, for example, prayed in Greek so long as Greek was spoken in Rome; in the Middle Ages she changed to Latin; today her liturgical languages are as diversified as the many living languages required for her expansion in the world. These changes presupposed courage and self-denial. We have had to abandon in large measure ways of expression of undeniable beauty in order not to smother, by unnecessary retention, that which they sought to express. We have had, as Father Congar said, "to be faithful to the principle in depth, and so be unfaithful to the forms which it has taken on the surface."[6] This is an example of a healthy change which was not the result of following fashion, of feebleness, or of a policy of concessions, all of these strangers to the Gospel.

Here, however, the bishop wishes to comment on these changes. These remarks are suggested by that charity which remains the supreme law of the Church of Christ.

Impatient people do not understand the slowness which seems to be impeding all the efforts of renewal, while the pusillanimous have the idea that the least change in detail undermines discipline and is even a danger for the faith. Where, then, are we going to find the true renewal? In a sincere seeking for the truth. There have always been explorers in the Church. Their presence is useful, even essential. Their vocation reminds us of that of the prophets in Israel. But the prophetic action did not, according to the design of Providence, supplant the role of the judges, the administrators, and the priests of the old covenant. In the Church prudence must inspire and balance the action of the bishops who

[6] Yves Congar, *Vraie et Fausse Réforme dans l'Eglise* (1950), p. 179.

22

have been chosen by the Holy Spirit himself to guide and sanc-
tify the people of God.[7] Impatience as well as inertia may compromise all real renewal which must, even if this involves delay
in its application, receive the approbation of the magisterium.

The Church has changed its ways of expressing the Christian
mystery through our mental categories. After the rabbinical sort
of exegesis of St. Paul and the early Fathers of the Church, after
countless confrontations with the Greek and Arab philosophers,
St. Thomas Aquinas wonderfully expressed the Christian faith
using the categories of Aristotle. We forget too easily the scandal
this genius provoked among his contemporaries. Thomas Aquinas
innovated, but his boldness merits the name of renewal because,
without losing a particle of the revealed truth, he crystallized a
whole movement in the renewal of theology in answering to the
needs of his century. It is this sort of boldness of which we have
need today.

Is this to say that a mere translation or even a transposition
of the thought of Aquinas into the modes of contemporary
thought can be considered as the substance of the renewal—a
renewal which the Church must quickly effect if it is going to
be able to answer to the questions of our contemporary world?
I do not think so. There is much more to be done than this.
What, then, must be said? The answer will be the result of your
work. For, just as the *Summa* of the Angelic Doctor is an effort
to synthesize both the secular and religious knowledge of the
Middle Ages, so the theologian in the final years of the twentieth
century must seek to harmonize our knowledge of the world of
satellites and electronic machines with the unchangeable, universal salvific will of God. I have the deepest conviction that
this effort cannot be done today by a single man, even though
he be a genius. Theologians must sooner or later work in groups
and organize laboratories of research, just as do the chemists
and the biologists who submit their hypotheses to the verification
of thousands of experiments before putting a single product on
the pharmaceutical market.

Take for example the question of the presentation of the doc-

[7] See Acts 20, 28.

trine of original sin. The theologian must take account of the findings of paleontology. And what does this new science tell us? It has pushed back the origins of man to the dim past of prehistory. We are forced to think in terms of millions rather than of the four thousand years of our little catechisms. On the other hand, the theologian must accept with respect a dogma which is based on the authenticity of the word of God. Holding onto these two links of the chain, the theologian must seek, with an effort which at times will demand heroism, to formulate the revealed truth in a way which will not contradict the findings of science. He may, in a sense, evaluate the findings of science, yet he must also respect them, because science has its own requirements and autonomy. But, on the other hand, his research must be in perfect harmony with the affirmations of the magisterium. If there was ever a case where the theologians should have recourse to the findings of the exegete it is here. But this is only one of a thousand such cases.

The Church has often changed its ways of dealing with nations. The Church of the martyrs under Nero, Domitian, or Trajan, could not suspect that there would come a day which would see the Edict of Constantine and the establishment of Christianity as the religion of the Empire. It would no doubt have thought it dangerous, as we today think it astonishing, to see Charlemagne kissing, one after another, all the steps of St. Peter's, and then entering the Basilica hand in hand with Hadrian the First. The vicissitudes of history, and even the errors of the past have given the Church and the nations some hard lessons. At the present time they are beginning to achieve a greater mutual respect in the understanding of the areas of authority, and a better understanding of freedom of the individual, especially where religion is concerned. This change in mental habits merits the name of renewal, for it applies the Gospel principles concerning the distinction of powers and the respect of conscience.

And here I must make mention of one of the most significant events of our time: the meeting of the Vicar of Jesus Christ on earth with the rulers of this world at the United Nations on

24

October 4, 1965. Pius IX resisted the kings who sought the territory of the Papal States. For him it was the way, at that moment in history, of being faithful to his role as the guardian of tradition, and in the political-sociological conditions of the time could he have acted otherwise? It is not up to us to say. But what a renewal in the attitude of a Church who now claims nothing else, nothing more, and nothing less than the liberty of proclaiming to the world the message of salvation, in its own proper role of the servant of God and the servant of humanity![8]

The Church has changed its behavior towards those who do not wholly share its faith. We are far from the time of anathemas, of the controversy over icons, and religious wars. Today the ecumenical movement discourages intransigence, condemnations, and fratricidal battles and seeks to replace them by the conversion of each to Christ, and by a common witness to the Gospel in a mutual love of truth and a profound spirit of charity. A renewal such as this may be called a revolution if we care to remember the words of Péguy: "A revolution is an appeal to a more perfect tradition."[9] I will return later to this point of such primary importance.

The Church has also gradually changed its attitude towards secular values, and has now opened herself to sources which are not ecclesial in the strict sense. More and more, as the Council says, the Christian community "realizes that it is truly and intimately linked with mankind and its history."[10] The distrust of the world and of progress—as well as an unwarranted spiritualized view of all earthly activities—appears to us today to be contrary to the spirit of the Scriptures. From the first page of Genesis, where man receives the universe as his portion, to the end of the Apocalypse, where he is promised a new heaven and a new earth, man is called on to complete the work of the Creation.

We need only a sense of history to understand that, in the

[8] See *Documentation Catholique*, 52 (1965), 1729–1738.
[9] Charles Péguy, *Cahiers de la Quinzaine, Oeuvres complètes*, XII, p. 187.
[10] *Pastoral Constitution on the Church in the Modern World*, art. 1.

past, the Church has renewed herself many times and, in the present, she is renewing herself before our eyes. It is a constant of her history. Why? Because it is a law of her life.

2. The biblical images which evoke the mystery of the Church make us see renewal as a law of her life, as much because of the normal evolution of all living beings as because of the perpetual relapses caused by human weakness and stupidity.

The grain of mustard seed develops and grows; the plant to which it gives birth renews itself without cease until it has reached perfection. The yeast in the dough stretches and extends its action until all is leavened. The spouse of Christ put all her joy into the preparations for the wedding day in order to find herself before him "without spot or wrinkle or any such thing, that she might be holy and without blemish."[11] The temple which builds itself through time, and which Christ is building constitutes, according to the words of Paul VI, "a fundamental conception of the life of the Church."[12] We do not have to destroy the Church to construct it anew in each century, but we would be wrong to believe that each one of the stones which have been put in place throughout the ages forms an integral part of its structure. We must have courage to knock down the now superfluous wall and useless tower. We must take care to see that we do not disturb the foundations or obliterate the outlines. Above all, we must understand that our duty is to know how to fit our century, like a living stone, into the spiritual edifice.

Sin in the Church makes a perpetual renewal necessary. The Church is a vine, some of whose branches do not always bear the fruit one expects; it is a field where the tares grow with the good grain; it is a net into which slip both good and bad fish; it is a gathering where the foolish virgins jostle the wise ones.[13] We must in all possible ways prune the vine, cultivate the furrows,

[11] Ephesians 5, 27.

[12] General Audience, November 16, 1966. See *Documentation Catholique* (December 4, 1966), 2039.

[13] See Matthew 21, 33–43; Isaiah 5, 1 and *passim;* Matthew 13, 24–30. 47–49; 25, 1–13.

26

again and again put down the nets into the sea, empty and refill the lamps which are going out. *Aggiornamento* is the natural state of the Church. The Fathers spoke of the *mysterium lunae:* the Church reflecting the light of Christ as the moon sends us that of the sun. The moon waxes and wanes. Our task is to renew the Church each time its light becomes less brilliant in the night of the world. "Christ summons the Church," says the Council, "as she goes on her pilgrim way, to that continual reformation of which she always has need, insofar as she is an institution of men here on earth."[14]

This situation of the Church which evolves because of the laws of life, and which must constantly be reassessed because of her weakness, is paradoxical since the Church has been established to continue forever as the great sacrament of salvation given to all men. The Church is thus at the same time made and to be remade; final and subject to change; one and divided; holy and sinful; universal and limited; apostolic and faithless. We go against the truth of Christ if we dare to say that in the Church nothing is permanent and everything is relative, as if we could continually rebuild it with new structures. It is just this paradox which makes the renewal of the Church a condition of her faithfulness. "The Church," says Newman, "must renew herself in the preservation of her type, and the continuity of her principles, with a power of assimilation, according to a logical sequence, with an anticipation of its future and a conservative action upon its past, in order to maintain its chronic vigour."[15]

3. For reform to be something more than mere change, and to become authentic renewal, we must serve the truth of the Spirit, the witness of the Spirit, and the unity of the Spirit.

(a) *The Truth of the Spirit.* Christ has told us two essential things concerning the Holy Spirit in the Church. He will "bring to your remembrance all that I have said to you,"[16] and "he will

---

[14] *Decree on Ecumenism,* art. 6.
[15] John H. Newman, *An Essay on the Development of Christian Doctrine.*
[16] John 14, 26.

27

guide you into all the truth."[17] In his book *The Mystery of Time,* Jean Moroux has an admirable echo of these words when he writes that the help of the Spirit creates at the same time in the Church both memory and prophecy.[18] When the Church takes account only of the present, she does nothing but change; if she looks only to the future, she does nothing but dream; only when she is conscious of being the living tradition of Christ is she truly renewed. When she considers the whole of time, past, present, and future, she gathers strength from the revelation she has received, she gives it to the present and so prepares for the tomorrow of God. Without the Holy Spirit we may see only what surrounds us and forget what has gone before. Distrust or ignorance of tradition no doubt stirs up confusion and change, but it does not promote renewal. On the contrary, it endangers it. Renewal demands that we should be humble before the times and not think more highly of ourselves than we ought.

The truth of the Spirit commands that we submit ourselves to a continual and rigorous self-criticism. It is easy to talk about necessary changes in the Church, to take note, for example, of the principles of renewal enunciated by the Council, to comment favourably, and even to eulogize the renewal now going on. It is more difficult to seek out the ways in which the renewal must correct our own short-comings, disturb our habits, and encourage our zeal. Without the Holy Spirit we will never get beyond words or become deeply and personally involved. The craze for change, especially in external matters, may easily become a first class excuse for putting off, into a more or less probable future, those real changes of the spirit and heart. If we judge with severity all meaningless routine, which all too often degenerates into a vain and empty succession of mere sounds, we must also be cautious in the face of changes which are not brought about in the course of that unique search for real holiness which is one of the marks of the Church.

(b) *The Witness of the Spirit.* Change which seeks the path of least resistance is not evangelical, and cannot claim the

[17] John 16, 13.
[18] New York, 1964, p. 219.

dignity of renewal. Renewal is never accomplished by laziness, parrotry, or complacency. Since Pentecost the Church has been placed as a prophet before men. We must take on ourselves all that this vocation entails. We have to speak to the world in a language which it cannot understand without a gift from God. If we dilute the Christian message to the point where it does not surprise anyone who hears us, we are no longer prophets. Renewal should make us abandon everything which, in our vocabularies or attitudes, hurts our brothers uselessly and impedes their progress towards the truth, but the desire to speak an intelligible language must not make us forget that we speak of things, and we must speak of things, which are beyond the bounds of reason. Without the Holy Spirit our testimony before the world is empty and without weight. We are always exposed to the danger of saying nothing in an agreeable way, but then we are, as Isaiah says, as seers who see not, and prophets who do not prophesy.[19] A true renewal cannot eliminate the folly of the cross, nor can it replace personal integrity.

It is by the witness of his life that a Christian best furthers the witness of the Spirit. Even if the Christian paradox allows that we can be for others the unworthy instruments of a good which we do not live ourselves, it remains true that, as Pius XI said, "when the zeal of the reformer has not personal integrity, but is the expression and the explosion of passion, he has muddied rather than clarified, destroyed rather than built."[20] It takes more than wishing to be a reformer! No one can arrogate to himself the right to renew the life of the Church. The Christian who sees himself placed in circumstances which tempt him to criticize the established order, and to set up new forms of thought, or prayer, or action, must first of all try to put himself in the presence of the Holy Spirit. If he fails in this, his action, even without ill-will on his part, can become a counterwitness. And it is thus that the unity of the Christian community is imperilled.

(c) *Unity of the Spirit.* The ecumenical movement dominates

[19] See Isaiah 30, 10.
[20] *Mit Brennender Sorge.*

the present scene and animates a great deal of today's renewal—unless it is more true to say that it is the renewal of the Church which has instituted the ecumenical movement and rendered it more effective. The tremendous effort of rapprochement among Christians, which can only come from the Spirit, carries more than one paradox with it. I cite only two of these. Ecumenism, no matter how outgoing it may be, is impossible without the fidelity of each of us to his own tradition, and the love of our own brethren.

If the ecumenical movement is to be a leaven of renewal, it must not encourage people to underestimate the disparity of the different Christian traditions in the interests of a supposed common heritage, satisfactory to all only so long as its nature remains vague and imprecise. Each one must, therefore, try to be as faithful as possible to his own Church. The Churches which renew themselves in order to be more truly themselves in faithfully following Christ will certainly one day be united, for their renewals arise from the same source, and their faithfulness converges. Paradoxically, unity will not be achieved unless each one, guided by the Holy Spirit, endeavours to be himself in Christ and to respect the other as an other. We do not have to copy each other to join together; it is enough to go to the end of the path laid down before us by our own tradition. Following that path we will, no doubt, discover that we are not so far from each other and, at the end, Christ will meet us in that unity which he has always willed.

Each Church must walk in unity towards unity. If the dividing line between the Churches is blurred today, it all too often, alas, permits the development within the different Churches of dangerous internal divisions. Enlightened minds have a tendency to rejoice too soon in their common victories against those they view as being the rear guard of their own community. If we must congratulate ourselves for having overcome prejudices, we must be careful not to provoke, in the name of an ill-conceived ecumenism, new divisions. Those who in the presence of ecumenism hesitate for valid reasons (such as the desire to be faithful to their Church), may in their hesitation prove to be a precious help in defining the objects to be attained. In any case, we will not arrive at unity by breaking up our own communities. Ecumenism between our Churches must rest on ecumenism within each Church, for the saying is still true, here more than elsewhere, that a well-ordered charity begins with oneself. The Church is a people on the march. All renewal hastens this process, and we must know how to create the conditions for a progressive and unified renewal.

We have seen how the Church, faithful to the truth, to the witness, and to the unity of the Holy Spirit, may fearlessly take the road to renewal which is a constant of her history and a law of her life. The renewal of the Church in her doctrine demands an effort of reflection which goes beyond what is possessed by even the most endowed of the theologians. Together, however, under the guidance of the Holy Spirit and in company with the whole Church, you may hope to shed some light on the most pressing problems.

Theology must become more flexible and diversified, and the progress in biblical research and the study of the Fathers of the Church has already made this clear. But, we must soon go further and deal frankly with the question of theological language in the face of a secularized world in order to move forward effectively with the renewal of the Church in her doctrine.

Theological language is indispensable. It is the necessary vehicle through which we understand and say what we can about God, Christ, the Church, sin, and redemption. Faith is not simply an ineffable response to the word of God, but it is social and must therefore be expressed in propositions which do not falsify it. Yet a constant vigilance must be exercised because modes of expression grow old quickly, and when it is too late we may find that they are empty. Father Karl Rahner reminds us that to do nothing in such a case is an indication of indifference to that very truth which one wishes to defend. It betrays a lack of power of appropriation and of practical assimilation which denotes a sort of concealed unbelief, and which he does not hesitate to call "a form of heresy . . . in which lifeless orthodoxy is only the

31

effect and expression of an inner indifference to truth."[21] We must nonetheless be wary of an iconoclasm which unleashes itself against every ancient formula, and be on our guard against idolatry which manifests itself in a worship of new forms.

In an area of such complexity, your discussion is the best way of serving the magisterium and the Church. The golden rule in all our work will be that dictated by an unfeigned charity. And for a theologian is it not true that the highest form of this charity will be expressed in a filial love of the Church, one and holy?

The true reformers have been saints. For them, the Church was before everything else a loving mother to whom they offered an unconditioned service. Their theological reflections were accompanied by hymns of praise in which they glorified their holy mother. The *Sancta Mater* was in their eyes the greatest and the most perfect of those works which showed forth the power and the mercy of the all-powerful God.

Today there is so much talk of changes being put into effect in the different areas of the life of the Church. But, as a certain bishop with his finger on the pulse of the Church's life confided to me with sorrow and disquietude, very little is spoken about sanctity. Perhaps we should question ourselves seriously during this congress in order to answer with speed, prudence, and confidence to the questionings of the Spirit and the world within this perspective of the search for holiness. We must never forget that the Spirit which gives us life is the Spirit of Holiness, and that the great lack of the contemporary world is that hunger of the soul for God without which there will be a return to a barbarism which could so quickly replace the highest forms of civilized life. History contains many lessons which could help us grasp the true meaning of renewal in the Church. Let us hope that the historians of the future who will examine our times will discover in them that wisdom which flowers into true contemplation. It is contemplation which enriches the robes of the Church, the pure spouse of Christ, whom he bought with his blood. It is contemplation which roots out our selfishness and allows us **to**

[21] *On Heresy,* New York, 1964, p. 61.

32

express that unity which Christ indicated to be the distinctive mark of his Church: "That they may be one, Father, even as you and I are one."[22] It is by contemplation that we find our way into the room of the bride, where Christ speaks to each one of us in an ineffable, incommunicable, and special way, and in which he says all with the words "I have loved you with an eternal love."[23] It is thus that the people of God, guided and sanctified by their pastors, will go forward towards the new heaven; and the Church "to which we are called in Jesus Christ, and in which we acquire sanctity through the grace of God, will attain her full perfection only in the glory of heaven. Then will come the time of the restoration of all things. Then the human race as well as the entire world which is intimately related to man and achieves its purpose through him, will be perfectly re-established in Christ."[24]

[22] John 17, 21.
[23] See Canticle of Canticles 1, 4; Jeremiah 31, 3.
[24] *Dogmatic Constitution on the Church*, art. 48.

1.

THEOLOGY IN ITS NEW CONTEXT

BERNARD LONERGAN, S.J.

THE general topic of the congress is the theology of the renewal of the Church. But any theology of renewal goes hand in hand with a renewal of theology. For "renewal" is being used in a novel sense. Usually in Catholic circles "renewal" has meant a return to the olden times of pristine virtue and deep wisdom. But good Pope John has made "renewal" mean *"aggiornamento,"* "bringing things up to date."

Obviously, if theology is to be brought up to date, it must have fallen behind the times. Again, if we are to know what is to be done to bring theology up to date, we must ascertain when it began to fall behind the times, in what respects it got out of touch, in what ways it failed to meet the issues and effect the developments that long ago were due and now are long overdue.

The answer I wish to suggest takes us back almost three centuries to the end of the seventeenth century and, more precisely, to the year 1680. For that, it seems, was the time of the great beginning. Then it was that Herbert Butterfield placed the origins of modern science, then that Paul Hazard placed the beginning of the Enlightenment, then that Yves Congar placed the beginning of dogmatic theology. When modern science began, when the Enlightenment began, then the theologians began to reassure one another about their certainties. Let me comment briefly on this threefold coincidence.

When Professor Butterfield placed the origins of modern

34

science at the end of the seventeenth century, he by no means meant to deny that from the year 1300 on numerous discoveries were made that since have been included within modern science and integrated with it. But he did make the point that, at the time of their first appearance, these discoveries could not be expressed adequately. For, the dominant cultural context was Aristotelian, and the discoverers themselves had Aristotelian backgrounds. Thus there existed a conflict between the new ideas and the old doctrines, and this conflict existed not merely between an old guard of Aristotelians and a new breed of scientists but, far more gravely, within the very minds of the new scientists. For new ideas are far less than a whole mentality, a whole climate of thought and opinion, a whole mode of approach, and procedure, and judgment. Before these new ideas could be formulated accurately, coherently, cogently, they had to multiply, cumulate, coalesce to bring forth a new system of concepts and a new body of doctrine that was somehow comparable in extent to the Aristotelian and so capable of replacing it.

In brief, Professor Butterfield distinguished between new ideas and the context or horizon within which they were expressed, developed, related. From about the beginning of the fourteenth century the new ideas multiplied. But only towards the close of the seventeenth century did there emerge the context appropriate to these ideas. The origin of this context is for Professor Butterfield the origin of modern science and, in his judgment, "it outshines everything since the rise of Christianity and reduces the Renaissance and the Reformation to the rank of mere episodes, mere internal displacements, within the system of medieval Christendom."[1]

Coincident with the origins of modern science was the beginning of the Enlightenment, of the movement Peter Gay recently named the rise of modern paganism.[2] Moreover, while this movement commonly is located in the eighteenth century, the

[1] Herbert Butterfield, *The Origins of Modern Science, 1300–1800,* New York, 1966, p. 7.
[2] *The Enlightenment, An Interpretation,* New York, 1966.

35

French academician Paul Hazard has exhibited already in full swing between the years 1680 and 1715 a far-flung attack on Christianity from almost every quarter and in almost every style.[3] It was a movement revolted by the spectacle of religious persecution and religious war. It was to replace the God of the Christians by the God of the *philosophes* and eventually, the God of the *philosophes* by agnosticism and theism. It gloried in the achievements of Newton, criticized social structures, promoted political change, and moved towards a materialist, mechanist, determinist interpretation no less of man than of nature.[4]

It would be unfair to expect the theologians of the end of the seventeenth century to have discerned the good and the evil in the great movements of their time. But at least we may record what in fact they did do. They introduced "dogmatic" theology. It is true that the word "dogmatic" had been previously applied to theology. But then it was used to denote a distinction from moral, or ethical, or historical theology. Now it was employed in a new sense, in opposition to scholastic theology. It replaced the inquiry of the *quaestio* by the pedagogy of the thesis. It demoted the quest of faith for understanding to a desirable, but secondary, and indeed, optional goal. It gave basic and central significance to the certitudes of faith, their presuppositions, and their consequences. It owed its mode of proof to Melchior Cano and, as that theologian was also a bishop and an inquisitor, so the new dogmatic theology not only proved its theses, but also was supported by the teaching authority and the sanctions of the Church.[5]

Such a conception of theology survived right into the twentieth century, and even today in some circles it is the only conception that is understood. Still, among theologians its limitations and defects have been becoming more and more apparent, especially since the 1890's. During the last seventy years, efforts to find

---

[3] *The European Mind,* London, 1953.

[4] The lasting influence of such enlightenment right up to the present has been illustrated rather fully by F. W. Matson, *The Broken Image,* New York, 1964.

[5] See Yves Congar, "Théologie," *DTC* 29, 432 f.

remedies and to implement them have been going forward steadily, if unobtrusively. The measure of their success is the radically new situation brought to light by the Second Vatican Council.

There is, perhaps, no need for me here to insist that the novelty resides not in a new revelation or a new faith, but in a new cultural context. For a theology is a product not only of the religion it investigates and expounds, but also of the cultural ideals and norms that set its problems and direct its solutions. Just as theology in the thirteenth century followed its age by assimilating Aristotle, just as theology in the seventeenth century resisted its age by retiring into a dogmatic corner, so theology today is locked in an encounter with its age. Whether it will grow and triumph, or whether it will wither to insignificance, in no small measure depends on the clarity and the accuracy of its grasp of the external cultural factors that undermine its past achievements and challenge it to new endeavors.

The topics, then, that I am to raise are not directly theological. For that very reason they are all the more apt to be overlooked in an age characterized by specialization. For the same reason it is all the more important to draw attention to them on such an occasion as the present, for the cultural context sets up an undertow that accounts for tendencies and exigencies that must be met, yet, if not understood, are too easily neglected or thwarted because they seem superfluous, arbitrary, perplexing, disquieting, or dangerous.

*   *   *

First, then, theology was a deductive, and it has become largely an empirical science. It was a deductive science in the sense that its theses were conclusions to be proven from the premises provided by Scripture and Tradition. It has become an empirical science in the sense that Scripture and Tradition now supply not premises, but data. The data has to be viewed in its historical perspective. It has to be interpreted in the light of contemporary techniques and procedures. Where before the step from premises to conclusions was brief, simple, and certain, today the steps from data to interpretation are long, arduous, and, at best, probable. An empirical science does not demonstrate. It accumulates information, develops understanding, masters ever more of its materials, but it does not preclude the uncovering of further relevant data, the emergence of new insights, the attainment of a more comprehensive view.

Secondly, this shift from a deductivist to an empirical approach has come to stay. One has only to glance at the bibliographies in *Biblica,* in Altaner's *Patrologie,* in the *Bulletin de théologie ancienne et médiévale,* and in *Ephemerides theologicae Lovanienses* to become aware of the massive commitment of contemporary Catholic thought to an empirical approach. But to understand this movement, to grasp the reasons for it, one must do more than glance at bibliographies; one has to get down to reading the books. Then one gradually discovers that the old dogmatic theology had misconceived history on a classicist model, that it thought not in terms of evolution and development, but of universality and permanence. Vincent of Lerins had proclaimed God's truth to be *quod semper, quod ubique, quod ab omnibus,*[6] and such a view was still quite congenial in the *grand siècle* of French literature.[7] On such assumptions it was quite legitimate to expect the theologian, if only he knew the faith of today, to be equally at home in the Old and New Testaments, in the Greek and Latin Fathers, in the writings of medieval, Renaissance, and more recent theologians. But today such an assumption appears fantastic and preposterous. In almost endless studies the writings of age after age have been examined minutely, and all along the line the notion of fixity has had to give way to the fact of development. Moreover, development is complex, intricate, manifold. Its precise character at any time can be ascertained only through detailed studies of the resources, the problems, the tendencies, and the accidents of the time. Where once the dogmatic theologian was supposed to range over centuries, now Scripture, patristics, medieval, and modern

[6] *Commonitorium,* II, Cambridge, 1915, p. 10.
[7] See Owen Chadwick, *The Idea of Doctrinal Development, From Bossuet to Newman,* Cambridge, 1957, pp. 17 ff.

studies are divided and subdivided among classes of specialists. Where once the dogmatic theologian could lay down an overall view that echoed the conciliar *semper tenuit atque tenet sancta mater Ecclesia,* now an overall view tends to be either a tentative summary of the present state of research, or a popular simplification of issues that are really not simple at all.

Thirdly, while theology has become largely empirical in its method, it has invoked a new vocabulary, new imagery, new concepts to express its thought. The Aristotelian analyses, concepts, words, that in the Middle Ages became part of the Catholic patrimony to resist both Renaissance scoffing and Protestant condemnation, almost suddenly in the twentieth century have gone out of fashion. With equal rapidity the vacuum is being refilled with biblical words and images, and with ideas worked out by historicist, personalist, phenomenological, and existential reflection. There is so much new in Catholic speculative theology that Karl Rahner felt the need to issue a *Theological Dictionary*[8] and Heinrich Fries organized over one hundred experts to collaborate and produce a two volume *Handbuch theologischer Grundbegriffe.*[9]

As the empirical approach, so too I believe, the new conceptual apparatus has come to stay. Religion is concerned with man's relations to God and to his fellow man, so that any deepening or enriching of our apprehension of man possesses religious significance and relevance. But the new conceptual apparatus does make available such a deepening and enriching. Without denying human nature, it adds the quite distinctive categories of man as an historical being. Without repudiating the analysis of man into body and soul, it adds the richer and more concrete apprehension of man as incarnate subject.

It would be far more than can be attempted within the limits of the present paper to attempt to communicate what precisely is meant by the contrast between nature and history or what is added to the couple, body and soul, by the phrase "incarnate subject." Summarily, very summarily, I may perhaps say that

[8] New York, 1965.
[9] Munich, 1962 and 1963.

such terms refer to a dimension of human reality that has always existed, that has always been lived and experienced, that classicist thought standardized yet tended to overlook, that modern studies have brought to light, thematized, elaborated, illustrated, documented. That dimension is the constitutive role of meaning in human living. It is the fact that acts of meaning inform human living, that such acts proceed from a free and responsible subject incarnate, that meanings differ from nation to nation, from culture to culture, and that, over time, they develop and go astray. Besides the meanings by which man apprehends nature and the meanings by which he transforms it, there are the meanings by which man thinks out the possibilities of his own living and makes his choice among them. In this realm of freedom and creativity, of solidarity and responsibility, of dazzling achievement and pitiable madness, there ever occurs man's making of man.

The wealth, the complexity, the profundity of this modern apprehension of man might be illustrated by pointing to its implications for philosophy, for human science, for art and literature, for education and psychiatry. But what must be mentioned is its significance for the notion of divine revelation. God becomes known to us in two ways: as the ground and end of the material universe; and as the one who speaks to us through Scripture and Tradition. The first manner might found a natural religion. The second adds revealed religion. For the first, one might say that the heavens show forth the glory of God; what can mere words add? But for the second, one must answer that, however trifling the uses to which words may be put, still they are the vehicles of meaning, and meaning is the stuff of man's making of man. So it is that a divine revelation is God's entry and his taking part in man's making of man. It is God's claim to have a say in the aims and purposes, the direction and development of human lives, human societies, human cultures, human history.

From this significance for revealed religion there follows a significance for theology. In the medieval period theology became the queen of the sciences. But in the practice of Aquinas it was also the principle for the moulding and transforming of a culture. He was not content to write his systematic works, his commentaries on Scripture and on such Christian writers as the Pseudo-Dionysius and Boethius. At a time when Arabic and Greek thought were penetrating the whole of Western culture, he wrote extensive commentaries on numerous works of Aristotle to fit a pagan's science within a Christian context and to construct a world view that underpinned Dante's *Divine Comedy*. To this paradigm theology today must look if it is to achieve its *aggiornamento*. Its task is not limited to investigating, ordering, expounding, communicating divine revelation. All that is needed, but more must be done. For revelation is God's entry into man's making of man, and so theology not only has to reflect on revelation, but also it has somehow to mediate God's meaning into the whole of human affairs. It is not a small task, but because it is not—in a culture in which God is ignored and there are even theologians to proclaim that God is dead—it is all the more urgent.

My reflections have come full circle. Not only does the cultural context influence theology to undo its past achievements, but theology is also called upon to influence the cultural context, to translate the word of God and so project it into new mentalities and new situations. So a contemporary Catholic theology has to be not only Catholic but also ecumenist. Its concern must reach not only Christians but also non-Christians and atheists. It has to learn to draw not only on the modern philosophies but also on the relatively new sciences of religion, psychology, sociology, and the new techniques of the communication arts.

* * *

I have been speaking of our renewed theology and now I must add that a renewed theology needs a renewed foundation. The old foundation will no longer do. But we cannot get along with no foundation at all. So a new foundation and, I should say, a new type of foundation is needed to replace the old.

First, some foundation is needed. If change is to be improvement, if new tasks are to be accomplished fruitfully, discernment

41

is needed and discrimination. If we are to draw on contemporary psychology and sociology, if we are to profit from the modern science of religions, if we are to revise scholastic categories and make our own the concepts worked out in historicist, personalist, phenomenological, or existentialist circles, then we must be able to distinguish tinsel and silver, gilt and gold. No less important than a critique of notions and conclusions is a critique of methods. The new largely empirical approach to theology can too easily be made into a device for reducing doctrines to probable opinions. A hermeneutics can pretend to philosophic neutrality yet force the conclusion that the content of revelation is mostly myth. Scientific history can be so conceived that a study of the narrative of salvation will strip it of matters of fact. If our renewed theology is not to be the dupe of every fashion, it needs a firm basis and a critical stance.

Secondly, the old foundations will no longer do. In saying this I do not mean that they are no longer true, for they are as true now as they ever were. I mean that they are no longer appropriate. I am simply recalling that one must not patch an old cloak with new cloth or put new wine in old wineskins. One type of foundation suits a theology that aims at being deductivist, static, abstract, universal, equally applicable to all places and to all times. A quite different foundation is needed when theology turns from deductivism to an empirical approach, from the static to the dynamic, from the abstract to the concrete, from the universal to the historical totality of particulars, from invariable rules to intelligent adjustment and adaptation.

Thirdly, I shall no doubt be asked to give some indication of the nature or character of the new foundation. To this topic I have elsewhere given considerable attention, first, to assure historical continuity, in a study of cognitional theory in the writings of St. Thomas,[10] then in a contemporary development entitled *Insight*,[11] to take into account the fact of modern science and

---

[10] Originally published in *Theological Studies* (1946–1949), and recently revised and reissued by David Burrell, C.S.C., under the title *Verbum, Word and Idea in Aquinas,* Notre Dame, 1967.

[11] *Insight. A Study of Human Understanding,* London and New York, 1957.

the problems of modern philosophy. On the present occasion I may be permitted, perhaps, to offer no more than a few brief approximations.

As a first approximation, to be corrected and complemented shortly by further approximations, let us consider the foundation of a modern science. It does not consist in any part of the science itself, in any of its conclusions, in any of its laws, in any of its principles. All of these are open to revision, and it is in the light of the foundation that the revision would take place. What, then, is the foundation? It is the method of the science. It is the method that generates the conclusions, laws, principles that are accepted today. It is the method that will generate the revision of conclusions, laws, principles tomorrow. What the scientist relies on ultimately is his method.

Now one might be inclined to think of method as a set of verbal propositions enouncing rules to be followed in a scientific investigation and, of course, it is true that there are the hodmen of science who carry out the routines prescribed to them by those who understand the purpose of an investigation and the manner in which it might advance scientific knowledge. But I wish here to use the word method to denote not the prescriptions given the hodmen, but the grounds that governed the prescribing. Such grounds, though perfectly familiar to the director, usually are not objectified or verbalized by him. Indeed, he cannot achieve such objectification with any accuracy, unless he is ready to devote as much time and effort to cognitional theory as he has already devoted to his physics, or chemistry, or biology. This does not happen. But, were it to happen, there would result the account of a normative pattern that related to one another the cognitional operations that recur in scientific investigations. There would be listed, described, illustrated, compared such operations as inquiring, observing, describing, problem defining, discovering, forming hypotheses, working out presuppositions and implications, devising series of experiments, performing them, and verifying. The greatest stress would be placed on the importance of personal experience of the operations, of identifying them within one's experience, and of finding within that experience not only the operations, but also the dynamic and normative relations that bind them to one another. In this fashion, you will agree, the subject as scientist would come to know himself as scientist. But the subject as scientist is the reality that is principle and foundation of science, of science as it has been, of science as it is, of science as it will be.

So much for our first approximation. It illustrates by an example what might be meant by a foundation that lies not in a set of verbal propositions named first principles, but in a particular, concrete, dynamic reality generating knowledge of particular, concrete, dynamic realities. It remains that we have to effect the transition from natural science to theology, and so we turn to our second approximation.

Fundamental to religious living is conversion. It is a topic little studied in traditional theology since there remains very little of it when one reaches the universal, the abstract, the static. For conversion occurs in the lives of individuals. It is not merely a change or even a development; rather, it is a radical transformation on which follows, on all levels of living, an interlocked series of changes and developments. What hitherto was unnoticed becomes vivid and present. What had been of no concern becomes a matter of high import. So great a change in one's apprehensions and one's values accompanies no less a change in oneself, in one's relations to other persons, and in one's relations to God.

Not all conversion is as total as the one I have so summarily described. Conversion has many dimensions. A changed relation to God brings or follows changes that are personal, social, moral, and intellectual. But there is no fixed rule of antecedence and consequence, no necessity of simultaneity, no prescribed magnitudes of change. Conversion may be compacted into the moment of a blinded Saul falling from his horse on the way to Damascus. It may be extended over the slow maturing process of a lifetime. It may satisfy any intermediate measure.

In a current expression, conversion is ontic. The convert apprehends differently, values differently, relates differently because he has become different. The new apprehension is not so much a new statement or a new set of statements, but rather new meanings that attach to almost any statement. It is not new values so much as a transvaluation of values. In Pauline language, "When anyone is united to Christ, there is a new world; the old order has gone, and a new order has begun" (2 Cor. 5, 17).

Though conversion is intensely personal, utterly intimate, still it is not so private as to be solitary. It can happen to many and they can form a community to sustain one another in their self-transformation, and to help one another in working out the implications, and in fulfilling the promise of their new life. Finally, what can become communal can become historical. It can pass from generation to generation. It can spread from one cultural milieu to another. It can adapt to changing circumstance, confront new situations, survive into a different age, flourish in another period or epoch.

When conversion is viewed as an ongoing process, at once personal, communal, and historical, it coincides with living religion. For religion is conversion in its preparation, in its occurrence, in its development, in its consequents, and also alas in its incompleteness, its failures, its breakdowns, its disintegration.

Now theology, and especially the empirical theology of today, is reflection on religion. It follows that theology will be reflection on conversion. But conversion is fundamental to religion. It follows that reflection on conversion can supply theology with its foundation and, indeed, with a foundation that is concrete, dynamic, personal, communal, and historical. Just as reflection on the operations of the scientist brings to light the real foundation of the science, so too reflection on the ongoing process of conversion may bring to light the real foundation of a renewed theology.

*   *   *

I met the question of theological renewal, of its *aggiornamento,* by asking how far we are behind the times. I went back three centuries, for it was then that dogmatic theology had its beginnings, and it has been towards a total transformation of dogmatic theology that the developments of this century have

45

worked. A normative structure that was deductivist has become empirical. A conceptual apparatus that at times clung pathetically to the past is yielding place to historicist, personalist, phenomenological, and existentialist notions.

I have urged that so great a transformation needs a renewed foundation, and that the needed renewal is the introduction of a new type of foundation. It is to consist not in objective statement, but in subjective reality. The objective statements of a *de vera religione, de Christo legato, de ecclesia, de inspiratione scripturae, de locis theologicis,* are as much in need of a foundation as are those of other tracts. But behind all statements is the stating subject. What is normative and foundational for subjects stating theology is to be found, I have suggested, in reflection on conversion, where conversion is taken as an ongoing process, concrete and dynamic, personal, communal, and historical.

2.

THEOLOGY'S TASKS AFTER VATICAN II

YVES M.-J. CONGAR, O.P.

THEOLOGY is a reflection on the faith intent upon reaching the status of a science. Theology, therefore, puts a rational method to work in order to construct intellectually a datum received in the Church on the basis of faith. It offers itself as a way open to all. Yet it must exist, and it does exist, as a certain service of the Church; of a Church which, in turn, performs a deaconry for men in view of their salvation, in other words: in view of the success of creation in God by Jesus Christ and his Holy Spirit. Hence the actuality of theology. Theology is not only actual in that today there exists a rather remarkable interest for it in a world that has hardly any religion. Here I have in mind the other fact, namely, that historicity and actuality are indeed an essential note of theology, at least if the word be taken in the full extension and vitality of its meaning. Theology, for that matter, can never be totally timeless. Each theologian performs his science with the resources of his own definite intellectual formation. And most of all, the theologian desiring faithfully to render *this* ecclesial service, finds himself conditioned by the resources offered to him, and the tasks imposed on him, through the cultural world in which he lives.

Hence we propose to consider, one after the other, the actual situation, the new resources offered to us, the vocation and the relatively new tasks with which theology is faced in consequence of all this.

THE ACTUAL SITUATION

The situation seems to be characterized, first of all, by the fact that the reality of the world, object of man's knowledge and his transforming action, has taken on a density and, we might say, an evidence beside which the positive affirmations of faith concerning a supernatural order, posited and revealed by God's initiative, sink into insignificance. This fact is not entirely new. It inspired the rationalism of the last two or three hundred years. But what is new is that now it has reached the Christians and threatens to shatter their faith. Does it not appear that a purely rational explanation can now be applied to everything, to the physical world, and to religious facts as well? If we follow Freud, where is there a place for transcendency? Another novelty is the triumph, achieved today, of the demand which was the soul of so many efforts in eighteenth-century Europe, the age of Enlightenment, the demand, that is, to build up a merely human and rational organization of social life as such. This demand is now fulfilled in the secularism of our culture and social life. Throughout the centuries the Church had penetrated culture and society, creating living space favoring faith and in harmony with it. Today we find ourselves more and more within a frame of life where there is no religious connotation. In 1935 we saw the major cause of modern unbelief in the fact that the totality of life was being constructed outside the faith. This fact has now grown into a mass phenomenon.[1] What is new, finally, is the ambition of modern thought to grasp the whole of reality and *reality as a whole*. The naïve objectivism, adequately distinguished subject and object, is being challenged; the subject is seen implicated in every one of his perceptions of reality.[2] The

[1] See my "Une conclusion à l'enquête sur les raisons actuelles de l'incroyance," *La Vie spirituelle*, 37 (1935), 214–249; English translation in *Integration*, August 1938, 13–21, and December 1938, 10–26.

[2] R. Johann, "Experience and Philosophy," *Experience, Existence and the Good: Essays in Honor of Paul Weiss,* ed. I. C. Lieb, Carbondale, 1961, pp. 25–38.

universe of modern rational explanation, therefore, is a universe of man; it is anthropocentric.

All this contains already a devaluation of the forms in which the Christian mysteries have been thought, expressed, elaborated, in accord with a culture which we seem to have left behind. Not that the old scholasticism has been refuted, but rather that it has been replaced by an entirely different set of considerations. These were conceived in the interest of man; they presented a different evaluation of man's ideas and proceeded from an interpretation of the individual's existential experience, from the analysis of his interpersonal relations, and so forth. Yes, that was it: a replacement of one culture by another, of one ensemble of cultural instruments and elements by another. The old instruments were not denied or rejected, but other considerations were brought forward which much intensified the interest and importance we usually attribute to a point of view. A good example is found in the matter of biblical studies. There was the discovery of the "economic," functional significance of a passage or notion which yesterday's theologians naïvely understood in an objective, ontological sense. Scholastic ontology, generally, has a bad press. We replace it by statements coined in words of personalist, existential, anthropocentric style. But often these statements keep to the standard of an essay, a suggestive sketch. However this may be, we surely are fond of "research," while our predecessors preferred firm conclusions. We like to keep to the stage and style of the essay, the tentative approach.

This is the situation. It entails two dangers. In the first place, there is a feeling of insecurity which is painfully shared by many. It is not so much a case of the religious realities themselves being questioned, but rather of the forms in which they have been proposed to us, intellectual forms, liturgical forms and last, not least, institutional forms. In a way, the conciliar *aggiornamento,* which did not create the situation but proceeded from a frank acknowledgment of its existence, has given cause to this insecurity. What hitherto was considered unchangeable now seems to be opened up for change; it is precisely at this point that an influence coming from the Council may be noticed. The Council did not create the questions but lifted the barrier which had prevented them from being asked freely. It has officially opened the way to change, not the foundations, but the forms, the expressions. It was an unexpected move when the Council led the Church out of a cultural and sociological world in whose proven frame Catholic faith and Catholic life had for centuries found their place, their expression, their vesture.[3] Many Catholics have the very painful impression that all of a sudden they have been thrown into incertitude. Without protection, they now feel to be, as it were, on the market-place or the highways, their hearth and home having gone. Where are we to go from here? Where shall we be in twenty years? I, too, feel almost every day a temptation of uneasiness in the face of all that has changed or is being called into question.

Secondly, it is easy to say—and there is good reason for saying—that these forms are all relative. But the absolute has been delivered, communicated, to us in these relative forms. This is why it is such a delicate task to criticize them even though it is legitimate, indeed necessary, to criticize and go beyond them. The example of the sixteenth century may illustrate, and cast a tragic light upon, what we are saying. It is averred that in those times it was necessary not only to reform a number of abuses, but also to disengage Christian life and religion from many superstitions. This is what the reformers set out to do. But they were not careful to salvage the valuable substance covered by these blameworthy forms. There was many an important matter where the proverbial baby was thrown out with the bathwater. Example: the religious life. A warning sign should be posted for our present day reformers: Beware! Do not repeat the old mistake when you envisage the replacement, legitimate *per se* and sometimes even necessary, of liturgical, theological, institutional forms by others that are more in accord with our world, our culture, our conditions.

[3] On this aspect see G. H. Tavard, *The Church Tomorrow*, London and New York, 1965.

NEW CONTRIBUTIONS AND RESOURCES

Philosophy has today abandoned the claim to furnish an interpretation of the cosmos on an ontological level different from the sciences. It has become a reflection on man's situation and existential experience. In this way it offers new resources to theology. These lie beyond Aristotle's physicism, but they are in harmony with the needs of Christian theology in a matter analogous to the way in which a philosophy of Platonic inspiration harmonized with the different needs of the Fathers. We know that a theology of the act of faith, the sacraments, marriage, the Christian community, can indeed find its resources in a philosophy of the subject and of interpersonal relations. What is less commonly known, is how to measure the limits of these contributions. If there were no limits, we should risk neglecting the historical and social dimensions of the human condition. Marxism has exploited this area, in a manner which seems to me an excessive systematization and simplification, but which we can neither ignore nor neglect. Neither can we ignore nor neglect the reasons for atheism. Atheism is for us a strenuous but profitable training. We have gone beyond a merely negative appreciation of it, which was either satisfied with a simple refutation, or indulged in a condescending and sometimes almost disdainful pity. Much talk has been going the rounds—the Holy Father himself took part in it—about the possibly purifying values of atheism. Atheism puts us under obligation not to short-sell God and his transcendency. It imposes upon us the burden earnestly to rethink a number of values and themes: freedom and responsibility, the grandeur of man's "project," our psychological conditioning, God's silence.

Modern scientific anthropology has not yet penetrated very far into theological consideration. We would first have to learn this science, even to practice it. But we are terribly short of time and possibilities. This means that we risk being ignorant of things which are more and more to condition the lives of men. On the other hand, historical sciences do indeed, already at this moment, have a deep impact on theological work, especially in the field of biblical studies which are farther ahead than any other branch of theology. It is impossible today to continue in a naïve understanding of the texts, impossible also to think that a good philology and good knowledge of the historical and cultural milieu will get us to the heart of a text. Certainly, these remain useful but, beyond all that, critical questions of a very delicate nature nowadays raise their head: the critical history of the literary forms and of the traditions, both preceding and following; the distinction between a literary product, from the writer's mind, and as constituting an original datum of facts or words transmitted to posterity; the distinction between the elements pertaining to the post-Pentecostal experiences of the community, and the historical events that happened before (the "historical Christ"). In short, we cannot ignore any longer the problems of critique which involve notions and views of a philosophic nature. Bultmann's program of demythologizing originated in a pastoral interest. He wanted to make acceptance of the biblical message possible for modern man. In implementing his program he used a specific kind of philosophy. He advanced a philosophical interpretation of the act of faith, conceived as a personal decision and an understanding of one's self. Scholars now almost everywhere take their starting point in Bultmann's analysis, as though this was an uncontrovertible datum, a Gospel truth itself. They combine this with the famous texts of Dietrich Bonhoeffer concerning the now irreversible transition to a secularized world and the need from now on to speak of God in a "non-religious way," or even not to speak of him at all, for his name is a name of transcendency, and our interest is man. Bonhoeffer, no doubt, would be the first to reject what people today retain or draw from his writings, to the neglect of all their positive elements. So it has come about that a new school of theology has been invented out of whole cloth, the "death of God" theology. Several writers have so been hailed as members of the same theological fraternity. But such a club was rather haphazardly put together. In truth its members have little enough in common.

52

Our epoch, then, clearly offers new resources to the theologian. But these, no doubt, generate new and difficult questions. We cannot in principle refuse to busy ourselves with them. Theology is a reflection on faith in the framework of a certain culture, taking up the problems and the resources of this culture. We cannot, *a priori*, exclude the philosophy of existence and of the personal subject, or the anthropological sciences, or the biblical criticism and the string of its corollaries. But all this brings forward both resources and questions. Our task is to be at once open-minded, receptive, and critical, that is, to exercise the critical function inherent in faith. This is an attitude very different from ignorance or disdain. It is an aspect of that contestation which faith, itself contested by the world, has to exercise in regard to the world. It is permissible to think that, not infrequently, Christians have failed in their duty to contest the society in which they lived, and which was, and more than ever is today, contrary to the Gospel, to contest the doings of potentates, and also to contest the forms of their own doings and their own organizations. Yet all this is a prophetic function of faith. To exercise it may perhaps be easier when the question presents itself from the outside and from far away. But it seems to me that not a few Christians fail to remember this duty when dealing with the requests and contributions of modern times. I am referring to such books as Paul van Buren's *The Secular Meaning of the Gospel* (New York, 1966), and W. van der Mauck's *Grundzüge einer christlichen Ethik* (Düsseldorf, 1967), to mention only these two. The first, it seems to me, shows an uncritical yielding to the conditions which a given philosophy of language sets up for a proposition to be considered valid; in the second, we notice a too simplistic acceptance of the social reference as the exclusive criterion of Christian ethical acting.

WHAT IS THE THEOLOGIANS' PRESENT TASK?

First of all—and it is important to note this—theologians still have to do what they have always had to do. Theology continues to be a reflection on the faith, using the valid resources of an intellectual culture, and this at an exacting and technical level. Moreover, theology is, and remains, a wisdom *constructed* on the ground of a datum. It is possible that this schematization (construct, datum) today presents itself under new conditions —we shall see about this later. Nevertheless, it is essential to what we call theology and might well serve here as the framework of what presently we have to say. Let us, then, investigate what, over and above the old tasks, the relatively new ones are in today's theology, first in regard to the datum, second in regard to the construct.

A. Concerning the Theological Datum

We shall, somewhat schematically, distinguish three levels: first, the level of Scripture; second, of Tradition (including the successive pronouncements of the magisterium); third, of the life of the Church and of men (past and especially present).

Today's biblical research has attained a remarkable density and quality. There is danger, however, that a gap may be opened between biblical scholars and theologians; the former pursuing their work in, so to speak, splendid isolation, taking little account of its dogmatic impact; the latter carrying on with scarcely any knowledge of exegetic research, and even less of the problems of textual criticism. There must be dialogue between the two. If I had a say, I should not hesitate to make it a law that no doctorate in ecclesiastical sciences should be conferred unless the candidate has published a work on a scriptural subject of at least the length of a review article; and this would be a work of exegesis proper, that is, research into the meaning of a text. To the effort of reading we must add, as we have seen, a very difficult reflection on the nature and the condition of historical truth, and on hermeneutic problems. This is more than just a matter of observing the rules of literary interpretation; it extends to historical interpretation, to *Realkritic*. What is it possible for us to know about the realities and the facts of which the sacred

54

authors speak? Is our reading of a story correct when under-taken in the light of what a later generation found in it? Does the experience of the Christian community contribute authentic information about the evangelical facts, or does this experience deform and exaggerate? This is the very question which Blondel in the days of modernism had already diagnosed as being at the heart of the controversy over the "Christ of faith" and the "Christ of history." He gave his answer in a meditation on Tradition, doubtlessly the profoundest view ever set forth in this matter. Tradition is the point of insertion of dogma in history.[4] The problem is still with us, as may be seen in *Wahrheit und Methode* by H. G. Gadamer (Tübingen, second ed., 1965). But there are other problems: how do we know and conceive realities belonging not to the order of our earthly, human history, but to an order which St. Paul calls "the Other Creation"? They have been in the past; they are now being and, in the future, will be inserted into *our* history. How do we conceive the resurrection of Christ, his ascension, and also the last judgment, purgatory, and our own resurrection? In the past, theology was able to reason on all this in terms of a naïve objectivism, making use of the ontological categories of a physics which today is super-seded. It is impossible to continue thinking in this way. Bult-mann's solution is simple but ruinous. Basically, for Bultmann all objectification is a myth. But our conjectures in new ways have scarcely begun. One of the terms of the problem still escapes us almost completely, namely, the nature and the time of that new creation, in other words, the eschatological order. We can scarcely speak of this order but in terms of earthly realities and of what happens here on earth; inevitably that partly implies a myth—if this word, so ambiguous but so difficult to replace, can be used.[5]

[4] Maurice Blondel, "Histoire et dogme. Les Lacunes philosophiques de l'exégèse moderne," *La Quinzaine,* 349–373, 433–458. Together with "De la valeur historique du dogme," *Bull. de lit. eccl.,* 1905, 61–67, these articles were reproduced in *Les premiers écrits de Maurice Blondel,* Paris, 1956, respectively pp. 149–228 and 229–245.

[5] So J. M. Paupert in his essay *Peut-on être chrétien aujourd'hui?,* Paris, 1966.

Turning to Tradition, we seem to be on more solid ground. However, this ground sometimes is supposed to be known rather than really explored. Who would boast of having a satisfactory explanation of the homogeneous development of dogmas? Today we recognize better the historicity of man; hence also the historicity of the Church, of her institutions, and the pronouncements of her magisterium (councils and popes). We know this better in principle. In fact, however, how often do we talk as though words always covered, and always will cover, the same content—which to be sure they do not? We are still wide of the mark in asserting historicity whenever indicated.[6] This ought to be done, and it will be done. But then the problems of continuity will be restated with renewed urgency. What is, and what is not, liable to be affected by historic conditioning? Vatican II reopened the question of the historicity of the pronouncements of the magisterium since more than once the Council said *something other* than had been said by the same magisterium previously.[7] People trained in historical studies and used to historical thinking will find nothing disquieting in this. But there are others with a monolithic, monarchic, and wholly divinized view of the Church who might be disturbed. Their view is a fallacy. It is a fact that in the Church the notion of infallibility has been used to an absolutely excessive extent, and this at the very moment when from a profoundly sacramental consideration of the Church—the Church submitted to God's present action—a transition was made to a juridical consideration, which Möhler expressed succinctly in his famous dictum of 1835: "God created the hierarchy, and thereby more than sufficiently provided for everything until the end of time." My personal conviction is that in regard to the life of the Church, the

6 Long ago we dreamed of a philosophical and historical commentary on Denzinger which would have *situated* the texts of this precious but dangerous collection in their historical and cultural conjuncture (vocabulary and so forth). If this is not done, it is hardly honest to use these texts detached from all their temporality.

7 For example, on the question of the Church as Mystical Body and, in connection with this, the problem of membership in the Church. Again on the question of the origin of the bishops' "jurisdiction," on religious liberty (one hundred years after the *Syllabus* of Pius IX).

use of the much more modest notion of indefectibility should be restored, and that of infallibility reserved for certain *acts* that have limits and definite circumscriptions. But to go into this further would carry me too far.

What are we to say about the life of the Church, her actual life, of course? Depending, as it does, on the life of the world, it too is a theological "locus," a source of knowledge interesting and pertinent to the theological task. Emphasis should here be given to the fact that this life depends on the movements, the problems, the contributions of the world, that is, on history.[8] Here, we again meet historicity, the condition already discussed above. Theologians like M.-D. Chenu, Edward Schillebeeckx, have long since recognized the fact that the Church receives from the world, from other men, elements of constitutive importance for her existence as the people of God. Vatican II vitally experienced this and formally admitted it in aiming to be a *pastoral* council, one envisaging the *pastoral* service of men.

In the present Church—to point out concrete examples— we come upon this fact twice, or better in two ways, the one perfectly consistent with the other. There is, first, *Gaudium et spes,* usually entitled *Pastoral Constitution on the Church in the Modern World.* I confess that, at first reacting to this title in the terms of the established and classic notions of theological criteriology, I was not enthusiastic about it; it was a novelty. Now I am better able to see its justification and importance. The point is that a doctrine was being proposed in matters for which the classic method of theology was inadequate. In dogmatic matters and, for the most part, in ethical and social matters as well, our theology normally proceeded by deduction. We applied established principles, with our attention fixed upon a firm doctrinal datum. But when Vatican II set out to speak of the Church in today's world, it realized that the starting point should be a set of facts. Hence an investigative, descriptive, and induc-

---

[8] See for instance my contribution to the colloquy between Marxists and Christians, Marienbad, April–May 1967: "L'Influence créatrice de la société et de l'histoire sur la développement de l'homme chrétien," *Le Christianisme social* (1967).

tive method was indicated. We grant that the Council did not altogether follow out its program, but its expressed intention was to do so. Moreover, the encyclical *Populorum progressio* enters into the same logic. The world indeed does give something to the very datum on which theology lives. And the same may be said about man's existential experience on the one hand, and the life of the people of God on the other. This fact must set in motion a corresponding theological epistemology. It seems to me that in this historical and social perspective we need a new elaboration of several chapters of our ethics, namely those dealing with the Christian engaged in the social and political movements which serve the construction of a *human* world, a world tailored to the measure of the whole man and of all men.

In this respect—this is my second example—it seems to me that the setting up of five Roman Secretariats, alongside of, and in addition to, the traditional Congregations, has an importance that goes beyond merely pragmatic or technical considerations; it has a theological relevance as well. I should even go so far as to say that it affects the method of theological science. The Council wants the Church to be opened up for dialogue. This openness has become something like the law of the Church's apostolic and pastoral system. When the Council began its deliberations, there was only the Secretariat for Christian Unity functioning as the organ for dialogue; and the tendency was to pass everything implying contact with "the others" to its desk, even if this Secretariat were not particularly competent in the matter. For example, it seemed that contact with the non-Christian religions through the Congregation *De Propaganda Fide* was most unlikely, and so the task of preparing pertinent declarations fell to the Secretariat for Christian Unity. Today there are five Secretariats in Rome: the Secretariat for the Unity of Christians, for Non-Christian Religions, for Non-Believers, for the Lay Apostolate, for Justice and Peace. All this represents a natural development. But my point here is that theological significance attaches to these new organisms. Theologically speaking, they give us to understand that the Church does not fulfill her mission by pulling all her knowledge and her

58

every pronouncement out of her own bosom. She must ask questions of the world; she must listen to the "others"; she has something to receive from them, and *Gaudium et spes* explicitly says so (art. 44). With this, new tasks are introduced into theology, and this on the level of its datum.

B. *Concerning the Theological Construct*

But, finally, what about the *construct?* What are the tasks coming to light in this field, demanding to be taken up by today's theology? Two preliminary remarks are in order at this point.

(1) Surely there is every reason for theological renewal. But this novelty will be such in a relative sense only. The aspect of continuity, and even of identity, is incomparably weightier. The task of theology remains what it always has been. It is still a reflection on the mysteries of faith. A theologian studying, for instance, the indwelling of the Holy Spirit in the souls of the just, or the sacramental character, no more wastes his time today than his colleague did yesterday. Moreover, theology today draws its decisive teachings from the same source, that is, from the very same faith, which nourished it yesterday and from its beginnings. Although obedient to the duty of being up to date and employing the means of culture offered by our present world (investigation, elaboration, expression), it remains in depth and substance the same "discourse" about God and the mysteries of salvation which it was in the time of Gregory of Nazianzus, Augustine, or Thomas Aquinas.

(2) At the same time, the renovation and the incontestable enrichment of the sciences investigating its datum, lay new duties upon theology. We have already spoken of the possibility— or should we say, rather, the existence—of a gap between exegesis and dogmatics. This would be a matter of extreme gravity. The problem is not simple. On the one hand, exegesis needs freedom in following out the methods of its work; on the other, the student of dogma in need of textual support from the Scriptures cannot wait—any more than can the magisterium itself—

59

till the exegetes have reached a consensus on an interpretation. Are not the texts of holy Scripture, first of all, a common good of the Church and of the faithful? Still, the so-called speculative theologian must make a new effort to be informed of all the techniques of knowing the datum, techniques that at the moment are being promoted fully and most auspiciously.

Theology is a reflection on the faith. As such it has value in itself, independently of any "usefulness." But theology has also a function in the service of the people of God, in the historical situation in which this people now finds itself. In a cultivated world, and to the extent that the world is cultivated, theology must show vitality if what faith proposes is to be announced effectively and completely. There is ground here for distinguishing two lines of theological research. In the first we reflect on the various articles comprised in faith; in the second on the overall situation of faith, that is, on how faith and the act of believing as such are possible, appropriate, and fitting, it being understood that we are dealing with the Christian and even the Catholic faith. In the first case we have the theology of the different theological matters; in the second we have fundamental theology or, as Karl Rahner says, formal dogmatics.

Whichever the case may be, theology today simply must develop the reference to man. Why? Is it that today man appears as the center and measure of everything? It is evident that a conversion of this kind to pure humanism cannot be the program of theology. Yet to the extent that a conversion to humanism is the soul of atheism and of its contestation of the faith and, moreover, in respect of atheism's positive affirmations rather than its negative repudiations, we must answer its objections by making ours whatever truth atheism holds up as its own. People today are drawing away from religion, and religion is losing its hold on life. The one root cause of this is that people are losing sight of the link between God or the mysteries and men. The supernatural realities are somewhere out there, a world in its own right, without relation to us. But if this is so—and I believe it has been so to a large extent—the responsibility lies with clerics, not with revelation. Revelation speaks at least as often of man as of God; or better, it never speaks of one without also speaking of the other. The God of revelation is the God of grace, a God for men, the Creator of man made to his image. That revelation is functional is today commonly admitted. It means that God reveals himself not as he is himself, but in what he does for us and in what he wishes to be for us. Being functional in this way is not to be taken as doing away with the real meaning of the affirmations concerning being. This we have shown and strongly emphasized elsewhere.[9] But this same functionality points to the fact—in my opinion a decisive fact and the key to a great many problems brought up at the time of modernism as well as today—that the true content of revelation, its *objectum formale quod*, is the truth of the religious relation, covenant, and filial adoption, which God proposes to conclude with men in Jesus Christ. This is the reason why revelation speaks jointly of God *and* man. They are the very terms of the religious relation. Concerning the one term, God, revelation tells us exactly what makes this relation true.

There are thus reasons for elaborating in our different theological treatises the relation between the mysteries, the Christian realities, and man; not only man in general, but the historic and social man, the man whom psychology and the anthropological sciences make known to us. Surely in this certain treatises will profit more than others, for instance, the treatises on marriage, on woman's place and role, and generally our ethics. Here, one of the most urgent tasks, as I mentioned briefly above, is the elaboration of an ethics of the social and historic man viewed precisely in the historic and social conditions of his actions and duties. The man of our current moral treatises is the individual subject loaded with obligations towards God and his neighbors; he is not the man engaged in the construction of the world and called to take position in the causes of justice and peace, of progress and organization. Sometimes priests are blamed for

[9] See my "Le Christ dans l'économie salutaire et dans nos traités dogmatiques," *Concilium*, 11 (1966), 11–26, and "Le moment 'économique' et le moment 'ontologique' dans la Sacra Doctrina (Révélation, Théologie, Somme théologique)," *Mélanges M.-D. Chenu,* Paris, 1965.

speaking too much of these things and for allowing the deeper and more traditional themes of spiritual life to go by default.[10] I should like to see the proof of this; but I think that if they speak much of "these things," they do so in very general terms, and without the guidance of carefully worked-out studies, because there are scarcely any.

This anthropological reference evidently is at the heart of a fundamental theology understood as a reflection on faith as such and hence interested in clarifying its credibility (that is, the conditions making faith acceptable to man) and its appropriateness (that is, the intimate relation between being man and having faith). Let me repeat, we are dealing with Christian and even Catholic faith. Such a fundamental theology was the intention of all great apologists, most especially of Maurice Blondel whose stature seems to be growing with the years. Others have intervened since; Karl Rahner, for example, follows Joseph Maréchal rather than Blondel. Rahner's idea is the elaboration of a "transcendental anthropology."[11] By this he understands the scientific effort to bring to light the conditions under which the affirmations of faith make sense to us. There is one method of apologetics more insistent on divine authority; there is another more insistent on human truth. The former, before everything else, establishes the divine revealing authority outside of us in a purely formal and external manner, thus bringing us to accept the affirmations of faith. The other method stresses the fact of God's addressing himself to us; here the accent falls on the truth of the relations between the great themes contained in revelation, and their unique addressee who is man. This latter is Rahner's method, a way of demythologizing. Not that Rahner adopts Bult-

[10] Reproach stated in particular by J. Maritain, *Le Paysan de la Garonne,* Paris, 1966.

[11] See Karl Rahner, *Hörer des Wortes. Zur Grundlegung einer Religionsphilosophie,* revised edition by J. B. Metz, Munich, 1963; ET *Hearers of the Word,* New York and London, 1968; "Formale und fundamentale Theologie," in *Lex. f. Theol. u. Kirche,* IV, 205–206; *Est-il possible de croire aujourd'hui?,* Tours-Paris, 1966, pp. 173–225; "Theology and Anthropology," *The Word in History: The St. Xavier Symposium,* ed. T. Burke, New York, 1966, pp. 1–23. This last text is of special interest.

mann's view of reducing revelation to man's self-comprehension, or to an existential interpretation of the decision which Bultmann identifies with faith. Rahner preserves intact the objectivity of the revealed affirmations. But he proposes to show their reference to the human subject by bringing to the fore the necessary or *a priori* conditions which are relevant to man and may capture man's interest. This will eventually result in making of anthropology a dimension of all the treatises of theology: Trinity, Incarnation, salvation, angelology, sacramentology, eschatology. In this way, a demythologizing will be obtained, effected not by a de-objectivation, but by a detailed clarification of the relations between the objects, or rather the realities, and the human subject who is always implicated in their comprehension.

All this is bound to give theology an air less purely positive, more philosophic than classical theology. Hence, considering that philosophic reflection is a rare gift among mankind, this theology could not but be the concern of some particularly endowed people. But—and experience confirms this—such a theology might again find favor with a world where philosophy is much appreciated when it professes to be a reflection on the existential condition and experience of many.

Several chapters of theology may thus be rethought with, and no doubt reanimated by, an anthropology which, like holy Scripture, does not dissociate man from the whole of creation nor from his entire history. This is the case in eschatology, too often treated as an ensemble of "things," while in truth its point is the future of man and the relation of this future to his present activities. Again take the chapter on the relations between nature and the supernatural, or the doctrine of what we call "salvation." What exactly is it? What is its relation with the reality of the present creation, with the human project, its successes as well as its limits and shortcomings?

This kind of reflection on the faith—investigating with particular care its relation to man as he endeavors to understand himself—can be conducted along lines apparently almost entirely philosophical. Clearly, it is a procedure that courts the dangers involved in constructing a theology of a new type, alongside of a theology of the traditional plan and structure which will continue to follow the ancient pattern, namely, exhaustive examination of the datum in Scripture, Tradition, and the magisterium and, after this and on the basis of it, a reasoned construction of the same datum. This design, I believe, is still valid. I myself have explained it both in the article "Théologie," in *DTC* (XV, cols. 398–502) and in *La Foi et la Théologie* (Paris, 1962). Is a synthesis of these two types possible? It is desirable but difficult. There are those who think that a choice is necessary, that two types of theology, the one open to the novelties of modern thinking, the other following the lines of our classical treatises and the ontological views of St. Thomas, who in his turn depended on Aristotle, cannot be combined in one coherent construction. Let me conclude with two remarks concerning this problem.

1. No one man can do all that has to be done. The appearance of a universal genius is a rare event. The more we go ahead, the more complexities we encounter and the more specialities we need. Why not, in these conditions, think of a sort of society or "presbytery" of theologians? Vatican II put forth the idea of a *presbyterium*,[12] that is, of a grouping of priests serving a local diocesan church among whom, with the bishop acting as first pastor and moderator, are distributed the tasks attaching to the priestly mission and function. There would be here no first theologian, not at least in the sense of there being one personal authority. But the very host of theological chores to be done would serve to integrate that one and unique function of reflecting on the faith. An ensemble of means, particularly reviews and conventions, would aim at promoting connections and exchanges between the particular tasks, and fostering a synthesis which no single theologian could achieve, but which might result from such a community of theologians. A review, perhaps like *Concilium*, a congress not unlike the present one, or that held in Rome in September, 1966, are excellent occasions of dialogue and exchange, all striving for the goal that ensures, in

[12] *Lumen gentium,* art. 48; *Presbyterorum ordinis,* art. 7 ff.

spite of a disparate variety of trends or tasks, the unity of all theological endeavor.

2. Concerning the Fathers, and particularly St. Thomas—not excluding any classical theologians—our concern is to seek out their more original perceptions, over and above their system of material implements which limits them to *one* age, *one* mentality, *one* intellectual construction. Of course, the classical theologians can only be studied in the context of profound historical investigations. These, thank God, are not wanting, and they can restore and renew for us the creative reaction, the innermost perceptions of those minds. The technical apparatus employed by these scholars may prove intractable to synthesis with other instruments of thought, those, for example, borrowed from modern philosophy. But in what concerns perceptions of reality, the same today and forever, all thought can converge into a common synthesis. Take, for example, St. Thomas's perception of man as a spiritual subject having, and even being, a reference to the Absolute—you will find this particularly developed in the Second Part of the *Summa*—this perception may well be brought into concerted harmony with modern thinking in psychology or phenomenology. The Fathers, the great Scholastics, together with the liturgy and other monuments of our tradition, are still a school for us, a school to which we can continue to return. But when, faced with the questions of the modern world, we make the effort to accept its new resources, we leave the ancient technical systematizations behind us.

No doubt this is a difficult program. The theologian is on the way to becoming more and more that "almost impossible man" of whom Lacordaire spoke over a hundred years ago.[13]

---

[13] "The Catholic Doctor is an almost impossible man. He must know, on the one hand, the whole deposit of the faith, the Scriptures, the written and unwritten Traditions, the Councils, the acts of the popes, and, on the other, what St. Paul calls the elements of this world" (*Mém. pour le rétablissement* . . . , ch. 4). See also Cdl. G. B. Montini, Preface to P. Veuillot, *Notre sacerdoce*, ed. Fleurus, 1954.

3.

RENEWAL AND THE SCRIPTURE-TRADITION PROBLEM IN THE LIGHT OF VATICAN II AND MONTREAL 1963

MAX THURIAN

DURING the Fourth World Conference of Faith and Order, the theological section of the World Council of Churches, held in Montreal in 1963, one of the major topics of study was the relation between Holy Scripture and Tradition. At the same time, the Second Vatican Council took up the same problem, and, at the end of 1965, its *Dogmatic Constitution on Divine Revelation, Dei verbum,* was promulgated. With no direct communication between Vatican II and Montreal, but thanks to the efforts of Catholic and Protestant theologians, who were kept in contact by their research, a certain agreement appeared in the solutions reached. Certainly, there has been no complete unity realized on these problems, but prejudices and false questions have been discarded. And this is a sign that the Holy Spirit is at work leading both parties towards visible unity.

1. THE SCRIPTURE IS A TRADITION

Christ fulfilled and promulgated with his own mouth the Gospel promised by the prophets. He gave to the apostles the mission of proclaiming it to all men. The Gospel of Christ as preached

66

by the apostles is, then, the unique source of the whole truth concerning our salvation. This means that we do not have to seek a truth concerning salvation which is not to be found in the Gospel as in its source; that we do not have to seek in the Gospel a human truth, but only that truth which concerns the salvation of man. Further, the Gospel is also the source of the discipline of our life, the framework within which our moral life is formed. The Gospel promulgated by Christ and proclaimed by the apostles is, then, truth and life, the source of all saving truth and of the whole moral life.

This transmission of the Gospel was faithfully accomplished first by the apostles of Christ. The Gospel consists of what they received from Christ when he spoke to them, lived with them, worked in their midst, and also of what they received from the Holy Spirit who recalled to them everything Christ had said (Jn. 14, 26). This transmission of the revealed Gospel the apostles accomplished by their oral preaching and by the example of their lives. Moreover, the Gospel was also transmitted by those who wrote the message of salvation under the inspiration of the Holy Spirit.

Furthermore, God foresaw the preservation and transmission of his Gospel in the Church after the death of the apostles of Christ and of the writers of the New Testament. This is how the apostles left successors after them, ministers, *episcopoi,* to whom they transmitted their own ministry of teaching the Gospel. This espiscopal ministry of supervision entrusted by the apostles has as its essential aim to keep the Gospel intact and to maintain it always alive in the Church. Here we see the two aspects of the apostolic mandate as regards the Word of God: to guard and to transmit. The *episcopoi* also have this apostolic ministry of preserving intact the deposit of truth and to transmit it faithfully so that it remains alive and active in the Church. Scripture accentuates the ministry of guarding the evangelical truth intact; Tradition emphasizes the function of transmitting alive this same truth.

The pastors of the Church, like the apostles, ought to be the guardians of Scripture and promoters of Tradition. In both, the

67

same Gospel is expressed, the only source of all saving truth. This is why the Council can say that Tradition (chronologically earlier) and Scripture (fixed later) are like the mirror in which the Church contemplates God, from whom she receives everything, and this as long as she is a pilgrim on earth, until the day when she achieves her aim, when she will see God face to face, as he is. Tradition and Scripture together, two forms in the Church of the single Gospel, the only source of truth and life, are compared to a mirror; this is to say that God cannot be contemplated there as he is, but only, as in a mirror, reflected. As long as the Church has not achieved her final aim, she cannot contemplate God save by the mediation of signs; she cannot know the truth but in the mirror of Tradition and Scripture. This image of the mirror and that of the Church in pilgrimage show that, in the contemplation of God and the knowledge of truth, the whole gift is not given at once, in the full light of a face-to-face. The Church must journey until the day when she will see God as he is; she should constantly seek to discern better the truth of God in the mirror which is Scripture and Tradition together. This mirror reflects at once the whole of saving truth, but the Church must examine it ever more deeply, with an attention ever more constant, discovering in it all its implications until the day when the mirror will disappear, yielding in the light to the face-to-face.

Here, we must consider a burning problem of today, namely, hermeneutics, or the interpretation of Scripture. Ever since Bultmann launched the method of demythologizing, one is tempted to judge in a condescending manner the exegeses of Scripture in the past. One usually thinks that our fathers did not know modern, scientific methods and treated Scripture as a code of historical truths which they interpreted to the letter, in a fundamentalistic manner. Now, this is to have an incompetent knowledge of the interpretation of the Bible throughout the ages. Biblical theologians have always tried to make the distinction between the fundamental message of Scripture, the very Word of God, and its historical or literary envelope. Hermeneutics and demythologizing are permanent problems in the Church and have been so since its beginnings. But evidently, questions which the Church is asked concerning Scripture are not the same in every age. We should not consider the Fathers of the Church or the theologians of the Middle Ages and of the Reformation as naïve just because new questions are presenting themselves to us today. Scripture always remains a mirror which reveals to us only a reflection of God, of his person, and of his action; indeed, it is a faithful reflection, but it is not the face-to-face encounter that is promised to us at the final resurrection. Because Scripture is this mirror and this reflection, it is just and permitted to seek its deep meaning by releasing it from its contingent envelopes, from its literary expressions, from the myths and images it uses, and even to discern truths as more clearly present in the faith of the primitive Christian community than in history. We certainly no longer think that creation took place historically as Genesis relates it: it is a question of a myth being used to affirm the work of God, a personal and loving creator. We certainly no longer think of God inhabiting the heavens, as if he were sitting on top of a vault; it is a case of a primitive image that contemporary science cannot allow to subsist, but which simply underlines the transcendence of God, who is the totally other at the same time as he is present among us and within us. But where can this demythologizing stop? Is not even the resurrection a mythical expression of the reality of the Lord living in spite of the cross and death? Here, the living Tradition of the Church brings its decisive help to the interpretation of Scripture; the living Tradition of the believing, praying, and obedient Church is also a mirror wherein the mystery of the living God is reflected. It belongs, therefore, to the faith of the Church, expressed in its living Tradition, to set limits for hermeneutics and demythologizing. Fundamental faith should thereby never be placed in danger. It is probably not essential to faith to believe that the temptation of Christ in the desert was a dialogue between Jesus and Satan, in the manner of two men speaking to each other. This representation can be interiorized while still keeping its deep spiritual value. But the fact that Christ really rose from the dead, in such a manner that the tomb was found empty, is fundamental to the Christian faith, and the living Tradition of the Church cannot consider it as a myth signifying the life of Jesus in spite of death.

Furthermore, this whole hermeneutic effort, often too presumptuous, ought to be accompanied by the humble certitude that the Word of God can do without exegesis and transmit itself equally through the most naïve interpretations. Some very effective and numerous present-day evangelical movements are there to prove it.

2. THE DIFFERENT MEANINGS OF TRADITION

The preaching of the apostles is expressed in a special way in the inspired books of Scripture; but even before the canon of the New Testament was constituted, the intention to preserve and continue the evangelical teaching was present in the Church; it was already in the spirit of the apostles. We see them exhorting the faithful to guard what they transmitted to them, having received it themselves from Christ and the Holy Spirit.

It is necessary to try here to understand the signification given to the word "Tradition." The Council did not provide a precise definition in any one phrase of the *Dogmatic Constitution on Divine Revelation*. When the Council speaks of Tradition, it generally designates Tradition as transmission of the Gospel of Christ by the apostles and their successors; it does not mean to signify ecclesiastical traditions, that is, uses or customs of historical origin.

Still, it would have been useful for the Council to give definitions, as did the Fourth World Conference on "Faith and Order" at Montreal in 1963. The report of Section II, in fact, said: "We have distinguished between a number of different meanings of the word Tradition. We speak here of the *Tradition* (with a capital T), *tradition* (with a small t) and *traditions*. By *Tradition* is meant the Gospel itself, transmitted from generation to generation in and by the Church, Christ himself present in the life of the Church. By *tradition* is meant the traditionary process. The term *traditions* is used in two senses, to indicate both the diversity of forms of expression and also what we call confessional traditions" (Montreal II, 39).

Transposed to the Montreal vocabulary, the Council wanted to speak of Tradition in the first sense, of Tradition of divine origin, of the Gospel itself, transmitted from generation to generation in and by the Church, and not of traditions in the third sense, that is, of purely ecclesiastical traditions, and the forms of their expression. However, the Council speaks also of tradition in the second Montreal sense, that of the process of tradition. Hence in the conciliar text the expression takes on the notion of Tradition of divine origin (the Gospel transmitted) and the notion of process of living tradition (the transmission of the Gospel).

In the light of Vatican II and of Montreal, we can give to the concept of tradition the three following meanings, which represent our ecumenical consensus today:

1. *The Apostolic Tradition* is the whole evangelical message, just as the apostles, who had received it from Christ, and the writers of the New Testament under the inspiration of the Holy Spirit, entrusted it to the Church to guard it and transmit it until the end of time. This apostolic Tradition is expressed in a special way in the inspired books of the New Testament, and it is carried in the living Tradition of the Church, in its dogmas, its sacraments, and its sanctified life.

2. *The Tradition living in the Church* is the whole of the dogmas, the sacraments, and the holiness of the Church, incorporated into the act which transmits the faith; this Tradition, from the time of the apostles and inspired writers, guards and transmits the apostolic Tradition which it carries; the living Tradition, in this sense, is at the same time the apostolic Tradition, the revealed content of that which is transmitted, and the process of tradition, the transmission of the revealed content. It is in this sense, we think, including both content and process, that the Council speaks most often of Tradition.

3. *Ecclesiastical Traditions* are the forms of expression which the tradition of the Gospel takes according to place, time, and culture, the better to achieve its aim, which is the communication of the Word of God to men.

71

We will now give special attention to the point of Tradition living in the Church. Tradition appears here as a life and a dynamism of faith which grows and deepens; Tradition is the very life of Holy Church in faith: "In her doctrine, in her life, and her worship, the Church perpetuates and transmits to all generations all that she herself is, all that she believes," says the Council. Tradition is here identified with the total life of the Church (doctrine, existence, worship); Tradition perpetuates and transmits the life and the faith of the Church. This is a vital and dynamic conception of Tradition, which is the life of the Gospel of Christ in the Church, under the form of doctrinal teaching, sanctified existence, and sacramental worship, insofar as they assure the continuity and accomplish the transmission of the very being of the Church and of her faith.

Montreal conveyed an analogous conception of Tradition: "In our present situation," said the theologians of Montreal, "we wish to reconsider the problem of Scripture and Tradition, or rather that of Tradition and Scripture. And therefore, we wish to propose the following statement as a fruitful way of reformulating the question. Our starting point is that we are all living in a tradition which goes back to our Lord and has its roots in the Old Testament, and are all indebted to that tradition inasmuch as we have received the revealed truth, the Gospel, through its being transmitted from one generation to another. Thus we can say that we exist as Christians by the Tradition of the Gospel (the *paradosis* of the kerygma) testified in Scripture, transmitted in and by the Church through the power of the Holy Spirit. Tradition taken in this sense is actualized in the preaching of the Word, in the administration of the Sacraments and worship, in Christian teaching and theology, and in mission and witness to Christ by the lives of the members of the Church. What is transmitted in the process of tradition is the Christian faith, not only as a sum of tenets, but as a living reality transmitted through the operation of the Holy Spirit. We can speak of the Christian Tradition (with a capital T), whose content is God's revelation and self-giving in Christ, present in the life of the Church" (II, 45–46).

72

This Tradition which comes from the apostles, which is the Gospel living in the Church, progresses under the assistance of the Holy Spirit. Assistance is not inspiration. Only the apostles and the biblical writers are considered by the Church as having been inspired in the transmission which they performed of the Word of God. The Church in her Tradition does not enjoy the inspiration but the assistance of the Holy Spirit. This means that the living tradition of the Church cannot add a revealed truth, under the inspiration of the Spirit, to what has been given completely and definitively by the apostles, in their oral and written Tradition, and by the writers of the New Testament, who alone enjoy the inspiration of the Holy Spirit. Revelation has been achieved by the apostles and the writers of the New Testament.

The assistance of the Holy Spirit permits the Church to penetrate revelation more deeply and to develop its implications, but not to add to this revelation truths not already present in apostolic Tradition or in the New Testament. Therefore, the Church in her tradition does nothing but recover and investigate under the assistance of the Holy Spirit, that which has been given once for all in the Tradition of the apostles and recorded by writing in the New Testament. When the conciliar text, then, says that "this tradition which comes from the apostles progresses in the Church," it refers to this penetration of revelation and to the development of its implications which is accomplished in the living Tradition of the Church, under the assistance of the Holy Spirit. This is not a matter of progress by quantitative addition of new truths, but of an organic growth of the conscience of the Church, which understands always more profoundly the whole truth.

3. THE UNION BETWEEN SCRIPTURE AND TRADITION

There is a tight link between Tradition and Scripture, which communicate one with the other; together they form a true unity and tend towards an identical goal, for they flow from the same

73

divine source. The Council is remarkably precise. There is but one and the same source of truth, which is the very revelation of God, the Gospel of Christ "promised first by the Prophets and which he himself fulfilled and promulgated from his own mouth" (*Dogmatic Constitution on Divine Revelation,* art. 7). We are not to see Scripture and Tradition as two distinct sources of revelation; we must go behind and beyond Scripture and Tradition to the Gospel of Christ himself, to the Word of God, which is the unique source of revelation. Tradition and Scripture flow from this unique source of the Word of God, they are its first original forms, its first and primitive manifestations in the Church, its authentic channels, profoundly united to each other, communicating with each other, both directed towards the same aim: the knowledge of the whole Word of God in the Church, and through her, in the world.

The Council describes the proper and different modes of Scripture and Tradition, as forms, manifestations, channels of the unique revelation of the Word of God (*locutio Dei*) as recorded in writing under the breath of the Holy Spirit. Scripture is the written record of the act of God speaking. Scripture thus contains the Word of God under the form of a written document, but this Word of God was first a living act, of which the Holy Spirit then inspired the recording. We see here how Scripture flows from the unique divine source, revelation. There is first the act of God speaking, then the inspiration of the Holy Spirit directing the act of writing, finally the Scripture itself which is the record of the living Word of God. Tradition in turn transmits the Word of God (*verbum Dei integre transmittit*), entrusted to the apostles by Christ the Lord and by the Holy Spirit; it is clear that Tradition is conceived here essentially as an act of faithful transmission of the Word of God. Tradition is not the Word of God in the same sense in which it has just been said that Scripture is the act of the Word of God recorded by the inspiration of the Spirit. Tradition carries the Word of God as entrusted to the apostles by Christ and the Spirit, and transmits it. We see here, then, how Tradition flows from the unique divine source, revelation. There is first the Word of God, then

74

the mandate of Christ and of the Spirit to the apostles, who constitute that which ought to be transmitted, finally Tradition itself, which is the transmission of the living Word of God.

If one compares Scripture and Tradition in this description, one notices that Scripture is the act of the Word of God recorded and that Tradition transmits the Word of God entrusted to the apostles. Scripture, then, is distinguished from the Word of God, or from revelation, only by the passage from the act of speech to the record by writing, and again this record is inspired by the Holy Spirit. Tradition is distinguished from the Word of God, or from revelation, in that it transmits the Word of God. Tradition is thus other than the Word, though it carries the Word and is linked to it by the very fact that it transmits it. Scripture *is*, Tradition *transmits*, the Word of God entrusted to the apostles by Christ and the Spirit.

The Council does not juxtapose Tradition and Scripture in an attempt to define what properly constitutes Tradition, but refers it to the unique source of the Word of God which it carries and transmits. This transmission of the Word of God brings the Word of God to the successors of the apostles, "that under the enlightenment of the Spirit of truth, in their preaching, they might guard this Word, explain it, and faithfully propagate it." The Council distinguishes between the Word of God, entrusted to the apostles by Christ and the Spirit, that is to say by inspiration, and the ministry of the Word of God, exercised by the successors of the apostles under the light of the Spirit of truth (*praelucente Spiritu veritatis*), that is to say, with the assistance of the Holy Spirit. The Word of God, transmitted by Tradition, is a fruit of the inspiration of the Holy Spirit; the ministry of the Word of God, exercised by the successors of the apostles, is a fruit of the assistance of the Holy Spirit. In the first case, the work of the apostles is constitutive of apostolic Tradition, by mandate of Christ and the inspiration of the Spirit; in the second case, the preaching of the successors is a service of the Word of God which they have received by Tradition, which they guard, expound, and spread faithfully, with the assistance of the Spirit

75

of truth; they cannot add anything objectively to the content of apostolic Tradition, to the Word of God given once for all.

An important addition was made to the conciliar text before the final vote: "Consequently, it is not from sacred Scripture alone that the Church draws her certainty about everything which has been revealed." The explanation of this addition given by Cardinal Florit, archbishop of Florence, affirmed that the text of the Schema remained unchanged in its substance, and that it was perfected in its expression. The two most important justifications of this addition may be summed up as follows:

1. The Catholic doctrine, sanctioned by the constant practice of the Church, maintains that the Church draws her certitude about revealed things from sacred Scripture always joined to Tradition; hence when Scripture alone is insufficient for the attainment of this certitude, Tradition can contribute a decisive argument.

2. The meaning of this affirmation ought to be judged and circumscribed by the general tenor of the Schema, according to which

(a) Tradition is not presented as a quantitative supplement to Holy Scripture,

(b) Holy Scripture is not presented as a codification of the whole of revelation.

We must first emphasize the importance of the word "certainty." It is not a question, in this addition, of the objective existence of revealed realities which absolutely are not found in Scripture and which would have to be sought in Tradition. The role of Tradition is to confirm the certitude of the Church about certain revealed things for which Scripture alone is not sufficient to provide this certitude; this is not to say that Scripture does not contain at all these revealed things, even implicitly, and that one cannot find them except in Tradition. There is no such thing as *sola Traditio,* any more than *sola Scriptura,* even for certain particular truths. The Church draws her certitude about Relevation from Scripture always joined to Tradition; and when Scripture is not sufficient for the attainment of a certitude, Tradi-

76

tion does not furnish the objective reality of a truth absent from Scripture, but a decisive argument for the certitude of the Church concerning this truth not made explicit by Scripture alone.

Tradition is not, then, a quantitative supplement to Scripture; there are no truths of Tradition to be added to those of Scripture; both carry the same revelation. Yet Scripture is not a codification of the integral revelation. The Bible is not a code fallen from heaven, all of whose affirmations are immediately evident. To say that Scripture is the Word of God recorded under the inspiration of the Holy Spirit does not mean that it can be understood immediately in all its parts, in its full signification, and all its implications. Scripture, fruit of the living Tradition of the Church just as it is fruit of the Holy Spirit, needs to be read and interpreted in the life of the Church, in conjunction with Tradition, in order to be fully grasped in its full signification and all its implications. Scripture, to be understood as the living Word of God, cannot, then, be isolated (*sola Scriptura*) from the life of the Church and from Tradition.

One may verify this affirmation by the study of certain truths of the Christian faith, the Trinitarian dogma, the Christological dogma and the Eucharistic dogma, for example. One cannot deny that in Scripture God manifests himself, speaks, and acts as only God, as Father, Son, and Spirit; but the Trinitarian dogma of the Christian faith appears as the résumé, assured and confirmed by Tradition of this Trinitarian truth present in the history of salvation, reported by Scripture. Nor can one doubt that in the Gospel Christ appears as the Son of God and as a man; but the Christological dogma of the two natures is an authentic explanation of Tradition which assures the faith in Christ, true God and true man, as he appears in Scripture. This is certainly true of the dogma of the real presence of Christ in the Eucharist. This real presence by which the Church lives in her Eucharistic liturgy since the apostles, brings a decisive light to the interpretation of certain brief texts of the New Testament which recount to us the institution of the Holy Supper by Christ. Here, the living Tradition of the Eucharist brings a decisive argument to our certitude on the real presence, implicitly attested by the Scripture in its eucharistic texts.

This reminds us of the Montreal text: "The Scriptures as documents can be letter only. It is the Spirit who is the Lord and Giver of life. Accordingly, we may say that the right interpretation (taking the words in the widest possible sense) is that interpretation which is guided by the Holy Spirit" (II, 52).

For the Vatican Council, the Holy Spirit is the soul of the living Tradition of the Church, and this Tradition ought to be joined to Scripture for the Church to achieve the fullest certitude on all revealed things.

No Christian confession gets away from this union of Tradition and Scripture. In fact, every Christian comes to Scripture with a formation he has inherited from the tradition in which he was born; each Church confirms the certitude of its teaching by Scripture interpreted in the light of its tradition. Who could claim to interpret Scripture by itself alone, without introducing into his interpretation the argument of tradition? Who could assert that he believes on the basis of Scripture alone? The Montreal conference said, not without a touch of humour: "We are more aware of our living in various confessional traditions, e.g., that stated paradoxically in the saying 'It has been the tradition of my church not to attribute any weight to tradition.' " To return to the example of faith in the Eucharistic presence, there is no doubt that the various Christian confessions, which often find themselves opposed to one another on this question of the real presence, do introduce into their interpretation of the pertinent scriptural texts arguments based not only on objective exegesis, but also on their particular ecclesial tradition, their own theological system, and their own liturgical experience.

Here arises the problem of the criterion, the principle of interpretation of Scripture and Tradition. The Montreal conference stated it as follows: "The necessity of interpretation raises again the question of the criterion for the genuine Tradition. . . . This problem has been dealt with in different ways by the various churches. In some confessional traditions the accepted hermeneutical principle has been that any portion of Scripture is to be interpreted in the light of Scripture as a whole. In others the key has been sought in what is considered to be the centre of Holy Scripture, and the emphasis has been primarily on the incarnation, or on the atonement and redemption, or on justification by faith, or again on the message of the nearness of the Kingdom of God, or on the ethical teachings of Jesus. In yet others, all emphasis is laid upon what Scripture says to the individual conscience, under the guidance of the Holy Spirit. In the Orthodox Church the hermeneutical key is found in the mind of the Church, especially as expressed in the Fathers of the Church and in the Ecumenical Councils. In the Roman Catholic Church the key is found in the deposit of faith, of which the Church's magisterium is the guardian. In other traditions again, the creeds, complemented by confessional documents or by the definitions of Ecumenical Councils and the witness of the Fathers, are considered to give the right key to the understanding of Scripture. In none of these cases where the principle of interpretation is found elsewhere than in Scripture is the authority thought to be alien to the central concept of Holy Scripture. On the contrary, it is considered as providing just a key to the understanding of what is said in Scripture" (II, 51, 53).

Once more, we see to what extent Montreal and Vatican II posed their problems in the same way. However, the major and decisive difference between them continues to be the question of the criterion of the authentic Tradition and of the correct interpretation of Scripture, that is to say, in the last analysis, of the magisterium. Which Church, and who in the Church, possesses the ministry of protecting the deposit of faith and of determining, in case of doubt or during a crisis, the exact meaning of Scripture and true tradition? But this is another problem which it is not my task to deal with here. If this problem of the magisterium of the Church and in the Church remains ahead of us in our ecumenical dialogue, we must nevertheless rejoice that Vatican II and Montreal 1963 have found it possible to draw together their points of view on the relations between Scripture and Tradition.

4. THE PROCESS OF TRADITION

We have seen how Scripture (revelation of God's Word to the Church) and Tradition (the life and transmission of this Word within the Church) are closely bound one to the other. We ought now to grasp *how* Holy Scripture is understood by and in the Church, in view of a faithful tradition, in view of an accurate transmission of faith down through the centuries, and for the salvation of men. I think that on the *how* of this handing on of faith we are also much nearer than ever. I will limit myself to a statement of three aspects of the process of tradition: tradition living in the Church, the tradition of the Gospel, or the transmission of faith, has (1) a universal, (2) a liturgical, and (3) a missionary character.

The universal Church, in its living tradition, seeks to explain the Word of God in an inclusive way so as to be understood by all the local Churches: this is the fundamental reason for calling the Churches together in Councils where the universality of tradition takes on a spatial quality. But the Church is universal in time too, and she also seeks to explain the Word of God in continuity with the past; this is why the living tradition takes into account the Church's secular experience; this is why she likes to return to primitive sources both liturgical and patristic: she wants to see her theological development from century to century. However, this attention to continuity does not prevent the Church from freely examining new problems arising and influencing her thought and life. For example, there is no doubt that modern, scientific development forces the Church's tradition to take another look at her interpretation of Scripture and to make a sound distinction between what is fundamental and what is literary, cultural, or mythic wrapping. In all these ways the universality of the Church is shown forth in tradition.

Secondly, the Church understands the Word of God in her common prayer, in her doxological adoration, in her liturgy. This is tradition in its doxological or liturgical form. God speaks to the Church in prayer through Scripture. And Scripture provides the Church with her response to God: in the psalms, in prayers woven out of a biblical vocabulary, in hymns or canticles charged with scriptural theology. In using Scripture in this way in her liturgy, the Church turns the Word of God into living experience. It penetrates that Word and transmits it. It is thus that liturgy is a privileged place for tradition.

Thirdly, the Church is always in the process of understanding the Word of God better, and she transmits it efficaciously to men in the measure of her attentiveness to the world, to its needs and its difficulties. This, indeed, is the world to which it is her duty to proclaim the Gospel. This is the missionary form of the understanding and of the tradition of the Word of God in the Church. Christ reigns in the world and prepares men in mysterious ways for their encounter with him. The Church must at the same time know revelation and be attentive to the signs that the Saviour of the World is preparing men for the Gospel. The dialogue of the Church with the world is also a form of tradition as the Church's actual understanding of the Gospel. This dialogue expands the Church to its catholic dimensions. In order that true tradition of the Gospel function, in order that the Word of God truly and actually reach men and the world, the Church must be profoundly presented to men and to the world. She must penetrate, understand, and utilize the values and the vocabulary of the time. By vocabulary is meant all means of expression: not just language, but images, signs, literature, the novel, the cinema, the theatre, song. The Church must look with optimism and gratitude on new techniques as on values. The Church has too often been pessimistic and puritanical about the world. Condemn and reject sin in all its forms—war, injustice, greed, pride, which exploit the values of this world for their own purposes—she must; but she must also be positive and hopeful about the world's values themselves as open to sanctification by the Gospel. The dialogue of the Church with a world whose language she understands and speaks can be the occasion for the Gospel's finding a new way of expressing and revealing its catholicity and its efficacy. Thus does the world, and all the authentic values which the Lord sustains and develops in it, share too in the tradition of that Gospel which reveals in every age the wealth of its treasures.

In the context of divided Christendom, but also of the ecumenical dialogue now going on, I should like to suggest still another possible aspect of tradition, one actually arising from our divisions yet struggling eagerly to discover visible unity. Our ecumenical dialogue, our common prayer for unity, our peaceful coexistence—more and more a pro-existence—our shared search for better communication of the Gospel to men, are not these an unexpected form of living tradition in our day? Is it not the case that our understanding of the Gospel deepens and progresses where our ecumenical awareness is the more lively? There is today a lively tradition of ecumenism in the Churches. Indeed it is to this deepening and developing of the tradition of faith in the sister Churches that Pope Paul VI called Christians on the occasion of his visit to Constantinople. We are no longer truly separated, rather we are already moving along the path of the visible unity of faith, when we live together this prodigious adventure, this ecumenical quest, wherein living tradition in the Church, understanding of Scripture by the Church, becomes richer and deeper and more advanced, even to the point of our one day drawing so close together that we may receive the same Eucharist—tradition *par excellence* of the Word of God, transmission of the Bread of Life.

4.

THEOLOGY OF RENEWAL
TALKS ABOUT GOD

EDWARD SCHILLEBEECKX, O.P.

THE Christian revelation, in the form in which it has been handed down to us, clearly no longer provides any valid answer to the questions about God asked by the majority of people today, and it would also appear not to make any material contribution to modern man's meaningful understanding of himself in this world and in human history. We could say that the great mass of people who, at an earlier period of history when the framework of society was taken for granted to be Christian, were sociologically speaking "nominal Christians" can, now that this framework of society has ceased to exist, be called as a mass "nominally atheist." I shall not consider here the question as to whether this has brought about a great existential change, but would prefer to direct attention to those members of modern society who still try to go through life as conscious *Christians.* It is at once evident that more and more of these people are becoming increasingly displeased and dissatisfied with traditional Christian answers to their questions. It is in particular their questions about God which are central, and there is unmistakable evidence of a growing desire everywhere for a new answer to be given to these new questions about God. The situation requires us to speak about God in a way that is *different* from our past speaking about God. If we do not do this, we shall perhaps still be able to experience God *ourselves* in obsolete forms, but *our own* witness of and speaking about God will clearly be greeted by most people of today with headshaking disbelief as incomprehensible mumb-jumbo. Partly because we are blind to the "signs of the times," God's word, in our speaking about God, is certainly returning to us empty—quite the opposite to what the Old Testament prophet assured us would happen.

The criticism of the traditional way of speaking about God which is being voiced within the Christian Churches today, both Protestant and Catholic, arises, on the one hand, from the deepest values which these Churches really aim to embody and, on the other hand, from the new rational and secular sphere of understanding within which people are now seeking a meaning for human life. I propose to analyze the second of these two affirmations first, and then to go on to analyze the first in terms of the older and the new way of "speaking about God."

1. THE CONSEQUENCES OF THE GRADUAL DISCOVERY OF THE RATIONAL SPHERE OF UNDERSTANDING

There are many different factors which prompt us to speak differently about God. I shall confine myself here to those factors which are connected with the growth of a rational sphere of understanding.

In the patristic and the medieval periods, man—despite the "antidote" of Albert's and Thomas's revaluation of the so-called *causae secundae* which was, in principle at least, injected into man—generally viewed and appraised everything in the light of the *causae primae et ultimae,* following the Augustinian world view. Medieval wisdom and science had little to offer him in the way of improving his life in this world, which was filled with the Church's ethical and explicitly religious values, and the ultimate perspective of a happy existence after this life. This was the real horizon of his life. The Church tried, of course, to alleviate misery in this world by works of charity, but man's intellect seemed not yet to have discovered its special task and its possibilities for the future.

Nonetheless, a glimpse of man's technical ability to improve his lot on earth became apparent in the twelfth century. These were not European discoveries, but the result of chance encounters with the East during the crusades which made the *ars mechanica* acclaimed with as much enthusiasm in the twelfth century as the first launching of a satellite has been greeted in our own age. The water wheel, which could perform the servile work of men and even of twenty-four horses, was (re-)discovered and windmills, levers, the compass, the mechanical time-piece and so on[1] all brought more humanity into the world. The world became a rather more human place to live in.

At the same time, however, man found out at once that technology could also be a source of new misery. All kinds of new and ingenious implements of war were invented, implements which were condemned as early as 1139 at the Second Lateran Council because of their murderous power. Then, as now, the "rise of technology" was interpreted by some as the work of the devil which claimed to improve on the work of God's creation.[2] This view persisted obstinately until the reign of Philip II of Spain. A suggestion was submitted to the country's administrators for making the rivers Tajo and Manzanares navigable and thus for creating greater economic possibilities for certain isolated groups of the population. It was rejected by the government commission. It was admitted that the situation in which these people lived was unsatisfactory and indeed untenable, but "If God had so willed that these rivers should be navigable," the commission said, at least in its explicit vindication of its

[1] See L. Mumford, Techniques and Civilization, New York, 1963; J. le Goff, *La Civilisation de l'Occident médiéval*, Paris, 1964, chapter 7, pp. 249–318; M.-D. Chenu, "Arts mécaniques et œuvres serviles," *Revue des sciences philosophiques et théologiques*, 29 (1940), pp. 313–315 and *La Théologie au douzième siècle*, Paris, 1957, pp. 19–51.

[2] *Ars mechanica* was traced back, by an etymological trick, to the root *moechia*—technology was a violation of human dignity. See P. Delhaye, *Le Microcosmos de Godefroid de S. Victor*, Lille, 1951, p. 115; M.-D. Chenu, "Arts mécaniques," *op. cit.*, pp. 313–315.

disapproval of the plan, "then he would have made them so with a single word, as he did formerly when he said '*fiat lux*' (let there be light). It would be a bold infringement of the rights of Providence if human hands were to venture to try to improve what God has left unfinished for unfathomable reasons."[3] This historical event depicts in its sharpest form a basic characteristic of medieval and Augustinian man—his affirmation of the static status quo of this world, the evils of which were absorbed as far as possible by works of charity. A rational understanding, as the principle on which to base a plan for the future within the world, was beyond the range of medieval man.

As a result of the later process in the West of rationalization in the service of mankind, modern man has discovered the world, and thus himself as well, in an entirely new way, that is, as a situated freedom which, together with others, has to give itself its definite character in a task which gives meaning in this world, so that justice, peace, and love may prevail among men. It can scarcely be disputed that *this* is the new pattern of life of mankind today, although it may or may not be explicitly formulated. But we must be critical in our attitude towards the possibility of its total realization. It is, after all, obviously intersected by equally unmistakable abuse and ultimately also by the "sin of the world."

This dynamism, together with its partial realization in many different spheres, has undoubtedly led to a diminution in the search for religious security. The uncertainties of the earlier "static" world, which, men believed, could not be essentially changed, have to a great extent ceased to exist. The new, rational sphere of understanding, which led to many sectors gradually being withdrawn from the domain of faith and theology, has not only caused a cleavage between man's new understanding of himself and his traditional Christian ideas about, practice of, and attitude towards faith, but has also ultimately raised the fundamental problem of the relationship between man's under-

[3] Quoted by M. Landmann in *Problematik, Nichtwissen und Wissensverlangen im philosophischen Bewusstsein,* Göttingen, 1949, p. 55, note 13.

standing of himself and his understanding of faith. It therefore poses the question of the legitimacy of our "speaking about God."

The recognition of an independent sphere of understanding within this world has had a very long growth. Leaving aside even earlier origins, the first clear signs at least of a Christian secularization can be seen as early as the twelfth and thirteenth centuries, when a horizontal creatural network began to be built into the traditional Augustinian theology of the exclusively vertical relationship with God coming only from without, the "extrinsic" relationship. This can be illustrated by two fundamental examples taken from many, the first at the ethical level and the second at the more general level of the theory of knowledge.

After a few initial attempts had been made by the theologians of the early Middle Ages, the thirteenth-century theologians especially began to build the human *natura* with an inherent *lex naturae* in "between" God (and his *Lex divina* that had been handed down by tradition) and man's conscience. This attempt had all the defects of any beginning, and we must therefore be especially alert to the intention that lay behind it and to what it aimed to do. The purpose was to humanize morality, to base it *in* man himself and thus to interiorize it, without denying its ultimate theist foundation. The second example is to be found in Albert's and Thomas's new attempt to build the horizontal structure of the *intellectus agens* into the medieval Augustinian doctrine of vertical "illumination." In this way, although it remained within the all-embracing understanding of faith, the legitimacy of a rational sphere of understanding was nonetheless established for the first time in the history of Christianity. Even more symptoms of this increasing "secularization" or humanistic interiorization could be quoted from Albert and Thomas. All the same, these new insights still remained a secularization within the one supernatural vision of life.

This view was radically changed in the last quarter of the sixteenth century. Apart from a few beginnings made round about the middle of the sixteenth century, a real division was made in the history of the West by Bellarmine, who was the first to teach with complete clarity the so-called *natura pura* theory,[4] in which the principle that man has both a supernatural destiny and a destiny within this world was affirmed for the first time in history. This meant a break not only with the patristic period and the Middle Ages, but also with the *sacral* extra-Christian and pre-Christian world. It was the beginning of what may be called "horizontalism" (a misleading image, certainly, but a suggestive one). I am not implying that the *natura pura* theory was the active origin of the modern tendency towards secularization. Probably quite the reverse is the case—the *natura pura* theory came about as an *interpretation* (albeit inadequate and unsuccessful) of a new understanding of man that had gradually arisen on almost all sides at the turn of the tide in the autumn of the Middle Ages and the spring of the Renaissance, when man was beginning to accept the full value and dignity of his being man within this world. The *constitutive* difference of this new sense of man and the world from the older biblical, patristic, and scholastic view of life is most strikingly revealed in the previously completely unknown theological idea of the *natura pura*. This theory affirmed that being man was independently meaningful, quite apart from any supernatural destiny.[5]

The Reformation returned to the biblical, patristic, and

[4] Henri de Lubac wrongly attributed the *natura pura* theory to Cajetan in his *Surnaturel,* Paris, 1946, as did J. H. Walgrave in *Geloof en theologie in de crisis,* Kasterlee 1967. This affirmation was correctly attacked by H. Rondet in "Le problème de la nature pure et la théologie du XVIe siècle," *Recherches de science religieuse,* 35 (1948), pp. 481–522 and by P. Smulders, "De oorsprong van de theorie der zuivere natuur," *Bijdragen,* 10 (1949), pp. 105–127. Cajetan certainly announced a different feeling for life by his minimalist interpretation of the natural longing for grace, but after the way had been prepared by the Louvain theologians (R. Tapper and J. Driedo) and by Bañez. the *natura pura* theory was created by Bellarmine.

[5] It is quite true that the emergence of the *natura pura* theory can be attributed to speculation in the sixteenth century about the gratuitous character of grace, but the belief that this theory was necessary to confirm the gratuity of grace certainly originated in a Renaissance context. Basically, then, Baianism was a reaction against this novelty in the idea of *natura pura* and it must be judged in this light.

88

medieval view of man's one religious, supernatural destiny and at the same time denied the importance of man's life within a purely rational sphere of understanding. All the same, it did contribute in quite a different way to further secularization, namely, by denying the Catholic view that it was possible in principle to say something meaningful about God within a rational sphere of understanding. This interpretation of Christianity, called "fideist" in Catholic circles, left the world, as world, in its complete secularity. The vertical religious life was thus placed really perpendicular to man's horizontal life in this world. This could, on the one hand, easily lead to "fundamentalism," but it could, on the other hand, equally well lead to a freer acceptance of the rational sphere of understanding in the non-religious field, and ultimately even in the field of Christian faith, at least as far as its content was concerned—in Bultmann's *was,* not in his *dass* of Christian faith.

The principle of the rational sphere of understanding—initially still a part of the sphere of understanding of faith, but raised in principle by the *natura pura* theory to a sphere of life which in itself provided a meaningful horizon of human life—has been constantly affirmed and substantiated more and more clearly, and in an increasingly all-embracing way by the tangible and effective results of the independent experimental natural sciences and the *Geistes wissenschaften,* and in our own times by those of what have come to be called the behavior sciences,[6] results that have shown themselves to be fruitful in making this world a place fit for men to live in.

The Enlightenment even broke with the *natura pura* theory, at least as an interpretation of the new, secularized idea of man. This theory itself had been a new secularization in comparison with the distinctively medieval form of secularization, which only implied a discovery and a recognition of the legality of the *causae secundae* by virtue of the *causa prima.* The newer form of secularization brought about by the Enlightenment was one

---

[6] In the Netherlands, the *Geisteswissenschaften* are called the alpha disciplines, the natural sciences are known as the beta disciplines, and the behavior sciences are termed the gamma disciplines.

in which man became explicitly conscious of the *process of sec-ularization* itself on the one hand, and took an active part in this process on the other. The rational sphere of understanding became all-embracing and rationality had the last word, even about faith, if this came into focus at all.

Against the background of the past, this process of seculariza-tion of course meant that religion, the Churches, and theology suffered a functional loss. A new, independent world came into being alongside the Church. The Church, however, continued to live in her old world until she had to discover how to live in a totally different world from the one in which very many people now live. The cleavage between the Church and the world thus gives the impression of two different worlds—the *world of past memory,* the Church, and the *world of the future,* dynamic mankind living within an all-embracing rational sphere of under-standing.

The confidence that men in need had previously placed in the Church was transferred, because of this functional loss, to the sciences, technology, politics, welfare work, and so on— all of them activities and institutions realized and furthered within a rational sphere of understanding. The traditional way of speaking about God and to God thus became gradually more difficult. Specialists in new sciences also began to concern them-selves with the religious phenomenon, a field in which previously only the theologian had appeared to be competent. The psyche of religious man was scientifically interpreted—depth-psycholo-gists interpreted faith and religion, an interpretation which is, moreover, at its own, relative level, quite legitimate. In the same way, sociologists also interpreted religion. Thus modern man was confronted with a certain ambiguity in his thinking about and his practice of faith. Religion became "suspect."

All this impaired the traditional way of speaking about and to God. Experience, too, seemed to confirm the growing doubt —diseases which apparently no prayer or miracle had been able to cure were cured by modern drugs, fields which had re-mained infertile despite sprinkling with holy water were made fertile by chemicals, and human needs were alleviated by various social provision and economic changes in the structure of society. Man ceased to speak about and to God in the way which he had previously taken for granted. Necessity, the "mother of invention," was radically conceived and, as borne out by experience, this approach proved to be much more *effective* than prayer in mitigating human needs. The result is that man today finds it not only more difficult than he did in the past to speak *about* God, but also to speak *to* God. Many people who have been brought up explicitly as Christians leave the Church without a sound, and those who still continue to believe authentically experience great difficulties in speaking about and to God.

What is more, believers, living in an increasingly pluralistic society, have made the initially disturbing discovery that those who do not believe are neither more stupid nor less virtuous than they are. They have found out, too, that Christians have specific faults and lack understanding in specific respects, and that a great deal of injustice has often been perpetrated "in the name of God." All this has meant that the very significance of religion, of speaking about and to God, and of appealing to God has been swallowed up in the mist.

This process, which is of course still going on, has now reached a stage where the historical background against which it has taken place has been forgotten, and different words are being sought to define its present stage. Instead of talking about secularization, sociologists are tending more and more to talk about *differentiation,* and the theory of "structuralism" is gaining ground in France. But, whatever name we give the child— and he has a right to many names— we should not neglect the other side of this social process. Secularization is, after all, also an expression of man's fundamental uncertainty in a world which he himself has designed. In the past, uncertainty and spiritual distress were the consequence of a status quo world on which man seemed to be unable to have any effect. Now, however, he is made anxious by the world that he has himself devised. The process of rationalization and man's increasing ability to manipulate the world are at the "instrumental" level, that is, at the level of the means and the sub-meanings of human life,

91

and not at the level of ultimate significance. This whole process has therefore been accompanied by a loss of significance, by an obscuring of the ends. A certain *insignifiance* has crept into human life and attitudes, and everything has become trivial. The result is that we have uneasiness, revolt, and demonstrations by restless young men like the *provo's* in the Netherlands. Paul Ricoeur has recently spoken about the "caractére d'insignifiance qui s'attache á un projet simplement instrumental."[7] All this should also spur us on to discover the meaning of religion in a new way, on the basis of secularization.

The most recent stage through which history is passing in this whole scheme of social change is indeed concerned with (apart from the many different forms of atheism) a radical reinterpretation of religion itself, of Christianity and of the Christian way of speaking about God. Without drawing any sharp dividing lines, it is possible to distinguish two tendencies in this reinterpretation—the first calls itself, paradoxically, "Christian atheism," the second is concerned with the various forms of the "Death of God" movement.[8] Both movements take as their point of departure the radical identity between the love of God and Christian human fellowship. The second movement appears to be concerned with the love of God in the exclusive form of *devotio* or dedication to our fellow men. Of the first group, those who call themselves Christian atheists, we may ask (not whether they are really atheists, but) whether they are not advocating a destructive absorption of the love of God in love of our fellow men, albeit in the sign of the man Jesus as our example.

These tendencies have made the arguments of D. Bonhoeffer, who had already challenged us with his ideas of a "secular interpretation of the Bible"[9] and "religionless faith,"[10] even more

[7] "Prévision économique et choix éthique," *Esprit*, 34 (1966), pp. 178–193.

[8] T. Altizer and W. Hamilton, *Radical Theology and the Death of God*, New York, 1966; T. Altizer, *The Gospel of Christian Atheism*, Philadelphia, 1966. See also H. Cox, *The Secular City*, New York, 1966 and *God's Revolution and Man's Responsibility*, Valley Forge, 1965; G. Vahanian, *The Death of God*, New York, 1961, and *No Other God*, New York, 1966.

[9] *Widerstand und Ergebung*, Munich, 1951, *passim; ET Letters and*

forceful. Even H. Braun's explicit affirmation that an existential interpretation of the Bible is possible without referring to God[11] appeals to many people, despite Bultmann's protest against this.

We should not imagine that these still rather vague forms of "Christian atheism," in other words, of Christian silence about God, are only theories which originated in scholarly circles and commenced their journey round the world from there. In my opinion, the very opposite is nearer to the truth—the theologians have simply thematized and expressed in a systematic way what many believers have been experiencing in their own lives since the war, whether they wanted to or not. This problem was thrust forcibly under my nose in a very suggestive way once, in circumstances in which I would least have expected it. A Dutch youngster, fully eight years old, was admonished by his father at lunch, "Hey! Say grace first! Thank God for what he is giving you to eat today." The boy's answer was immediate. "God isn't giving it to me. All of *you* work to give it to me." And this was said with a nonchalant shrug of the shoulders, as if to say, "how old-fashioned you all are still."

What is new in this experience is that it is taken for granted, and that it has spread all over the world. In other civilizations, a process of secularization has taken place in the present, and similar phenomena have even occurred in the distant past. It is, for example, possible to regard the philosophy of ancient Greece as a demythologizing interpretation of the gods of Olympus, and Titus Lucretius Carus, the Epicurean, wrote things in his *De rerum natura* [12] of which whole pages could be quoted and the modern reader would, if the author's name were suppressed,

---

Papers from Prison, London, 1967, *Prisoner for God,* New York, 1957. See also G. Ebeling, "Die nicht-religiöse Interpretation biblischer Begriffe," *Zeitschrift für Theologie und Kirche,* 52 (1955), pp. 296–360.

[10] *Widerstand und Ergebung,* especially pp. 178 ff. See also H. Zahrnt, *Die Sache mit Gott,* Munich, 1967, pp. 170–178, 196–214.

[11] *Gesammelte Studien zum Neuen Testament und seiner Umwelt,* Tübingen, 1962, pp. 243–309, especially p. 297. On the basis of a narrowly empirical linguistic analysis, Paul van Buren also makes the same affirmation in *The Secular Meaning of the Gospel,* London, 1963.

[12] Published in Zurich, 1956. See also a brief outline of Lucretius in G. Hasenhüttl, *Der unbekannte Gott,* Tübingen, 1964.

think that they had been written by such people as Harvey Cox, William Hamilton or Thomas Altizer, or even Karl Marx or Roger Garaudy.

I need to analyze the present situation no further. Is it leading to the end of Christianity, or to the end of what has been called "conventional Christianity"?[13] And, if the latter is the case, will authentically Christian aspects therefore not disappear at the same time? I propose now to answer the question, or at least to try to answer the question as to how we, as believers, can still speak about God in our contemporary, secularized world. Before I do this, however, I must first answer a preliminary question, as it is quite evident that the problem of our speaking about God cannot be solved unless we listen to and discuss with the world what is in fact happening among men in the world at the moment. It is precisely one-way traffic between the Church and the world that makes the message of God that the Church has to take to the world incomprehensible. Not only has the Church something to say to the world—the world also has something to say to the Church, something that can have important consequences not only for the way in which the Church speaks to the world, but also for the way in which the Church speaks about God.

2. A PRELIMINARY QUESTION

It is right that we should ask the preliminary question as to whether the *aggiornamento* of our speaking about and to God is, in the first place, to be an adaptation "to the world," or whether it is to be a readaptation of our speaking "to the Gospel," a re-evangelization of our expressions of faith by a definite return to the inspiration of the Gospel. This dilemma, put in this way, is, however, watched by two different snakes in the grass. On the one hand, not everything that is to be found con-

[13] W. van de Pol, *Het einde van het conventionele christendom,* Roermond and Masseik, 1966, and *Op weg naar een verantwoord Godsgeloof,* Roermond and Maaseik, 1967.

94

cretely in "the world" can in itself be reconciled with faith, since although it is true that man is essentially a "potential for good," he is also—although only as the other side of this potential for good—at the same time a "potential for evil," and we know that this must also be present here and now in the concrete form of what we essentially regard as good, our existential experience of the modern, secularized world. On the other hand, however, a return to the Gospel can easily become a form of biblicism and fundamentalism, points of view which are as little evangelical as an uncritical and frank affirmation of everything that is put forward under the name of "secularization." The dilemma—either adaptation to the secularized world, or readaptation to the biblical message—would therefore seem to be a false one. This difficulty must first be cleared out of the way.

It is, of course, clear to Christians that the inspiration of the Gospel is a guiding principle—in the context of our secularized world, we once again *question* the apostolic witness of Christ. The new question that we ask thus arises from the situation and the problem of our concrete life today. For what reason do we question the Bible again? Precisely because experiencing God in our modern age and speaking about, and above all to God have become a problem for many people. From the point of view of this problem, we ask the Gospel new questions which previous generations of Christians *could not* ask, simply because they were not living in a secularized world like ours. What is more, a new question requires a *new* answer which the Bible itself, as a message to men of *that* time, cannot immediately provide in its literal text, because it was providing an answer to questions that were *different* from those which we ask it today. And yet the Bible itself, as the crystallization of God's revelation, must inspire in us an answer to these questions. The question itself thus poses the problem of making the Gospel relevant again to our time. The Gospel does not answer questions that are not asked. And not every time is ripe for every question. Every generation asks the Gospel its own questions from the context of its own life, and the Gospel itself must provide an answer to

95

these questions which naturally goes further than a material or literal repetition of what is in Scripture.

We too, living in a secularized world of the twentieth century, thus question the Gospel, and the answer that the Gospel gives us will therefore be *new,* but at the same time also *evangelical.* This presupposes that we should be ready to allow our questioning itself in the light of Scripture to be subjected to criticism, and ready even to change, extend or correct our questioning in the light of Scripture and biblical interpretation given during the Church's whole history throughout the centuries. We must allow ourselves to be called into question by God's word, which we shall nonetheless continue to believe while *interpreting* it (within the community of believers and available to the Church's leaders, our pastors).

It follows from what I have said previously that the dilemma had been presented wrongly. The re-evangelization of our speaking about and to God essentially implies a *confrontation* with the modern achievements in man's striving towards full humanity and in his care for his fellow men, and with the values which these achievements have brought to light in our own times. The primary demand—Jesus himself, as proclaimed by the faith of the apostles, is our guiding principle in all readaptation and reinterpretation—can only be realized *in confrontation with* our modern, secularized world. If we divorce our questioning from the inspiration of the Gospel from our concrete, contemporary existential experience, then our questioning will, in the end, be without content and meaning, and the only answer that we can expect from it will be one that is not relevant to our contemporary situation.

I have, very briefly, tried to situate the heremeneutical background to our problem because there are two tendencies in the books and articles that deal with our "speaking about God" which ought, in my opinion, to be avoided. It is possible to describe these two tendencies, not completely accurately, but certainly suggestively, with the well-known terms "naturalism" and "supernaturalism." The first, "naturalism," tends to let God remain *implicit* in our human existence, and to experience religion only in the form of care for the world, and our fellow man, while excluding every form of explicit religiosity. The second, "supernaturalism," tends, on the other hand, to regard God as in competition with man, and to reduce authentic religiosity to the Church's explicit homage to God in the liturgy or to man's interpersonal experience of God in prayer. As the Second Vatican Council so rightly said, a division of this kind between life and religion, whatever direction it decides to take, is the most serious drama of our times.[14]

3. ACTIVE SILENCE ABOUT GOD AND SPEAKING ABOUT AND TO GOD

What in the first place characterizes our new image of man and the world is that our older image of God has evaporated and that we can no longer live with it because it is associated with our older image of man and the world. But even more characteristic is our apparent inability to form for ourselves a new image of God, an inability that is clearly reflected in the books and articles—both those carefully thought out and the more impetuous ones—that have been written about the "death of God." In the past, Christian thinkers have always been clearly conscious of the fact that God was unapproachable, that he could not be expressed, and that man was basically unable to speak about God and to imagine him in an adequate manner. In the average theology, spirituality, and preaching of the past, however, God was in fact often experienced as someone who intervened in the world and the predicamental ideas about God were manipulated too frequently as adequate concepts—"concepts of God." In this, man's religious experience continued to be authentic, but it was contained within a social and cultural context which has now been superceded, but which certainly inwardly coloured man's religious experience. Concepts such as

[14] *Pastoral Constitution on the Church in the Modern World,* art. 43. See also E. Schillebeeckx, "Foi chrétienne et attente terrestre," *Gaudium et spes. L'Eglise dans le monde de ce temps,* Tours, 1967, pp. 117–158.

"religionless faith" are therefore extremely ambiguous because they fail to make sufficient distinction between faith and its essential functioning within a social and cultural context, which does not mean that faith itself was less authentic in the past than it is now in our new social and cultural situation. Why should we assume airs and claim that our present age has authentic faith, when in fact all that is being disputed is a different relationship between man and the world? We often make unconsciously religious statements when we should in fact be making statements about man and society. Certain events in the past which gave rise to a direct appeal to God's intervention seem now, on the basis of our present knowledge, to have been based on a lack of human knowledge, technique, and so on. Was the faith of the Fathers for this reason, given their circumstances, any less authentic? Man's religious experience has always been partly conditioned by social factors, just as it is for us today. Man has no need to wait for authentic faith until the scientists are ready with their conclusions! In our modern world, so transformed and conditioned by science, we simply have different reasons and incentives to experience religion from those of the past.

We are today conscious, not only theoretically, but also practically, of the fact that we have no concepts of God and that every concept that is really put forward as a concept of God is in fact godless, because it denies God's transcendence. Thus, on the rebound, God threatens to become a marginal concept, a "void."[15] In the past God was an accepted idea—he was the world mover, the last cause, he upheld the moral and political order of the world, and even maintained social stability. In the modern world God has ceased to be an idea and has become a question which both believers and non-believers are never tired of discussing in ordinary conversation, in the newspapers, in books and articles, and on the radio and television. Now that we can no longer feel secure with ideas of God, God himself is the subject of our conversations. Whatever solution is offered, whether we talk about an atheist, a theist, or a post-theist "God

[15] See C. Verhoeven, *Rondom de Leegte,* Utrecht, 1966, p. 163.

after the death of God," or even if we give a post-Christian answer, the question itself will not let us go. It has, as a matter of fact, become clear to at least some people that it is not enough simply to get rid of illusions, pseudo-ideas and out-of-date images in order to reach a more pure truth. "The image of God does not become in any way clearer, nor does faith in God become any easier by exposing the idols. The aim is to make faith cleaner by clearing the idols out of its way, but no one knows whether it can then still turn to God."[16] The question is, have we in our new problem of God not forgotten our human predicament? Whoever is looking for truth must take the risk of a certain element of falsehood. Anyone who is looking for God must risk a certain idolatry—he must accept a false idea of God into the bargain, because God without ideas threatens to become a void. Even the idea of the "Wholly Other" makes God into a being so elevated and far from us that it is difficult to see how he could influence our life. As C. Verhoeven has correctly said, "The reflective slenderness of a faith that is directed towards the pure God reaches out into a vacuum and suffocates in a convulsion. God is not obtainable separately from the world and from the idols."[17] To orientate one's life exclusively and directly towards God would have no explicit, concrete content and would therefore involve the risk of chasing a void. The only approach to any truth whatever is via the world of human experience. There is no other mysterious source of knowledge outside human experience. How could any revelation of God which lay outside the sphere of human experience be heard—how could it, in other words, be a revelation made *to man*? The fact that perception is the basis of all human knowledge means that our conscious being in the world is our only access to explicit knowledge here and now of all other possible reality. Hence we know primarily only the material world and *thus* everything that is connected with this material world (and insofar as it is connected with the world), that is, firstly ourselves and our fellow men, precisely

16 *Ibid.,* p. 165.
17 *Ibid.*

as beings in the world, and then God, as the creator of this world and, possibly, as manifesting himself *in this world.*

Thomas Aquinas said long ago that all our ideas of God and all our explicit affirmations about God were derived from our experiences within the world and with the history of salvation.[18] God was never called the *subiectum philosophiae* in medieval theology, but the *principium subiecti philosophiae.* Although he was regarded as the *subiectum theologiae* (that is, *Sacrae Doctrinae*), he was only regarded as accessible within an *oeconomia,* that is, in the history of salvation as condensed in the human life of Jesus, the Christ.[19] The *theo-logia* was to be found only in the *oeconomia,* never outside it.[20]

This has become even more obvious in our new, secularized existence. If God speaks, then he does so *in* and *through* man together with all his world and history. We have to let the voice of his revelation be raised in the world and history of man. We may therefore say that the Bible only really comes to life and only begins to speak to us when we ourselves have encountered its essence somewhere *within our own lives,* just as we may also say that we only really get on to the track of the message of the Gospel through our own authenticity. Man has always given *content* to his ideas of and his affirmations about God in the light of his own existence and history. Our life in the world nourishes, as it were, our understanding of God, just as God lets himself be known to us in and through our history in the world of men and things. Religious and Christian faith essentially means that our *concrete* existence is a divine promise of salvation. Speaking about God and speaking about man in the world are therefore always correlative, although they cannot be called identical.

[18] *Summa Theologica,* I, q. 1, a. 7, ad 2.

[19] *Ibid.,* I, q. 1, a. 7.

[20] See, for example, Y. Congar, "Christ in the Economy of Salvation and in Our Dogmatic Tracts," *Concilium,* 2, Glen Rock, 1966, pp. 4–15; E. Schillebeeckx, "La 'theologia' nous est donnée à travers une 'oikonomia'," *Révélation et théologie* (Approches théologiques 1), Brussels, (1965), pp. 331–339, and "La nouvelle tendance de la dogmatique actuelle," *ibid.,* pp. 364–377.

This means, therefore, that the problem of whether man has an indirect or direct relationship to God is a false problem. It also means, therefore, that secularization may not be identified with the secularization of religion itself, because this would also imply the dehumanization of man, who transcends this world in the world. For a Christian, secularization which would exclude religion as a human existential possibility is a misconception, a new paganism. But having made this essential distinction between Christian and "pagan" secularization, we must continue to be conscious of the fact that the living God can only express himself in a way that we can experience explicitly in our lives *from* our lives with our fellow men in this world. This means, then, that we may indeed affirm a direct and interpersonal community with God, but it also means that this relationship with God is *mediated,* as far as its concretely real and expressive content is concerned, by the human realities of the world and of our fellow men. Precisely because it is *divine,* the immediacy of God's reality for us cannot be placed on the horns of a dilemma with, or in opposition to these human mediations of the world and of our fellow men and, of course, the mediations of the Church as well.

This is, moreover, most evident in man's relationship with Jesus, the Christ. This interpersonal relationship *is* at the same time a direct living relationship with God experienced in faith, because God's will to be God for us *in a human way* has been made apparent in Jesus Christ. Immediacy and mediacy are not mutually exclusive in man's relationship with God—it is in this that God manifests his transcendence. But it also means that religion cannot be defined as an "exclusive relationship with God." It must rather be defined as a specific way of approaching the *totality* of reality and of realizing this in God's active, absolutely close (and therefore never available) presence. This is undoubtedly the authentic aspect that can be distilled from the new way of speaking about God in our own times—a way of silence which allows God to speak in our care for our fellow men and in our welfare work.

However, this active, caring, and committed silence does not imply that the older way of speaking about God, often called in the pejorative sense "theist," has nothing more to teach us, at least in its fundamental intention. This older way of speaking about God contained an authentic basic direction which we cannot dismiss if we want to remain on firm Christian ground. Our interpersonal relationship with God can never take place on its own because it would then be an *empty* relationship without explicit content. The love of God always has a point of contact and experience in the world and in our fellow men, and has this even by definition. This, however, does not in any way imply that explicitly thematic religiosity, as expressed in silence with God (in personal prayer), and in the explicit worship of the Church (in the liturgy of the Word and of the Eucharist) is a consequence of obsolete "theist supernaturalism." Anyone concluding, from the assertion that man's living relationship with God is always nourished by his relationship with his fellow men in this world and is embedded in this relationship, that we have to make every effort to humanize mankind by humanizing the world and have consequently to be *silent* about God is, in my opinion, causing a fatal short-circuit. After all, anyone who states *explicitly* that our relationship with God is implicitly present in our relationship with the world and with our fellow men is already at the level of explicit confession of God. He must therefore draw the consequences of this explicitness if he is to go on being consistent with himself. If the Christian is conscious that the implicit relationship with God makes his service to the world and his fellow men worship of God, and that everything that he does—"whether eating or drinking" (1 Cor. 10, 31)— can be done in God's honour, then the fullness of this reality, precisely because it is a gift, requires to be *expressed* in praise and thanksgiving. Anyone who in his daily life really gives and receives love also requires to *express* himself in a gesture, the only meaning of which is to declare his love and gratitude. The Christian's explicit confession of love, praise, and thanksgiving in prayer and the liturgy will, of course, be worthless if the underlying reality—our relationship in service with our fellow men in the world (the relationship that is made explicit in all its

102

depth in prayer and the liturgy)—is not really present. In that case, the whole of the Church's liturgy, our prayer, and our speaking about and to God are left hanging in the air and are no more than a separate superstructure and a lie, while the person who authentically devotes himself to his fellow men, although outside the perspective of God, does possess the religious *reality* at least, even though he cannot express this and thus realize himself more deeply precisely as a religious man. Our expression of God's majesty and love of man in praising God forms an essential part of the total structure of our love of God in the form of love and care for our fellow men. It is the authentic essence which we have to distill from the obsolete "theist" image of man and the world of our fathers in faith. That is why Thomas, bearing witness to the whole Christian tradition, was able to say that the *virtus religionis* was essentially not a separate virtue existing alongside the other virtues, and that human fellowship —"visiting orphans and widows in their affliction," the typically medieval form of social care for one's fellow men—was "worship" of God, but also that this did not do away with the need for explicit praise of God and *eucharistia*.[21] Two points emerge quite clearly from the whole of Thomas's treatise on prayer:[22] on the one hand, his interpretation (expressed in formulas that had already become standard) of our care for our fellow men in the world as holiness and prayer;[23] and on the other hand, his insistence on the need for this form of prayer also to be openly confessed in explicit "thematic prayer" or in praise and thanksgiving, as expressed in the great eucharistic prayer especially as *anamnesis* in the singing of the *magnalia Dei,* God's miraculous deeds.[24] The eucharistic prayer as *anamnesis* and as praising and giving thanks to God is thus orientated towards the future, and our actions in the future are thus considered both from the point of view of universal worship of God in the world, and from the point of view of worship in the narrower

[21] See, for example, II-II, q. 81, a. 1, ad 1; a. 3; a. 4, ad 2; a. 8.
[22] See especially II-II, q. 83.
[23] II-II, q. 81, a. 8.
[24] II-II, q. 91, a. 1, ad 1 and ad 2.

sense, namely, our association with God in prayer as a thematization of what is the most profound reality of our active being in the world outside the church, that is, the building itself. In this way, we *celebrate* inside the church what is achieved in human history—what may be called the history of man's salvation—outside the church. *Homo mundanus* must be *homo religiosus*.

I have, I believe, in this way rescued the two authentic elements—on the one hand, the element that is present in what has been called, by Christians themselves, "Christian atheism" and, on the other hand, that which is present in what has been called the "older theism"—from the possibly inauthentic expressions that may be present in both the older and the more recent ways of presenting the Christian faith. I believe, moreover, that we shall have to take these two authentic elements into account when we speak, as Christians *about* God and when we speak *to* God in the future, and also that we shall only then be able to say: "theology of renewal talks *right* about God."

5.

THE JEWISH NOTION OF GOD
AND CHRISTIAN RENEWAL

RABBI ABRAHAM HESCHEL

THE title of my lecture as proposed in the original invitation read like this: "The God of Israel and Christian Renewal." Upon reading these words, I first recoiled. Who am I to speak with such a voice? Upon second thought, I realized that to decline such an invitation would be an act of irreverence. Is it not a moment of blessing that this congress of illustrious Catholic theologians is willing to submit the great movement of Christian renewal to a confrontation with Jewish understanding of the meaning of the God of Israel?

On the way to the printer, the power of the title was emasculated. The magnificent biblical saying, "the God of Israel," was replaced by a scholastic missaying, "the Jewish notion of God." Realism was replaced by notionalism. Biblical words were pushed out by the jargon of manuals.

NAMES AND NOTIONS

"The God of Israel" is a *name,* not a notion, and the difference between the two is perhaps the difference between Jerusalem and Athens.

A notion applies to all objects of similar properties; a name applies to an individual. The name "God of Israel" applies to

105

the one and only God of all men. A notion describes; a name evokes. A notion is attained through generalization; a name is learned through acquaintance. A notion is conceived; a name is called. Indeed, the terms "notion" and "the God of Israel" are profoundly incompatible. All notions crumble when applied to Him. A more appropriate title might be: "The Jewish experience of the collapse of all notions in relation to God." The God of Israel is "a devouring fire" (Deut. 4, 24), not an object of abstraction or generalization.

To be sure, we are given certain ways of understanding God, ways that point to Him, that lead to Him. "Hear, O Israel, the Lord is our God, the Lord is One" (Deut. 6, 4). "The Lord, the Lord, a God merciful and gracious, slow to anger and abounding in love and faithfulness" (Ex. 34, 6). Yet the adequacy of our understanding these ways depends upon our sensitivity to its inadequacy.

A notion is definitive, finished, final, while understanding is an act, the intention of which is to receive, register, record, reflect, and reiterate; an act that goes on forever. Having a notion of friendship is not the same as having a friend or living with a friend, and the story of a friendship cannot be fully told by what one friend thinks of the being and attibutes of the other friend. The process of forming an idea is one of generalization and abstraction. Yet such a process implies a split between situation and idea, a disregard for the fullness of what transpires, and the danger of regarding the part as the whole. An idea or a theory of God can easily become a substitute for God, impressive to the mind when God as a living reality is absent from the soul.

The prophets of Israel had no theory or "notion" of God. What they had was an *understanding*. Their God-understanding was not the result of a theoretical inquiry, of a groping in the midst of alternatives. To the prophets, God was overwhelmingly real and shatteringly present. They never spoke of Him from a distance. They lived as witnesses, struck by the words of God, rather than as explorers engaged in an effort to ascertain the nature of God; their utterances were the unloading of a burden

106

rather than glimpses obtained in the fog of groping. To them, the attributes of God were drives, challenges, commandments, rather than timeless notions detached from His Being. They did not offer an exposition of the nature of God, but rather an exposition of God's insight into man and His concern for man. They disclosed attitudes *of* God rather than notions *about* God.

I am not going to speak about notions. To quote from Isaiah, "You are My witnesses, says the Lord, I am the Lord" (Is. 43, 10. 11).

There are no proofs for the existence of the God of Israel. There are only witnesses. You can only think of Him by seeking to be present to Him. You cannot define Him, you can only invoke Him. He is not a notion but a name.

Now there are voices in our own days, all over the country, suggesting that we eliminate and get rid of the traditional name, God, to refer to the ultimate Presence. After all, who needs that word, that name? This is being done for the telephone exchanges in the United States: to get rid of names! So let us abolish names altogether. Let us call every human being by a number, and worship zero.

You know what goes on in our days about words. Certain chapters from certain books are considered obsolete because the words are not understandable anymore. For example, "The Lord is my shepherd; I shall not want." An impossible verse; who has seen a shepherd? Children grow up without ever having heard of a shepherd. I therefore offer an emendation and suggest that we read: "The Lord is my plumber, I shall not want." In the same spirit, artificial fertilization may substitute the test tube for the mother. There will be no mothers. All men will be organization members.

The supreme issue is not the question whether in the infinite darkness there is a ground of being which is an object of man's ultimate concern, but whether the reality of God confronts us with a pathos—God's ultimate concern with good and evil; whether God is mysteriously present in the events of history; whether being is transcended by creation; whether creation is transcended by care; whether my life is dependent on God's care; whether in the course of my life I come upon a trace of His guidance.

God is either of no importance or of supreme importance. God is He whose regard for me is more precious than life. Otherwise, He is not God. God is the meaning beyond the mystery.

How can I speak of a notion? To speak adequately about God one would have to sense all the horrors and all the joys of all creatures since the beginning of time, and to intuit how God is relevant to all this.

The ambiguities are numerous and drive us to despair— almost. Yet the God of Israel does not leave us to ourselves. Even when He throws us into darkness, we know that it is *His* darkness, that we have been cast into it by *Him*. Thus we do not pretend to know His secrets or to understand His ways. Yet we are certain of knowing His Name, of living by His love and receiving His grace, as we are certain of receiving His blows and dying according to His will. Such is our loyalty, a loyalty that lives as a surprise in a world of staggering vapidity, in an hour of triumphant disloyalty.

The Covenant is a holy dimension of existence. Faith is the consciousness of living in that dimension, rather than an assent to propositions. Important as is the intellectual crystallization of faith in terms of creed, what characterizes Judaism, I believe, is the primacy of faith over creed.

Faith is both certainty and trial: certainty in spite of perplexities, a trial demanding sacrifice, strain, wrestling. For certainty without trial becomes complacency, lethargy, while trial without certainty is chaos, presumption, as if God had never reached us, as if history were always a monologue. Faith is a mode of being alive to the meaning beyond the mystery, commitment of total existence, and the dynamics of faith is the ongoing shaping and modification of one's existence. Faith also involves fear: fear lest He discard us, lest He forsake us. Then we must learn how to despise the convenience of belief. We have again and again experienced His wrath. "Thou hast made us like sheep for slaughter . . ." (Ps. 44, 12–13).

108

We remain faithful in spite of the demonic darkness that often engulfs us, in spite of the vapidity of the holy that often affects us. God is one, but man is torn to pieces by temptation and ambiguity. We are both haunted and exalted by the words of Job: "Though He slay me yet will I trust in Him" (Job 13, 15).

Faith is a high ladder and at times all the rungs seem to have been taken away. Can we replace the rungs? Can we recover the will to rise? And if the rungs cannot be replaced, shall we learn how to reach the truth at the top of the ladder?

Let me illustrate. In 1492, the Jews of Spain were placed before the choice: to be converted or to be expelled. The overwhelming majority left their homeland. Ships overcrowded with fugitives found difficulty landing, because disease had broken out among them on board ship. One of the boats was infested with the plague, and the captain of the boat put the passengers ashore at some uninhabited place. There most of them died of starvation, while some of them gathered up all their strength and set out on foot in search of some settlement. There was one Jew among them who struggled on foot together with his wife and two sons. The wife grew faint and died, not being accustomed to so much difficult walking. The husband picked up his children and carried them in his arms until he and they fainted from hunger. When he regained consciousness, he found that his sons had died also. In great grief he rose to his feet, raised his eyes to the heavens, and cried out: "Lord of the universe, much have you done to make me desert my faith. But know this of a certainty, that a Jew I am and a Jew I shall remain! And nothing which you have brought upon me, or are likely to bring upon me, will be of any avail!"

The meaning of the saying "the God of Israel" differs essentially from a phrase such as "the God of Aristotle" or "the God of Kant." It does not mean a doctrine of God conceived of or taught by Israel. It means God with whom Israel is vitally, intimately involved, an involvement transcending the realm of thinking, not reducible to human consistency, and one which

109

does not simplify itself in order to accommodate common sense.

Furthermore, the saying "God of Israel" has no possessive or exclusive connotation: God belonging to Israel alone. Its true meaning is that the God of all men has entered a Covenant with one people for the sake of all people. It is furthermore clear that "Israel" in this saying does not mean Israel of the past, a people living in ancient Palestine which has long ceased to exist. Israel is a people in whom the past endures in the present tense. The exodus occurs now. We are still on the way, and cannot accept any event as a final event. We are God's stake in human history, regardless of merit and often against our will.

Israel is a people that shares the Name of God. Of the two words in Hebrew for the Jews, "Israel" and "Yehudi," the "el" in Israel means "God," whereas the Hebrew word for "Jew," "Yehud," has the three letters that combine to make up the four in the ineffable name. It is a people that can only endure in a world in which the name of God is revered. The disappearance of God would mean the disappearance of the Jew. But we know of God's commitment and of His faithfulness.

CHRISTIAN RENEWAL

The term "renewal" has many meanings, but I shall suggest only briefly that what is taking place in the movement of Christian renewal is certainly a shift from evasion to confrontation, a willingness to recognize the validity of principles long disparaged or disregarded, which it is unnecessary to enumerate here.

It is clear, however, that renewal is not an act carried out once and for all, but rather a constant happening, *semper a novo incipere*. It is furthermore a process, not only in relation to others, but above all one that affects the inner life and substance of the Christian.

I believe that one of the achievements of this age will be the realization that in our age religious pluralism is the will of God, that the relationship between Judaism and Christianity will be one of mutual reverence, that without denying profound diver-

110

gencies, Jew and Christian will seek to help each other in understanding each one's respective commitment and in deepening appreciation of what God means. And I should like to make some suggestions in the hope they will be taken in the right spirit. Although I may be critical, I shall be offering the critique of a friend.

My own suggestion, first, is that Christian renewal should imply confrontation with Judaism out of which it emerged. Separated from its source, Christianity is easily exposed to principles alien to its spirit. The vital challenge for the Church is to decide whether Christianity came to overcome, to abolish, or to continue the Jewish way by bringing the God of Abraham and His will to the Gentiles.

Now, in a real sense, I believe there is a battle going on in this twentieth century which centers around the Hebrew Bible. The prohibition and suppression of the Hebrew Bible in Soviet Russia is symbolic of that battle.

There is an old challenge to the Christian church going back to Marcion, a challenge that has never died out. The recurrent tendency to bring about a disengagement of the New Testament from the context of Judaism in which it came into being is evidence of what may be an unresolved tension. Marcion's spirit resounds in words recently uttered by a distinguished Catholic writer, that "it would be inexact . . . to suppose that the Christian *Theos* is the same" as the God of the Old Testament.[1] Marcion's criticism of the Old Testament or the Hebrew Bible proceeded from his conviction that the Gospel was something absolutely and utterly new. However, the Catholic Church of the second century appreciated the heritage, and rejected the one-sidedness of Marcion's doctrines.

Although I do not presume to judge matters of Christian doctrine, it seems utterly strange to assert that the community of Israel, "the Synagogue," did not have the capacity to determine the canonicity of holy Scripture. If this were the case, there could not have been any legitimacy in the scriptural text which the New Testament, and Jesus as depicted in it, quoted to authenti-

[1] Leslie Dewart, *The Future of Belief,* New York, 1966, p. 183.

cate their claims. Without the existence of a scriptural canon which is presupposed by the New Testament, the arguments of Jesus would be bereft of their foundation. And to turn a disagreement about the identity of this "Anointed" to an act of apostasy from God Himself seems to me neither logical nor charitable.

I would go beyond that and make a suggestion that what I believe the hour calls for is a renewal of understanding, renewed acknowledgement of the primacy of the Hebrew Bible. It was the Torah and the prophets that Jesus himself expounded, preached about. It was the Torah and the prophets that he revered as sacred Scripture, and it is in the words of the psalmist that Christians pray. To be sure, according to conciliar doctrine, equal reverence is required for all books, both of the Hebrew Bible and of the New Testament. And still, what lingers on in theology is the assumption that the worth of the Hebrew Bible is in its being a preparation, a prehistory, not in its own grandeur.

Let me mention an example. At Vatican Council II each morning after Mass, an ancient copy of the Gospel was carried down the nave of St. Peter's Church and deposited on a golden throne on the altar. It was the Gospel only and no other book.[2]

According to Karl Rahner, "ultimately God effected the production of the Old Testament books to the extent that they were to have a certain function and authority in regard to the New Testament,"[3] not in their own majesty and preciousness,

[2] See *Dialogue on the Way*, edited by George A. Lindbeck, Minneapolis, 1965, pp. 137 and 222.

[3] Karl Rahner, *Inquiries*, New York, 1964, p. 56. Equally astonishing is Rahner's statement:
"Now the Synagogue, unlike the Church, does not have the authority to testify infallibly to the inspiration of the Scriptures. Even prior to the death of Christ, there existed no authoritative teaching *office* in the Old Testament, in the sense of a permanent institution formally endowed with inerrancy. There were individual prophets, but no infallible Church, for the eschatological event, the final and irreversible salvation act of God, had not yet occurred. It was possible for the Synagogue to apostatize from God, to turn a "No" to him and to his "Anointed" into its own official "truth," thus bringing about its own end as a divine institution" (*ibid.*, p. 54).

112

but only to the degree to which they plan a role in the New Testament. Now this statement reminds me of the proof of divine providence that was offered in the seventeenth century by an Anglican bishop. He said, "You see, you can see Divine Providence in the fact that wherever there is a city, Providence supplied a river . . ." I think this is a perspective that makes the infinite power of the Hebrew Bible conform to a rather narrow ecclesiastic principle.

Why is the Hebrew Bible indispensable to our existence? It is because the Bible urges us to ask and to listen: What does God require of me? And if there is any validity to my claim to be human, it is is the fact that I am aware of this problem: What does God require of me? It is through the Bible that I learn how to say "Here I am!"

The place and power of the Hebrew Bible is so important, because all subsequent manifestations and doctrines, whether in Judaism or Christianity, derive their truth from it, and unless they are continually judged and purified by it, tend to obscure and distort the living relationship of God to the world.

Now, the Bible is absent from contemporary thinking. It is quoted for edification, as a pretext for a sermon. It does not live as a power judging our lives. The Bible is respected as a source of dogma, not as living history. The Psalms are read, but the prophets are not. They are revered as forerunners, not as guides and teachers.

The Bible is on-going disclosure. Yet the word will not speak in a vacuum. It is a sledgehammer to the prophet, when he knows how to be an anvil. The words speak. The words are not signs, but outcries. The words stand for Him, they extend from Him, pleading unceasingly. The words are gates disclosing possibilities, possibilities of engagement to Him and the staccato of His presence and His concealments.

An important root of contemporary nihilism is the age-old resistance to the Hebrew view of the world and of man. The Hebrew Bible has destroyed an illusion, the illusion that one can be an innocent bystander or spectator in this world. It is not enough to be a consumer in order to be a believer. The

113

Bible has destroyed the ancient tradition in which the relation to the gods came with ease, in which gods accommodated themselves to our notions and standards, in which religion was above all a *guarantee*.

God is Judge and Creator, and not only Revealer and Redeemer. Detached from the Hebrew Bible, people began to cherish one perspective of the meaning of God, preferably His promise as Redeemer, and become oblivious to His demanding presence as Judge, to His sublime transcendence as Creator. The insistence upon His love without realizing His wrath, the teaching of His immanence without stressing His transcendence, the certainty of His miracles without an awareness of the infinite darkness of His absence—these are dangerous distortions. To believe too much is more perilous than to believe too little.

With your permission, I should like to say that it is difficult for a Jew to understand when Christians worship Jesus as the Lord, and this Lordship takes the place of the Lordship of God the Creator. It is difficult for a Jew to understand when theology becomes reduced to Christology. It is significant that quite a number of theologians today consider it possible to say, "we can do without God and hold on to Jesus of Nazareth."[4]

The overriding issue of this hour in the world and western civilization is the *humanity of man*. Man is losing his true image and shaping his life in the image of anti-man. Is there anything in the human situation today that makes reverence and responsibility a vital necessity? Is being human a supreme purpose? Does not man cease to be human if reverence and responsibility are gone?

The task of Christian renewal, I should like to hope, is above all the renewal of man, and the renewal of man is the *renewal of reverence*. How shall we prevent and heal man's discarding

[4] "We do without God and hold to Jesus Christ." Thomas Altizer and William Hamilton, *Radical Theology and the Death of God,* New York, 1966, p. 33.

114

the power of freedom, his massive disposal of his power to decide? How shall we teach him to be involved in living engagement with the challenge and mystery of what being alive demands of him? The task is to deliver the mind from the illusion that availability and transparency are the exclusive attributes of being. False lucidity misguides us more than plain obscurity.

THE RENEWAL OF MAN

The renewal of man involves a renewal of language. To the man of our age, nothing is as familiar and trite as words. Of all things they are the cheapest, most abused, and least esteemed. They are the objects of perpetual defilement. We all live in them, feel in them, think in them, but since we fail to uphold their independent dignity, they turn waif, elusive—a mouthful of dust. When placed before the Bible, the words of which are like dwellings made of rock, we do not know how to find the door. There is no understanding the God of Israel without deep sensitivity to the holiness in words. For what is the Bible? Holiness in words. And we destroy all the gates of the Bible by the on-going desecration of the power of the word. The effect, I believe, is that we are all engaged, all involved, in the process of liquidating the English language. Promiscuity of expression, loss of sensitivity to words, has nearly destroyed the fortress of the spirit. And the fortress of the spirit is the *dabar,* the word. Words have become slums. What we need is a renewal of words.

The hour calls for *the renewal of the antecedents of faith*. The task is pre-theological. Revival and cultivation of basic antecedents of faith will help us to rediscover the image of man.

The renewal of man involves renewal of the sense of wonder and mystery of being alive, taking notice of the moment as a surprise. The renewal of man must begin with rebellion against reducing existence to mere fact or function. Why do I speak about the renewal of man? Because the Hebrew Bible is not a book about God. It is a book about man. Paradoxical as the Bible is, we must accept its essential premise: that God is concerned about man. If God had asked me for advice, I would have told him right after the first experience with Adam and Eve, "Don't bother with that species." But He goes on patiently, waiting for man. I say we need a revival of the premises and antecedents of faith because it is useless to offer conclusions of faith to those who do not possess the prerequisites of faith. It is useless to speak of the holy to those who have failed to cultivate the ingredients of being human.

Prior to theology is depth theology; prior to faith are premises or prerequisites of faith, such as a sense of wonder, radical amazement, reverence, a sense of mystery of all being. Man must learn, for example, to question his false sense of sovereignty.

The biblical message remains unacceptable unless seen in the context of essential attitudes and sensibilities. The tendency to rely completely, in our religious thinking, upon the so-called "contemporary experience" must be questioned. Contemporary experience is stunted experience, it is largely devoid of the higher qualities of experience.

Human beings have never been so bewildered about issues that challenge them most deeply. The famous dictum of Dietrich Bonhoeffer "that a world that has come of age . . . could live without the tutelage" of God presupposes a view of our world which is, I believe, naïve. Can you regard a world of Auschwitz and Hiroshima, of Vietnam and intercontinental ballistic missiles as a world that has come of age?

The most radical question we face does not really concern God but man—has not man proved to be incompatible or incongruous with the civilization that has emerged? Contemporary consciousness has not come to terms with its own experience. Overwhelmed by the rapid advancement in technology, it has failed to develop an adequate anthropology, a way of insuring the independence of the human being in the face of forces hostile to it.

The level of experience is wide but shallow. Man is gradually losing his ability to be in charge of his own life. He is beginning to regard himself not only as a self-contradiction but as an impossibility. To what degree is the predicament of man of this civilization, which is shaped by Judaism and Christianity, due to the failure of the Jewish and the Christian faith? Too many events happening too rapidly bombard our consciousness too frequently for us to be able to ponder their significance. Contemporary experience is lacking in adequate corresponding reflection. In facing the tension between faith and the everyday world, we must not forget that our everyday experience is a problem rather than a norm. It is not assumed that we must renounce technology, but rather that we must ask whether man's image can be derived from technology.

I mention all this because, where ancient religions were concerned with single aspect or some aspects of the human, the Hebrew Bible is concerned with all of human existence. In a sense, there is no preoccupation with the "religious" in the Bible; in the Bible what counts is the secular.

SACRAMENTAL—PROPHETIC

I should like here to touch briefly on a few other subjects I believe of concern to us here. Men of faith frequently succumb to a spectacular temptation: to personalize faith, to localize the holy, to isolate commitment. Detached from and irrelevant to all emergencies of being, the holy may segregate the divine.

Is the world of faith a realm of its own, an oasis of peace in the wilderness of the world? Is its task accomplished in being concerned for the holy, in offering spiritual comfort, while remaining aloof from the material and secular issues of this world?

In Israel there are two orientations, I believe, two directions of living for the sake of God, exemplified by the prophet and by the psalmist. I would suggest, therefore, that the right goal would be to bring about some kind of balance or polarity,—the proper polarity of the sacramental and the prophetic.

The psalmist is mostly guided by personal impulse. His own life, his concern for his spiritual situation, form the background of his experiences. His attainments, his insights, and his purification constitute self-enhancement of significance to his existence as an individual. He exemplifies the individual's secret love affair with God.

The prophet's existence, by contrast, involves public affairs. Its content, aim, and events have an eminently super-personal character. Prophecy is not a private affair of the experiencer. The prophet is not concerned with his own salvation. His aim is not personal illumination, but the illumination of the people; not spiritual self-enhancement, but leading the people to the service of God. The prophet is nothing without his people. The prophet is a person who holds God and man in one thought at one time—and at all times.

When the people Israel arrived at the wilderness of Sinai, the Lord called to them out of the mountain, saying: "You shall be to me a kingdom of priests and a holy nation" (Ex. 19, 6). A whole nation of priests? A people who so recently were slaves are told to be priests! And yet to Moses, our teacher, the charge was not radical enough. His vision of what the people ought to be was of a grandeur unsurpassed in the history of self-reflection. When Joshua the son of Nun, the minister of Moses, appealed to him to curb the prophetic outpourings of Eldad and Medad, Moses said to him: "Would that all the Lord's people were prophets, that the Lord would put His spirit upon them!" (Num. 11, 29).

The two central ideas proclaimed in the Bible are *demand* and *promise*. Theologically, the demand precedes the promise. God first said to Abraham: "Go from your country . . . to the land that I will show you," and then ". . . and I will make of you a great nation . . ." (Gen. 12, 1–2).

Existentially, the commandment is the link of man to God. Man's existence has a touch of eternity if God is waiting for his deeds. God's expectation, God's waiting for man, comes to expression in His commandments. Indeed, the transcendence alluded to in man's existence is that mysterious waiting, that divine expectation.

The Hebrew Bible records God's "mighty acts" in history.

118

What is overlooked is that on every page of the Bible we come upon God's hoping and waiting for *man's* mighty acts.

This the meaning of human existence.

The world is unredeemed and deficient, and God is in need of man to be a partner in completing, in aiding, in redeeming. Of all the forms of living, doing is the most patent way of aiding. Action is truth. The deed is elucidation of existence, expressing thirst for God with body and soul. The Jewish *mitzvah* is a prayer in the form of a deed. The *mitzvoth* are the Jewish sacraments, sacraments that may be performed in common deeds of kindness. Their nature is intelligible if seen in the light of God's care for man. The good act, ritual as well as moral, is a *mitzvah,* a divine offer, a divine representative.

Ultimate issues confront us in immediate situations. What is urgent for the Jew is not the acceptance of salvation but the preparing of redemption, the preparing *for* redemption.

The prophet Samuel would not abide in the security of his own home, of his piety. He moved from place to place, mixing with those who were not pious. In sharp contrast, Noah stayed at home, waiting for others to come to him. He and his family were saved, while his generation perished.

The urgent issue is not personal salvation but the prevention of mankind's surrender to the demonic. The sanctuary has no walls; the opportunity to praise or to aid has no limits. When God is silent, man must speak in His place. When God is hiding His compassion, man must reveal His love in this name.

Words become stale, and faith is tired. Unless we labor in helping God to carry out His promise—to be a father to those who are forsaken, a light to those who despair in secret darkness —we may all be forsaken by Him. Man must be involved in redeeming the promise: Nation shall not lift up sword against nation, and there shall be no war any more.

From the Jewish point of view, any doctrine that downgrades the demands and merely proclaims the promise is a distortion. An influential Protestant theologian has said: "The key to the ethics in the New Testament is contained in the following passages: Romans 6, 7, and the beginnings of Romans 8. Here,

119

as nowhere else, we perceive in great clearness and detail the identity of the central points in dogmatics and in ethics. The Sermon on the Mount, on the other hand, although it is the necessary presupposition of Christian ethics, is not its foundation. Its relation to Romans 6 is that of the Law to the Gospel."[5] I cite this viewpoint because it is utterly alien to the Jewish mind.

MESSIANIC EXPECTATION

I should like to offer a rather controversial—and perhaps heretical—idea: that Christians have become less and less messianic; there is very little waiting. I may be mistaken. I hope I am. In primitive Christianity, there was a waiting for the second coming. In the consciousness of the Christian today, there seems to be no such awareness, no such waiting. Where is the promise of redemption?

Perhaps I can illustrate my point with a story told by a Christian pilgrim in the great drama by Maxim Gorki. There was once a man who was very poor and very old, who lived in Siberia. Things went badly for him, so badly that soon nothing remained for him to do but to lie down and die. But still he did not lose courage. He often laughed and said to himself, "It makes no difference—I can bear it! A little longer yet will I wait, and then I will throw this life aside and go into the Land of Justice." It was his only pleasure, this Land of Justice. At that time there was brought to Siberia an exile, a man of learning, with books and maps of all sorts. And that poor old sick man said to this great sage: "Tell me, I implore you, where lies the Land of Justice? How can one succeed in getting there?" Then the learned man opened his books, spread out his maps, and searched and searched, but nowhere could he find the Land of Justice. Everything else was correct, all the countries were shown, only the Land of Justice was not to be found.

The old man would not believe him. "It must be there," he said. "Look more closely! For all your books and maps,"

[5] Emil Brunner, *The Divine Imperative,* Philadelphia, 1947, p. 586.

said he, "are not worth a whistle if the Land of Justice is not shown on them." The learned man felt himself insulted. "My maps," said he, "are absolutely correct, and a Land of Justice nowhere exists." The other was furious. "What," he cried, "have I now lived and lived and lived, endured and endured, and always believed there was such a country. And according to your maps there is none! That is robbery! You good-for-nothing knave! You are a cheat and no sage." Then he gave him a sound blow over the skull, and still another. And then he went home and choked himself. "There must be a Land of Justice," he said, "there must be and will be an Age of Justice."[6]

I would like to conclude with one more point. We Jews have gone through an event in our history which is like biblical history continued. The Jewish people everywhere have entered a new era in history. Jerusalem, the City of David, has been restored to the State of Israel. It is an event of high significance in the history of redemption. It is therefore proper, I believe, for me to share a few remarks with you on the subject.

But first: How should a Christian view this event?

According to the Book of Acts, right at the very beginning, the disciples to whom Jesus presented himself alive after his passion, asked him: "Lord, will you at this time restore the kingdom to Israel?" And he said to them: "It is not for you to know times or seasons which the Father has fixed by his own authority." (Acts, 1, 6. 7)

Now, what is the meaning of this question and this answer? It was a time when Jerusalem was taken away from the Jewish people, the holy temple was destroyed, Jews were sold into slavery. Pagan Rome ruled in the Holy Land.

But there was a hope, a hope of deliverance from the pagans, there was the promise offered by the prophets that Jerusalem would be returned to the kingdom of Israel. So, when the disciples saw Jesus for the first time in these extraordinary circumstances, it is understandable this was the first question

[6] Maxim Gorki, *A Night's Lodging* (or *Submerged*), Act III.

121

they asked, their supreme concern: "will you at this time restore the kingdom?" In other words, they asked the question about the restoration.

Jesus' answer was that the time of the fulfillment of the divine promise was a matter which lay within the Father's sole authority. So, earlier, he had assured them that he himself did not know the day or the hour of his parousia. "But of that day or that hour no one knows, not even the angels in heaven, nor the Son, but only the Father" (Mk. 13, 32). A similar awareness is common in Rabbinic literature. "Nobody knows when the house of David will be restored."[7] According to Rabbi Shimeon the Lakish (c. 250), "I have revealed it to my heart, but not to the angels."[8] Jesus' answer is as characteristic of the Rabbinic mind of the age as is the question itself.

However, this passage is generally interpreted in a different way. Reflecting a dichotomy in early Christian thinking, the position of the Galilean disciples was different from that of the hellenistic Christians. The original hope of the disciples was that the kingdom was at hand in the apocalyptic sense, but the hellenistic Christians, who in the end conquered the Empire, preached the Gospel as having present importance for each individual apart from the eschatological kingdom.

Thus Augustine explains that the meaning of the question was that, after the resurrection, Jesus was visible only to his followers, and that they were asking whether he would now make himself visible to everyone.[9] Calvin maintains that "there are as many errors in this question as there are words."[10] Mod-

[7] *Mechilta,* to Exodus 16, 32.

[8] *Sanhedrin* 99a.

[9] F. J. Foakes Jackson and Kirsopp Lake, *The Beginnings of Christianity,* Part I, *The Acts of the Apostles,* vol. IV, p. 8.

[10] He points out that apostles were gathered together when this question was posed, "to show us that it was not raised through the foolishness of one or two but through the concern of all. Yet their blindness is remarkable, that when they had been so fully and carefully instructed over a period of three years, they betrayed no less ignorance than if they had never heard a word. There are as many errors in this question as there are words. They ask Him concerning the kingdom; but they dream of an earthly kingdom, dependent upon wealth, luxury, outward peace,

ern commentators assert that the question reflects the spiritual ignorance and hardness of hearts of the disciples,[11] "the darkened utterance of carnal and uninspired minds,"[12] and that the answer of Jesus was a rebuke.[13]

However, the simple meaning of the entire passage has a perfect *Sitz im Leben,* and both question and answer read like a *midrash.* The apostles were Jews and evidently shared the hope of their people of seeing the kingdom of God realized in the restoration of Israel's national independence. So now, hearing their Master speak of the new age, they asked if this was to be the occasion for restoring the kingdom to Israel. We can scarcely fail to realize or to understand the naturalness of their question. The expectation was burned into their very being by the tyranny of the Roman rule. The answer confirms the ex-

---

and the blessings of this nature. And while they assign the present as the time for restoring this kingdom, they desire to enjoy the triumph before fighting the battle. Before setting hands to the work for which they are ordained they desire their wages; they also are mistaken in this, that they confine to Israel after the flesh the kingdom of Christ which is to be extended to the farthest parts of the world. The whole question is at fault in this, that they desire to know things which are not right for them to know. No doubt they were well aware of what the prophets had said about the restoration of the kingdom of David, for they had often heard Christ speaking of this, and it was a common saying that in the depths of the captivity of the people every man's spirit was revived by the hope of the kingdom to come. They hoped that this restoration would take place at the coming of the Messiah, and so the apostles, when they saw Christ raised from the dead, at once turned their thoughts to this. But in so doing they betrayed what poor progress they had made under so good a Master. Therefore Christ in His short reply briefly reprimands their errors one by one, as I shall presently indicate. To 'restore' in this passage means to set up again that which was broken down and disfigured by many ruins. For out of the dry stock of Jesse should spring a branch, and the tabernacle of David which was miserably laid waste should rise again." *Calvin's Commentaries, The Acts of the Apostles,* Edinburgh, 1965, p. 29.

[11] "The hardness of the disciples' hearts is apparent here as in Mark's Gospel; they awaited a material kingdom, for the Spirit was not yet poured out on them to give them a more enlightened conception of it." C. S. C. Williams, *A Commentary on the Acts of the Apostles,* London, 1964, p. 56.

[12] G. T. Stokes, *The Acts of the Apostles,* New York, 1903, p. 29.

[13] R. B. Rackham, *The Acts of the Apostles,* London, 1901, p. 7; A. W. F. Blunt, *The Acts of the Apostles,* Oxford, 1922, p. 132.

pectation that the kingdom will be restored to Israel—an expectation expressed again and again in ancient Jewish liturgy. It is the point in history at which that restoration will take place that remains the secret of the Father.[14]

It is very likely that, following Daniel and Esdras, calculations were made to predict the time of the coming of the restoration. However, most Rabbis disapproved such computations which deal with "a time, two times, and half a time" of Daniel 7, 25. Jesus' answer is not a rebuke of the apostles' hope, it is rather a discouragement of messianic calculations (see Lk. 17, 20–21).

Jesus' expectation that Jerusalem would be restored to Israel is implied in his prediction that "Jerusalem will be trodden down by the Gentiles, until the times of the Gentiles are fulfilled" (Lk. 21, 24). Some commentators see in these words a prediction of "the re-establishment of Jerusalem as a capital of the Jewish nation." By "the times of the Gentiles" is probably meant "the period God has fixed for the punishment of the Jews."[15]

Several weeks ago I was privileged to be in Jerusalem, and upon my return I wrote my impressions of Jerusalem and particularly of what the Wall, the western Wall means to us. In the following personal remarks, I shall attempt to show what Jerusalem means to my people.

JERUSALEM

I have discovered a new land. Israel is not the same as before. There is a great astonishment in the soul. It is as though the prophets had risen from their graves. Their words have a new

[14] F. F. Bruce, *Commentary on the Book of the Acts,* Grand Rapids, 1954, p. 38.

[15] William F. Howard, *St. Luke (The Interpreters Bible),* p. 308; E. Earle Ellis, *The Gospel of Luke,* London, 1966, p. 245. Alfred Plummer, *Commentary on . . . St. Luke* (The International Critical Commentary), New York, 1896, p. 483, lists six possible meanings.

ring. Jerusalem is everywhere; she hovers over the whole country. There is a new radiance, a new awe.

The great quality of a spiritual moment is not in its being an unexpected, unbelievable event in which the presence of the holy bursts forth, but in its happening to human beings who are profoundly astonished at such an outburst.

My astonishment is mixed with anxiety. Am I worthy? Am I able to appreciate the marvel?

I did not enter the city of Jerusalem on my own. Streams of endless craving, clinging, dreaming, flowing, days and nights, midnights, years, decades, centuries, millennia, streams of tears, of pledging, of waiting—from all over the world, from all corners of the earth—carried us of this generation to the Wall. My ancestors could only dream of you, to my people in Auschwitz you were more remote than the moon—but I can touch your stones! Am I worthy? How shall I ever repay for these moments?

The martyrs of all ages are sitting at the gate of heaven, having refused to enter the world to come lest they forget Israel's pledge given in and for this world: "If I forget thee, O Jerusalem, let my right hand forget its cunning!" They would rather be without heaven than forget the glory of Jerusalem. From time to time they would go on a pilgrimage to the souls of the Jewish people, reminding them that God Himself is in exile, that He will not enter the heavenly Jerusalem until His people Israel will enter Jerusalem here.

Jerusalem, I always try to see the inner force that emanates from you, enveloping and transcending all weariness and travail. I try to use my eyes, and there is a cloud. Is Jerusalem higher than the road I walk on? Does she hover in the air above me? No: in Jerusalem, past is present and heaven is almost here. For an instant I am close to Hillel who is here. All of history is present.

You see Jerusalem only when you hear. She has been an ear when no one else heard, an ear open to the prophets' denunciations, to the prophets' consolations, to the lamentations of the ages, to the hopes of countless sages and saints, and to the prayers flowing from distant places. And she is more than an ear. Jerusalem is a *witness,* an echo of eternity. Stand still and listen. We know Isaiah's voice from hearsay; but these stones have heard what he said concerning Judah and Jerusalem:

> It shall come to pass in latter days . . .
> out of Zion shall go forth the law,
> and the word of the Lord from Jerusalem.
> He shall judge between the nations,
> and shall decide for many peoples;
> nation shall not lift up sword against nation,
> neither shall they learn war any more (Is. 2, 3, 4).

Jerusalem was stopped in the middle of her speech. She is a voice interrupted. Let Jerusalem speak again to our people, to all people.

The words have gone out of here and have entered the pages of holy books. And yet Jerusalem has not given herself away. There is so much more in store. Jerusalem is never at the end of the road. She is the city where the expectation of God was born, where the anticipation of lasting peace came into being. Jerusalem is waiting for the prologue, for the new beginning.

What is the secret of Jerusalem? Her past is a prelude. Her power is in reviving. Her silence is prediction; the walls are in suspense. It may happen any moment: a shoot may come forth from the stump of Jesse; a branch may grow out of his roots (Is. 11, 1).

THE WALL

At first I fainted. Then I saw: a Wall of frozen tears, a cloud of sighs.

The Wall. Palimpsests hiding books, secret names. The stones are seals.

The Wall. The old mother crying for all of us. Stubborn,

loving, waiting for redemption. The ground on which I stand is Amen. My words become echoes. All of our history is waiting here.

The Wall. No comeliness to be acclaimed, no beauty to be relished. But a heart and an ear. Its very being is compassion. You stand still and hear: stones of sorrow, acquaintance with grief. We all hide our faces from agony, shun the afflicted. The Wall is compassion, its face is open only to those smitten with grief.

When Jerusalem was destroyed, we were driven out; like sheep we have gone astray; we have turned, each one to his own way. The Wall alone stayed on.

What is the Wall? The unceasing marvel. Expectation. The Wall will not perish. The redeemer will come.

Silence. I embrace the stones. I pray: "O, Rock of Israel, make our faith strong and your words luminous in our hearts and minds. No image. Pour holiness into our moments."

Once you have lived a moment at the Wall, you never go away.

For more than three thousand years we have been in love with Jerusalem. She has occupied our hearts, filled our prayers, pervaded our dreams. Continually moaning her loss, our grief was not subdued when celebrating festivities, when arranging a dinner table, when painting our homes. No meal was concluded without imploring, "Build Jerusalem, speedily, in our own days . . . ". The two most dramatic occasions of the year, Seder on Passover and the Day of Atonement, found their climax in the proclamation: "Next year in Jerusalem." And on the Sabbath we implored Him:

> When will you reign in Zion?
> Speedily, in our own days
> dwell there, and for ever!
> May you be magnified and sanctified
> in the midst of Jerusalem Thy city
> throughout all generations and all eternity.
> Let our eyes behold Thy kingdom . . .

Jerusalem, our hearts went out to you whenever we prayed, whenever we pondered the destiny of the world. For so many ages we have been lovesick. "My beloved is mine, and I am his," Jerusalem whispered. We waited unbearably long, despite frustration and derision.

In our own days the miracle occurred. Jerusalem has proclaimed loudly: "My beloved is mine and I am his" (Song 2, 16).

How shall we live with Jerusalem? She is a queen demanding high standards. What does she expect of us, living in an age of spiritual obtuseness, near exhaustion? What sort of light should glow in Zion? What words, what thoughts, what vision should come out of Zion?

The eyes of history are upon the city of David, upon "the faithful city"; authenticity cannot be borrowed.

What is the mystery of Jeusalem? A promise: peace and God's presence.

First there was a vision. God's vision of the human being. Then He created man according to His vision, according to His image. But man's resemblance to God's image is fading rapidly.

God had a vision of restoring the image of man. He created a city in heaven and called it Jerusalem, hoping and praying that the Jerusalem on earth might resemble the Jerusalem in heaven.

Jerusalem is a recalling, an insisting, a waiting for the answer to God's hope.

> Your eyes will see Jerusalem,
> a quiet habitation, an immovable tent,
> whose stakes will never be plucked up,
> nor will any of its cords be broken.
> But there the Lord in majesty will be for us
> a place of broad rivers and streams,
> where no galley with oars can go,
> nor stately ship can pass (Is. 33, 20–21).

128

At that time Jerusalem shall be called the throne of the Lord, and all nations shall gather to it, to the presence of the Lord in Jerusalem . . . (Jer. 3, 17).

. . . my house shall be called a house of prayer for all peoples (Is. 56, 7).

6.

THE CONCEPT OF TRINITY
AND OF CHRISTOLOGY
IN THE EASTERN LITURGY

It is self-evident that the relationship which exists between the tripersonality of God and the Incarnation is so close that the conception of the latter is conditioned by the conception of the former. As is to be expected, the so-called Antiochene-Greek Trinitarian theology offers a perspective on the understanding of the Incarnation of the Logos which differs from that of Alexandrian-Latin theology. The difference is crystallized in the question: Has the man Jesus a different relationship to the first divine Person than to the divine tripersonality? In the background of this question is, of course, the oneness of the activity and relationship of the three divine Persons with respect to creation, that is, *ad extra*.

On the basis of the explication of revealed truth concerning the Christ-event as it has been formulated with the aid of philosophical notions by the Church in the great councils, the content of faith may be presented as follows. There is only one God. This is the basic truth attained to in the revelation of the Old Testament. However, the historical Jesus of Nazareth, the son of Mary, of the house of David, crucified in Jerusalem, raised from the dead on the third day, is truly the Son of this living God, the Son of Yahweh. Indeed, he is himself truly God. This Son of Yahweh became true man at a time destined by

God; and this not by transformation into creaturely existence, but by assumption of manhood into his own eternal divine existence. He remained, thereby, one and the same Jesus Christ. Thus one must say: Jesus Christ is perfect God, as is Yahweh, his Father; he is also perfect man. Gregory of Nazianzus expresses this in the formula: Christ is not ἄλλος καὶ ἄλλος (that is, not "someone" and "someone": two persons), but ἄλλο καὶ ἄλλο (that is, "the one" and "the other": two natures). Nevertheless, he is one and the same.

Thus there is in Christ a unity based on the unity of the personal. On this basis, the man Jesus is truly Son of God, and vice versa, the true Son of God is truly man. This means, however, that he leads an integral human life equal to us in all things but sin; that is to say, a life of genuinely human freedom and human consciousness.

The one divine Person of the Logos acts both through the divine nature which is identical with him and through the human nature which he has assumed. The one divine Person of the Logos possesses two natures, the divine and the human, albeit each is possessed in different ways. The human nature is concrete, individual, integral. It is in no sense a defective or deficient human nature.

The faith-content thus outlined gives rise to many difficult questions. First of all, there is the question as to how the human nature of Jesus Christ can be a truly integral human nature if it does not exist in its own personality but in the personality of God. Secondly, how is one to understand the relationship of the human nature which exists in the personality of the Logos to the divine nature which is identical with the Logos? Connected with these two questions is a whole further series of questions, for instance, whether only the Person of the divine Logos or any one of the divine Persons could in this manner have become the personal ground or basis for subsistence of a human nature? Or, how is this structure of the man Jesus Christ related to the Christ-centredness of the cosmos, above all, to the Christ-centredness of human history; or again, of what significance is

131

this structure of Jesus for the understanding of the Church, of grace, or of the problem of eschatology?

With regard to the first question, we must consider the notion of the personal. According to the customary definition, the personal comprises self-possession, self-determination, and self-responsibility. These three elements were supplemented by psychological reflections in the philosophy of the nineteenth century. The thesis was then established that self-possession, self-determination, and self-responsibility take place in the dimension of conscious life. This assertion implies an important complementation of the purely ontic doctrine through which the ontic is led over into the ontological. However, were the ontic basis as foundation of the psychological overlooked or undervalued, we would have in effect a destruction of the notion of person. Again with respect to the ontic, one must not remain with a purely static interpretation of personhood, as it is expressed in the three elements previously mentioned. Thomas Aquinas emphasizes that man possesses himself by continuously returning to himself. Thus self-possession is something dynamic. Man possesses self by continuously entering into self, apprehending self, as it were. His self-possession is his self-apprehending. Man accomplishes his self-determination and self-responsibility by reaching beyond himself, by transcending himself with respect to matter, but more especially with respect to person. It is only in clearly demarcating that which he is not, above all in relation to person, that man gains his self-consciousness, his ego-consciousness. In this self-consciousness is necessarily included the consciousness of the "you." Man cannot say "I" without the "you" likewise resounding. Consequently, the relationship of the "I" to the "you" is essential for the personal. And this means dialogue. However, were the personal merely seen in the dialogue-character or in the "dialogueness" of man, then the ontic basis would vanish and the partnership would hang in the air without any solid foundation. The ontic and ontological basis is the precondition for the essential element in personal being which is dialogue and partnership. On the other hand, this ontological basis would not raise itself to the full heights of the personal if it did not express itself in dialogue. It is only in dialogue that the personal expresses itself in a recognizable and authentic manner.

A further element must here be considered. In claiming that man accomplishes his self-possession in the act of self-apprehension, we do not wish to uphold an exaggerated actualism in the sense of man constituting himself as person from one act of self-apprehension to the other. Man is at all times *person-al*. His personality is so essential to him that it can neither be lost nor interrupted. Of greatest significance for the understanding of the personal is the fact that it reveals itself in man's self-apprehension through self-reflection. This means that he sets self over against self. In his self-apprehension man sets up, so to speak, a certain bipolarity in himself. He makes self an object of self and by so doing becomes nature with regard to himself. Through this analysis of self-possession and self-apprehension we gain not merely the aspect of the personal, but also that of nature. Insofar as man is the object of his self-apprehension he is nature.

Nature can be extended for man by his apprehending of things in his environment, whereby they become objects of his knowing and acting. There is nothing in the environment of man that he is not capable of making the object of his knowledge and activity. He is even capable of making other persons objects; and to some extent, he cannot help but make them objects of his knowing and acting. However, were he to treat person as object alone, he would not do justice to the decisive element, that is, to the personal. If he wishes to recognize and acknowledge the other in his individuality, he must approach him differently than he would the non-human world, the world of things. The latter is only nature to him. This means it is exclusively object and cannot be the occasion for a genuine and valid encounter. In consequence of the identity which man has with self, and despite all bipolarity in self, one can say that the personal consists in the subsistence of the human essence. As is clear from Boethius's definition of person, the intellectuality of the human being is *the* essential element in the under-

133

standing of person. It must, however, be borne in mind, that it would be wrong simply to identify the spiritual with person and the material with nature. It is precisely the unity of the spiritual and the material, the unity of body and soul, which can be termed the nature of man, insofar as man considers this nature the object of his self-apprehension. This is the nature through which man is active as an "I," as a person. He is active both through his corporeal and spiritual nature, through the totality of his being. Although it is by virtue of the personal aspect that man transcends self, it is still his nature which both renders possible and mediates this act of transcendence.

When we apply these reflections to the true humanity of Jesus Christ, we gain the following insights. (It must be borne in mind at this point that the divine Persons for their part can be understood only as relations; relations, that is, which are identical with the divine essence, and which precisely by virtue of this identity with the divine essence have the element of subsistence which is basic for personhood.) According to the New Testament witness and the theological explication of later centuries, the God of the Old Testament is Father, or first Person in that reflecting upon himself he gives expression to self, and in so doing, produces a real Word which is over against himself. In this Word he sets himself over against himself. This implies that the Father who is expressing himself, and the Word who is expressed, are identical with the divine being; although—in order not to merge into complete identity but to preserve the true contradistinction—they must be virtually (Thomas Aquinas) or, more probably, formally (Duns Scotus) distinct from the divine being. In the Holy Spirit as the unifying love between the Father and the Word, Father and Son are shown to be a "we," that is, a "we" precisely in the Person of the Holy Spirit. The Holy Spirit can exist only as the expression and as the sign of this "we" of Father and Son. He owes his distinction to the relation, but his personality, the element of subsistence, he owes to his identity with the divine being which must also be attributed to the Holy Spirit. It can thus be said that each of the three divine Persons is in a certain sense a concretization of the one divine being. God exists in the *manner* of the three divine Persons. This thesis receives its full significance if one favours the Greek conception of the Trinity, which maintains that the one God, witnessed to in the Old Testament, is the *sourceless source* of the Son and the Holy Spirit. Without the richness and fruitfulness of the divine being, the one God—who constitutes himself in the inner-Trinitarian procession as first Person, as Father—could not accomplish the act of bringing forth. At any rate, if we take our point of departure from the one God of the Old Testament—as it suggests itself from the point of view of salvation history, and as is the procedure in the Greek interpretation of the Trinity—then we must make some distinction between personhood and beingness without in any way sacrificing the real identity of personhood and beingness. God is real. He is the absolute God; and in no other manner than in that of tripersonality. The absolute being, of its very essence, is Trinitarian. The aspects of unity and tripersonality in God are of fundamental importance for the understanding of the hypostatic union. The unity is significant with respect to the fact that the three divine Persons are active in their *creative self-emptying* as a single operative principle. All the works of God *ad extra* are performed by the tripersonal God as by one single efficient cause (*causa efficiens*). This thesis is not merely theological speculation. It is a dogmatic statement of the Church, and it must be reconcilable with the statement that the three divine Persons are active according to their own proper characteristics. The activity is the activity of the divine Persons in virtue of the divine nature. The divine nature determines the manner of the activity. Thus the unity of the divine activity which is asserted by dogma refers to the fact that the Persons act through one and the same divine nature. They can, however, only be active through this divine nature in that particular characteristic which is proper to each of them. A consequence of this basic thesis would be the statement that each human being is created by the one tripersonal God. What is true of every man is true also of the man Jesus Christ. The man Jesus Christ was also created in the womb of his mother

135

by the tripersonal God. Because of the virginity of conception and birth, that is, because of the absence of male seed, the efficacy of God in this particular instance and in this instance alone is an activity of a special kind. The human nature brought forth in a unique act by the three divine Persons was determined from the outset for the Logos and not for either of the other two divine Persons. It was intended to be assumed by the Logos into his own person. Augustine expressed this once in a somewhat obscure statement: the human nature, he maintains, was not created and then assumed into unity with the Logos; rather, its assumption into unity with the Logos is its very creation. Since the act of assumption can be an act only of the Logos, and since the creation is an act of the tripersonal God, it is no easy matter to explain this statement of Augustine in a logically unobjectionable manner. One would have to understand it in the sense that already in the act of creation there is contained the activity of the assumption which belongs solely to the Logos. The idea of the "assumption" of the human nature was widespread in the patristic period. It involves the danger of a Nestorian independence of the human nature with respect to the Logos. Such a conception, however, is foreign to the thesis of Augustine. If we designate the Logos as the recipient of the human nature created by the tripersonal God and declare that he has assumed human nature, then we are no longer operating in the area of efficient but of formal causality. It is, however, to the former that the dogma as to unity of the divine activity applies.

The most important example for formal causality in our experience is the relationship of soul to body, or of spirit to matter. As the Council of Vienne declared, the soul is *forma corporis*. This means the soul does not produce the body or the matter as its efficient cause; rather, as the formative reality the soul imprints its own structure upon matter without detriment to that structure which is peculiar to matter. Consequently, the spirit presents itself in the body in a certain manner. The body is the manifestation of the spirit. From a different point of view, one can call the body the instrument of the spirit. Yet one must

136

not overlook the fact that it is precisely the body which imposes restriction and limitation upon the spirit. It is, however, the spirit, the soul which is the determining reality for the body; and so determinative is it that the body cannot simply and clearly be differentiated from the spirit, nor the spirit from the body. The soul is spirit insofar as it is limited, restricted, and characterized by the body. The body is matter inasmuch as this matter is stamped by the spirit, which is relatively distinct from it. The spirit is nevertheless the superior. All this is involved when we term the soul the formal cause of the body. If we apply this notion to the relationship of the Logos to the human nature which is assumed by him, then we attain to the insight that it is the person of the Logos which determines the manner of subsistence of the human nature of Jesus, without estranging it from its own essence. The human nature remains what it is. It remains a truly human nature with the spontaneity, freedom, self-responsibility, intellectual power, and the capacity for both corporeal and spiritual development which is proper to human nature. That which is other in this human nature is its manner of existing; that is, its manner of subsisting. Not that which subsists changes, but its *mode* of subsisting; for the human nature is a concrete reality. It is concretely itself through the subsistence of the divine Logos. The divine Logos, or rather the subsistence of the Logos, is the basis of subsistence for the human nature of Jesus. This is the core of the mystery, the unique and incomprehensible fact regarding the man Jesus; namely, that he is in all respects fully man apart from the fact that he does not, as every other man, bear within himself his ground of subsistence. His ground of subsistence comes to him "from without," from a reality distinct from his human reality. The man Jesus has his subsistence from the divine Logos.

Considering this situation from the aspect of the divine activity, it must be concluded that this relationship is dynamic and not static. The human nature of Jesus is not assumed in a momentary, point-like action, but in an act which is continuously being accomplished. Since God is pure act, the assumption of the human nature on the part of the Logos, from the first moment of its realization, must and can only take place in endless, uninterrupted activity. The divine Logos assumed the human nature of Jesus in the totality of its human life. With the exception of sin he embraced its human destiny to the very heights of suffering and death. Just as there was never a moment in the existence of the man Jesus in which the nature of Jesus was not completely dominated by the ego of the Logos, so there will never be an end to this condition. From the very first moment of his existence, Jesus is God; that is, assumed into the unity of the Logos. It is certain theological teaching that this unity will experience neither interruption nor end. From the viewpoint of man, the Incarnation, in the ontic as well as the ontological sense, is a continuous "being-taken-possession-of." From the viewpoint of the Son of God, the Incarnation is a continuous "taking-possession" of the human nature.

One may ask whether the human nature, in being assumed by the Logos, forfeited its own proper existence, whether from the outset its proper existence was withheld from it. Under no circumstances may one deny it its reality. It is not merely some manner of appearance, some disguise of the Logos. It is as real a human nature as is any other. The question is whether one can speak of a real nature without at the same time speaking of an existing human nature. Such a question is decidedly legitimate. One cannot simply brush it aside because a reality, according to our experience, is always an existing reality. In the Middle Ages the problem of being was approached in widely varying ways. In one instance being was denied God since it was seen as limiting him. In another instance it was denied man since one would then attribute to him something divine. Thomas Aquinas admittedly found a solution with his distinction between essence and existence, between being and being-thing (that which is). This solution was questioned, however, in the mystical theology of Meister Eckhart. However the case may be, one may under no circumstance deny nor diminish the reality of the human nature of Jesus and the dynamism of this reality.

The following considerations may permit us some insight into the mystery of the Incarnation, although they will not be able to

138

explain it completely. Man exists only in his orientation to the other. Every human existence is necessarily coexistence, it expresses itself in the capacity to speak and in speech. When this relatedness of human existence is enacted in friendship and in love, then he who transcends self, steps out of self, as it were, and enters into the "you" he encounters. The "you" receives him, unless choosing to close himself. In this way the "I" is formed and transformed by the "you." The doing, thinking, willing, becoming, judging of the "I," all receive new orientation from this encounter with the "you." Thus the "I" lives in and out of the "you." What we find to be true of friendship and love in general, takes place in a profound and incomparable manner in the union of man with the divine Logos. In this union the Logos becomes the personal force which permeates and dominates the human ego. Here the words of St. Paul find inimitable application: it is no longer my ego that lives, but the ego of Christ, that is, of the Logos that lives in me (Gal. 2, 20). The human ego is formed by Christ to such an extent that Paul can speak candidly of the death of the old "I" which had been formed by the world, and of the resurrection of the new "I" or ego. Through the self-communication of the Logos to the human "you" in the Incarnation, the human "you" received such force that it was thrown, so to speak, out of its own centre. In place of its own, it received the centre of the divine Logos. Its ego is no longer that which is immanent to man, but the transcendent ego of the Logos. This transcendent ego of the Logos so fully took possession of the man Jesus, that despite all transcendence and without any loss of transcendence, it became the "I" which is immanent to man. So totally true is this that the divine Logos is active in and throughout the human nature, whose actions are the actions of the divine Logos.

Another manner in which we might obtain entry into the mystery of the Incarnation is as follows. The word of man is a power which can move and mould the heart and mind of another person. Although this is not true of every word, it is decidedly true of that word which has reached a certain height or intensity. A word which is capable of entering into the interior of another

139

has the power to enrich, to move deeply, to transform, to re-create. With this in mind we can consider the unequalled power of the pre-existent Word of God, that word of God which "is living and active, sharper than any two-edged sword, piercing to the division of soul and spirit, of joints and marrow, and dis-cerning the thoughts and intentions of the heart" (Heb. 4, 12). God has spoken many words. He spoke mightily to the bearers of revelation, penetrating their consciousness so forcefully that they were convinced this was no human or worldly power speak-ing to them, but one who was other than all others, other than anything other. Into the human nature of Jesus the Father spoke out his personal word, that word which he speaks eternally, which expresses and represents him. The human nature of Jesus Christ is most profoundly possessed and moved by this powerful, all-embracing, personal word. The transformation and re-creation effected by the personal word of God is such as knows no likeness. So totally possessed and permeated is the human nature of Jesus by this word, that it does not have its own power of subsistence, but can subsist only in the power of the Logos. In a certain sense, the Logos is the "I" of the human nature of Jesus, forming one dynamic unity with it.

Such analogies lead us on to the notion of the transcendence of God. As was previously explained, the human nature of Jesus was so created by the tripersonal God that the creating was identical with the assuming. Thus the Logos, and he alone, exer-cises the hypostatic function with respect to the human nature of Jesus Christ. In creation God communicates himself to man, making himself manifest in this act. His creative act remains in him, since the creative activity of God is identical with him. Consequently, the work of creation itself simply cannot be separated from God. Thomas Aquinas once made the statement that creation has its place in God himself. With this he wished to express the intimate union between God the Creator and creatures. This is the union we are referring to when we speak of the self-giving of God to creatures in the act of creation. Ad-mittedly, this self-giving is distinct from the self-giving of God through grace. Nevertheless, in a certain sense one may use the notion of self-giving also with regard to the creative act of God. On the other hand, one may and must say of creatures that they are open to God. Just as every man, in consequence of his personhood, is open to the other and attains his true being only in encounter with the other; so he is of his very essence open to God the Creator.

Patristic and medieval theology develops this idea in reflecting on the scriptural word that God created man in his image. In man God himself is mirrored. Consequently, man can only then realize himself when he realizes self as the reflection of God. This is implied in the notion that man is open for God's entry into his innermost being. When God communicates himself to man in ever new ways, the human is not impaired nor impoverished; on the the contrary, he attains to greater humanity. Man attains to greater being, the more he transcends self. According to the theory of evolution, this self-transcendence can take place in a future-orientated manner. It can and must, however, also take place vertically, be it into one's own depths or into the heights. It must at any rate be a transcending to the God who is other, who is distinct from man. Thus the forward or future-orientated movement unites with that into the depths to form one single movement. One of the basic insights of Teilhard de Chardin's theory of evolution, as of every theory of evolution, is that man in transcending himself gains greater being. In view of our consideration so far, we may say that precisely in this forward moving act of transcendence, man transcends self simultaneously in a God-ward movement, a movement into the depths; for God is not only in and with and behind man, he is also before man. He constantly beckons him forward. Thus when man transcends himself, it is God who is calling him into the future.

Since God presents himself analogously in his creative activity, even realizes himself analogously, it is not meaningless to say that in every coming-to-be of a human being there occurs an incarnation of God. One may not, for instance, categorically deny some element of meaning to the ideas of Far Eastern religions that every human being is an incarnation of the divine.

141

This process of becoming man, becoming world, takes place continuously. One must remain aware, however, of the essential difference between this "becoming-man" of God and the singular and unrepeatable incarnation of God in Jesus. Yet it would be advisable not to overlook the continuity within the radical discontinuity.

In Hegel's theology of history we find an unusual conception of the incarnation of God. According to this thesis, God is the Absolute or the Idea which evolves to the fulness of the world, above all to his own self-consciousness in man, indeed, in the state. The incarnation of God takes place in a great historical process. According to Hegel, God becomes himself only in and through the historical process. This historical becoming is projected into God himself. Fundamentally, this would mean that God is no longer God. However far removed scriptural revelation of the incarnation of God is from the ideas of Far Eastern religions and the thesis of Hegel—since both contain pantheistic tendencies—these nevertheless provide some aid in our approach to scriptural revelation. In the light of such ideas, scriptural revelation does not appear strange, miraculous, or absurd. It is seen, rather, in a much wider context. The history of religion discloses a widely-held inchoative understanding of the incarnation of God, of the divine. The true incarnation in Jesus thus becomes intelligible as climaxing something which is to be found in the religious thought patterns and processes of numerous peoples. It is intelligible as the fulfilment of the dream of humanity, whose dreamers are not conscious of the fact that they are dreaming. In the incarnation God communicates himself with such creative immediacy that a human being who is distinct from him comes to be, and although distinct, yet so intimately one with him that one must speak of a hypostatic unity, since the subsistence of God is communicated to man.

Any interpretation of the incarnation in the sense of a transformation of the infinite into the finite would be disastrous and mythological. The self-communication of God to the man Jesus in no way eliminates the distinction between God and man. On the contrary, it sharpens the distinction, despite the fact that in surrendering himself to God man gains greater being. It is clearly evident from the foregoing, that the distinction between God and man from the ontological point of view can never be overcome. The abyss remains. Unity and dissimilarity grow in equal measure. It is precisely in living his own life that the man Jesus, who is distinct from the Logos, is drawn progressively into the life of the Logos. At the same time it becomes increasingly apparent that the abyss between God and man simply cannot be eliminated. Jesus is an individual and concrete human being by virtue of the fact that he has been assumed by the Logos, who exercises for him the function of hypostatizing, that is, subsisting. The Logos, the divine sonship, constitutes the personal character of the man Jesus.

Now the eternal Son exists solely in relationship to the Father. He is nothing other than subsisting relation to the Father. This is why the human nature is taken into relationship with the Father. In this way the man Jesus is Son of the heavenly Father in as true and real a sense as is the eternal Word. On the other hand, the first divine Person is the Father of the man Jesus just as he is the Father of the Logos, in whose subsistence the man Jesus subsists. From eternity the Father generated his Son, the Logos, as the one who was to assume the human nature of Jesus as his own. Thus in the generation of the Son, the Father made himself also the Father of the human nature of Jesus, that is to say, of the man Jesus. The eternal generation by the Father has its term in the human nature of Jesus which exists in the person of the Logos. The incarnation appears thus as the prolongation, indeed as the goal of the Trinitarian life. The fatherhood of God focuses in, as it were, upon Jesus and in and through him, upon the Church and the entire creation.

In the patristic period that union of the divine and human in Christ which is grounded in the Person of the Logos, was characterized as a being-in-one-another, as *perichoresis* of the two natures. This expression has its origin in Gregory of Nazianzus. Maximus the Confessor, in his defence against monothelitic tendencies, compares the relationship of the natures of Jesus with the interpenetration of body and soul, and the mutual

143

permeation of word and the meaning of the word. The human nature of Jesus cannot be active without the divine because of their unity in the hypostasis. The term *perichoresis* is found for the first time in a strictly technical sense in John Damascene. It is used both in a Trinitarian and Christological context, above all in the latter. He speaks of a being-in-one-another, not of a fusing-into-one-another. He posits the one nature as the basis for *perichoresis* in the Trinity and the one Person as its basis in the hypostatic union. In the Middle Ages we find also the expression *circumincessio*. It is used by Albert the Great as well as by Franciscan theologians, for example, Duns Scotus, Peter Auriol, and Francis of Meyronnes. Here it is used solely in a Trinitarian context. John Gerson, on the other hand, applied it Christologically, but its use in this sense was later discontinued. One can distinguish here also between a static and dynamic viewpoint. The dynamic point of view considers that the act of mutual permeation takes place continually. Through this act the state of permeation is uninterruptedly being established anew.

The assumption of the man Jesus by the divine Logos takes place first of all in the ontic dimension. The question must now be asked whether the man Jesus was conscious of the fact that he did not possess a human but a divine subsistence. Did Jesus know that he was God? To what extent did he know that he was God? It would indeed be strange if the divine subsistence of the man Jesus, the decisive element of his personality, did not enter into his consciousness; that is, if the ontic did not become an ontological element. In his human self-consciousness Jesus lived the inexpressible experience of knowing himself to be the only-begotten Son of the heavenly Father. His whole inner life was moulded by this consciousness. Consequently, his religious experience was like that of no other man. On the strength of this he could declare, according to the witness of Mt. 11, 25–27, that no one knows the Father but the Son, and no one the Son but the Father; he was able to give a revelation of God which bore absolute character. Jesus could have no human consciousness of self without knowing God to be his Father.

At this point we must consider a question which has given rise to much animated discussion in current theology: the question as to the self-consciousness of the man Jesus. May we assume that the man Jesus possessed also a human self-consciousness, or are we only permitted to concede him a divine self-consciousness? Might we say that he had a double ego, a human and a divine; that in his human knowledge he knew of his divine ego only by virtue of the fact that he saw as an object, so to speak, the Trinitarian God, and thus the Logos, with whom he is united?

This intensively studied question is not simply a problem of matter but also of terminology. It can in no way be denied that Jesus had also a human centre of activity. If it could be agreed terminologically that his human centre of activity expresses itself in a human self-consciousness, then one could speak in this sense of a human ego-consciousness. The ego-consciousness, however, does not have the character of a personal consciousness. It is—if one agrees with this manner of expression—the awareness of the centralization of human spontaneity and freedom.

To carry through this idea one would have to accept a gradation with respect to the notion of person. One would have to distinguish between, even consider separable, the psychological and the ontological element. Since in the Middle Ages little stress was laid on the psychological element, it does not seem theologically impossible from the outset to make such a distinction. In other words, one could attribute to the man Jesus a human ego-consciousness without at the same time attributing to him a human personality. However, it might be more in keeping with the unity in Jesus Christ if one were to declare that the personal element, more precisely, the subsistence of the divine Logos, penetrates into the ego-consciousness of the man Jesus so that his ego-consciousness comprises both the human centre of activity, as well as the divine subsistence. In this way the ego-consciousness would be gradated without falling into duality or multiplicity. It is a composite and yet undivided consciousness in which is contained the consciousness of being

145

genuinely man, as well as the consciousness of subsisting in the subsistence of the divine Logos. The thesis formulated at the Council of Chalcedon as to "undivided" and "unmixed" would thus remain wholly preserved. The man Jesus, insofar as he is man, can never experience himself to be God. On the other hand, he can never know himself as a human person. Were he to interpret himself as a human person, he would fall victim to ontological self-deception.

In speaking of a composite ego-consciousness, one must note that it is not a case of heterogeneous elements being placed alongside one another. The human and the divine in Jesus permeate one another without mutual destruction, without the one being transformed into the other. It must further be noted that the divine is superior so that in the ego-consciousness of Jesus the primary consciousness is that of being the Son of God, the Son of the Father. This results from his being conscious of subsisting in the subsistence of the divine Logos.

On the other hand, precisely at this point one must say that the consciousness in Jesus of being truly man is neither suppressed nor diminished. Jesus knew himself to be fully and truly man, bearing the full burden of human destiny and called to a genuine human life unto death, even to the death of the cross. This consciousness is in no way obscured by his consciousness of being the Son of God; on the contrary, it is made more acute. It is precisely in this composite consciousness that the man Jesus is truly, wholly, concretely man.

In medieval theology the question was posed as to whether a divine Person other than the Person of the Logos could have become man. This statement of the problem presupposes a purely abstract notion of God which ignores the salvation history viewpoint of Scripture. It is reminiscent of the idea of *potentia* or *potestas dei absoluta,* that is, that God in his absolute power could act arbitrarily, which was held by several theologians in the late scholastic period. Such a conception of God is quite foreign to the thought of Thomas Aquinas even when we find the question posed and answered by him in a positive sense. It would appear that this late scholastic conception of an arbitrary God must be referred to, if one is to attempt to understand the question as posed by Thomas Aquinas. In a salvation history outlook on Scripture, neither the posing of the question nor a positive answer to it is possible. One may even ask whether it would not contradict the meaning of the tri-personal divine life if one were to declare it appropriate that a Person other than the Logos become man. As we have seen, by the incarnation is understood the self-communication of God to creatures. This self-giving is of such nature that the communication of the Father to the Son is extended to the divine self-emptying into creatures. However, if the Father communicates himself directly to the creature, then the Son and the Holy Spirit remain, in a certain sense, outside this movement of divine self-communication. This would result in the Father expressing himself, in his inner-trinitarian life, univocally in the Son and analogously—in a sort of mechanical parallelism—in creatures. Both self-expressions, then, would take place unrelatedly.

Concerning the Person of the Holy Spirit, we may speak of him as unifying principle in an extended sense. His task as uniting factor within the inner-Trinitarian life is extended to the uniting of the man Jesus and the divine Logos in the hypostatic union. It is further extended to the uniting of the whole of humanity with Jesus whereby a brotherly relationship with him is established. It is to this end that he is sent by Father and Son into the world. This corresponds to the peculiar character of the Holy Spirit as it is intimated in Scripture and as it has developed theologically in the course of the centuries. In both Greek and Latin theology he is called "gift." Augustine was deeply concerned that this denomination might result in the Holy Spirit being too closely entangled with the world. He suggested, therefore, that the term "gift" be used only from that moment in which he is concretely given to man, whereas in his eternal existence he should be characterized as "givable." According to this interpretation, there is in the Holy Spirit a certain orientation to creatures, or rather to their sanctification, which does not deny or compromise the immanence of the

147

Trinity as a whole. Augustine declared that the first gift of Love is Love. When Father and Son send the Holy Spirit into humanity, they send that love which first of all unites the man Jesus with the divine Logos and, in a different manner, unites all of mankind, indeed all of creation with the Logos. Thus the incarnation of a Person other than the Logos appears not only improper, but impossible. The incarnation of a Person other than the Logos would, in effect, be meaningless.

These considerations bring out more clearly the Christ-centredness of creation. All of matter is orientated towards spirit. This orientation finds its highest realization in the human person. Furthermore, all of creation is orientated towards God. The whole development of the universe has its term in a special oneness with God as Creator, a oneness which was not there from the beginning. This development, which is immanent to the world-process, has reached its goal in Jesus Christ. This did not take place in a natural, but in a grace-directed manner. This graded guidance of God was intended from the very beginning. The termination of the development of the world in union with himself was the reason for the creation of the world. It was not that the world was first planned and then its goal determined; rather, its goal was set and the world so planned that it was capable of attaining its goal. The most perfect realization of this orientation of creation towards union with God is found in Jesus Christ. So intimate is this union of creation with God in Christ that no other unity between God and creature would be possible without its verging over into pantheism. In this unity dissimilarity is preserved. This dissimilarity does not imply distance; on the contrary, it is characterized by the most intimate proximity. It is of the utmost significance that Jesus be not considered an isolated figure. Even if the grace-directed development of the world was but once to achieve that unity realized in Jesus, it was designed that Jesus be the representative of all men in this unity with God. According to Scripture, the intimacy of this function of representation is frequently expressed in the word "brotherhood" (Mt. 12, 49. 25, 40. 28, 10;

Mk. 3, 33 ff.; Lk. 8, 21; Jn. 20, 17; Rom. 8, 29; Heb. 2, 11 ff.).
It was intended that Jesus be the brother of all men.

If all men are called brothers because they are bearers of
humanity or because they are all created by the same God in
heaven, this does not of itself account for the deepest reason
for human brotherhood, nor does it constitute its greatest intensity. Both of these are to be found in Jesus Christ. Transcendence, it is true, has attained its zenith in Christ. But in
transcending to God, the man Jesus did not distance himself
from the rest of men; he rather opened himself to them. Man's
self-transcendence to God and God's self-communication to
man reaches its most perfect realization in the resurrection of
Jesus. The resurrection does not imply an alienation of the man
Jesus with respect to his humanity. Divinization is not dehumanization, it is rather, the attainment of the most perfect form
of human existence. It implies the total opening of the man
Jesus towards his brothers. By virtue of his resurrection he is
closer to them than would ever have been possible in his historical existence. Human life implies a simultaneity of distance
and proximity. However man might wish to open himself to the
other in love and friendship, he is inexorably closed within self.
It is precisely this self-confinement that has been overcome by
the resurrection.

As a consequence of the unification of all men with Jesus as
their representative, indeed as their brother, all participate in an
analogical manner in the sonship in which Jesus is related to
his Father. Thus God becomes the Father of all men, his fatherhood being mediated through Jesus. He ceases to be Judge and
becomes the Father who calls his children into his own divine
life. Jesus gave graphic expression to this when, according to
Jn. 14, 2, he says: "In my Father's house there are many
rooms; if it were not so, would I have told you that I go to
prepare a place for you? And when I go and prepare a place
for you, I will come again and will take you to myself, that
where I am you may be also." The brothers of Jesus belong
in the house of the heavenly Father. One must emphasize again
in this context that through the gathering together of men into

149

the sonship of the one brother who represents them all, they are in no way alienated from true human existence. On the contrary, it is precisely because of this participation in the sonship of Christ that their true humanity is guaranteed; for in their awareness of a brotherly relationship with Jesus, they are not only obliged, but also enabled to live in a spirit of brotherliness with each other. If partnership is an essential aspect of human existence, then it is in the man Jesus that it will be found most deeply rooted for all men. Through this brotherhood with Jesus men are clearly directed towards and obliged to an existence in fraternal charity. They fulfill this brotherhood to which they are committed in a variety of ways, more exactly, in the form of their historical activity. Thus we are led to conclude that, as a consequence of the incarnation, God himself has a history; that is not in the pantheistic theology of history as propounded by Hegel, but in a form in which the Chalcedonian terms of "unmixed" and "undivided" are validly maintained. God has a history by virtue of the history of his Son Jesus, who led a genuine human life and through his life, death, and resurrection injected into human history a dynamism which remains inexhaustible. The consummation of the life of Jesus in his brothers, that is, in humanity and through humanity in all of creation, will only then reach its term when everything is perfected at the final manifestation of the resurrected Christ. The incarnation of God, therefore, implies both an obligation to historical activity and an endowment of the capacity to discharge this obligation, that is, to act in such manner as befits brotherhood amongst all men. Now resurrected and with his Father, Jesus also lives in this dynamic sweep of history. At the endpoint of this process he awaits, as man's representative, the arrival of all men to unity with him in the Father. He represents the Father before all men until that hour of perfection when the Father will reveal himself. Thus the incarnation guarantees the secularity of the world as well as its divinization. Historical activity implies that ever new forms of economic, social, cultural, and political community living must be strived for. There is no absolutely valid form with which man could be fully satisfied. What today might be

150

considered a genuine expression of brotherhood may tomorrow—in consequence of a new outlook, new scientific and technological developments—be considered outmoded, inhibiting, unbrotherly. It is precisely the believer in Christ who can never consider himself dispensed from tirelessly seeking those new cultural and political forms of life which changing times and conditions demand. He must work towards their achievement without falling victim to the restless drive for innovation. The norm is not any *a priori* ideology; it is the human community as brotherhood, and the individual in this community as brother.

At this point, the question imposes itself upon us as to whether the Holy Spirit is drawn into the history of Jesus. Our point of departure must be the fact that he is sent in a concrete manner as is the Son (Gal. 4, 6). According to St. Thomas, the mission implies a temporal mode of existence of the Person sent. The Person enters, in a certain sense, the temporality of creatures without himself becoming temporal. At the baptism of Jesus, the Holy Spirit entered into salvation history and remained thereafter with Christ. One might also refer to the fact that since the incarnation of the Logos, it is the incarnate Logos who together with the Father brings forth the Holy Spirit; not insofar as he is man, but nevertheless as the incarnate Logos. The Holy Spirit is continuously active in the man Jesus. The *pneuma* accompanies the man Jesus and thus has a history in and through him. Since the Spirit remains effective in the Church, the community of Jesus, he has also in this community and in the historical activity of its members, a history.

It is apparent from these considerations that the incarnation is itself of great salvific significance. Already through the incarnation redemption has become a reality, for in the Word-made-flesh human nature has once for all and unconditionally been assumed by God to an immediate communion of life. In and through Jesus the way to participation in the life of God has been opened to all of humanity. However, the redemptive acts of Christ, his death and resurrection, are by no means superfluous or insignificant; for the assumption of the human nature by the divine Logos also implies an identification with an inte-

151

gral human life. In this way all acts in the human life of Jesus Christ are self-realizations of the man Jesus who is hypostatically united with the Logos. They have redemptive significance. Whatever Jesus does he does in absolute communion with God, he does it as representative of all mankind. With the exception of sin his life is lived in a manner proper to the sons of Adam, to the very point of death. His frightful and shameful death on the cross is the result of sin which broke into human history. Therefore, functional and ontological Christology, that is Christological and soteriological elements in the traditional sense, are most intimately interwoven and condition one another. The ontological element includes the functional element and the functional element is expression of the ontological element.

Consequently, because of the incarnation, and because of the function of the incarnate Logos as brotherly representative, all who are one with him are sons of that Father whose eternal Son he himself is. When we say "our Father," we do not have in mind the tripersonal God in his paternal attitude towards creation, as would seem to correspond to the Latin conception of the Trinity. It is, rather, the first Person of the Trinity, the God and Father of Jesus Christ, whom we address. It is, then, only within the framework of Greek Trinitarian theology that the formula which expresses the structure of Christian existence becomes truly meaningful: through Christ, in the Holy Spirit, to the Father.

7.

THE HISTORY OF SALVATION AND THE HISTORICITY OF MAN IN THE RENEWAL OF THEOLOGY

M.-D. CHENU, O.P.

A CHANGE of schedule has advanced my paper to this first day of our gathering. This is really a happy circumstance in that it invites my giving, as part of my assignment, a somewhat fuller comment on the proper object of this congress, as suggested in its very name, that is, "theological renewal." Renewal refers to time, to time on the march, to history. If theology, taken not only as any knowledge, but expressly as the Word of God, has a capacity for renewal, it is because it bears a reference to time and to history *in its very object,* this object being the very reality of God. Herein lies the paradox.

Such a reference to time and history has not been added to theology. It inheres in its very nature in that a relation to time *enters right into* the Word of God. Moreover, the same reference to time and history qualifies man who is both the hearer and the hero of this Word. Herein appears the historical density of this "renewal" applied to the rather original kind of knowledge that theology is. Renewal is not a reshaping from without, but an understanding from within.

The impact of the Council in its profound sense, in its permanent compass, will be found in this: that renewal is not a process of bringing something to light two or three centuries later on (this kind of thing would have to take place every fifty years); it is, rather, a permanent state of *re-formatio* in the etymological sense of the word.

Renewal, aggiornamento, better yet, *re-formatio* (a term which, despite its ups and downs, has a rich tradition): these words, like all words expressing lively feelings and raising great hopes, run the serious risk that their very warmth will turn to lukewarmness. They must be maintained in their strict meaning, according to the stated theme of this congress. Let us say, then, that it is our task to construct theology out of them. We must discover how the Word of God, *theo-logia,* on all the levels of its perception, of its expression, of its elaboration, implies in its very nature (and so in fidelity to itself), a permanent *re-formatio.* Let us, to speak like Aristotle, observe how the genesis of things is homogeneous with their nature (*genesis-phusis*), so that to observe genesis is the best way of knowing nature (I Pol. 2, 1252, 24–26). It is in the very nature of the Word of God that we find the intelligible principle and the laws of its "renewal" in the community of believers.

Indeed, the internal logic of this operation was at work in an extraordinarily direct way in the Council. This was all the more perceptible the more the Council's spontaneous charism overrode its institutional preparations. It was by becoming aware of its *nature* that the Church, at Vatican II, found again the law of its *aggiornamento,* which had been John XXIII's project conceived on the spur of the moment. The theology of this operation should provide us today not only with an opportune application, but also with a solid, bold, and clear-sighted grasp of it.

Two bishops out of three, taking the floor during the recent Council, justified their interventions by the observation, sometimes fearful, sometimes hopeful, that there was a general change taking place in the world, which was affecting the condition of man himself to its very depths. "Today," says the introduction to the Constitution *Gaudium et spes,* "the human race is passing through a new age of its history. Profound and rapid changes are spreading by degrees around the whole world. Triggered by the intelligence and creative energies of man, these changes recoil upon him, upon his decisions and desires, both individual and collective, upon his manner of thinking and acting, with respect to things and to people. Hence we can already speak of a true social and cultural transformation, one which has repercussions on man's religious life as well" (art. 4).

Such a transformation, far from provoking a stiffening of defensive lines, soon presented itself as a challenge to the Church, and so she was led to become aware of her existence in the world and in history as a constitutive condition of her mission, and so of her very being. Everyone remembers the intervention of Cardinal Suenens at the end of the first session (December 4, 1962), immediately accepted by Cardinals Frings and Montini. Out of a confused and unwieldy agenda paper, he extracted the decisive line of the Council: the Church has to define herself within herself, but also outside herself in a "dialogue" with the world. This was the launching of the famous Schema XIII, a charismatic shock from which emanates the whole theology of renewal. "When the Church takes thought of herself, she becomes missionary," as Paul VI said soon afterward.

To consent in this way to changes in the world and to the movement of history so that the Word of God may speak *today* did not come about without disturbing that security which is the necessary and spontaneous reflex of every living being. Within the Church, it is fidelity to tradition conceived as a deposit which effectively brings this necessary security to the Community and to each believer. But the sociological accretions which gradually form around this assurance which goes with faith often atrophy that power, which the tradition of the Word has to be permanently present to the continuity of history. We indulge in "restorations" rather than a "renovation." This tension, which might have provoked a mere adroit compromise, instead led the Council to define the objective dialectic which measures the historical dimension of Christianity, a dimension entirely determined by the coming of God into history. The decision for *aggiornamento,* then, did not proceed from a pastoral opportunism. However legitimate this might have been for the preach-

155

ing of the Gospel message, it would have been deficient in thought and in action. Instead, *aggiornamento* emanated from a lively consciousness that to be present to its own time is, for the Church of God-made-man, the elementary law of growth and of existence.

THE HISTORY OF SALVATION

Salvation history: this profound expression, which has passed through many variations in the history of theology, seems capable of carrying and communicating all the elements in question, the objects as well as the methods of theology. Its usage at the Council clearly gives its meaning: "that mystery which affects the whole history of the human race" (*Optatam totius,* art. 14). And a little later, this link between *mystery* and *history* is considered the principle of renewal of the theological disciplines: "Other theological disciplines should also be renewed by livelier contact with the mystery of Christ and the history of salvation" (*ibid.,* art. 16). This text, which may be considered one of the rules for the renewal of theology, is found, it is true, in a minor decree, one concerned in a practical way with the formation of young priests; however, this pedagogical statement not only touches the teaching of theology, but emanates in its depth from the very substance of the constitution of the Church, as defined by *Lumen gentium* as well as by *Gaudium et spes*.

Further, these pedagogical statements ought to be read, meditated upon, and applied, as in their radical context, in the light of the constitution *Verbum Dei,* the great text, so sharply debated, on the Word of God as the structure of the Church. The vocabulary there, too, is extremely significant, even in the subtle discussion in which it was chosen. The word "Christianity" in the primitive schema (1963) was replaced by "*oeconomia christiana*" (Report of June 3rd, 1964, no. 4, *in fine*). The expression that prevailed implies a constitutive reference to time, to the earthly development of the Church, as well as to her eschatological fulfilment. The "definitive" (*ibid.*)

156

character of the evangelical revelation within the fulness of Christ, far from being incompatible with development, requires it: the mystery of Christ is always in act, not only in projecting old lights into new situations, but by an immanent presence in the community of his Body. The Church is the historical form of grace.

What is, then, as underpinning of the conciliar text, the profound meaning and the content of salvation history, as object of faith and as theological locus of the Word of God?

At the beginning of this analysis, we ought to distinguish and articulate clearly two ways of referring to God: God the creator of the universe, and the God of history. In the most common belief of the faithful, God is primarily creator of the world, the God of origins, who has subsequently spoken "many times and in many ways to our fathers through the prophets" (Heb. 1, 1), revealing himself to the Jewish people and finally becoming incarnate in Christ. So Christianity appears primarily as an explanation of the world and of man; it gives access by proof, or at least by a spontaneous inference, to the existence of a supreme Being, the cause of all reality.

On the contrary, if we examine the biblical tradition, it is the God of history who presents himself face to face, manifesting himself not by the realities of the universe, but by and in "events" from the promise to Abraham to his personal coming into history, which will only be consummated in his second coming. The faith of Abraham, of Isaac, and of Jacob, is profoundly and entirely respectful of the transcendence of God, of the Most High God; but this religion is not the source of the biblical faith and knowledge of the "true God."

It is certainly necessary to keep in mind the complementary character of these two roads, but also the difference in their movements. In a summary fashion, we might say that Vatican I, faced with the errors of the time and provided with the rational methods of post-Tridentine scholasticism, followed the first route, which we might call the metaphysical one (the timeless schema of proofs for the existence of God, and so forth). Vatican II, thoroughly penetrated with the biblical renewal, with the

157

liturgical mystery, with missionary evangelism, and with escha-tological sensitivity, found its path in the definition of the Church as the Body of Christ in history. By their very diversity in genesis and final form, the two constitutions *Lumen gentium* and *Gaudium et spes* show most clearly their unity of intention and doctrine.[1] The constant use of historical categories in the draft-ing of the texts, already significant in itself, in its novelty, is but the consequence of a fundamental plan.

Christianity is an economy rather than a system. It is an economy in the rich density of that word as used by the Greek Fathers to designate the plan of salvation history. But Chris-tianity is not primarily a system, even though in its second phase, as known in faith, it develops normally and fruitfully into a system, or better, into a "scholastic" knowledge. This is per-fectly obvious if we consider that the revelation of the old covenant begins with the violent opposition between God, who directs the actions and conduct of his people, and the gods of surrounding—and infectious—clans who make idols of the forces of nature. Creation itself is presented in a framework of historical thought: description of the origins of the world, episodic narratives of the daily developments of a first great week, and so forth. Creation is not envisaged as a metaphysical operation in the order of essences, but as the commencement of a great history. And so the road to knowledge of the tran-scendence of God goes by way of man, by way of this history in which God summons him. God speaks by events.

The denouement of this "sacred history" among the messianic people is the coming of God himself into history. Not an

---

[1] This is not merely an afterthought in the text of *Gaudium et spes.* "The schema does not start from the natural order to wind up later in the supernatural order, as if the human person had two vocations, one laid upon the other from the outside," said one of the principal drafters of the text, Bishop Haubtmann (interviewed in *La Croix,* September 30th, 1965). This obviously poses for the theologian, builder of the understanding of the faith, the problem of coordinating the mystery of creation and the mystery of incarnation within a single divine economy, and consequently, in the very existence of the Christian in the world, the problem of coordinating within himself his participation in the building of the world and his communion in divine life in the kingdom of Christ.

extravagance, not a wasteful super-miracle, but an operation whose logic ratifies and consecrates all the preparations for it. All Christianity stands on this *event,* which is not the strange, transitory episode of a fleshly birth of the Son of God, but a personal investment of God into the community of men, into a chosen people which henceforth extends to the human race as a whole. And because this *event* occurs in two times, the incarnation in the time of Caesar Augustus and the parousia at the end of time, it is realized in an accumulative and progressive process of incorporation of all those men whom faith has taken hold of, more or less consciously. And so the eschatological future is already present in a way, as the immanent object of hope, as the very essence of Christian existence.

Such, then, is the economy of revelation in the old and in the new covenant: not a history in which a revelation occurred, but a history itself revealing. This introduces a serious problem for theology. It will oblige theology not to occupy itself solely with ontological relations and with definitions of essences, but to be primarily a reflection on a becoming, on a plan of salvation. It is within a history that theology encounters the problem of ontological relations. The theologian, then, in the use he makes of the documents, will have to respect both their authority and their origin, and this he cannot do except by integrating them into an historical pattern of thought rather than using them merely as a point of departure.

This revelation, this investment, this mystery, is accomplished in its fulness in the humanity of the risen Jesus. Consequently, the unfolding of the history between the two comings is not in itself the medium of revelation or of salvation. Every development, in thought or in action, is within the total truth of Christ and of his Gospel. Still, one cannot say that after the event of Christ, the future is henceforth entirely behind us, as if history after Christ has done nothing but pass by, and has not been *realizing* itself. Tradition is not an arrested history in a preserved past; it is the "authentic" emanation of this "definitive" truth, by the help of the events of the world, according to the

159

rhythm of the civilizations in which the Church implants herself in the course of the centuries.

How is this? In the continuous thread of this history, every reality, every value, every truth of thought or of action, whereever it is and whatever its source, is "recapitulated" in the *man*-God, who divinizes wherever humanization takes place. The mystery is in history. The Church is in the world.

The Church is in the world of our time. She is here by a sociologically visible existence; she is here in the expression and interpretation of the very truth of the revealed datum; the Word of God speaks *today* in the hierarchical and magisterial community of which it is the living architecture. Thus we are not at all concerned with an "adaptation" of the Word of God preconceived in abstract purity. We are not dressing up or stripping dogmatic formulas. It is a rereading of Scripture that progressively reveals its appropriate significance in each generation of the Church, thanks to the light which the present moment throws upon the past when past and present confront each other, open to the future. It is a permanent reinterpretation, within the regulating community and as conditioned by its magisterium, of truths within the unchangeable identity of their intentionality.

Before seeing how this statement governs theology at work, at the work of renewal, it is important to measure in the dynamism of history the curve of this relation between the Church and the world, between the evangelical message and the civilizations. With a fearlessness that disconcerted many, the Council followed out the logic of its position: the Church *receives* from the world, from the human enterprise of building the world, from the progress of humanization, and cultures. "The Church," said the Council, "can be enriched, and is effectively enriched, by the unfolding (*evolutio,* says the Latin text, despite the opposition of certain bishops) of the social life . . . and she does not ignore all she has received from the history and the evolution of the human race." For the sake of anyone who would see this cooperation solely in pastoral practice, not in the understanding of the faith, let us read from another part of this famous article (44) of *Gaudium et spes:* "The experience of past ages,

160

the progress of the sciences, and the treasures hidden in the various cultures, which open new roads to truth, are likewise useful to the Church. In fact, from the beginnings of her history she has learned to express the message of Christ with the help of the concepts and the languages of various peoples, and moreover has endeavored to enhance it by the wisdom of the philosophers." This is not a lucky accident; it is "the law of all evangelization." For better reason, we ought to say here that it is the law of all theology. Thus, a consciousness of human values in terms of the progress of civilizations in all their diversity leads to a consciousness of the implications of the mystery and of the truths expressing it.

We are now in a position to proceed with our present investigation: the renewal of theology finds its principle, its profound reason, its laws and rules, in the very nature of the economy of Christianity as revelation, since the mystery of renewal becomes real in the unfolding of history. Theology, on all its levels, from the kerygmatic proclamation of the message to its scientific construction, articulates and develops its knowledge according to the very law of the Word of God, the understanding of which is its special province: under the light of and with the discernment of faith, it adopts the objects, the methods, the discoveries, the disputes of the human spirit at work in its very timeliness. It is wrong for a theologian to isolate, to "put in parentheses" as it were, his contemporary thought, in order first to determine exactly what has been revealed, and only then, as a second step, to translate it into contemporary language.

To anyone who is surprised at this earthly engagement of the science of God, let me say that this position is taken by the most classical theology: God, speaking to man, uses the language of men, conforming to the geography of civilizations and the development of history as much as to the psychology of individuals. "God, when speaking to men, speaks in the manner of men" (St. Augustine, *De civitate Dei,* 18, 6, 2). And St. Thomas declares that knowledge of the faith follows the mode and methods of the human subject, not the dignity of the divine object. Basically, this is the reason for the *aggiornamento*. The

161

evangelical message is not an archaeological document which one "brings to light"; rather, it is announced and proclaimed this very day. Let us not miss this specific dimension. Like the Church whose intellectual consciousness it is, theology is *semper reformanda,* according to the famous phrase whose historical ambiguity must not be allowed to obscure its truth.

Consequently, to understand the "places" of the Word of God in the world, the first requirement is not to deduce its applications from an abstract and extratemporal analysis, as we have long done, but "to scrutinize, to discern, to interpret" in history, in the Church in act, "the multiple languages of our time" (*Gaudium et spes,* art. 44), or in the now classic expression of John XXIII, taken up by Paul VI and expressly recorded by the Council (*ibid.,* art. 4) "to scrutinize the signs of the times."

"Signs of the times": here without a doubt we have the key phrase, the theological category which will function as a pivot, not only for analysis of the pastoral *aggiornamento* of the Church, but much more for the renewal of a theology conscious of the historical dimension of its object.

It is quite true that the events which constitute the thread of history do not enter into the object, nor into the light of revelation at all, no more than they result, of themselves, in the coming of the kingdom. Neither nature nor history has the capacity to reveal the mystery of God; his Word comes "from on high" by the initiative of a gratuitous love, engaging itself in a loving communion. Grace is grace, and profane history is not the source of salvation. Human enterprises, the conquering of nature, the increasing awareness of peoples, the cultivation of minds, and education of hearts, are only the material occasions or the extrinsic conditions of the individual and collective life of grace. The economic and social advancement of the labouring classes, the entrance of women into social life, the liberation of colonized peoples, the world-wide dimension of development, and in general all the phenomena of socialization—enumerated by John XXIII as so many signs of the times—all these, in their human density in the context of the march of history, make

162

possible capacities for the concrete understanding of the plan of God, of God the creator as well as of Christ the recapitulator of every value. The first verses of Genesis on the domination of the world by man assume a new significance and pose new questions to the theologian in a time when this domination is being realized in an extraordinarily powerful manner. The evangelical aspirations to universal brotherhood increase their theologal clarity when "neighbor" is defined in terms of a world-wide socialization. The solidarity of the world and the diversity of its civilizations form, in the laborious creation of a "human community," an admirable picture, and, as it were, a challenge for the catholicity of the Church, which has been too long confined, her theology included, to the West. The theologian finds here something like a second inspiration of the transcendence of the Word of God. These are so many "signs of the times" of God, spelled out in profane realities.

Does not this kind of historicity ruin the speculative construction of theology, or will it not at least reduce theology to a rather artificial superstructure? The blunders of a sort of pseudo-evangelical positivism might make us fear so. But let us leave them to their failure. Let us rather observe that any articulating of a "speculative" science on history, that is, in the present case, any constructing of a science-theology on the history of salvation, will not proceed without problems nor without risk. It is *kalos kindunos,* noble risk, if it compels the theologian to dig more deeply into the soil of a faith whose roots and branches are alive, and in process of being discovered in the community of the Spirit. The deeper the digging about the roots, the more the tops, including their "scholastic" trimmings, will be stimulated with light and health.

THE HISTORICITY OF MAN

It is not by chance that the Christian is becoming more attentive to the peculiar character of the economy of salvation at the moment when man is becoming vitally aware of the historicity of his own nature. This is a normal convergence, if it is true that faith, incarnate in the human subject, adjusts itself to man's structures and evolutions. We observe this, moreover, in the Council. To the extent that the Council elaborated its Christological vision of a universe in movement, it experienced the need, a need albeit inadequately satisfied, for an anthropology. Now, in this "Christian" anthropology, as it is being set forth more or less explicitly in theological statements, three attributes, three coessential attributes of man are emerging: first, that man is by nature social; second, that he is so linked to the universe that the very matter of the cosmos is engaged in his destiny; and third, that man exists in history. This threefold value for better or for worse—and fear of the worse in the case of all three aspects hovered over the deliberations of the Council Fathers— this threefold value, written into man's nature and in some way, too, issuing from it, let us take as something distinct from abstract analysis, or from anything resembling either a timeless idea or an unchanging definition. It is thus that, even in its vocabulary, the Council speaks rather of the human *condition* than of human *nature* as such, by contrast with Vatican I. Without setting aside an essentialist philosophy, one can readily have recourse to existential analyses.

On the point that interests us, then, what is the direction of this anthropology? And how will anthropology, as it is more vigorously elaborated, come to the aid of the renewal of theology?

It would be quite superficial to see in the Council's proceedings, as some have feared, an attempt to accommodate the Christian faith to some ideology of progress, to some theory on evolution. It was only at the end of an inductive analysis, in which were recorded the many elements of change in the world and in society, that the experts came to grips with the *cause* of these changes, causes which have up to now been only too often dealt with in the Church as a simple occasion for pastoral accommodation or for an opportunistic apologetic. These changes are, of themselves and as met with even in their unhappiest manifestations, the signs and the effects of an undefined perfectibility of humanity according to the very design of the Creator, who did not turn man out like a ready-made garment, but placed in his hands the future of his own perfection, not only individual, but collective. Humanity was not made up of monads set out side by side, each with only exterior relations with the others. Humanity is, and ought increasingly to be, a society, in which each individual is constantly becoming more jointly responsible with all the others. Each stage of this socialization, or more exactly each successive awareness of the progress of this socialization is the crossing of a threshold as notable in its own way as any threshold of prehistory. The present stage, passing into the scientific and technological civilization now taking shape, has been justly compared with the neolithic era.

So the historicity of man is the expression of a double condition of man: first, man exists only in society, today a community of global dimensions; second, this sociability proceeds at bottom from the fact that man is consubstantially linked to matter (this, at least, is the anthropology of St. Thomas, more up-to-date than ever), and that he only has being, consciousness, and perfection, to the degree that he experiences existence-in-the-world. History, society, matter: theirs is an inseparable homogeneity. In the course of the centuries, if not always in theory, at least in mental outlook and behaviour, Christian "spirituality" (the word is significant) has almost always inclined, more or less consciously, towards the existence in the soul of a region that is free from the body and the place for the encounter with God—timeless Christianity, in a Christology more or less monophysite. In any case, it is a psychological dualism which results not only in a depreciation of the body in an indifference to presence in the "world," but also in an insensitivity to history. It is a timeless conception of man which, in the Christian, atrophies both the sense of the economy of salvation and the eschatological vision of the faith. For the last four centuries, generations of theologians have put together manuals in which sacred history is treated as a preliminary study, left for the exegetes as an "auxiliary" discipline (to use the terminology of the *ratio studiorum*), and in which eschatology, when one reached it, consisted of a puny treatise *de novissimis*. During this period, we were fully "scholastic" in the pejorative sense of the word. One might speak of it as an essentialist theology leading to the kind of "spiritualism" which has been justly denounced by the humanism, atheist or not, of contemporary civilization.

Whatever the lucubrations of evolutionism of whatever kind, whatever the danger of a summary historicism, it would be senseless not to recognize in this historical understanding of man a significant enrichment, and one fully homogeneous with a philosophy that affirms both man's natural sociability and his consubstantiality with matter.

This is not the place to develop the consequences of such a position for a theology of man and of the world. There is obviously a perfect—and promising—homogeneity between a theology whose object is the history of salvation and a Christian anthropology which appreciates the historical dimension of man. All the biblical realism of "sacred history" comes to the support of this high conception.

There is here an admirable convergence to delight the theologian in depth of the mystery grasped and contemplated in history: for while, on the one hand, a new light on modern man comes to support a rediscovery of the incarnation as the historical humanization of God, on the other, the Christological center of gravity of Christianity places man under another new light. Anthropology and Christology, Christology and anthropology, together become, one by means of the other, the geometrical locus of theology in the full understanding of the mystery.

Against an unconscious Docetism which has too long nourished an abstract, timeless, and acosmic "spirituality," the interest in the concrete and historical humanity of Christ leads to rediscovery of man as God's partner in the history of the world. "God being made man, man is henceforth the measure of all things." (Karl Barth)

Yes, truly, the history of salvation and, in support of it, the historicity of man, are at the basis of the renewal of theology, in its method as well as in the perception of its object.

166

8.

THEOLOGICAL REFLECTIONS ON THE PROBLEM OF SECULARIZATION

KARL RAHNER, S.J.

THE concept of secularization appears first of all, historically and objectively, as a concept which has reference to the Church as something in the social order. Certainly, one can distinguish —for example in German—between "secularization," "secularizing," "secularism" (cf. *LThK,* IX, 248–254). By this last term, "secularism," is meant the phenomenon of a "world become worldly and profane," of an understanding of the world theoretically and practically without God. But it is more precise to begin with the concept of secularization insofar as it refers to the development of the world (as creation of man). This concept, then, denotes for us the world's taking its distance from the Church, the growing separation of *sacerdotium* and *regnum,* the ever increasing profaneness of the world in contrast with the time when religion, as institution and social life, Church and world, formed a relatively homogeneous unity.

This secularization or mundanity in relation to the Church need not be simply identified with an atheistic profaneness, for the world itself bears witness in its own way to a certain "religiosity," is within the universal salvific will of God, and can under certain conditions attain salvation. These two realities, secularization as the world's taking its distance from the Church and the process of secularization as the endeavour of atheistic profanity, are naturally bound up with one another.

But we do not intend here to speak of this relationship. We

shall limit ourselves to the concept of secularization insofar as it denotes a separating from the Church. So we are not speaking of the atheistic understanding of the world in its many forms; nor are we speaking of the "world without religion" (Bonhoeffer), of the theology of the death of God, of the non-religious interpretation of biblical concepts (Ebeling), of the world worldly as such (Metz), nor of the world's coming of age, inasmuch as we presume as already given such a diastasis between the Church and the world. Even when we have thus delineated our subject, only some among the many questions which arise can be treated.

We presuppose here the results of recent work on the problem of secularism and secularization: the biblical and theological concept of "world" (including the world in the sense of world perfected by man, of hominized milieu, of sinful world of this "Aion," and so forth), the worldly development of the world, legitimate and gradually coming to realization in the course of history in virtue even of the dynamism inherent in Christianity, and so forth. These presuppositions, in addition to assuming the fundamental distinction "in itself" always given between the world (society, state) and the Church in the sense of Leo XIII, also affirm that this distinction itself has, in theory and practice, a history, and a history which continually pursues further clarification, and therein a clearer manifestation of the world and the Church in themselves and in their mutual relationship.

We will present our reflections in the form of five theses or propositions.

First Thesis: there appears frequently in the history of the Church a false integrism in opposition to which secularization has an authentically Christian claim.

We must examine here in particular the concept and nature of integrism, for as attitude and mentality it has far from disappeared from the Church, and for this reason a critique of it can help us grasp more clearly a legitimate form of secularization with its very concrete consequences.

In speaking of "integrism," we are not thinking of any particular historical phenomenon, such as the anti-modernist group which under the direction of Monsignor U. Benigni played a role in the last years of Pius X, or similar movements which were still to be found after the second world war ("integrism" in opposition to "progressism" in France, "Catholics of the right" in opposition to "Catholics of the left" in Germany, and so forth). We are here concerned with the nature of a phenomenon which can be called integrism (but which could be given another name) insofar as it refers to a particular conception of the Church's relationship to the world (in culture, society, and State), a relationship which would reject every kind of secularization. In this sense, integrism is the theoretical or (non-reflexive) practical attitude according to which the life of man can be projected and directed in every detail from universal principles proclaimed by the Church and controlled by her in their application. An integrism of this kind (without saying so) considers the world and history as the transparent and docile matter in which praxis is nothing but the execution of theory, nor does it recognize that "practical reason," which to the extent that it is meaningful cannot be a deduction from principles, but can be given only in the very interior of an active and confident decision of liberty. Integrism presupposes that the Church is always in possession of these principles, at least sufficiently for all that is of importance; thus it denies that there is a true historical evolution of dogma and of theology, at least on the level of principles of action. Integrism tacitly implies that at that point where no clear and legitimate objection based upon the *general* principles of the Gospel and the "natural law" can be sustained against a particular way of acting, this action would be *eo ipso* profane, so much so that it would be morally indifferent, and the question as to whether or not it is salvific would no longer come to mind. Once it is granted with integrism that the Church has the role of proclaiming and interpreting these general principles so understood, it pertains to her at least *de jure* (inasmuch as she can lay claim to this right) to direct the world. Furthermore, this integrism was not yet left behind when it was stressed from Leo XIII to Pius XII that the Church

169

recognizes the relative autonomy of the world, the State, and the domain of culture, and that only *ratione peccati* does she claim competence in these areas of human existence. We shall for the moment pass over the fact that integrism actually claims too little for the Church, and in an attempt to completely escape its influence, turn our attention to answering two questions about this directive or indirect *potestas* of the Church over the world.

First question: in marking, in terms of the *ratio peccati,* the boundary between what is morally permissible and what is immoral, should the Church (1) determine specifically how the world must act here and now; or should she rather (2) provide, at least in principle, for a variety of possibilities within which the world can make her own decisions responsibly and autonomously, and this without loss to the human significance and moral importance of the decision? The second alternative must be the proper one, but there is no need here to further justify it. Integrism tacitly accepts the first alternative, while still maintaining at least the words of indirect or directive *potestas* of the Church; this is precisely how it can establish indirectly for the Church (at least she can claim) a real authority of direction over the world. Suffice it to say this: it is a false presumption to think, in regard to a free act, that what is no longer determinable from general principles is by that very fact without moral importance; to think, in other words, that the knowledge of what is moral as such can be obtained only from general principles and that there is no "logic" proper to an individual ethic.

Second question: it must be asked whether integrism is right in making another tacit presupposition, namely, that one knows what he must do when he knows (owing precisely to the Church and to her interpretation *ratione peccati*) what he must not do. But in fact, a "no" from the Church, the possibility and legitimacy of which ought not to be questioned, does not offer *eo ipso* and in principle a concrete and positive plan of what can and must be done. It can so happen in many simple and common instances of an individual every day morality, but not in principle, and especially not in the "political" ethic of great social and historical events. Here, in spite of the *ratio peccati* administered by the Church, the world is thrown back upon itself in a manner altogether different than integrism would imagine. Here, the *casus complexus* can become, should it occur, a terribly serious thing for which theoretical moral theology, subtle as it might be with its concepts and *quaestiones disputatae,* is of no help to us, and in which the Church once again has to leave the world to itself. For example, no pope, no council has been able to say concretely how one can practically and effectively withdraw from the vicious circle of the atomic balance of terror, or how the world-wide population explosion ought to be coped with. Solutions which must be found here and now must be "self-derived" in constant respect for all the ever valid principles; but such principles offer no concrete solution. Fundamentally, the question still remains whether those ends, proposed by the Church's principles as being those towards which it is necessary to tend asymptotically in the development of history (individual and collective) and which have normative value, should perhaps be realizable at each moment of history. Could not one, should the occasion arise, and being aware of it, live short of these ends and nevertheless sin not formally, but only materially in attaining the best possible here and now? Whatever answer is given to this question which really engages the historicity of man in his moral task, the foregoing reflections show that the Church cannot at all determine with precision the moral quality of the moral decision to be taken in every new situation in the world, and that in fact she does not claim to be able to do so, even when she emphasizes the obligatory character of her principles which always basically signify the marking out of boundaries. The Church is not at all, and does not at all want to be the absolute director of the human and the moral in the world. She is not the sum of what is human and moral, but an element in this sum; and this sum, by its nature, is already "pluralist" by reason of the historical situation which cannot be fully projected in an adequate way, by reason of the principles of the

Gospel and the natural law, and by reason of the concrete decision, ever unique, yet always subject to moral obligation. Once again, the unity, sought and realized, of these different elements in the concrete action does not fall under the judgment of the Church, but under the judgment of God alone (otherwise why, for example, does the Church avoid making a moral judgment on the policy of the United States in Viet-Nam—if she could, she would indeed be bound to do so). Ecclesial integrism has not only never proven to be practicable, it is false. All this means that the Church herself withdraws the world from her own tutelage and constantly returns it to its mundanity and to its own responsibility (in that which concerns not only execution, but also the search for the imperatives which command its decision). This "mundane" as such retains no less of its moral importance and its significance for salvation; this "mundane" is not the profane and in itself indifferent matter "on the occasion of which" a Christian action is realized; but this "mundane" is itself also a Christian action (not *the* Christian action) which cannot be controlled by the Church. In this secularization, the Church's own enterprise, she offers to the world her grace, her principles, and her ultimate horizons, but it is the world itself which must bring forth human and Christian action on its own terrain and on its own real responsibility.

Second Thesis: the legitimate secularization of the world implies an altogether new task for the Church, namely, to create within herself as a whole and in her particular communities a new ecclesial integration among the faithful themselves.

The second thesis simply intends to draw a simple but in itself not unimportant consequence of the new task of the Church in her own field of concern. The Church, as the whole of the faithful and the faithful gathered around the local altar, must form a community. But this cannot happen simply in virtue of the formal juridical structure of the Church, including the profession of common faith, nor by the fact itself of the common celebration of the liturgy (even if the liturgy in the mystery of the Eucharist, by the power of the sacrament, tends towards the formation of community). The Church and the local ecclesial community were able, formerly, without special effort, to constitute such an integrated community even on the sociological level; the reason for this was that the Christian community (with its inner dynamic tending to the building of a community: juridical structure, confession of faith, cult) could take for granted an already socially integrated group coming to her from the secular domain. This group possessed a culture impressed equally upon all, constituted a politically homogeneous and unpluralistic society, was equipped with a common moral teaching, self-sufficient and much more than abstract moral principles, and so forth; in short, the group possessed the bases of a stable and homogeneous society, everything which integrates the individual into society, sets bounds for him, and offers him the security which liberates. This fact, just as truly, had repercussions on the specifically ecclesial factors of the Christian community: the confession of common faith was also a social witness, the formal authority of the magisterium was thereby unburdened, cult was lived as the sacred crown of the unity of secular community.

Now things are different. The society which now comes to the Church, which must form a community in her, and which formerly brought with it the bases essential for forming this community, is today the "secularized" world, a world which is secularized in this sense, among others, that it no longer naturally provides, as it formerly did, the substratum which could be the basis of ecclesial community. This world is pluralist in its visions of the world, composed of men among whom no individual any longer has at his command the totality of knowledge, of culture, of control over the future, things which are found only in society as a whole. Despite the considerable growth of mass education, despite the information explosion, despite the power of communications media, society as a whole has become more confused and less tractable than ever, and no longer sees where the future is leading; in short, society is less integral, with all the consequences this implies for the individual and for society itself. Whence arises for the Church an altogether new task in regard to her own self. She must provide for herself what formerly she could presuppose as the social, "natural" substratum of her own passage to Christian community. It is important to understand what is meant here: it cannot be a question of the Church retransforming the secular and pluralist world into the homogeneous society of another age which brought to the Church its own integration. If the Church were to try that (and the temptation is always present and considerable), she would make a ghetto of herself, and would tend, from the point of view of the sociology of religion, to develop into a "sect." Even within her walls, the Church must remain, or rather become, an "open society"; she must not practise a negative selection by which (in a non-reflective but nevertheless real way) she would, within the secular and pluralist world, seek to approach, meet, and win over only men of a particular social and cultural strain; she must find room for conformists and non-conformists, for men of different political tendencies, for philosophers with the most diverse ideas, for Catholics of the right and of the left, and others; she must deal with this pluralism without falling into integrism; she must learn to see it and live with it as something positive. But, we repeat, this certainly does not mean that the Church is left without a task of integration of an order higher than the spiritual and social pluralism which remains. If she were to fail to recognize and undertake this task, she would then become a sect for the satisfaction of merely individual religious needs, in truth she would become again an exclusively clerical Church (the clergy alone finding it possible to satisfy their religious needs, and the faithful, as an unintegrated mass capable of being only recipients of the saving action of the Church, despite every theoretical assertion which would have one believe that they are something more; this was the real situation of the Church for a long time). The Church would not be in a position to undertake as Church a world-responsibility and world-mission.

But how is this "integration" of the Church as community

174

to be understood and realized if it must not take the form of an homogenization of the pluralist world after the pattern of an intra-ecclesial integrism, nor of a restoration of the ecclesial society's former integration, nor a pious ideological superstructure of the sort: "We *are* already the Body of Christ"?

This question, bearing as it does on an as yet hardly discovered task of the Church, is difficult to answer. Yet three elements of an answer can be suggested.

1. Attention can be drawn to all the social work (in view of the new integration of society) which the Church accomplishes (can and must accomplish) in a spirit of collaboration with secular society. One could say that it is precisely this work which, though seemingly profane, the Church must carry on in favour of her own baptized members (for example, for her children, adults, aged, each one of whom in his own way must be integrated into society, and there find room and security).

2. In this context, one could hope for a true democratization in the Church. This word "democratization," in fact, understood properly, does not so much mean in profane society "liberation" from all constraint; it means rather the institutions, behaviour patterns, directive images, rules of the game, which must be created in a society which is and is to remain pluralist, that it might truly constitute *one society* and not a radically unintegrated mass of men and factions. It does not at all follow as a consequence that "democratization" in the Church be understood as a battle cry against the full powers of the hierarchical function; it should be understood rather as the keynote for the integration in the Church of this secular and pluralist society, the existing and permanent substratum for the formation of the Church.

3. Attention could be drawn now in this context to what must be said in our third thesis about an entirely new function of the Church as a whole in relationship to profane society. But this will be developed later.

What has been said so far about the subject of the second thesis is necessarily very abstract because, on the one hand, the task which we have indicated and which is imposed on the

175

interior life of the Church by secularized society has as yet hardly been discerned; and, on the other hand, practical proposals in the field of "pastoral theology" cannot be proffered here because of lack of time and competence.

Third Thesis: precisely because she cannot manipulate society in its concrete decisions in an integrist way, that is in the name of her doctrine and law, the Church has an altogether new task vis-à-vis society returned to its pluralist secularity by the Church herself. This task can be described as "prophetic," but that presupposes the new ecclesial-social building up of the people of the Church already mentioned in the second thesis.

The thesis is difficult and must be explained. Secularization, upon which we have tried to cast some light in the first thesis, seems, straightway and at first sight, to affirm a vast incompetence of the Church in face of the world: the Church can indeed mark out certain boundaries *ratione peccati,* she can proclaim general norms; but against every subcutaneous tendency to integrism, she cannot, by means of her valid doctrine or her pastoral function (as *potestas jurisdictionis*), concretely manipulate the history of the secularized world. Has, then, the real relationship between the Church and the secularized world been fully defined in virtue of these negative determinations? Can the Church, solely as "grace," through the intermediary of individual Christians acting as individuals and to the extent that they have been transformed by grace and the Gospel mentality, exercise a greater influence in the construction of the secularized world? I believe that this question has not been answered clearly even at the Second Vatican Council (not in *Lumen gentium,* nor in the decree on the apostolate of the laity *Apostolicam actuositatem,* nor in *Gaudium et spes*); for the activity of the Church is there still considered, at the point where it is no longer merely activity of individual Christians, far too much as doctrinal support, and so as "mediation of principles"; and that in contrast with the idea, developed in a copious supply of words, of the Church's cooperation with all men of good will and with their social institutions.

Our third thesis is intended to give an answer to this question

176

and to say: the Church as Church can play in the world more than the role of counselor by virtue of the proclamation of her principles, or of collaborator, and this can be realized, it is clear, only by the work of individual Christians within profane institutions (certain unimportant exceptions aside). To see what this means positively, one must first reflect on what follows: in a democratic and pluralist society which functions well, each group (informal and formal) desires, and has the right, to make itself heard in the maturing of the inevitable decisions which concern the whole of that society, and does so by every legitimate means from discussion about publicity to legitimate use of power. But this is always on condition that such a group has, in regard to these common decisions of society about society, an "opinion" about what is to be done here and now. Such a "program of action," though in itself a very complex structure, is, nevertheless, in the practical "will" of the group, a unity. It includes (and must include) a rational, reflective element, a measured calculation about what should be done which is used to inform others and to win them over; a rational element of this kind exists for the end to be attained as well for the appropriate means of attaining it. But a group "program of action" always includes, beyond such a rationale, an element of creative imagination; it is "creation" which makes the utopian possible; it is decision in freedom which, perhaps with very little reflection, chooses one among many possible and imaginable objects, wills it, seeks to impose it, creates history without being merely its creature, in that undeducible praxis which has its own evidence not adequately received from theoretical reason. It is just such a group in the midst of secular and pluralist society that the Church can and must be (in relationship to this secularized society). Pluralist society cannot itself prohibit such an undertaking on the part of the Church. For only a society absolutely totalitarian in structure can have the intentioin of tolerating social groups only insofar as they are prolongations of that society's functions, legalized and governed as it is in a totalitarian and authoritarian way from a single center. An "open" pluralist society, which does

177

not establish in law from a single vantage point all the powers which reside in it, as does a "closed system," can have nothing *a priori* against such a community of faithful which is continually and freely reforming itself, provided that this community (this is our presupposition) respects the society's "rules of the game" and the mechanism of its decision-making, that is to say its "praxis."

The Church is permitted to engage in such a project. It is not here a question of discussing whether the Church is in a position to do so, how she can be capable of doing it, what social unity she must have, and how she can forge this unity within herself so as to be able to be in her entirety "subject" of a project of this kind. Nor are we asking to what point she can effectively succeed in realizing such a project in profane society, in making her "program of action," totally or in part, the action-principle of profane society. Nor do we claim that such a program of action, at its beginning and from its origin, can be the achievement only of "explicit Christians." The grace of God can inspire the same program just as well in others. First of all, for theological reasons, the Church can and must have such a plan, such a program of action, if she can bring it about. She has a mission to the world; she does not exist for herself, but is the sacrament of the world's salvation, she must be the leaven of the world; for the Christian, to act in the world and to work out his salvation are not two materially and adequately distinct levels of his activity, they are (at least in part) two aspects of one and the same self-realization; yet this realization is essentially effected in intercommunication and in the spatio-temporal dimension of history in the midst of a concrete society. The Church as "visible" is a concrete historico-social quantity which necessarily has, even if she wished it were not so, repercussions on the whole of society; and these repercussions proceed not only from her "eternal" essence, they proceed also from her contingent and inevitably concrete form, repercussions for which the Church must answer. In fact, the Church as such has already exercised such a deliberate influence over the world (by her doctrine and the individual action of Christians), and given this fact it cannot be seriously suggested that the Church now renounce in principle such influence (to withdraw to the "sacristy"). The only remaining question is this: *what form* must the Church give today to this legitimate influence in face of a secular world?

These suggestions as to the legitimacy and necessity of such an influence of the Church in the world (over and above the teaching of principles and the individual action of Christians) will have to suffice for now. What is of greater importance here is

1. to attempt, to a certain extent, to determine more precisely the nature of this influence (and no longer negatively as has been done so far); and

2. it is essential to reflect on this question: how must the Church herself be presented in her concrete structure and in the mentality of her members if she wants to exercise in fact an influence such as this on secular society? To provide the beginnings of an answer to the first question, it would be advisable first of all to reflect a little on the distinctive trait of certain encyclicals of John XXIII (*Mater et Magistra, Pacem in Terris*), of Paul VI's encyclical *Populorum Progressio* and especially of the pastoral constitution *Gaudium et spes* of Vatican II. What is characteristic of these documents?

They contain, to be sure, a good number of fundamental, theoretical, and ever-valid "doctrinal" truths (with good reason, it must be said, and necessarily), but the salient point of these texts, what in them is stimulating and "shocking" for the pure theorician, rests in their intention which can be described first of all as (in the terminology of Vatican II) "pastoral." Nevertheless, one would underestimate and misconstrue this "pastoral" element in its essence by understanding it as a series of purely practical consequences whose certain and compelling deduction from general principles the merest glance at the actual situation of the world would suffice to bring about. The intent of these documents is clearly present in "imperatives," in emphases, in an historical programmatic which calls the world to decision. It is a result of the fact that analysis of the present

179

situation, in which their pastoral character is rooted, is neither a datum of revelation, nor so simply arrived at that this situation could be seen as *factum brutum* which no one might doubt; this analysis is inseparably bound to the sphere of practical action in which knowledge of the situation and historical reaction form a unity and are reciprocally conditioned. For example, proposals for the establishment of a super U.N. (*Gaudium et spes,* art. 84) and for the formation of a world assistance fund for the developing peoples (*Populorum Progressio*) suggest, beyond any doubt, eminent objectives which can very well be justified objectively; but they are clearly not things which can be deduced from revelation as *conclusio theologica,* convincing to everyone in such a way that every Christian would have to make them his own. Rather, they are programs of action, optive in character, which are drawn up by practical reason insofar as it is not deducible from *intellectus principiorum;* they are options which the Church does not conceive purely and simply as execution of her own principles, but chooses as a realization, determined and non-deducible in character, of these principles, and by this choice, influences secular society as a concrete group in its midst. The discovery of this imperative addressed to society can be described, considering the nature of the Church, only as "prophetic," not excluding but including all the other elements of such a discovery such as ordinarily occur on the occasion of a decision in the socio-political order. A pastoral directive is, then, when it fully realizes its deepest essence, a prophetic directive of the Church, in the sense of a decision which, ultimately, is not historically deducible, and is addressed to the secular world. A directive of this kind is, naturally, restricted to what the Church can ask of the world in view of its salvation. But within these limits, it is beyond doubt such a directive.

The question now (it is the second asked a moment ago) is whether the Church in her present concrete constitution is the subject which, as one of the groups within the secular pluralist world, can, and with some prospect of results, address such a program to the world. To be sure, this hope cannot be founded merely in the chance that the program of action might in one form or another recommend itself (more than ancient Jeremiah's program of neutrality), or in the fact that others might proclaim the same word of order. This hope and chance of an effective influence of the Church on the secular world comes up against a twofold difficulty: first, the official Church, which here, by the nature of the Church, cannot be more (but she must be this) than the *herald* of a prophetic impulse given, as a rule, in the Church, or at most more than *one* of the doors through which the spirit erupts into history, has "authority" over and effective influence on the world to the extent that the Spirit (in a thousand ways) comes to the group called Church; secondly, the official Church cannot, by virtue of the formal authority of her magisterium or her power of jurisdiction, oblige her faithful to follow these prophetic imperatives which she issues. Indeed, analagous situations are found within the Church: the Church can, for example, recommend indulgences; but what real significance would remain in the Tridentine doctrine of indulgences if the majority of the faithful, taking advantage of their holy and just freedom as sons of God (Paul VI, *Indulgentiarum Doctrina*), decided to refrain from gaining indulgences? The Church as people of God must "be with" these prophetic imperatives of the official Church if they are to have a real effect on secular society.

It is now clear that the Church is (in principle) and must become (in practice) something more than the institution of the truth of theoretical reason (with its necessary consequences, including administration of the sacraments and administrative apparatus): she must be the institution of the truth of practical reason, the "discernment" and act of which also belong to the institution which God's revelation has created; this institution, the Church, is the pilgrim people of God which must and wants to imprint its eschatological hope on the structures of terrestrial life by the concrete orientation of her travels which are not charted once and for all on the map of theoretical revelation; she is this people which, for one, must and wants to have a voice in the progress of the secular world, without being able to determine it in a doctrinal or even frankly integrist fashion.

181

But how much still remains to be done in the Church that this task might be accomplished with the necessary efficacy! It would be necessary to develop a principled "political theology," that is, to develop theology (as content) in its entirety and ecclesiology in particular in their socio-political and history-shaping significance; it is necessary to rise above the reduction of revelation to the salvation of the individual alone. It is necessary to engender among the faithful not a mentality which confronts the magisterium with the dilemma of making declarations which either oblige doctrinally or are deprived of interest, but rather a mentality which is disposed to take prophetic impulses seriously, to make contingent attitudes its own, to share in formation of not only the mind, but also the will. It is necessary to develop in the hierarchy the readiness to welcome prophetic impulses in the Church (and not only on the level of the specifically religious, as, for example, the developing of new forms of devotion); for although the greater number of these impulses become really efficacious in the Church as a whole, and thus in the world only through the mediation of the hierarchy, yet only very rarely do they find their origin among the hierarchy. It is necessary to promote within the Church that social integration which was discussed from another point of view in the second thesis; this integration alone can help the Church have an influence on the socio-political level. Here again we must admit that all this has been very abstractly and formally expressed. But it really is not possible to do more here.

Fourth Thesis: the relationship of the Church to the secular world requires today within the compass of "practical theology" the establishment and development of a special theological discipline which, provisionally and for want of a better term, we will call "practical ecclesiological cosmology."

What does this mean? Taking for granted that this "cosmology" is to be understood from the outset as a discipline which forms a part of "practical theology," let us first of all say a word about "practical theology," which is usually called "pastoral theology" (even at Vatican II). "Practical theology" is not a mere collection of "practical" maxims flowing as of

THEOLOGICAL REFLECTIONS ON THE PROBLEM OF SECULARIZATION

themselves from dogmatics, moral theology, and canon law; it is even less a collection of maxims useful for the "pastoral" work of the ministering clergy. "Practical theology" is rather an autonomous science because neither its object nor its method can be simply drawn from the "systematic disciplines" of theology. It asks, methodically and reflectively, what at this very moment is possible and required that the whole Church be fully realized in her every dimension (not only among her clergy). It is also distinct from the other disciplines which are concerned with ecclesiological questions because they can consider only the permanent nature and essential structures of the Church's self-realization as they are communicated by revelation, or because these other disciplines reflect upon the *jus conditum* and its history, but not (in an adequate way) upon the *jus condendum*. To understand the Church's self-realization, required here and now, and far beyond the application of permanent principles and of the *jus humanum* of the Church, we must proceed to a theological analysis and to an interpretation of the present (internal and external) situation of the Church. Precisely because no other theological discipline is able to make this analysis, one is here faced with an altogether specific object of theology, since it is not "revealed"; this requires in addition a special theological method which is not merely that of the profane sciences such as sociology, contemporary history, or cultural criticism. For all these reasons, "practical theology" forms a truly original and distinct theological discipline even if it presupposes all the other theological disciplines. These remarks about the nature of practical theology will have to suffice for now.

Now within the self-realization of the Church, the relationship of the Church to the secular world occupies a place which, though not unique, is very important. This relationship, a consideration of which in its permanent essence is insufficient, for it must be continually rediscovered, is even so important that it requires separate treatment, with precision and method, in practical theology. This relationship cannot, in virtue of the general reasons which establish the autonomy of practical theology, be treated in the other theological disciplines. For it evolves with the rhythm of the transformation of the secular world, which constitutes the situation of the Church. But this situation cannot be object of the systematic theological disciplines; and because of its complexity, it escapes the simple, pre-scientific experience of individuals. In addition, this relationship calls for decision of a prophetic character and cannot at all be understood by any combination of theoretical ecclesiology and concrete knowledge of the situation. Such a study of the ever new situation-conditioned relationship of the Church to the world, which forms a part of practical theology, has no name. As a result, this nameless task of theology goes unnoticed, and its full implications and urgency are not understood with sufficient clarity. It is not identical with the Christian sciences, for these consider the ideal structures of profane society (of economy, law, political constitution, and so forth) in order to say what they should be according to Christian principles. Nor is it merely a division of dogmatic ecclesiology which can at best treat (please God that it do so) only of the stable structures of the Church's relationship to the world. Nor is this nameless study identical with "political theology," which J. B. Metz calls for as urgent today, for in "political theology" the permanent social implications and social relevance inherent in the revelation, the doctrine, and the hope of Christianity as such are considered, but not the form which the Church's relationship to the world as it actually is must take here and now. This study really has no name and, as a result, does not yet exist in the Church and in theology. One becomes aware of this fact the moment he reads *Gaudium et spes,* resisting the temptation to reduce it to pure dogma, moral theology, and the social sciences, seeking rather the "prophetic," and *then* wonders to which of the distinct theological disciplines this "pastoral constitution" properly belongs as a whole and in its specificity. None of them can be singled out because the proposed theological discipline has no name and as yet has not been established at all as a distinct discipline. For want of a better name, let us call this science which we are trying to identify, and which belongs to practical theology, "practical ecclesiological cosmology," trusting that the term "cosmology" will be taken in its biblical sense of *kosmos* and that no one will confuse this cosmology with the discipline of the same name in "philosophy of nature."

Such a "cosmology" would today have an almost limitless field of investigation. We are still naïve enough to think that we know in what world we are living, that we understand its structures, its disintegrative factors, its ideologies, its hopes and impulses, a world in which we are given the simultaneous co-existence of diverse historical strata. But each of us, because of his individual historical limitations, can know only a random segment of this world. We think we know who these men are whom the Church addresses in her specifically religious mission and, beyond that, in the contribution she makes to ameliorate the lot of the world and the future of society. We do not know these men, or at best we know a chosen few with whom only our outdated bourgeois ecclesiastical mentality brings us into contact. One need note only once the tone, the perspective, the choice of subject in the statements of the magisterium to wonder what men these utterances can reach; then one realizes that the Church, despite her good will, does not really know well enough the man of today (otherwise would it be possible even today to speak so candidly of the "fire" of purgatory, as Paul VI has recently done?). In this cosmology there would be vast areas to consider concerning the relationship required to-day between the Church and the secular world. The directly religious mission of the Church certainly does not belong to *this* part of practical theology. Still, this cosmology would already have quite enough for reflection in the Church's relationship to the world. To be sure, many particular subjects belonging to this sphere of inquiry are already under theological discussion, those, for example, which are treated in the second part of *Gaudium et spes* and which always imply a responsibility of the Church towards the world. But have all the special subjects been thereby seized upon? Are there not still many other subjects about which the Church has really expressed only a purely theoretic and dialectic "on the one hand, on the other" without

185

risking a concrete imperative in the form of prophetic directive, or to which the Church answers with such a timid and theologically subtle imperative that it could easily not be understood, even, I would say, formulated with the secret hope that it will not be understood and that there will then be an alibi without anyone being offended? Such a cosmology certainly cannot itself posit imperatives; but it could prepare them and be their scientifically critical and aroused conscience; it could keep alive in the Church the realization that she cannot much longer be satisfied with being a mere organization for the quieting of religious anxiety over individual salvation. For the Church neither is, nor may she be an integrist force seeking to manipulate the world; but she must, in the area here under consideration, recognize the secular world as free partner in open dialogue; she must understand herself as authentic *part* of this secular world, part, certainly, which from within cooperates in the history of the world sovereignly directed by God alone, but part which cannot attribute to itself a monopoly in being *the* representative of God in this history.

Deliberately limiting our matter, we have thus far attempted to consider that form of "secularization" in which the Church and the world proceed to a greater, epoch-conditioned diastasis, thus being led to try to establish between them a new positive relationship which might be neither integrism, nor merely negative distance, nor criticism by the Church of the world. May I be permitted, lastly, to expand this theme a little to consider the distinction between the secular world and grace, it being understood that the Church is only the efficacious sign of grace without for that being identical with it. Consequently, we are considering the world as worldly, and not any longer as distinct from the Church and in relation to her, nor vice versa, but the world in itself. But we do not intend to raise again the questions about the worldliness of the world—from the beginning we have left them aside as settled; but we want to try to make a theological statement about this world (always and in every age worldly) which might enable us to deepen and further the debate. This statement brings into play some old theological data which in scholastic theology seems to have become dull and of no interest, but in our context their importance becomes evident once again.

Fifth Thesis: we are given in our secularized world a pluralist situation of concupiscence, but unconsidered involvement in this situation is not in itself sin. It imports, in all the dimensions of human existential realization (including the gnosiological), the postulate and the place of the Christian's human existence; an existence which is agonal and threatened by sin (by forgetting God); an existence which must be accepted by the Christian such as it is, in its permanence, and which must be borne realistically without an integrist ideologizing of this world.

To understand the meaning of this thesis, we must begin with a few words about man's "concupiscence," taken in its theological sense. Properly understood, "concupiscence" means an interior pluralism of man in all his dimensions, levels, and impulses of such a kind that man, insofar as he is (in his deepest self) a free and personal being, can never adequately and radically integrate it in the one decision of freedom (for or against God). This "state of disintegration," which cannot be abolished, is manifested in all the dimensions of human existence (not only in moral action in the strict sense, but also in the dimension of knowledge which as such is always at the same time "praxis"), and appears in its bitterest and unconcealed manifestation in the state of disintegration of death and of life as *prolixitas mortis*. It is impossible for man to rise above this state of "carnal" disintegration, even if this fact doesn't exclude, on the contrary, that the historical orientation of human existence must always tend towards full integration considered as a terminus which, within the world, is approachable only asymptotically. It would be a mistake to be satisfied with conceiving of this concupiscence as an "inner" datum which does not extend beyond the limits of our body, of our "skin," so to speak. Man is an open system, in constant contact with the world; he is constantly exteriorized in the world; the world is in him, he is in the world; and what we call the "milieu" of man is man himself in the spatio-temporal exteriority in which he finds himself,

187

hidden from himself and sharing this alienation of his self with the others (in identity). The "concupiscent," "inner" constitution of man and the constitution of his world necessarily correspond. That is why what is properly called "concupiscence" is really to be looked for in the world rather than in a "psychological" introspection.

This concupiscence has its history precisely as history of man standing fast against the powers of disintegration while never able to overcome them completely. It is perfectly permissible, then, to interpret traditional theology's statements about concupiscence as statements of theology about the secular world; for the secular world as man's space and corporeality extended bears in itself exactly the same fundamental and epochal properties as man's "interior" concupiscence: plurality of realities and dimensions; their disintegration; man's permanent inability, which can be overcome only asymptotically, to pass beyond this pluralism from a center of unity of which he would be master; the historicity and history of this concrete pluralism and of efforts at its integration (under a single idea, under a single representative of power, and so forth). And so the statements of theology (Catholic and heterodox) about concupiscence are indeed theological statements about the world. The Christian's interpretation of the world, and so of his relationship to the world, can, as a result, be borrowed from theological statements concerned with the interpretation of concupiscence. Accordingly, we venture to call special attention to the three basic statements of the Council of Trent about concupiscence and read them as statements about the secular world.

1. The unintegrated pluralism of human reality called "concupiscence," and thus also the pluralism of the secular world, is not "in itself" sin; but (let us add) it is a stage of salvation history, open ended and directed towards an integration which will be given only in the completion of man and of the kingdom of God. This "declaration of innocence" is not as evident and insignificant as might seem at first sight. To realize this we have no need to consider the heterodox interpretations of the world such as gnosticism, manicheism, and so forth, which on the level

188

of lived Christianity continue a kind of subliminal existence, albeit not theoretically reflective, at least in regard to certain particular dimensions, varying according to the times, of human existence. This innocence does not need to be denied thematically, it is already denied on the level of the realization of human existence as lived. Where an *a priori* preference is given to an environment or to a style of life singled out as specifically Christian—to the "plain and simple" life, to the life which does not pursue "dangerous" learning, to a puritan life which has qualms about the sexual, or the happy enjoyment of life; where certain specific potentialities of life are *a priori* taken as suspect and as really unfitting for a Christian—the military life (formerly!), the life of a politician and of political appointment ("dirty work"), the life of comedian and of artist in general, and so forth: there, secretly at work, is such a non-thematic denial of the pluralist world's innocence. It is an attempt to escape from the unintegrated pluralism of the world by excluding from the start certain of its dimensions and saying as human or Christian "this is out of the question"; it is an attempt to "simplify" life so as not to have to bear and to overcome unintegrated "concupiscent" pluralism. But such simplifications can be made only if the disjointed, and thus complex, plural world can be considered a "culpable" world which can rightly be disavowed. *Gaudium et spes,* art. 25 sees clearly the difference between, on the one hand, the disturbances (*perturbationes*) which result from the natural tensions (*tensio*) of economic, political, and social realities (thus from their tension-bred pluralism), and, on the other hand, disturbances which have their origin in sin. When man declares the first "disturbances" and tensions culpable, he undertakes an exercise of exoneration, because then the objectifications of its sin add absolutely nothing else or new to this sinful world, but are simply its expression.

2. Concupiscence is imposed upon man *ad agonem.* In other words, the plural and secular unintegrated world of man is not an abode of "peace" in the enjoyment of an integrated world (which could be established with a little good will), of a world "reconciled" in itself in harmony; the secular world is the place

of an agonal existence (that is, an existence-for-death). This *agon,* to be sure, tends towards a terminus, towards the integration of the whole of reality in the perfected love of God "face to face"; but towards a terminus which is never accessible here in this age, which is always ahead of us and which is thus constantly opening the way to new possibilities. Yet this *agon* must first of all be accepted (*viriliter,* says the Council of Trent). But it is not so accepted when man at bottom refuses to accept and to bear the unintegrated plurality of his existence and the impulses which dwell in him, within which he is, so to speak, continually situated. For example, he does not accept the concupiscent gnosiological situation of his existence who sacrifices the open confronting of his plurally diverse and irreducible "sources" of experience and knowledge in favour of a "system" in which some science (be it even theology or metaphysics) intends simply to rule the others, without allowing itself to be challenged or historically transformed by them in "open dialogue"; or in favour of a universal science which tries to absorb and integrate every science of every school, and which fears not knowing everything, which does not want to be surprised by the "unheard of," by a foreign science for which, unless it is willing to change itself, it has provided no place within its own system; but it is well known that in fact the "areopagus" of the mind is an "open society" with an ever unstable balance of forces. The *agon* amidst the concupiscent, plural, and unreconciled world is not accepted when one thinks he is not allowed to have "interests," joys, prior decisions, which have not yet passed through criticism and undergone selection by an explicitly religious "supernatural" motivation. The *agon* in the secular world is not accepted (though, of course, it remains as disowned and suppressed, and precisely for that reason becomes more dangerous) when, upset by its disunity, one attempts to rebuild this ambiguous life on a stubbornly and austerely "Christian" model, as if we ourselves were required to reduce its disordered cacophony to harmony here and now in an integrism which (not now the Church, but) the Christian himself on his own would manipulate.

3. In the third place, concupiscence means impulse to sin

("*ad peccatum inclinat*": DS 1515). This is not the place to consider concupiscence (and thus the plural, unintegrated world) in all its aspects, its origin ("original sin"), and its consequences (personal sin and its individual and collective objectifications in the world). Let us take note of one thing, because it pertains directly to the subject of "world." We have no need to go elsewhere for knowledge of what sin is, sin which threatens us in the concupiscent world; it follows from the worldly concupiscent situation itself. Sin consists precisely in not supporting, not bearing this situation of man in his private and public dimensions. Not to have at his disposal an absolute fixed point in the unintegrated instability of the openness which is human existence—it is precisely that which anguishes man. Because he cannot control it, he dare not abandon himself to the unique unity of this whole (unintegrated, which is and remains pluralist), unity which is open backward (towards its obscure beginning), forward (towards the unforeseeable future), on high (in the infinity of transcendence), below (in the obscure factitiousness of the material). In order to egress from this "anguish of death" (Heb. 2, 15), some one of the elements of the unintegrated world is postulated, in theory or (and) in fact, as absolute, that is, it is made, arrogantly and timidly at the same time, the unique and controllable point of reference for the alleged and autonomous integration of the world. This comes to pass theoretically in bad ideology, and practically in what is simply called sin. To the extent that the theoretical and practical activity of man is itself a fragment of the world, and that the original free decision of man is necessarily realized in the otherness of the corporeal and social objectifications of this freedom (although this freedom is not simply reducible to these objectifications and so remains ambiguous), to that extent and in virtue of the arrogant claim, always destined to fail, to integrate the world, the world itself is changed, it becomes the world of sin, "this Aeon" in the biblical sense. The "objective conditions are flawed by the consequences of sin" (*Gaudium et spes,* art. 25). In this regard we shall make two remarks.

(a) As long as the integration of the world, which must

191

come from God, is delayed, man continues to yield (though freely), in one fashion or another, to the pressures of the un-integrated world. This he does in two essentially different ways: either by a pseudo-integrist absolutizing of a moment of the world, radically engaging his liberty ("mortal sin"), or by freely slackening the dynamic which tends towards authentic integra-tion, given always as charge and approachable only *progres-sively* and asymptotically ("venial sin"). These two ways of yielding to the pressure of the unintegrated world cannot be clearly distinguished from one another in the concrete.

(b) An attempt to differentiate sharply in the world between inculpable concupiscence and disintegration imprinted by sin (sin as pseudo-integration is intensification of disintegration) is again an exercise in arrogant integration (for one would have to know "on what he must fasten" as undisputed Good harmo-nized in itself).

These two remarks show why the secular world is the unity, beyond our manipulation, of inseparably interwoven plural realities: world as good plural creation; world as plural, legiti-mate achievement of man; world as objectification of the sin of man who, as integrist, would arrogantly put the world "in order." In short, the secular pluralist world is (and can so be as *history,* not as static "system") the "world" known by Scrip-ture. Thus the secular world is exactly the world which the Christian expects, makes, and suffers from in his properly Chris-tian understanding, as a result of which he does not ideologically, as integrist, alienate this world, but sees it as it is.

9.

SECULARISM AND THEOLOGY

E. L. MASCALL

It is always well to begin a discussion by defining one's terms. I shall use the word "theology" in its usual sense, to denote the study of God and of other beings in their relation to God, and for the most part the theology of which I shall be speaking will be Christian theology. By "the secular" I shall mean that whole body of human thought and action which is concerned solely with man's life in "this world," a life which begins with the fertilization of an ovum by a spermatozoon and ends with bodily death. Thus I exclude from "the secular" any concern that a man may have with a possible future life after death, and any concern which he may have even in "this life" with an order of reality (if such there be) that transcends the experience of the senses; this is the point of the world "solely" in the last sentence. Thus the word "secular" will roughly correspond to one of the uses of the word "natural" by Christian theologians, namely, that use in which "natural" is contrasted with "supernatural." By "secularism" I shall mean the view that "the secular," as defined above, is the only reality that there is, or at any rate, the only reality of which human beings need to take account. "Secularism" will thus be more or less synonymous with "humanism," as that word is commonly—though, I would hold, improperly and misleadingly—used today. As the adjective correlative to "secularism" I shall use the word "secularist,"

193

and this must be carefully distinguished from the adjective "secular."

The first point which I wish to make is that the culture in which we live—the technological and technocratic culture which derives from the scientific revolution of the seventeenth and the industrial revolution of the nineteenth century, which is dominant in Europe and North America and is spreading irresistibly into other parts of the world as well, is, in the sense above defined, a secularist culture. This I believe to be true in spite of the official establishment of one form of the Christian religion in England, and of the fact that in the United States 63 per cent of the nation in 1962 were enrolled members of some religious organization and 45 per cent attended church every week. I cannot argue the point in detail here, but I would refer any who are in doubt to the impressive work by the sociologist Mr. Brian Wilson entitled *Religion in Secular Society*. What tends to obscure the issue is the fact that the secularist culture in which most of us live is not totalitarian but pluralist, that is to say, one in which men and women are free to adopt any philosophy of life and to follow any mode of conduct that they please, subject only to the condition that in doing so they do not cause too much inconvenience to other people. It is thus possible for people who are genuinely religious to practice their religion without interference by the state, and for the state, when it suits its purpose, to garnish with the externals of religion policies that are in essence purely secularist.

It is my purpose in this paper to consider the kind of theological thinking to which Christians are called in this secularist situation. I will begin by recalling that theology, like the Church itself, has a double orientation; first to its own members and then to the world without. These we might describe as edification and evangelization respectively. While distinct, these are mutually related and at points they overlap; it will be well to keep them distinct in our minds even while we discuss them together. It is, as we all know, argued by a vociferous and much noticed body of theologians today that in a secularized culture theology itself must become secularized, that is to say, it must

194

conform its own thinking to the secularist outlook, express as much of the traditional theology in secularist terms as it can and jettison the rest. A comparatively moderate programme of this kind was outlined, though not very coherently, by Dr. J. A. T. Robinson in his best-seller *Honest to God;* it has been given an extreme and more consistent expression in the "death-of-God" theology of such writers as Paul van Buren, William Hamilton, and Thomas Altizer. When forced to these lengths it produces a very paradoxical result. It begins with a denunciation of the traditional religious institutions as introverted, heedless of the world and its needs, and concerned only with their own perpetuation. However, when it has trimmed down the Christian religion to the point where its sole concern is with the secular, there is nothing for religious institutions to do that cannot be done more professionally by institutions that have no religious labels or attachments; there is, in brief, nothing for the Churches to do except to commit suicide, unless they are to make their own self-perpetuation the object of their existence. The wheel indeed comes full circle.

There are, I believe, two reasons for this movement on the part of many theologians and clerics. There is first the tendency of fallen men (which infection of nature, to use the words of one of the Anglican Articles of Religion, doth remain, yea in them that are regenerate) to want to be "in the swim," "with it," "switched on," or whatever the passing idiom may be. In a situation in which theologians and clergymen find it increasingly difficult to get taken seriously, this can easily take the form expressed in the maxim, "If you can't beat them, join them." There is also—and this is more creditable—an understandable reaction from a theological phrase in which the Christian religion has been assumed to be concerned exclusively with the salvation of the individual, and the secular order has seemed to be either so squalid that the pure minds of theologians ought not to be sullied by it, or else simply irrelevant to theology and capable of minding its own business.

However, to return to our main theme, we must ask our-

195

selves what is the right attitude for a Christian theologian who wishes to do his duty in that state of life unto which it has pleased God to call him, when he is living in a secularist society. As a Christian, he is not bound to justify himself to the secularist society; it should be a matter of indifference to him whether or not his secularist contemporaries see usefulness or relevance in his job. It is, however, important that he should be able to justify himself before God, unless he is one of those oddly-styled theologians who deny that there is a God, in which case it seems impossible for him to justify himself before anyone whatever; since if there is a God after all, his position is false and clearly unjustifiable, and if there is no God, his position is correct, but there can be no justification for theologians.

The first duty of the Christian theologian, I would maintain, is to set his own thinking firmly within the great tradition which he has inherited from the Church and its thinkers, *sentire cum ecclesia*. This means something much more than mere memorization and parrot-like repetition of verbal formulas, be they those of Denzinger, the Thirty-nine Articles, or the Augsburg Confession. It lies deeper than the level of words and concepts, though words and concepts are inevitably involved in its articulate expression. It is basically a knowledge by *connaturality*, by identifying oneself with the life of the body of Christ, by living in and as a member of the Mystical Body. The task of the individual theologian is thus to be seen as the translation into human idiom, according to the needs of the time, of some fraction of that knowledge which is possessed in its totality, in one unified contemplative act, by the Head of the Body, the ascended Christ. Brother Gabriel Moran is, I believe, entirely correct when he writes as follows, in what I believe to be one of the most penetrating and potentially fertile theological books of recent years:

The risen and glorified Lord is the one place where revelation continues to happen in fullness. . . . There is no question of adding objective truths to the deposit of faith, nor is there question of going beyond Christ. What is of utmost importance is that the revelational

196

process first accomplished in Christ should now be participated in by all Christians through a continuing revelational process.[1]

And again:

The Church as a whole is the recipient of God's revelation, and each individual participates in revelation according to his position within the community. . . . The whole church has from the beginning a human understanding of God's self-revelation. . . . Within the believing Church and within the mystery of revelation, God's guidance has been promised to the entire people of God.[2]

Thus I would maintain that it is the duty of the theologian to bring to articulate expression, according to the needs and opportunities of his time and place, some fragment or aspect of the revelation which is apprehended as lived reality by the Church as Christ's body, and which is beheld as an undiscursive and utterly simple subject of contemplation in the mind of the glorified and ascended Christ who is the Body's Head.

If, then, one pole of the theologian's activity is provided by the ascended Christ and his Body the Church (and Brother Moran reminds us that the Church is a prolongation not primarily of the historical Christ, but of the heavenly Christ[3]), its other pole is provided by the concrete historical situation in which his own individual life and work are set. The aspects and implications of the revelation which need emphasis and development in the fourth century will not be the same as those that need emphasis and development in the twentieth century; nor are the verbal and conceptual complexes which will make it intelligible to one age identical with those which will make it intelligible to another. There is thus an inevitable relativity about doctrinal expressions which arises simply from the limitations of human languages, even the most subtle and sensitive; and there is an inevitable partiality about doctrinal understanding which arises from the limitations of human minds, even the

[1] *Theology of Revelation*, New York, 1966, p. 75.
[2] *Ibid.*, p. 140.
[3] *Ibid.*, p. 117.

197

RENEWAL OF RELIGIOUS THOUGHT

most brilliant and devout. Some qualifications need, however, to be made.

First, the inevitable inadequacy and coarse-structuredness of human thought and language, in comparison with the richness and complexity of the objects to which it refers, does not imply that statements and thoughts cannot be perfectly true. The metaphysical essence and the zoological constitution of feline nature may forever elude me; nevertheless, I may be making a perfectly true statement when I say, "The cat is on the mat." It is not true that I cannot know anything about anything unless I know everything about everything, or even until I know everything about something. Thus I do not need to have an exhaustive knowledge of Godhead and manhood in order to be able to say with perfect truth and accuracy, "Although he is God and man, yet he is not two but one Christ," or in order to recite intelligently and honestly the Nicene Creed.

Again, the difficulty of finding an exact bi-unique correspondence between one language or conceptual system and another does not make it impossible to distinguish accurate translation or transposition on the one hand from sheer confusion and reductionism on the other. The existence of difficult borderline cases does not provide a legitimate reason for denying the distinctness of instances in general. The fact that it is difficult or impossible to decide whether certain organisms belong to the animal or the vegetable kingdom does not throw doubt upon either the meaningfulness or the truth of the statement that a kangaroo is not a plant but an animal, while an aspidistra is not an animal but a plant. Nor does the inevitable looseness of fit of linguistic expressions make it impossible to distinguish between the translation of a statement from one language to another and its substitution by a statement with a different meaning. The English word "cat" and the French word "*chat*" have not entirely the same extension, since "cat" is of common gender and "*chat*," in the singular, is of masculine. Nevertheless, I am justified in saying that "*Le chat est noir*" is a translation of "The cat is black" and not of "The dog is brown." The point is important because in recent years some theologians have pro-

198

duced what they allege to be translations of traditional Christian formulas into modern idiom in a quite scandalously cavalier way. When, for example, it is maintained that "Jesus was born of the Virgin Mary" means, in modern terms, "God acted in history, and monogamous marriage is civilization's most important social institution,"[4] I can only reply that it no more means that than it means "Prague is the capital of Czechoslovakia." All that I shall say here is that the task of translating Christian truth into a new idiom is important, difficult, and extremely delicate; it is not to be done by taking expressions of secularist humanist views and announcing that these give the "real meanings" of the traditional formulas. This is in fact a task which the Church and its thinkers have pursued throughout history, and like all human enterprises it has met with various degrees of success. It is particularly difficult today, for, now that the world has moved into a secularist culture, the contemporary idiom is very ill fitted for talk about transcendent realities. Nevertheless, the task must be attempted; but it is not being attempted if we simply produce secularist formulas and say that they express the "real meaning" of the Christian ones.

It will, I hope, be clear that in saying all this I am not suggesting that Christian theology has no concern with the secular order; the precise opposite is the case. It is because I believe that it has quite characteristic and special things to say about the secular order, quite different from those that secularism has to say, that I have protested against the substitution of the latter for the former. It is largely because the type of theology dominant in recent years has had so little to say about the secular order that we are now confronted, by an understandable but deplorable reaction to the opposite extreme, with a so-called "theology" that has nothing to say about anything else. The central Christian tradition has in fact contained a theology of the secular, or as would more usually be said, of the natural order, but it has failed to keep pace with the tremendous developments of the technological age. The principles are none-

[4] T. Boslooper, *The Virgin Birth,* Philadelphia, 1962, p. 234.

theless there, and because they refer the natural order to its ground in the supernatural, they provide it with a value and a hope that no secularist doctrine can offer it. It is the belief that the world is God's world and that man is God's creature, made in God's image, fallen through sin, and redeemed in Christ, that has inspired the great body of social thinking represented in my own country by such men as Maurice, Gore, and Temple and elsewhere by St. Antonino of Florence, the great social papal encyclicals, and the longest of the decrees of the Second Vatican Council. The detailed application of the insights of the Christian faith to concrete human problems needs a combination of theological understanding and technical expertise that no single body of theorists can provide; it requires the respectful and cordial cooperation of theologians with sociologists, educators, economists, lawyers, medical men, politicians, and experts in every walk of life; such cooperation has already produced notable results, though it has as yet hardly passed beyond the initial stages. There are welcome manifestations among the practitioners of the various disciplines of a recognition that without the understanding of man that belongs to Christian theology, work for the welfare of man tends to become self-frustrating, uncoordinated, and unable to justify its own existence. On the other hand, the Christian theologian must be ready to recognize and welcome selfless service for the welfare of man on the part of many who ignore or repudiate the faith; this will be all the easier for him since he knows the grace of God to be universal and not confined in its operation to the visible structure of the Church. The empirically verifiable features of the contemporary human situation, so far from causing him embarrassment or dismay, will provide material for theological discrimination and interpretation. Man's amazing dual constitution of spirit and matter, bound together in a mysterious and intricate unity, his aspiration to eternity linked with a physical death like that of the beasts, his need to incorporate pieces of matter into his own body in order to maintain its life, the propagation of his species through an act whose character oscillates between the noblest and the most squalid impulses of his nature—all these and many other features known by mere experience or by scientific research in no way disquiet him as they have constantly disquieted those who profess a purely spiritual religion. With his belief in the resurrection of the body and the life everlasting he can avoid romanticism and escapism on the one hand, and hedonism and cynicism on the other. While bringing his Christian understanding of the human condition to bear upon the unlimited range of human possibilities and predicaments, he will nonetheless be humble and cooperative in his dealings with experts in the various secular disciplines, for he knows that, while God has revealed in Christ the great basic truths about man's nature, destiny, condition, and resources, he has left it to man himself to discover the details of his own constitution and of that of the universe of which he is a part. His conviction that it is the ultimate destiny of the secular order not to be abandoned or destroyed, but to be transformed and glorified in the final consummation of God's creative and redemptive work, will preserve him from the fate of the pietist on the one side, and of the advocate of a secularist Christianity on the other. For he will recognize the God-given character of both the natural and the supernatural order and also—this is of central importance—the organic relation between them.

Unless I am altogether mistaken, the most urgent task for Christian theology is that of its own renewal within the context of the contemporary situation. We have to speak the word of God to the world of our time, but first of all we must be sure that it is the word of God that we are speaking. It is in this latter respect that the advocates of "religionless Christianity," "the secular Gospel," "Christian atheism," and the like have so tragically misunderstood their task. For the primary need of a world that has ignored God is that God should be presented to it. The advocates of secularized theology are no doubt impelled by the highest motives and we must honour them for their honesty and candour. Objectively considered, however, their project seems to me to verge upon apostasy and to weaken and hinder the Church's mission at its very heart. In spite of the

201

amazing revolution which man has brought about in the realm of the secular, modern man is anxious, disturbed, and perplexed in his soul. Over the triumph of his achievements there hangs the unanswered question whether humanity as a whole or men as individuals have any ultimate future and significance in this world or any other. Many of our most perceptive playwrights and novelists have depicted with unsparing realism "the plight of man in a world that is neither of his making nor his choosing," the meaninglessness and absurdity of a godless world. It is in such a situation that the proclamation of a supernatural Gospel—the Gospel of a God who saves—may come with relevance and power. Karl Rahner may well be right in saying that, for all we know, faith may be on the point of returning to the world. The disillusionment of an affluent society may in the end be no less receptive of the Christian Gospel than the privations of an underprivileged one, and both of these exist in the world of today. If, as I believe, contemporary man has a God-shaped void in the heart of his being, no godless religion will be able to fill it. In leading so many Christian theologians today into the desert of atheist theology, Satan is performing his traditional function of deceiving the very elect.

In M. Jean-Paul Sartre's famous novel *La Nausée* the climax comes in the episode in which the central character—one can hardly call him a hero—Antoine Roquentin, who is naturally a complete atheist, has a sudden revelation of the basic character of the world as his glance falls upon the black, knotty roots of a chestnut tree. What he finds himself forced to recognize is the complete lack of reason for its existence, and he expresses this by describing it as "superfluous," "contingent," "gratuitous," and—this is most significant—"absurd." The first three of these adjectives are precisely those on which a traditional Christian theist might base an argument for the existence of God— St. Thomas's Third Way, in fact. The fourth adjective—"absurd"—expresses precisely what one is left with if one does not take the final step of affirming God's existence. In Antoine Roquentin's experience we have what might be described as a "lived manifestation" of the meaninglessness of the world if one is determined to take it as the only reality there is. It is well known that Sartre insists that this meaninglessness must not be resolved, because he knows that belief in God is the only way of resolving it and he is determined at all costs not to believe in God; this topsy-turviness is easy for an existentialist, for whom belief is a matter of sheer decision and not of argument. It may well be, however, that in the tortured groanings of the atheistic existentialists and the exponents of the absurd we can discern what another modern writer, the poet Martin Skynner, has described as "the pins and needles of returning faith."

Not all existentialists are atheists; some, following in the footsteps of Søren Kierkegaard and Martin Heidegger, are avowed Christians, and it may indeed be argued that their attitude is so different that it is misleading to apply the same word "existentialist" to both. Dr. F. T. Kingston has discussed this question in his very able book *French Existentialism*. Some Christian existentialist writing may be welcomed as a healthy reaction from the bleak and bloodless character of much Christian ethical and ascetical writing in the post-Reformation era. Much of it, however, expresses a deliberate exaltation of the will over the intellect and a corresponding lack of concern with truth as such; it can, for example, treat the existence of God as something wholly dependent on the decision of human beings (or of some specially qualified human beings) to recognize him, so that if they refuse to recognize him the resulting situation will be described by saying that God is no more or that now he has died. In the case of Bultmann and his school, existentialism comes in as a highly convenient rescuer from the ravages of New Testament form criticism; if nothing of consequence can be known about the life and teaching of Jesus, there are obvious advantages in basing religion simply on the existential reactions of the Christian congregation to the prophetic declamations of their preacher. Leaving aside such instances as these, with their obvious *parti pris*, there can be no harm in experimenting with the existentialist idiom in order to see whether it can or cannot provide an effective medium for addressing the contemporary world. Karl Rahner appears to have made good use of it in

203

addressing a German-speaking public, in spite of the fact that, in English translation, his writings convey little of their very genuine insight and originality to readers who are unfamiliar with it. It is perhaps significant that one of the most brilliant English-writing theologians who has thoroughly experimented with the existentialist idiom as a vehicle of Christian thought, Dr. John Macquarrie, has, in his recent most impressive work *Principles of Christian Theology,* confessed to its inadequacy unless it is supplemented by an ontological insight. I would add that, while existentialism emphasizes man's situation *in* the world, it never quite reconciles itself to the fact that he is *part* of it. We might perhaps express this by saying that existentialism in the Heideggerian sense cannot do without existentialism in the Thomist sense as well.

It is frequently asserted with a large measure of truth that when atheists explicitly deny the existence of God, the God whose existence they deny is often not the God of Christian theism at all, but some false and quite unworthy image that they have conjured up for themselves, or that they have derived from the utterances and the behaviour of ignorant or insincere Christians; Vatican II itself suggested as much. That this is so is a matter of shame for Christians and an impelling reason for the opening up of a dialogue between Christians and atheists. It must not, however, be assumed that if and when they are presented with the genuinely Christian image of God, they will wholeheartedly rush to embrace it; that may or may not be the case. Still less should it be assumed that sincere professing agnostics and atheists are really Christians at heart, in the sense that what they ultimately believe in is the Christian God although for some reason or other they have never recognized this. Again, this may or may not be the case; and if we assume that it necessarily is, we may be doing a grave injustice to the intellectual integrity of our collocutors, and provoking quite justifiable irritation. For the fact is that, much as we should regret it, there are many people who know quite accurately what Christian theism is and sincerely believe it to be false. In recognizing that this is so, one is not in the least degree denying that the grace of God and of Christ may be vigorously active in the lives of such sincerely mistaken persons.

In saying that we must resist all temptations to secularize Christian belief in order to make it palatable to a secularist culture, I do not imply that we shall not find ourselves able to agree and collaborate with our contemporaries on a variety of human issues; the opposite is true. Although we must always be ready for divergences to appear, many of the values for which humanists stand are those for which Christians should stand as well. We may explain this by saying that the humanist himself is living on the last dregs of a vanished Christian culture, or we may say that the fundamental principles of the natural law are still operative in the heart and mind of fallen man. Where we shall often find ourselves differing from him, even when we are in agreement on a matter of practical action, is about the ultimate ground and justification for the action in question. My impression, for what it is worth, is that many humanists have a deeply rooted respect for human beings as such which they would find it difficult to justify rationally, and that their decisions are directed by a kind of pragmatic utilitarianism which meets each crisis as it comes and tries to solve it in the way which may produce as much happiness and prevent or abolish as much suffering as possible. And this, however difficult it may be to justify it theoretically, is not a policy to be despised; Christians, in spite of their wider access to truth, do not always do nearly so well. When we turn, however, to the theoretical aspect we may well find ourselves wondering how long a scientific humanism will be able to maintain itself in the world of the near future. The one value which the humanist holds as supreme is that of the human being as such, and it is just at this point that the new discoveries and techniques of science are likely to intervene. The really new and frightening feature in the situation is that science, which has for the last four centuries been adapting the world to the requirements of man, is now finding out how to interfere with the material basis of human personality itself. If one stresses this, one is frequently accused of having read too much science fiction and finds it difficult to get oneself taken seriously.

205

However, to get this impression one need not read science fiction; one need only attend to the utterances of scientists. In 1963 and in 1966, that admirable organization the CIBA Foundation published the reports of conferences held under its auspices in which biologists, sociologists, lawyers, medical men, and other specialists, including two theologians, met together to discuss the ethical problems raised by such matters as the manipulation of human genetic material, the influencing of brain processes and personality by surgical, chemical, and electrical means, the transplantation of bodily organs from one person to another, the separation of procreation from sexual intercourse and the consequent destruction of the human family, all of which are either already possible or only just round the corner. It is interesting to see how many of the scientists were seriously perplexed about the ethical problems that they had raised, and how often they seemed to expect theologians to have at any rate some contribution to make towards their solution.

Behind all these specific and individual problems there lies one basic issue: what grounds are there for holding that the essential nature of man ought to be preserved and not to be changed by scientific manipulation into something radically different? The attempt has been made to find the justification in the evolutionary process itself; a notable instance is provided by Dr. C. H. Waddington in his extremely interesting book *The Ethical Animal*. Ingenious as it is, it seems to me to fail for the simple reason that no process can furnish a criterion for its own assessment. Man is now both the manipulator and (if the word may be allowed) the manipulatee of the evolutionary process; how can the process tell him what to do with it? Some transempirical criterion must be found and this is provided by Christian faith. If God has made man in his own image and, by taking man's nature himself, has ratified and confirmed his creative act, if the God-man is the originator and head of the renewed human race, so that by incorporation into him men can find their own human nature renewed and transformed, mankind is certified as having a dignity and a destiny which no merely evolutionary doctrine can assure him. This does not mean that the scientific account of man's prehistory and history is incorrect; it does mean that science cannot speak the last and most important word about him.

To sum up this discussion, then, I would simply say that, as I see it, the task which confronts theology in this secularist culture is to work out a contemporary expression of the classical theological principle that grace neither ignores nature nor destroys it, but needs it, establishes it, perfects it, and transforms it.

10.

TEILHARD DE CHARDIN IN THE CONTEXT OF RENEWAL

HENRI DE LUBAC, S.J.

ALTHOUGH differences continue to be considerable from one country or from one continent to another, certain traits, certain aspirations, certain hopes are today shared by most men who observe and think.

For the first time in history, and despite the ravages of the world wars and the conflict of great ideologies, an aspiration for unity is becoming clear. Despite misery and distress of every kind, great hope is placed in the progress of science and the conquests of technology for the betterment of human life. Despite great selfishness, lack of understanding, inertia, and disheartening experiences, the great effort continues on every side to promote economic, social, and cultural development, and to work in spite of constantly reborn obstacles for the "building of the world."

And we know how the Catholic Church is encouraging all her faithful along this road, in the very name of love for men, of the "cult of man" inspired by our faith.[1] We know the great enthusiasm which the recent Council has raised in the Church, the new projects that are springing up, the signs of renewal that can be seen almost everywhere.

Now if the work of Teilhard de Chardin has found such an

[1] A new sign of this has just been given by the encyclical *Populorum Progressio*.

208

echo, in the Church and outside it, it is certainly, at least in great part, because people have discerned in it this same aspiration, hope, effort, and because they have found in Teilhardian theory something capable of giving them direction.

1.

One of the principal characteristics of Père Teilhard, in fact, one of the marks of his genius, is that he was a generation ahead of his contemporaries. What we feel today, what is tending to become the common consciousness of men, what is sometimes almost commonplace for us already, he felt and expressed in his solitary meditations half a century ago! It was during the First World War, when men were torn apart as never before, that, during days of rest from combat, he set down in his copy-books the first statement of this great dream of unity[2] whose structure and conditions he was to try progressively to define. "The building of the world" was precisely the title he gave to the first part of one of his writings[3]:

The world builds itself. This is the fundamental truth which we must first understand, and understand so well that it becomes a habitual, natural form of our thought. At first sight, beings and their destiny may appear to us disposed by accident, or at least arbitrarily, on the face of the earth, . . . as if the universe, from the beginning to the end of its history, forms a sort of garden plot in time and space, in which the flowers are interchangeable at the whim of the gardener. This idea does not seem sound. The more we reflect, with the aid of every source of knowledge, each in its own sphere, science, philosophy, and religion, the more we find that the

[2] He was to write in 1957 on the essence of the mystical feeling: "Essentially, the mystical feeling is a sense and a presentiment of the total and final Unity of the World beyond its present and sensed multiplicity."

[3] In his "L'Esprit de la Terre," 1931, *Oeuvres* 6 (Paris, 1962), p. 46, he wrote "to build the earth." He was also to speak of an "organic future" of Humanity in "La Foi en l'homme," Oeuvres 5 (Paris, 1947), pp. 5, 237.

world is comparable, not to a pile of elements in artificial juxta-position, but rather to an organic system, alive with a general move-ment of growth . . . There is a process in the universe, working toward an end, for which we know no better comparison than gestation and birth: the birth of a spiritual reality, formed by souls and by the matter they carry with them. Laboriously, through human activity and in favor of it, the new earth gathers itself together, emerges, and becomes distinct. No, we are not comparable to separate sprigs of a floral bouquet, but to the leaves and blossoms of a great tree, on which everything appears in its own time and place, proportioned to and summoned by the Whole.[4]

But also, if the Council involves us in this task of the "con-struction of the world," it is not to lose us in it, but to show us, in the first principles of our faith, the only foundation, the only spirit, the only conditions, the only End which we can envisage. And this is also precisely what Père Teilhard tried to do. We have seen this in the passage just quoted: the birth for which he hoped, this birth of a "new earth," he saw not simply as result-ing from the immanent transformation of the species in a tem-poral future; it was for him the birth of "the spiritual reality formed by souls" which are chosen and united in their divine homeland. This passage is taken from an essay entitled "The Meaning and Constructive Value of Suffering," which shows that its author did not avoid the most austere conditions which alone can make the great dream of unity something more than a utopia.

We are invited by the Council in view of this end to reflect on the relations between the Church and the world. Now, one of the governing ideas of Teilhard was that of the necessary union of these two great realities which come both from the same God, Creator and Redeemer. He came back to this in every period of his life. I will quote from some of his letters, the intimate letters which he wrote to his friend Père Auguste Valensin, as to a true spiritual director. "The Lord has led me on roads so unforeseen that I must count on him to make the best use of me for his

[4] "La Signification et la Valeur constructrice de la Souffrance," 1933, *Oeuvres* 6, pp. 61–62.

glory. May I simply be able to serve the great cause in a small way, the cause which alone possesses me in the depths of my heart, the cause of the explicit fusion of the Christian life with the 'natural' sap of the universe" (Holy Saturday, 1922). Again, some years later: "I think it can be useful to the Kingdom of God that at the bottom of our hearts there be an explosive union of the passion for the world and the passion for God" (June 27, 1926). And later: "Instinctively, especially in the last ten years, I have offered myself to Our Lord as a sort of experimental field, so that he might work there, on a small scale, the fusion between the two great loves, of God and of the World—a fusion without which, I am convinced, the Kingdom of God is not possible" (December 31, 1926).

Already in the introduction to the first work of his that we possess, entitled *La vie cosmique,* writing at the front in 1916 he said, "I am writing these lines . . . because I love the universe, its secrets, its hopes; and because, at the same time, I am devoted to God, the only Origin, the only Result, the only End." And it is to this point that he returned, in one way or another, all his life. Always, the "majesty of the universe" made him recognize and adore "the primacy of God."[5]

How we must conceive objectively, following our faith, the relation between the world and the Church, or the construction of the world and the coming of the Kingdom of God, or the temporal development of humanity and its eternal destiny; what resources the work of Teilhard offers us in this regard; how this work proposes to us a view of the future, and even more, a "will for the future"[6] which, being founded on the "substance of the Christian faith," rescues us from sterile pessimism and from "progressivist nonsense"[7] of the right and the left: this I have tried, like others, to deal with elsewhere. I have also said what

[5] "Esquisse d'une Dialectique de l'Esprit," 1946, *Oeuvres* 7 (Paris, 1963), p. 158.
[6] See Dietrich Bonhoeffer, *Letters and Papers from Prison,* London, 1953, pp. 146–147: "The optimism which is will for the future should never be despised. . . . It is the health and vitality which a sick man should never impugn."
[7] The expression is J.-M. Domenach's.

weaknesses may be discerned there (for in an "experimental field," one does not register only successes), and what criticisms of him seem to me legitimate.[8] My purpose here is different. It is to see how Teilhard's work, however it is judged, contains on some most important points the antidote which can protect us against certain maladies which even today threaten to abort the enthusiasm of which I spoke by corroding the Christian conscience. Or, if you prefer more positive language, I propose to examine the support that each of us can find in his work for a fruitful, properly oriented action. What I have said up to now has had but one aim, to prevent an ambiguity. I do not at all intend to offer negative criticism, nor to take an attitude of reserve, but on the contrary, I shall try to enter fully into the road traced by the Council; I shall, when necessary, push aside with the audacity of faith, any obstacles standing in the way.

2.

It would be vain to try to ignore the fact that for several years signs have been multiplying of a spiritual crisis such as has rarely before shaken the Church. It is the counterblow, no doubt inevitable, of the crisis of civilization which rapid progress and profound upheavals of every kind, beginning with the war of 1914, have accelerated. Neither in its basic causes nor in its essential characteristics does it derive from the recent Council. The Council was convoked, by a sort of divining instinct in which John XXIII rightly recognized the action of the Holy Spirit, in order to surmount it as a crisis of growth in the only effective way: not by condemnations, but by an appeal for

[8] Henri de Lubac, *La pensée religieuse du Père Teilhard de Chardin*, Paris, 1962; ET *The Religion of Teilhard de Chardin*, New York, 1967. *Teilhard de Chardin. The Man and his Meaning*, New York, 1965. *Pierre Teilhard de Chardin, Maurice Blondel. Correspondence*, New York, 1967. *Teilhard missionaire et apologiste*, Toulouse, 1966. *Images de l'Abbé Monchanin*, Paris, 1967. See Bruno de Solages, *Teilhard de Chardin*, Toulouse, 1967. See also the collection *Théologie d'aujourd'hui et de demain*, Paris, 1967, ch. 1–2.

internal renewal of the whole Church. For the rest, it suffices to read the conciliar documents—although frequently weak in their wording, sometimes lacking in precision, reflecting the very situation for which they are seeking remedies—to ascertain the wisdom, balance, sense of tradition which always accompanies the boldness of this appeal. Transcending frozen conservatism, it is always to the most central tradition, which alone carries the promises of life, that the Council sends us back. It has produced an impact, like a rough awakening—others have called it a thaw—whose effect will be salutary. As I mentioned already at the beginning, felicitous new projects born of the Council are springing up everywhere. There is no room for alarm, nor even for wonder, if in this great workshop some disorder appears; if backwaters take shape in the wake of such a great vessel. But the present crisis is more serious. It owes nothing to the Council; it threatens to reject it. Here or there under the name of the post-conciliar Church, or of the "New Church," there exists a Church quite other than that of Jesus Christ, and it is even seeking to be "established"—if one can speak of establishment in reference to a phenomenon which is above all destructive.

It is not just those who are nostalgic for the past, the stubborn traditionalists, opponents on principle, who are warning us of this. It is not the "integralists," nor the gloomy, nor the fearful. We are being warned by some of the great builders of renewal, by men who have given proof of the greatest daring, by men who labored effectively at Rome or elsewhere in the spirit of the Council, and who remain today determined to use every means to complete its work. Suffice it to mention, among many others, that hardly unique and strongly motivated cry of alarm that came from Dr. Josef Ratzinger at the *Katholikentag* of Bamberg in July of 1966; or those articles on "Changes and Continuity in the Church" published this year by Father Yves Congar; or the moving pamphlets, inspired by a pure and profound Christianity, which Dr. Hans Urs von Balthasar issued between the publication of his great works as so many appeals to our conscience. It seems needless to add that Paul VI himself, as tactful in regard to persons as he is rigorous in regard

213

to doctrine, continues to multiply, along with encouragement to renewal, his warnings. In spite of his clear vision and the authority of his words, there have been many, even within the last year, who have hesitated to echo him in public for fear of increasing the trouble by imprudent "alarmism." But today one would have to be not only blind, but deaf as well, not to recognize the extent of the epidemic. An Anglo-Saxon observer wrote recently that there was a time when one might have supposed that the Catholic Church alone, thanks to her solid structure, would escape the universal crisis of our generation; but *this is no longer so,* and she now faces the formidable question, "Does the Catholic Church herself remain among men as a witness to God, or is she too going to become an anthropocentric society?"

Once again, in these days after the Council, small pressure groups are raising their bids, as was the case a century ago (though with a completely different orientation) after the First Vatican Council. Many are trying to exploit the current period of transition to advance their own views rather than give their cordial support to the decisions of the Council. The efforts of many who have good will, but poor coordination, result in a certain anarchy. These are phenomena too human to cause surprise. It is nevertheless sad to have to state that today, as a century ago, men seem to want "to employ themselves, by their inconsiderate language, with troubling those little ones who believe in Christ, and of . . . destroying those for whom He died." Newman, who wrote these words,[9] also gave warning at about the same time of the danger he saw rising on the spiritual horizon: "the spread of that plague of infidelity, that the Apostles and our Lord Himself have predicted as the worst calamity of the last times of the Church."[10] But Newman could not

[9] *Letter to the Duke of Norfolk,* 1874 (published January 1875), *Certain Difficulties Felt by Anglicans in Catholic Teaching,* New York, 1896, II, 300.

[10] Address of 2 October 1873, at the opening of the seminary of St. Bernard at Olton. *Catholic Sermons of Cardinal Newman,* London, 1957, p. 121. See Louis Cognat, *Newman, ou la recherche de la vérité,* Paris, 1967, pp. 288, 292.

imagine that in a future day these two evils, scandal and contempt, would combine into one more dangerous, which threatens to install unbelief in the very heart of the Church of Christ. Today's threatening danger is no longer simply that of apostasy through immanentism, but as M. Jacques Maritain rightly diagnosed, that of an "immanent apostasy."

Our hope is not affected. We are not pessimists. We know that the Spirit of Christ watches constantly over his Church. But it is nowhere written that the Church will always be spared ravaging. This very day, not on account of some powerful idea logical in its errors, but by a sort of collective vertigo, every vital point seems menaced at the same time; all the Church's problems seem suddenly to have been uncovered, as if they had never been noticed before, and as if the most destructive measures were necessary in every area. When by reason of a contempt that is sometimes as pretentious as it is ignorant, the Catholic conscience is becoming isolated from its past, from what is of yesterday and forever, it is finding itself betrayed, destitute, defenseless against all the solicitations from outside. It no longer knows how to see itself, save in the conception which an unbelieving world has formed of it. Without discrimination it adopts, receives from anywhere, everything that can cast doubt on the faith from whatever bias. Sometimes it is not only the intelligence that is affected, but the heart as well; then it turns away from the Church, from her tradition, from the interior life, from the Christian virtues, and is satisfied with their caricatures. It no longer has a taste for, nor understands the Gospel.

Where such a state of the spirit prevailed, or even where it only insinuated itself, there would be no call for surprise that the teachings of the Council should be distorted. *Aggiornamento,* openness to the world, adaptation, rejuvenation, ecumenism, the spirit of dialogue, all excellent things when rightly understood, when developed on the firm basis of the faith as the fruits of a living faith, can in fact become the pretext for their opposites, covering up a more or less general surrender. Everyone with eyes even a little open can find examples of this. It is

215

clear that if we were to let ourselves slide on this slope, yielding to the pressures which bear upon us, there would soon be no renewal or progress to talk about, only liquidation. The hope raised by the Council would be swallowed up.

To sum up in a few simple propositions (for this is not the time for subtlety), I will say that in the situation of the present time resulting from the confused mixture which has just been described, the objections which confront us, the trials which beset us, the obstacles which we must overcome, concern principally three fundamental objects: faith in a personal God; faith in Jesus Christ; faith in the role of the Church of Christ. These three objects are for us practically interdependent; and when the Christian faith loses its vitality, the process of its death follows an order which has been well analyzed by Madeleine Delbrêl: contrary to what may seem logical, "a world which de-Christianizes itself seems to empty itself out from within, first of God, then of the Son of God, then of what he gives of divinity to his Church; and it is usually the surface that collapses last."[11]

Now, to protect us from this catastrophe without leaving us either rigid or closed, it has seemed to me that we could find in the work of Père Teilhard de Chardin, as in his personal demeanor, an effective aid. On the three fundamental points I have just enumerated, he expressed himself many times, and the very organization of his thought places them in strong relief. He wrote in 1944, in his brief *Introduction to the Christian Life:* "A threefold faith is necessary and sufficient as the foundation for the Christian attitude: 1. Faith in the (personalizing) Personality of God, the focus of the world. 2. Faith in the Divinity of the Christ of history (not only prophet and perfect man, but object of love and adoration). 3. Faith in the reality of the Church as a phylum, in which and about which Christ continues to develop in the world his total personality." One can certainly criticize many things in Teilhard; but even one who cannot stand him need not be afraid to follow him in such a program. I can here just supply a few brief

[11] *Nous autres, gens des rues,* missionary texts presented by Jacques Loew, Paris, 1966, p. 29.

hints; only the careful reading of his work will bring out fully its cogent force. For the rest, I do not claim that the thought of Père Teilhard, who was constantly at his research, always got properly expressed; even less do I claim that his thought is completely adequate, that it has an answer for everything. Père Teilhard de Chardin is only one voice, partial and very imperfect, in the great Catholic concert which is constantly recalling us to our only master, Christ.

3.

Père Teilhard de Chardin once denounced "the sophism which consists of corroding the solid bases of the Christian faith under pretext of promoting their development."[12] Let us gather his remarks together. The Second World War reinforced in him a conviction already acquired in the war of 1914. He wrote from Peking in December 1939: "At the root of the grave troubles in which the nations find themselves involved, I believe it is possible to discern that humanity is going through a change of age."[13] There was taking place, he felt, a genuine *mue,* a "moulting" or "sloughing off," a "mutation" as the constitution *Gaudium et spes* was to put it,[14] and this ought to affect even "religious perspectives" and ought to entail a renewal of the very method of presenting the Christian faith. This renewal, this "renovation," he said,[15] ought to be the effect of an authentic development (Teilhard had meditated hard on Newman)[16]; it ought to proceed not from some relaxation, but

[12] Letter of 20 July 1922.
[13] "L'Heure de choisir," 1939, *Oeuvres* 7, p. 21. See "La Foi en l'homme," *Oeuvres* 5, p. 237: "Let us observe . . . the new world which is being born around us in the spasms of war."
[14] Art. 5: "Today's spiritual agitation and the changing conditions of life are part of a broader and deeper mutation."
[15] *Christologie et Evolution,* Tientsin, 1933, Conclusion.
[16] Newman's essay on development was to inspire him to long reflections about the development of doctrine and of life in the Church, as well as, by transposition, cosmic evolution. He was never to admit anything but a homogeneous evolution, and he rejected all "illegitimate evolution of dogma" (1929).

217

from a deeper penetration of traditional faith.[17] "Should my faith unhappily slacken, the light goes out at once and everything becomes dark, then falls apart."

This faith was, first and fundamentally, faith in God. At the same period when he diagnosed for the human species a "change of age," Père Teilhard also perceived—and this is a surprising observation at first sight—the cause of the world cataclysm in man's despairing of the personality of God.[18] He also revealed to his superiors his desire to become fully engaged in "the battle for a personal God."[19] The opposition he habitually noted between the two mystiques which, he said, divided the whole world, those of East and West, springs from the opposition between the mystique of the impersonal, which Teilhard rejected, and the "mystique of personality."[20] In his thought, it has been written, "everything rests on the primacy of personality."[21] While explaining the necessity of seeing God at work at the heart of the cosmogenesis which extends into nöogenesis, he insisted always that it is important "in the first place to maintain at all cost his primordial transcendence," his "transcendent reality."[22] One day, in the midst of disaster and ruin, he cries out, in spite of all, his "triumphant joy, born of [his] conviction of the transcendence of God."[23] And he knows that this God is a loving and provident God, capable of revealing himself, and who has in fact revealed himself. That

[17] See Bernard Towers, *Teilhard de Chardin,* Richmond, 1966, pp. 7–8: "He was not a 'revolutionary' but rather an 'evolutionary.' That is, his thinking represents a genuine 'development of doctrine,' wholly within the Christian tradition. . . . He was never a relativist where knowledge and thinking were concerned."

[18] To M. Teillard-Chambon, 18 October 1940, *Letters from a Traveler,* London, 1962, p. 269.

[19] To Père Schurmans, Vicar General of the Society of Jesus, 1940.

[20] "Le Christianisme dans le Monde," 1933, *Oeuvres* 9, pp. 138–139: "The road to the West"; if seen clearly, they are both inverted forms of the spirit.

[21] Madeleine Barthélemy-Madaule, *Bergson et Teilhard de Chardin,* Paris, 1963, p. 352.

[22] "Un Seuil mental sous nos pas: du Cosmos à la Cosmogénèse," 1951, *Oeuvres* 7, pp. 270–271. Texts in de Lubac, *Teilhard. The Man and his Meaning,* pp. 23–28.

[23] Letter of 9 April 1916, *The Making of a Mind. Letters from a Soldier-Priest, 1914–1919,* London, 1965, p. 98.

is for him the supreme truth. Neither his Christian faith, nor his reflection, nor his intimate experience left him open for an instant to the puerile antithesis which some propose as the last word and coming of age of critical thought, the antithesis between an interior God and a God regarded as "external" and "spatial." He knew, he saw only too well, that if the real is a sphere, God is at once the center and the circumference, that he "occupies the whole sphere"; that he embraces everything "and imprisons nothing"[24]; that he is only at the heart of our being because he is infinitely beyond it, at the same time near and far, intimate and incomprehensible. Many times he gave in his own way the words of the great Augustine: "*Deus, interior intimo meo, et superior summo meo!*" "Real centre" and "unifying energy" of the Cosmos, "*rerum, Deus, tenax vigor*"—God cannot be this unless he is a Being "distinct from the Cosmos," "independent" of it, so that the conjunction of the Cosmos and God, the supreme end of creation, will always be "a conjunction hierarchically arranged."[25]

On the other hand, Teilhard knew "the antipersonalist complex that paralyzes us."[26] He observed it especially in the world of scientific thought. One of his principal concerns was to show its vanity. He wished to see again "in our most modern world, the *face* of God."[27] Hence his insistence on doing away with "*evil* anthropocentrism,"[28] on rejecting the caricatures produced when Christian life is down to the standard of mediocrity, and which transform the personal Absolute into a big, all too human Individual[29]; hence also his care to distinguish between a certain type of paternalism and evangelical faith in

[24] "La grande Monade," 1918, *Ecrits du temps de la guerre (1916–1919)*, Paris, 1965, pp. 247–248. In contrast with the material Universe: "Raising their eyes to the total shape of their world, they (human beings) see themselves *encircled*" (p. 242).
[25] "On the Possible Bases of a Universal Human Creed," *The Future of Man*, London, 1964, pp. 76–81. "L'Union créatrice," 1917, *Ecrits*, pp. 181, 184. See de Lubac, *La Pensée religieuse*, pp. 261–262.
[26] *The Phenomenon of Man*, New York, 1959, p. 266.
[27] "Man's Place in the Universe," *The Vision of the Past*, London, 1966, p. 231.
[28] *The Phenomenon of Man*, p. 35.
[29] See de Lubac, *Teilhard. The Man and his Meaning*, pp. 13–19.

the divine Paternity, and his insistence on solidly establishing the classical distinction between individual and person.[30] Hence his demonstration, incessantly reiterated, and confirmed for believers by his relating it to St. Paul, on the final union of this Person and the whole.[31] Hence Teilhard's doctrine that without the vivifying and inspiring reality of a Love who is a Person,[32] it is impossible to affirm, even in our terrestrial society, a truly human order, or to maintain in a man of clear vision the taste for progress, or in the case of each one of us, to love others in the concrete. Hence also his efforts towards an understanding, or at least a glimpse, of the correlation that exists between the idea of a "condensing Infinite," the only real Infinite, and the mystery of divine Personality ("Hyperpersonality"), a mystery of which the believer is doubly assured by the revelation of the Trinity[33]; a mystery which, far from blocking thought, gives it endless momentum towards knowledge and adoration of the *Deus semper major*. Teilhard here is near to Gregory of Nyssa, Augustine, and Anselm: "God," he said, "does not present himself to our finite beings as a thing ready to be grasped. He is for us, rather, eternal Discovery and eternal Growth. The more we think we know him, the more he reveals himself as other; the more we think we grasp him, the more he withdraws, drawing us into the depths of himself; the more we approach him, by all the effort of nature and grace, the

[30] *The Phenomenon of Man*, pp. 257–263. "Esquisse d'un Univers personnel," 1936, *Oeuvres* 6, pp. 67–114. "L'Energie humaine," 1937, *ibid.*, pp. 141–200. On Teilhardian personalism, see Barthélemy-Madaule, *La Personne et le drame humain chez Teilhard de Chardin*, Paris, 1967.

[31] Letter of 15 August 1936.

[32] *The Phenomenon of Man*, p. 269: "Love . . . dies in contact with the impersonal and the anonymous." "The Human Rebound of Evolution and its Consequences," *The Future of Man*, p. 207. "La Centrologie," 1944, *Oeuvres* 7, p. 126. "L'Atomisme de l'Esprit," 1941, *ibid.*, p. 54. "Sauvons l'Humanité," 1936, *Oeuvres* 9, pp. 189–190. "The Heart of the Problem," *The Future of Man*, pp. 264–265. *Introduction à la vie chrétienne*, 1944, p. 6. *Trois choses que je vois*, 1948, p. 11. "Esquisse d'un Univers," p. 101. "L'Energie humaine," pp. 187–188. *Le Christique*, 1955, p. 13.

[33] *Introduction à la vie chrétienne*. Likewise, as Hans Urs von Balthasar says in *Herrlichkeit*, "a figure infinitely determined."

more he increases his attraction over our powers, and, in the same movement, the receptivity of our powers to this divine attraction."[34]

Teilhard's saneness and realism did not permit him to be distracted by apparently subtler speculations. He understood perfectly what a marvelous tool analysis is, but not for the purpose of penetrating into knowledge of being; he understood equally well that intellectual criticism, a legitimate function necessary in every area, is neither the only, nor the highest, use of the intelligence.[35] These two instruments of progress must themselves be criticized and put in their proper place. If they become exclusively dominant, they become the agents of the worst kind of retrogression; they destroy man in destroying his object. "The personal elements of the universe," said Teilhard, "would return to disorder, that is, to nothingness, if they did not encounter the Suprapersonal, itself already actualized, to be dominated by it. There must be found in the world about us, not only the expectation, but the very face, already to be recognized, of a Universal Personality. Nothing less will do . . . to preserve the accumulated powers in the heart of the individual, of societies, and of the world itself, from going completely astray."[36] It was in complete faithfulness to his thought as a whole that he repeated in private conversation: "God is person! We must think of him as of a person. A God who was not personal would not be God."[37] And again he said: "The spiritual value of a man . . . depends on the *degree of*

[34] *The Divine Milieu,* New York, 1960, pp. 119–120. See "Forma Christi," 1918, *Ecrits,* p. 341, on the subject of revelation. One can say that this page is Anselmian: for St. Anselm, God is not only the being *quo majus cogitari nequit,* but the being *majus quam cogitari possit* (Prosl., c. 15). See also St. Thomas, *De veritate,* q. 2, art. 1, ad 9m.

[35] "Science et Christ ou Analyse et Synthèse," 1921, *Oeuvres* 9, pp. 45–62.

[36] "Esquisse d'un Univers," p. 89. Teilhard, then, undertook to restore "not more sentimental or instinctive, but intimately linked to contemporary evolutionary views (provided that man is not excluded from them!), the traditional conceptions of God intellectually influential upon the immortal monads distinct from himself" ("L'Esprit de la Terre," p. 56).

[37] To Père Pierre Leroy. In Claude Cuénot, *Teilhard de Chardin. A Biographical Study,* Baltimore, 1965, p. 244.

reality which God has achieved for him, not his degree of speculative, or even affective, perfection, but, I repeat, the degree of reality."[38] These are words which every believer may meditate upon, but which every theologian and every Christian philosopher ought particularly to reflect over.

At the basis of this realism, there is with Teilhard a "sense of being," a "faith in being," a "taste for being," a "feeling that Being is infinitely richer and more renewing than our logic," which give his thought its stability and at the same time its enthusiasm.[39] The same realism inspires his whole faith. Teilhard, who undertook his theological studies in the time of the modernist crisis, who read Tyrrell, and Loisy, and many others, nevertheless always kept himself "a total stranger to modernism."[40] A stranger, but one who gave it a full hearing. While he was not caught up in the details of the exegetical problems, it would be a mistake to think that he was ignorant of them. He uncovered and criticized myopic historicism, as well as the formless mysticism of the modernism of his time; he would certainly be no less hard on a neo-modernism often more superficial and more pretentious. Modernism, he declared, "evaporates Christ, dissociates him in the world." He noted for himself: "I am fundamentally other, with God's help."[41] And not long ago, in 1950, he agreed joyfully with what a young friend

[38] See his letter of 9 March 1940: ". . . to give to God, who made the Saints, a true value of reality" (*Nouvelles lettres de voyage,* Paris, 1957, p. 45). In his retreat notes he remarks, "What we lack is the sense of the reality of God, the full Faith." Compare this with Newman who wanted to "realize" the truths of faith.

[39] See de Lubac, *Teilhard missionaire,* pp. 97 f., letter of 7 January 1934. On 28 May 1919, he noted "a certain taste (subjective) and flavour (objective) of the Being." In *Comment je vois* (1948), he was to speak of "respect for the value of being."

[40] Georges Crespy, *La Pensée théologique de Teilhard de Chardin,* Paris, 1961, p. 168.

[41] Note of 9 June 1919: "As for me, on the contrary, I am trying to concentrate the World in Christ. And the difference is not merely verbal. I believe (positively, I hope) that if Our Lord (Jesus Christ) does not have a personal and objective reality, the whole Christian religious current fails."

wrote to him: "To prevent dogma from evaporating into symbolism—excellent!"[42]

His whole religious thought, derived from his faith, was founded upon the historicity of Christ, upon what he called "the tangible and demonstrable truth of the evangelical event."[43] For, he was not concerned with just any historicity, but with the historicity of the Incarnation, that is, of the divinity of the historical Christ. God "descended into nature to superanimate it and recall it to himself"; "the Transcendent made himself partly immanent."[44] In his individual conscience, Jesus united the total Man: "this is the inaccessible secret of his agony, and also the incomparable force of his death on the cross."[45] Teilhard's realism is thus at once historical and dogmatic; it is likewise an interior realism. Just as he would not allow the evaporation of dogma, he would not allow the sugar coating of the spirituality which flows from it. Those who see in Jesus nothing but a "friend" or a "perfect man" incur his reproach: "God Our Lord is ravenous!"[46]

He knew quite well, on the other hand, what the unbelieving intelligentsia of his age thought of Christianity. He summed up lucidly the essential points of its criticism. "It is easy to criticize in the abstract this paradoxical mixture of primitive anthropomorphism, wondrous mysticism, and gnostic daring."[47] But he is not at all disturbed by it. He found in all that the Gospels tell of Christ, in the extraordinary sequence of the two interwoven Testaments, and in the immense fact which has its origin in the faith of the first disciples of Christ risen and glorious, "an extraordinary finality, which is in itself a serious indication

---

[42] To Georges Soulages, 29 September 1950. Note of 1 May 1916: ". . . One cannot be a Christian by only believing absolutely and *positively* in *all* the dogmas. The *least restriction* on the *extension* or the *understanding* makes *everything disappear.*" See Newman, *Apologia.*

[43] *The Divine Milieu,* pp. 94–95, 106.

[44] "Esquisse d'une Dialectique," pp. 155–156. "What Should We Think of Transformism?," *The Vision of the Past,* p. 160.

[45] "Mon Univers," 1924, *Oeuvres* 9, pp. 90–91. "La Mystique de la Science," 1939, *Oeuvres* 6, p. 220.

[46] A personal note.

[47] *Le Christique.*

223

of divinity."[48] To the triple criticism formulated by the ideologists who made themselves incapable of seeing or appreciating the living reality, he opposed a triple answer, showing with admiration the miraculous and efficacious association in Christianity of three characteristics: "tangibility, attaching to the experimental order; expansibility, to the universal order, assimilatory power, to the organic order."[49] These he considers solid criteria which confirm him in his faith. There is no fideism here. Already the idea of a personal God working in the world, to which he came by rational offort,[50] made him see as possible, even probable, the eventuality of revelation: "a Presence is never mute." Then, examining history,[51] he recognized the authentic signs of this revelation in Jesus Christ. He contemplated its fruits. He observed in the Christianity of Jesus a doctrine, a perspective, a force "for universal transformation."[52] In the body of Christians certain maladies can insinuate themselves which momentarily change this force of transformation, and consequently slow or even stop the drive of Christian penetration. For forty consecutive years, Teilhard never stopped deploring what he saw as the principal malady of the Christians of his time, and to beg the authorities of his Church to remedy it: a certain loss of the meaning of the human. In itself, of course, Christianity preserves its power intact, provided that it remains integrally itself and that it spreads in its integrality. But should it come to lose one of the three elements of that "paradoxical mixture" denounced by the unbelievers—in other words, should the disciples of Christ come to doubt one of the three aspects of the Christological dogma, should realism come

[48] Retreat notes, meditation on the Nativity. Note of 20 January 1925.

[49] *Le Christique*. The triple characteristic, the effect of the triple reality of the Incarnation, the Resurrection, and the cosmic Power of Christ incarnate and risen—the triple and unique reality of Christ, characterized as he just said by the unbelieving intelligentsia.

[50] See de Lubac, *Teilhard missionaire*, ch. 2, "Du monde à Dieu et au Christ."

[51] *Comment je crois*, 1934. See de Lubac, *Teilhard. The Man and his Meaning*, pp. 178–185.

[52] "La Mystique de la Science," p. 220.

to be stripped of one of its three components—then the Christian fire is quenched.[53]

May today's Christians, all of them, receive this warning of Teilhard.

4.

Under the action of a criticism which spreads everywhere today by the thousands of voices of the mass media, certainly an undertaking of psychological action, many Catholic consciences can be affected. We are not speaking of serious research which is indispensable for the life of faith and should never be forbidden. On the contrary, we should like to see research take longer and freer strides during the next few years.[53a] But what we are witnessing in many places is quite another thing. The corrosive subjectivism of a certain pan-psychology, joined by many other by-products too often uncritically absorbed, menaces at once their faith in Christ and in God himself. If this train of thought were to spread, the Church would be nothing but a façade, destined itself for collapse. But we also know that the effect can be quite different, that confidence in the Church of Christ can effectively protect the faith; and on occasion, even restore its vigor. This also seems to be the first condition of all renewal and all progress—something that Père Teilhard de Chardin never forgot. It is a lesson, perhaps the major lesson which we might learn from him to overcome the present crisis.

One word sums up today a whole stream of tendencies, "secularism"; an obliging word, stretchable at will, passing from the accessory and provisional to the essential, and in the end covering the whole field of the ecclesial institution and the whole of faith. From an observation of fact, a sort of fascination makes

[53] *Le Christique.*
[53a] In *Etudes*, September 1967, the article by Edouard Pousset, "Remettre sa foi en question?", opens avenues of research with as much philosophical depth as fidelity to the direction given by the teaching of the Constitution *Dei verbum* on divine revelation and on the act of faith.

our minds slip to the conviction of a fatal evolution, and soon of progress to be promoted. It is not at all, then, a question of a "legitimate secularization of the world," of "taking hold of it from a distance with respect to the Church." But the Church is then dissolved into the world, the religious into the profane, the eternal into the temporal, and the mystery into a totally human ideology. But the tendency of Teilhard is the reverse. He certainly saw as well as anyone the diminished place held by the Church in this vast world; he ascertained the weakness of its radiance, analyzed its causes, and expressed his insights, sometimes even brutally.[54] He was aware of the fact that most of the men who surrounded him seemed quite closed to the whole religious problem. He knew the interpretation given to this situation by unbelievers. "There is a growing number of systems," he wrote, "in which the fact of religion is interpreted as a psychological phenomenon connected with the infancy of mankind. Maximal at the beginnings of civilization, it ought gradually to evaporate and give way to more positive constructions from which God, especially a personal and transcendent God, would find himself excluded." What is his answer? "Pure illusion!" And he undertook to show that the more man becomes man, the more the need for the absolute is imposed on him, and the more religious he must become. For faith in God, the absolute End, is "the only possible mover of a thoughtful life."[55] He cannot be reproached for "falling on the unfortunate in the moment of their greatest weakness, to exercise a sort of religious coercion over them."[56] For him, as for every true Christian, religion was no mere stopgap, and this is why no amount of purely human fulfillment will account for its decline.

But he recognized another objection, this one concerning the Christian form of religion: "Christianity, a remarkable species

[54] Letter of 7 January 1934: "We have *ceased* to be contagious because we no longer have a *living* conception of the World to contribute. It is a situation that strikes your eyes as soon as you leave churches or seminaries."

[55] "L'Esprit de la Terre," pp. 52–53.

[56] See Bonhoeffer, cited by Robinson.

of religion, to be sure; but one among many others, and only temporary: this is what is said, more or less explicitly, these days, by an enormous majority of 'intelligent' people."[57] Not for an instant did he yield to this illusory philosophy. Here his dynamic and unified vision of the world cooperated with the absoluteness of his faith. As he saw the meaning in cosmic evolution, he saw the meaning in the religious history of mankind. This history is one, it tends to one end, it ought to evolve about one privileged axis. "Our Lord has provided the centre, the nucleus, the axis. . . . There is no outlet for the Noosphere outside the Christian axis."[58] This axis is the Church which Christ founded and in which he continues to live. As the Incarnation is unique, so is the Church unique. Teilhard, with his habitual method of objective phenomenology, observed: "At the very heart of the social phenomenon, a sort of ultra-socialization is in progress, by which the Church forms itself little by little, spreading life by its influence and collecting all the spiritual energies of the Noosphere in their most sublime form. The Church, the portion of the world which has reflexively become Christ; the Church, principal focus of inter-human relationships by supercharity; the Church, central axis of universal convergence and fixed point of explosive encounter between the Universe and the Omega Point."[59]

Another image frequently recurs in Teilhard, that of the phylum. As naturalist and paleontologist, he naturally borrows from his discipline certain analogies which serve him in thinking about his faith, but performing the same "corrections of analogy"[60] which he always admits in passing from one order of reality to another. For him, Christianity has the structure of a

[57] *Le Christique*, p. 5.

[58] Note of 11 January 1919 (Strasbourg). Letter to the Abbé Gaudefroy, 16 June 1929. See *The Phenomenon of Man*, p. 142, on "the precise *orientation* and privileged axis"; p. 164, "the existence . . . of a definite axis of evolution . . ."; and pp. 180, 227, 292–294.

[59] *Comment je vois*, no. 24.

[60] For there is nothing more false nor more sterilizing than the "pretended uniformity of laws and of forms of evolution to all its degrees," as Teilhard said in *Comment je vois;* this, even within the same order of things (here within geology). See "L'Energie humaine," p. 194.

phylum; it develops from a "revealed nucleus" as a phylum develops. It is a living organism, capable of undergoing extraordinary mutations without losing its substance. In a beautiful formulation, in which I cannot but find a Bérullean tone, he calls it "a phylum of love and Nature."[61] But precisely this phylum ought to have an axis to assure its homogeneous development by maintaining its right direction. This axis, as we have said, is the Church. Its first benefit is to preserve Christ for us. Teilhard makes mention, in a personal note, of his conversation with a friend who "wanted to have Christ without the Church." "But," answered Teilhard, "without the Church, Christ evaporates, or crumbles, or disappears!" Without the Church there is always the pressing menace of "liberalism." Teilhard employs the word pejoratively, as does Newman. The Church alone gives us Christ "in his traditional and *fruitful* form."[62] And she alone assures the growth of the total Christ. All the best that the religious effort of humanity has been able to produce—and all the best that the human effort of progress is still producing—ought to yield to her attraction and gather around her. "The Church is phyletically essential for the achievement of the Human."[63] She is "the axis of universal union," "the very axis upon which the awaited movement of union and convergence can and should be built."[64]

Let us note in passing another "convergence," that which exists between these texts of Teilhard and certain conciliar texts. In article 9 of the dogmatic constitution *Lumen gentium* it is said: "This messianic people, although it does not actually include all men, and may more than once look like a small flock, is nonetheless a lasting and sure seed of unity, hope, and salvation for the whole human race."[65] There is a convergence

[61] *Introduction à la vie chrétienne*, 1944, p. 18; "L'Energie humaine," p. 195.

[62] Note of 4 November 1916. See the letter to Père Auguste Valensin, 31 December 1926: "I find myself in the state of being unable to breathe without Our Lord—and of understanding that without the historical and traditional revelation Our Lord evaporates."

[63] Letter of 16 August 1951.

[64] "Le Goût de vivre," 1950, *Oeuvres* 7, p. 249 n.

[65] *Constitutiones, decreta, declarationes* (1966), ch. 2, pp. 108–109. See ch. 1, p. 93: "Cum autem Ecclesia sit in Christo veluti sacramentum

228

also between both and what we read in the old authors, like St. Ireneus or the author of the Letter to Diognetus. If the "messianic people" always looks like a "small flock," if, through our fault, the little flock seems to be so little "contagious," was the Church of Christ as numerous and powerful when St. Ireneus declared that it was called upon to "animate all creation"?[66] Or when the author of the Letter to Diognetus called the community of Christians the soul of the great body that is the world, capable of keeping it in existence?[67] The audacity of faith is no less evident in Teilhard than it was in these Fathers, or than it is today in the Church.[68]

But if this audacity is not to be an empty utopia, there is one indispensable condition: that the Church remain herself in faithfulness to her Founder and Lord; that her will to live remain intact. "The Church," said Teilhard, "cannot fail to consider herself the very axis, the living and organic axis"; her "liberating spirit" is "indissolubly linked with her existence and corporate organization." She has a "structural requirement." "From all the evidence, if Christianity is destined, as it professes and feels itself to be, the religion of tomorrow," it will not be so, except by fulfilling this requirement.[69] Only in that way will "the uniting properties of the Christian phenomenon" be able to act. Only in that way can the "synthesis between the ancient Credo and the views which have recently emerged in the human conscience continue to be maintained." Only in that way can the universal integration in Christ take place through the ages by "segregation," "convergence," "transformation," and "conversion"—these words are Teilhard's. Only in that way will the Church preserve her "unique power of divinization."[70]

---

et signum et instrumentum intimae cum Deo unionis totiusque generis humani unitatis . . ."

[66] *Adversus haereses* III, 24, 1.

[67] Ch. 6 (*Sources chrétiennes,* 33, 65–67).

[68] Only the dynamic viewpoint of the modern texts is different; it is not explicit in the ancient ones.

[69] "Le Goût de vivre," p. 249. *Introduction à la vie chrétienne,* 1944, p. 19. Note of 4 November 1916.

[70] See de Lubac, *Teilhard missionaire,* pp. 49–51; *Paradoxe et mystère de l'Eglise,* Paris, 1967, pp. 143–146; Teilhard's *Lettres à Léontine Zanta,* Paris, 1965, p. 108.

Nothing is more opposed than this to the idea of a "secular Christianity" which comes to consider nothing but "service of mankind," conceived without reference to God, and which orients thought and the Christian life towards profane reality.[71] Such a "secularism" leads us, if not immediately to the abdication of our faith, at least to a slackening, a bending, and almost to the dissolution of its substance. In any case it quickly reduces to nothing its power of assimilation.[72] Père Teilhard took a contrary position, admiring the strong structure of Catholicism—and more precisely, when the opportunity arose, of Roman Catholicism.[73]

In all his testimony on this subject, one statement is particularly significant. In October of 1948, for the first time in his life, he was called to Rome to hold conversations with his superiors. Although he was received there with much respect, this sojourn must have brought him, on the practical level, nothing but disappointment. He did not fail to note, humorously, the human weaknesses, the backwardness, the illusions he seemed to see in the representatives of the government of the Church.[74] Nonetheless, in the letters he addressed at that time to his friends, the dominant sentiment, compensating for all the rest, is one of profound admiration. Writing from Rome, for example, to

[71] See Jean Ancagne, "Urbanisation et théologie," *Travaux et jours*, Beirut, 1966.

[72] See Bonhoeffer, *The Cost of Discipleship*, London, 1959, pp. 105–107: "Ye *are* the light. . . . Flight into the invisible is a denial of the call. A community of Jesus which seeks to hide itself has ceased to follow him. 'Neither do men light a lamp and put it under a bushel, but on the stand.' . . . The bushel may be the fear of men, or perhaps deliberate conformity to the world for some ulterior motive, a missionary purpose for example, or a sentimental humanitarianism. But the motive may be more sinister than that; it may be 'Reformation theology' which boldly claims the name of *theologia crucis*, and pretends to prefer to Pharisaic ostentation a modest invisibility, which in practice means conformity to the world."

[73] *Introduction à la vie chrétienne*.

[74] "As it presents itself at this moment, this centre or focus of spiritualization completely lacks connection with the human World in movement about it. Around Rome, it is not an iron curtain, but a quilted curtain, which deadens all the noise of discussion as well as human aspirations." Things have changed much since then!

Abbé Henri Breuil, he said: "I have been impressed (and strengthened) by the extraordinary, truly imperturbable, confidence of Christianity in the unshakableness of its Faith and Truth. Here there is a very remarkable phenomenon, on the whole unique in all the world."[75] His impressions were crystallized when he entered St. Peter's. He does not pause to describe the monument, nor to criticize the "orgy of marbles and carvings." The feeling that filled him then, he says, was one of "the security (let us not say 'fixity') of a faith that cannot be confused"; and he adds, "I think this is the principal experience I will bring away from my visit here, and it alone was worth the journey."[76] At St. Peter's, as he later said, constantly using a vocabulary suggested by his scientific thought, "I have truly sensed what is formidable in the Christian phenomenon. I would say it is this assurance, safe from confusion, unique in the modern world, of being in direct contact with a personal Centre of the Universe. This, I repeat, from a planetary and biological viewpoint, is a phenomenon of the highest order, and quite unique."[77] I still recall the profound impression I experienced on receiving his letter. In short, at St. Peter's he recognized in the Church, by a sort of sense evidence, "the Christic pole of the Earth."[78]

For Père Teilhard, the Church is practically a continuous tradition and a present authority. He knew that nothing good could be attempted in the religious sphere without being in continuity with that tradition and without, in the end, receiving the approval of that authority. To mention this here is not only to recall the example given by a true believer; it is to continue

[75] 28 October 1948, *Letters,* p. 302.

[76] To Joseph Teilhard de Chardin, 19 October 1948 (Rome), *ibid.,* p. 300.

[77] To Henri de Lubac, 9 November 1948 (Paris).

[78] To Joseph Teilhard de Chardin, 7 October 1948 (Rome), *Letters,* p. 299. Newman, in *Loss and Gain,* describes the state of mind of his hero Charles Reding on the morrow of his conversion: "It was such as to throw him back in memory on his earliest years, as if he were really beginning life again. But there was more than the happiness of childhood in his heart; he seemed to feel a rock under his feet; it was the *soliditas Cathedrae Petri.*"

to show an essential point of his thought.[79] In fact, nothing was more deeply rooted in him than this twofold conviction, perfectly consistent with his most intimate ideas. "The living tradition of the Church," her "practical instruction," her "universal and practical influence," her "empirical and complex attitude" observed through the centuries, the "marvelous treasury of religious experience" accumulated in her: this is what he wished to trust.[80] He declared himself "absolutely convinced" that there was in this treasury "infinitely more of truth than in all our simplifying philosophies." The practice of the Church, "the solid platform constructed by two thousand years of Christian experience," is for him "the fundamental, the surest course, which all the philosophers can only illustrate, with more or less verisimilitude."[81]

These are not, one rightly suspects, the remarks of a timid conservative devoid of creative imagination. The more Teilhard became conscious of his vocation as a seeker, which made him live "constantly stretching forward,"[82] the more he felt the need to respond to the needs of new times, to enter into new ways, and consequently, the more he felt the need to relate his efforts to the great Christian tradition of all times. When he struggles for the doctrine of the "Universal Christ," it is not to change anything in the apostolic teaching, nor even to add anything; rather, he explains, "I desire with all my strength that the elements of truth universally believed and professed in the Church touching the action and the universal presence of God and of Christ be, in the end, considered in their entirety, without attenuation."[83] If he desires, foresees, and awaits the coming of

[79] It has been said that "the lines of his piety do not match those of his system at all points." The assertion would have to be verified. Here, in any case, it is not only "piety" that is at issue.

[80] Letter of 15 October 1916 in *The Making of a Mind*, p. 132. *The Divine Milieu*, pp. 19, 59. *Lettres à Léontine Zanta*, p. 108.

[81] *The Divine Milieu*, p. 15. See also de Lubac, *Correspondence*, ch. 7; *Teilhard: The Making of a Mind*, p. 302.

[82] See de Lubac, *La Pensée religieuse*, pp. 323–325.

[83] "Mon Univers," 1918, *Ecrits*, p. 279. "I am convinced that the dogmas and practices of the Church have for a long time now placed the elements of this conquest in our hands." He would always return

some "new saint" who will give Christians of our time "the lived formula and the example of a form of adoration and perfection which they vaguely see, but which they cannot formulate for themselves,"[84] he knows perfectly well and shows, for example, in his analysis of the "growth of the Divine Milieu," that this new saint will follow the saints of all times, the saints whose example, "though difficult to rationalize, . . . ought to be the model for our attempts at systematization, and will always outrun them."[85]

Père Teilhard wrote one day to his friend and confidant Père Auguste Valensin: "If I may venture to use a word which could have an unacceptable meaning, I consider myself hypercatholic."[86] It could have more than one acceptable meaning. It indicated first his opposition to the mentality of a certain involuted "Christian world," which transformed into systems and sects what was for him the great universal axis "of progression and assimilation."[87] It could also signify his habitual attitude towards the authority of the Church. If he devoted his life "to the service of the universal Christ," it was, as he made immediately clear, "in absolute fidelity to the Church"[88]; for, "I cannot see Christ except as I myself paint him, . . . but I cling to his integral identity more than to the colors I give him."[89] When in doubt about the value of the results of his reflection—and this happened more than once—or when he found himself faced with a decision against it, he observed

---

"to the better currents of the Catholic Tradition"; see the Introduction to "Forma Christi," 1918, *ibid.*, p. 325. One may debate the success of the enterprise, but it would be wrong to take this as a mere formula, so unconventional is it.

[84] Letter of 25 August 1947 in Cuénot, *Teilhard de Chardin,* p. 403.
[85] de Lubac, *Correspondence,* ch. 7. See *The Divine Milieu,* p. 113.
[86] Letter of 29 June 1926.
[87] In a similar sense, he said further: "The Catholic attitude is exhaustive and synthetic of the charm and of the value of all other doctrines . . .", 20 March 1916.
[88] Letter of 22 September 1954 in Cuénot, *Teilhard de Chardin,* p. 366.
[89] In the Exergue to *Christologie et Evolution,* and on 8 October 1933: "I have decided to sacrifice everything rather than to injure, in me or around me, the integrity of Christ."

simply, "Time and obedience will disentangle more clearly whatever there is of the immortal and the essentially Christian in the ideas that have been censured."[90] He would not risk detaching himself ever so little from the community of the faithful and "becoming the 'tinkling cymbal' that Scripture speaks of."[91] For he knew that he, like all men, was fallible: "How lucky we are to have the authority of the Church! Rudderless, where on our own would we drift?"[92] Let it not be said that he exaggerates. He knew well that the questions of conscience which face a Catholic thinker are not always simple. If sometimes the restrictive measures he was meeting were acceptable as having a serious dimension of their own, they were not always so acceptable in their origins and background. In such cases, when he was dealing with things within his competence, Teilhard maintained (evidently not without turmoil) the proper course. "Do not fear," he confided to a friend on July 13, 1925, "I hope to find the middle term, which seems to be a sort of loving docility towards what there is of truth outside of each of us in the totality of the Church, joined to a sovereign respect for what there is of truth shown to my individual mind. . . . Pray the Lord that he help me to act in these circumstances in conformity with the faith which he gave me and which is what I hold most precious in the world, faith in his omnipresence in all the forces in the world for those who love him."

Meanwhile, he was simply obedient. "I am too sure that the world cannot reach its completion without Christ, and that there is no Christ without fidelity to the Church, for me to experience the least hesitation . . ." (September 25, 1947). He remained faithful to what he wrote one day: "all progress in the Church comes from prayerful, common seeking." In bringing a close to these reflections, may I quote the words which Teilhard's manner of conducting himself inspired in an English author. "Others who seek, these days, to 'bring Christianity up

[90] To Père Valensin, 11 August 1920.

[91] To Père Valensin, 2 April 1930 and 26 February 1933.

[92] To Bruno de Solages in 1935. See de Solages, *Teilhard de Chardin*, p. 341.

to date' by the jettisoning of established doctrine, and in pursuit of contemporary fashions (temporary only, precisely because they are 'contemporary'), destroy the foundations of the Christian religion, would benefit by studying carefully the life and the works of this Jesuit scientist who was maligned at times by some as the archheretic of the age. His acceptance of the restrictions imposed on him . . . represent[s] an object-lesson to us all."[93]

---

[93] Towers, *Teilhard:* "Others who seek, these days, to 'bring Christianity up to date' by the jettisoning of established doctrine, and in pursuit of contemporary fashions (temporarily only, precisely because they are 'contemporary'), destroy the foundations of the Christian religion, would benefit by studying carefully the life and works of this Jesuit scientist who was maligned at times by some as the arch-heretic of the age. His acceptance of the restrictions imposed to him . . . represent an object-lesson to us all."

235

11.

ON BEHALF OF THE HANDMAID

THE encyclical letter of Pope Paul VI, *Ecclesiam suam*, contains an appeal unlike anything I remember reading in any pontifical document. Confronted with the spread of communist atheism, especially under its Marxian form, the Pope, moved by a deep feeling of spiritual distress, directly challenges each and every one of us to bring to a stop the process of the "politico-scientific atheism" that voluntarily refuses to proceed beyond a certain point, and to accept, beyond science, the reality of a universe inhabited by the presence of God. "Will there be no one, among us, victoriously to overcome that alleged duty to stop at a certain point?" In order to break the offensive of that politico-scientific atheism, the Pope thus was charging us with the task of defining "a new affirmation of the supreme God at the level of metaphysics as well as of logic."

These are clear words, but they are also distressing ones. Logic and metaphysics are on the front lines of those maids whom, in the words of Proverbs 9, 3, Wisdom *sent to invite to the tower*. After working at that tower for nearly two thousand years, those handmaids are to be excused for wondering what is wrong with them. Have they failed to find objectively valid demonstrations of the existence of God? If they have failed, what hope is there that we shall convince our own contemporaries that there is for the mind an obligation not to stop at the conclusions that science is able to demonstrate, but rather to proceed beyond the demonstrations of science up to affirmations justified by their sole logical and metaphysical necessity. Particularly disturbing is the obligation laid upon us by the Pope to find a "new affirmation" of God. For indeed, if the old ones are not convincing, what chance have we to discover a more convincing one?

If one is a simple professor of philosophy, who has worked for over sixty years in the service of those noble handmaids, he cannot help feeling personally challenged by the solemn exhortation of the Pope. If we are all called upon to find in logic and in metaphysics, beyond science, a compelling demonstration of the existence of God, how is it that I feel a kind of discouragement before tackling that task? And if I myself have such proofs of God's existence, how is it that what is convincing for me fails to convince the minds of other men? To these questions, I propose to suggest as an answer that perhaps we are expecting from the handmaid more services than she can possibly render, especially given the circumstances under which we are now obliging her to work.

A first remark seems to me of decisive importance. There have been proofs of the existence of God, of some God and, at least, of the gods, but these proofs have never pretended to reveal to men the notion of the divinity; on the contrary, they have all presupposed the common belief in supernatural beings, whose notion had to be purified and whose existence had to be demonstrated by philosophy. Such belief had nothing to do with Christianity, nor with what we call faith, nor with any kind of revelation in the Jewish and Christian sense of the word. A highly instructive witness on this point is Aristotle. Thomas Aquinas makes profession of borrowing from him at least four of the initial propositions of his celebrated *quinque viae;* his own first way in the *Contra Gentiles* is an elaborate dialectical construction integrating elements scattered through the writings of Aristotle himself to the effect that there is one immovable spiritual substance which, as desired for its perfection, moves the world. Aristotle does not exclude the possibility of a plurality of such astronomical gods. At any rate, he is fully conscious of

237

operating a metamorphosis in consequence of which a spontaneous popular belief is raised to the status of a demonstrated scientific certitude. To Aristotle, the whole religious order is mythological; his speculation turns it into a rationally demonstrated system of scientific truths.

Anticipating and justifying beforehand the future attitude of Averroës some fifteen hundred years later. Aristotle already says, in his *Metaphysics* XII, 8, 1074 b: "Our forefathers in the most remote ages have handed down to their posterity a tradition, in the form of a myth, that these bodies are gods and that the divine encloses the whole of nature. The rest of the tradition has been added later in mythical form with a view to the persuasion of the multitude and to its legal and utilitarian expediency. . . . But if one were to separate the first point from these additions and take it alone—that they thought the first substances to be gods—one must regard this as an inspired utterance, and reflect that, while probably each art and each science has often been developed as far as possible and has again perished, these opinions, with others, have been preserved until the present like relics of the ancient treasure."

In reading these lines, if we remember that in the nineteenth century, Catholic theologians consistently opposed "traditionalism" in the name of the peripatetic tradition, we will feel slightly uneasy about the whole situation, for indeed, Aristotle himself accepts the notion of the divinity as handed down to him and to us by more than primitive mythologies. His own job, as a metaphysician, is to establish the existence of a first immobile mover, belonging in a transnatural order and origin of the motion for the universe of the physical bodies. As to proving its divine nature, he does not feel qualified to do so on merely philosophical grounds. Men have always called "gods" those celestial movers, the stars. Whence did that notion of god come to them? Aristotle does not say; he says only that this was with them an "inspired utterance." Obviously, the Philosopher is here nearing the border of a properly religious order, different from that of the metaphysical one. He himself would not have thought of calling gods those first metaphysical substances, if

238

an ancient mythological tradition had not taught him the notion, and the very name, of divine beings.

The case of Aristotle is particularly important because the theology of the Common Doctor of the Church has established intimate relations with his doctrine. In the *Metaphysics* the notion of God antedates by a literally infinite number of millenaries the philosophical and scientific demonstration of his existence. A kind of divine inspiration is the only explanation for the presence of the notion of God to the minds of men whose generations indefinitely succeed one another in an eternally existing universe. Of course, the Christian notion of creation in time, which Thomas holds on faith alone, precludes the possibility of such a traditionalism, but he, too, discreetly proceeds to a distinct operation at the end of each one of the *quinque viae* when, after scientifically demonstrating the existence of a prime term in a given series of essentially ordered terms, he simply concludes: And that is what all men call God. Obviously, the notion of God is anterior to the proofs of his existence; it has been there all the time while the philosopher and theologian was affirming God's existence on the strength of his demonstration.

As long as that primeval notion of God has been present to the minds of men, there have been efficacious demonstrations of the existence of God. In his *Les nourritures terrestres,* the French novelist André Gide devotes one chapter to what he ironically calls "the round dance of the proofs of the existence of God." And indeed, the collection of the classical proofs of God's existence is fairly extensive. The problem has been approached by way of the presence of truth in the mind, of the very notion of God in the mind, of the ordered relations of causes in nature, then of beings, then of means and ends in the universe. A primitive revelation has been invoked, a universal consent of mankind, an immediate evidence of common sense, even the testimony of moral conscience under the form of duty, and so on almost indefinitely. Naturally, the desire to submit new proofs usually suggests a certain dissatisfaction, or incomplete satisfaction with the older ones; yet the older ones have given full satisfaction to their authors. One cannot be more pleased with a demonstration than St. Anselm was with that of the *Proslogion,* of which Thomas suggested that it is not a demonstration at all. On their own side, the authors of the new proofs were rather surprised to see their arguments opposed by other philosophers and theologians old and new. As often as not, they were opposed by the Church: Descartes felt convinced of having demonstrated the existence of God more certainly than any mathematically demonstrated truth, and his name was put on the *Index librorum prohibitorum;* so also was, after him, Nicholas Malebranche, the greatest metaphysician France ever produced and, incidentally, a priest of the Oratory; and after Malebranche, Rousseau and Kant (both of them Protestants); but Bautain, Rosmini, Gioberti (all of them Catholics and priests) have been likewise condemned, not for denying the existence of God, but rather for failing to demonstrate it in an officially approved way—more precisely, for failing to demonstrate it in the way considered by some theologians as the officially approved one. The overall picture of these events suggests a twofold hypothesis: first, that the philosophical certitude of the existence of God is, in a large measure, independent of its demonstrations; next, that the present failure of the same proofs to convince modern minds has little to do with the rise and spread of science. The ancients knew full well the difference between the scientific demonstrations of the mathematico-physicists and the dialectical conclusions of the metaphysicians; still, as has just been seen, an Aristotle did not hesitate to speak of the divinity as of a really existing being. Descartes and Leibniz, two mathematical geniuses of the first magnitude, still remain two classics in the field of natural theology. In our own time, we have seen the perfectly pagan mind of Henri Bergson slowly rediscover the meaning of the notion of God, to the point of expressing his regret at not feeling morally free to ask for the baptism of Christ. And who ever gave evidence of a greater respect for the requirements of scientific demonstration than Bergson constantly did? I have read and studied that man; I have seen and listened to that man. If he was not a kind of philosophical genius, I don't know what the word means. He knew and understood more science than nine-tenths of those who discredit as non-scientific the proofs of the existence of God, and yet he did exactly what *Ecclesiam suam* invites us to do. He showed himself and us that the scientific conception of the modern world of evolution should not stop where it does, but should boldly proceed beyond positive science, blossom into the notion of a cosmos inhabited by the divine presence, and put on our lips the whispered words of a grateful prayer. The *Creative Evolution* of Bergson was naturally put on the *Index librorum prohibitorum,* but for the young Catholics of my generation, that masterpiece achieved its purpose. It established beyond all possible doubt that, even in the twentieth century, the notion of God and the proof of his existence still were meaningful in a mind entirely and exclusively formed by the methods of positive science and of traditional metaphysics. For the philosopher, according to the heart of the pagan Bergson, has always been the pagan Plotinus. Only the pagan Plotinus had a mind naturally turned towards things divine; the presence in him of the notion of God inspired him with the desire to know him better and better; in short, like all the minds open to the notion of God, that of Plotinus, as after him that of Saint Augustine, or, in our own times that of Henri Bergson, was moved by love to investigate the mysterious object inhabiting our thought without our being able to know how it got there. Without claiming any philosophical authority, much less any theological one, I venture to suggest that new proofs for the existence of God will continue to be discovered as long as the human mind will spontaneously conceive the notion of a supreme being and realize it as meaningful. The fact that education and school teaching instill it into us does not make any difference, for in any case a moment comes when each and every one of us is called upon to recognize the truth of the notion and to make it his own by consenting to it. About those who reject it, more will be said presently; just now I am concerned with those who silently consent to it and embrace it in the secret of their hearts. Of such we can be sure that they will

241

delight in finding rational justifications for their inner certitude; hence the extraordinary historical spectacle of the "round dance of the proofs of the eixstence of God." Had I to submit a personal opinion about them, I should say that each of us should be entitled to his own proofs of the existence of God; they all are good inasmuch as they all express a valid experience in the order of the natural religiosity of the human mind. The trouble with the handmaids is that they are quarrelsome. Could they but keep peace among themselves, I should go so far as to say that they all are good. The poorest among them serve their purpose, which is rationally to justify in our own sight our spontaneous certitude in the existence of a God; in short, my advice to theologians is: don't be too hard on the handmaid; she usually does what she can.

Turning now to those of our contemporaries who, speaking of set purpose, deny the validity of all demonstration of the existence of God, I beg to ask them: What do you call a demonstration?

Scientific demonstrations are either experimental or mathematical. An experiment is an observation either provoked, or simply invoked, in order to verify a hypothesis. Now an experiment or an observation is something falling under sense cognition, and since the objects of theological knowledge belong, by definition, in a transphysical order, they escape sense perception. Taking the word experiment in its scientific sense, therefore, there can be no such thing as a metaphysical experiment. All the speculations concerning religious experience and metaphysical experience ultimately relate to personal and intransmissible psychological experiences, or, at most, to intellectual experiences none of which constitutes a properly so-called "experiment." We call "physical" the proofs of the existence of God which, like those of Thomas Aquinas, start from objects of sense knowledge. His reason for preferring them is that, in his Aristotelian noetics, all knowledge has its beginning in sense perception; but no proof of the existence of God, Thomistic or otherwise, concludes on a sense perception of the divine being.

242

Only the mystics claim to have an experience of the divine, but mystical experience is no experiment.

Excellent minds, even apart from Descartes, Malebranche, and Leibniz, have attempted to turn the existence of God into a mathematically demonstrated conclusion, but to no avail; for if we had a mathematically evident demonstration of the existence of God, we should not have to look for a new one. Mathematics is a perfectly formalized language. It is so precisely because its objects are not things, but mental signs created by the mathematician. In a sense, like the God of Aristotle, the mathematical mind is a self-thinking thought. In the words of a contemporary mathematician, "mathematics is radically non-ontological in nature." Again, "mathematics brackets ontology; the mathematical discourse is like unto a net, of which the mesh, however tightly knit, will always let pass the metaphysical fluid." To which the same penetrating mind presently adds: "Perhaps the awareness of the fact explains why great philosophers no longer want to become mathematicians."[1]

After physics and mathematics comes logic. Much of what was considered metaphysical in the Middle Ages, was, in fact, logical demonstration. But true logical reasoning is just as non-ontological as is mathematical reasoning. In the terse words of Thomas Aquinas, "the logician considers the mode of predication of the thing, and not its existence." (In VII *Metaph.*, lect. 17). Now, of course, like all ways of reasoning, theological reasoning must be logically valid in order to be conclusive, but its demonstrative value is not derived from its logical validity. "God or absurdity," a highly esteemed modern theologian used to say. I personally wish it were so, but when it bears upon such notions as those of efficient causality and of being, the metaphysical substance too easily runs free through the mesh of logical reasoning. Had we no other choice than God or logical absurdity, there would be fewer atheists.

After physics, mathematics, and logic, metaphysics remains.

[1] André Lichnerowicz, "L'activité mathématique et son rôle dans notre conception du monde," *Bulletin de la Société française de philosophie,* 59 (1965) 4, pp. 188, 192.

And indeed, the only kind of demonstrations theology can rightly expect are metaphysical demonstrations. Cajetan has been credited with saying that, "without analogy metaphysics is impossible and *a priori* without metaphysics theology is impossible." The nearest approach to this statement I have been able to find in Cajetan himself is the second sentence of his *De nominum analogia*: "*Est quidem ejus [analogiae] notitia necessaria adeo, ut sine illa non possit metaphysicam quispiam discere, et multi in aliis scientiis ex ejus ignorantia errores procedant.*" I beg to disagree with the first part of the proposition: it is perfectly possible to be a metaphysician without subscribing to the analogicity of being. Scotus always rejected it, and he was a metaphysician. But I quite agree with the second part of Cajetan's sentence, and that is precisely the reason why I am not a Scotist. Being can be either univocal or analogical; it cannot be both at the same time. At any rate, neither Thomas, nor Scotus, nor even Cajetan ever said that without metaphysics theology is impossible. Only the speculative theology of the scholastic type is impossible without metaphysics. Thomas Aquinas particularly never said that no theology was possible besides his own. Every medieval theologian was surrounded by other theologians whose theology differed from his own on many points, of which some happened to be important. Moreover, the handmaids themselves introduced an element of diversity, for all of them, and not only metaphysics, were being invited by him to collaborate. Now those liberal arts he had in mind were what we now call the positive sciences, and science is at all times the less stable element of philosophical knowledge. But, at all times, such a scientifically organized theology must ultimately resort to metaphysics, which is the queen of the sciences because it is the knowledge of the principles of human knowledge. So every speculative theology hangs for its truth on that of its own interpretation of the first metaphysical principles. That the speculative theologies should be free does not mean that their truth value is the same, and here we are confronted with what seems to me a distressing yet inescapable fact.

The metaphysical conclusions are valid and cogent only for

244

minds naturally open to the kind of evidence proper to the order of metaphysical notions. Is it fair to ask from the handmaid that she should convince unmetaphysical minds of the cogency of metaphysical demonstrations? Moreover, can it be expected from her that she will succeed in making all metaphysicians see in the same way principles of which the very nature entails that their common truth can be perceived differently because it appears different when seen at different degrees of depth? Many of us know from bitter experience that the possibility of universalizing metaphysical conclusions is limited by the very nature of their demonstrations. We know the sorry plight of the professor in charge of introducing pupils to metaphysics. Confronted with notions which he himself feels hard to grasp and to keep immobile under the gaze of his own intellect, he turns them into logical concepts and engages in a sort of abstract juggling with terms which naturally fails to carry conviction. As they do not understand the real meaning of the words, those who hear the proofs say they are not conclusive. What can the handmaid do with people who, trained from youth to mistake logical reasoning for metaphysical thinking, have become permanently unfit for the practice of prime philosophy? Minds exclusively dedicated to the pursuit of scientific knowledge often find it as difficult to go beyond the point where Pope Paul VI urges them to proceed. In the Preface to his own *Ontologia,* Christian Wolff spoke before Kant of the time when, following the triumph of the Cartesian philosophy, metaphysics became an object of contempt to be ridiculed by all. In the same work (#321), Wolff uses a very penetrating expression: "if Descartes had not been seized by a loathing for metaphysics."[2] In the same spirit the French philosopher Jules Lagneau has rightly observed that "there is no metaphysics in Spinoza; his system is a minimum of metaphysics, just as Judaism is a minimum of theology."[3] Is it fair to ask the handmaid to demon-

[2] *Philosophia prima sive ontologia,* p. 253. The second edition (Leipzig, 1736) was recently reprinted by Georg Olms, Hildersheim, 1962.

[3] *Ecrits de Jules Lagneau* réunis par les soins de ses disciples, Paris, 1924, p. 240.

strate the existence of God to minds still more completely blinded than Descartes and Spinoza to the meaning of metaphysical notions and, like Kant, totally unable to see them?

The same supremely abstract nature of its objects likewise accounts for the apparent disorder that obtains in the field of metaphysical knowledge. The proofs for the existence of God are not wanting; one rather would say, as Gide's irony suggests, that there are too many of them and that a single one would be better, if it were good. But they are all good. Their multiplicity is unavoidable, for all of them ultimately rest on the consideration of being, of which the notion is analogical. Even before descending into the categories, metaphysical being diffracts itself in the transcendentals, which all are being with the addition of a *quatenus,* that mysterious adverb without which prime philosophy would simply not be possible. Hence the rise of several different metaphysics such as those of unity, of truth, of order, of love, and of beauty. Ever since the time of Plato, then of Plotinus, the One has been for philosophers a favourite approach to being.[4] Because it goes deeper into the reality of being, the Thomistic approach is the better one, but it ultimately justifies all the other approaches to the problem. The theological pluralism often denounced, and regretted, by modern theologians is perhaps less real than it appears to be. At any rate it certainly is more superficial than the bitterness of the doctrinal controversies between theological schools invites to believe. Though formally different, the proofs of Augustine, Boethius, Anselm, Bonaventure, Thomas, and Scotus are more mutually complementary than opposed, because the root of their differences lies in the metaphysical possibility of various transcendental approaches to being.[5] The metaphysics of Saint

[4] See *Being and Some Philosophers,* ch. I, "On Being and the One."

[5] This would be best substantiated by an analysis of St. Bonaventure's *Itinerarium mentis in Deum,* wherein the two names of God, Good and Being, are successively related to Plato and Aristotle, wisdom and science and, in fine, Moses and John. I still am of the opinion that Thomas was right in subordinating Good to Being, but the meditation of Bonaventure vividly exemplifies the virtual pluralism inherent in the metaphysics of being.

246

Thomas is absolutely true, not by mode of exclusion, but of inclusion, for the notion of being permits it to justify all the other ones, whereas no other one, taken by itself, is able to justify it.

To conclude, leaving aside the men suffering from a sort of congenital metaphysical blindness and whose antiphilosophism is incurable,[6] and even granting (*dato non concesso*) that the modern school system will turn out a much larger number of

[6] At that level, it is possible to subscribe to the remarks recently made by an author quite favorably disposed towards Thomism: "I fail to see why such systems as nominalism, Kantian and Hegelian idealism, even positivism could not, despite the peril of deviations they present, provide a certain understanding of faith." Jean-Marie Paupert, *Peut-on être Chrétien aujourd'hui?*, Paris, 1966, p. 190. I should go so far as to say that, if it helps them to believe, and if no better philosophy is intelligible to them, those who find satisfaction in such doctrines should not be disturbed in their peace of mind. I once knew a priest for whom philosophical truth was the system of Octave Hamelin. I knew two others to whom Occamism gave full satisfaction, including Occam's opposition to the temporal authority of the popes. Abbé Bautain took pleasure in the thought that, according to Kant, there are no demonstrations of the existence of God. It seems to me that, nearer to us, Auguste Valensin, S.J. is of similar opinion: "Ethics demands God as it demands my personal immortality." Since for him nothing can be more solid than this affirmation, he goes on: "I shall believe in God as long as I shall believe in the absolute character of Good and Evil. One does not progress in the understanding of the moral proof through a dialectical *processus* and an exercise of the understanding, but by keeping faith with Duty; here sight is solidary with life" (*Auguste Valensin, textes et documents inédits*, Paris, 1961, p. 217). Unfortunately, like all those who share this disposition of mind (since the time of Martin Luther), Valensin is anxious not to understand in order that he may believe. He is inclined to feel that faith is in inverse proportion to understanding: "If there were a demonstration capable of convincing unbelievers, one could teach belief as one teaches the sciences. This would be unseemly" (p. 389). I am not now concerned with the almost obtuse misconception of the problem which underlies such remarks. My point here, however, is that, while a Thomist is willing to let every man go to God as best he can, men like the above are unwilling to let anyone go to God the way Thomas recommends and the Church prefers. Their anti-Thomistic intolerance is rooted in a radical anti-intellectualism which is perfectly consistent with personal salvation, but which does not foster the peace that proceeds from wisdom. Were it not that the issues at stake were so all-important, one might find more than one comical side to the situation.

qualified metaphysicians than could be done by the mediaeval universities, there is no reason to hope that the proportion of the metaphysically gifted minds will not remain the same.[7] At a time when the disinterested nature of true scientific knowledge is less and less appreciated, the contemplative vocation of the metaphysical speculation will be less and less understood. We already have a *pop-psy;* we shall perhaps have to do with a *pop-the.* However, the theologian cannot feel entirely responsible for the difficulties of the situation.

In his remarkable tract *On Humanism,*[8] Martin Heidegger has multiplied the warnings against the peril. Ever since it has lost its primitive autonomy, as a speculative discipline, to the benefit of doing and of making, philosophy has felt the need to justify its existence in the sight of the sciences; metaphysics itself is haunted by the fear of losing caste if it is not considered a scientific discipline: "Not to be a science is resented by philosophy as a deficiency." The mark of its shame is "not to be a science." To which Heidegger adds: "As an element of thought, being is allowed to get lost in that technical interpretation of

---

[7] See "Thomas Aquinas and our Colleagues," in Anton C. Pegis, *A Gilson Reader,* New York, 1957, pp. 279–297. My excuse for quoting myself is that those pages which I did then and still do take very seriously, have often been mistaken for some sort of paradoxical joke. But the fact is that the problem is almost tragic. How much good, or harm, has been done, and is still being done, by teaching to the millions what are alleged to be demonstrations, but which neither students nor, in some cases, masters really understand? I think the "five ways" provide valid openings for all metaphysically gifted and trained minds. But each way is a proposed plan for personal meditation, each successive step of which requires a distinct effort of assimilation. The formal necessity of the reasoning, though required, *is not the substance of the proof.* Because so many students fail to grasp the meaning of the ways and are aware of their failure, they turn to any pseudo-scientific theology, even to atheistic Marxism, and with it undertake to "carry on a dialogue." But Marxism is resolved to concede nothing, because the slightest concession to any form of theism would mean its own death. Of course, there are rational approaches to the problem of God. These should be taught as rational approaches not as *scientific proofs,* nor as *metaphysical demonstrations.* There are such demonstrations indeed, and first of all the "five ways." But they are conclusive to metaphysical minds only. To provide a pedagogical answer to the question escapes the competence of the metaphysician.

[8] M. Heidegger, *Über den Humanismus,* Paris, 1957.

248

thought. *Logic,* as the sanction of that interpretation, was at work already at the time of the Sophists and of Plato. We now judge thought after a standard not appropriate to it." And more significantly still: "That way of judging it is like pretending to appreciate the nature and the capabilities of fishes from their ability to live on dry land. For an already long time, for much too long a time indeed, thought has been stranded."[9]

It is not in our power to make metaphysics easily accessible to the millions. At any rate, that would be a way back to being, not to God. The only true way to God, apart from faith in a supernatural revelation, starts from the fact that man is a religious animal for the very same reason that he is a rational animal. His mind naturally produces the notion of some divinity. Even granting that the notion of God comes to us from society, we must still explain whence it came to society itself. The old notion of the *consensus universalis* has long been mistaken for a proof of God's existence. It is no such thing, but it is very important, for it provides the basis on which all the proofs of the existence of God can be erected. It is not a demonstration, but rather that which the metaphysical reason undertakes to demonstrate. Nothing is more able than religion to keep that notion alive in the hearts of men; nothing is better qualified than theology to strengthen in us the desire to understand its meaning[10]; only metaphysics can provide for us such an understanding, but even the noblest of the handmaids cannot serve if we first oblige her to abdicate her own essence, to cease to be metaphysics in order to make herself a science of nature, and to work, as a formal logic, for a dead wisdom instead of the living wisdom it makes profession of serving.

9 *Op. cit.,* pp. 28–30.
10 To those who are leaning backwards lest they fall into "fideism," I beg to quote Vatican I on this precise point: "*Huic divinae revelationi tribuendum quidem est, ut ea, quae in rebus divinis humanae rationi per se impervia non sunt, in praesenti quoque generis humani condicione ab omnibus expedite, firma certitudine et nullo admixto errore cognosci possint*" (Denz., 3005). The notion, as well as its justification by the divine design to ordain man to his supernatural end, are borrowed by Vatican I from Thomas Aquinas, *Summa theologiae,* I, 1, 1. See *Summa Contra Gentiles,* I, 4.

12.

THE NOTION OF MAN
IN THE CONTEXT OF RENEWAL

ANTON C. PEGIS

1.

UNDER a very large title I propose to consider a limited but important question. What does St. Thomas's notion of man, which is today some seven hundred years old, have to contribute to the theology of the Church in the modern world? The question needs to be asked for many reasons, but especially because St. Thomas's influence and popularity have noticeably declined in the last two decades. It is, of course, easy to lose contact with St. Thomas across seven hundred years, and to experience many misdirections in trying to return to him. What is certain is that the road back to St. Thomas himself and to his world has proved difficult for historians to follow. Many things in the world of St. Thomas have been dead for centuries. What can we find in his pages if we return to them and try to understand what he has to say about man, and especially about the unity of the human person?

We can agree, certainly, that we are not living in the world of St. Thomas, if this means that we are not living in the Aristotelian physical universe. Galileo destroyed it in the sixteenth century, Descartes in the seventeenth, and Newton at the turn of the eighteenth. But even in the thirteenth century, St. Thomas was not living—and did not intend to live—in the Aristotelian world such as Aristotle had created it in his classical writings.

250

St. Thomas did not live in an eternal and divine world, forever re-enacting its divine sameness. He lived in that mysterious world of creatures in which the first mystery was the reason for its existence. He lived, in other words, in the Christian world of salvation, in the mystery of the kingdom of God in history, and in the promise of eternal beatitude that the Incarnation had thrust into history. This was St. Thomas's world as a Christian theologian, and were he alive today this is the world that he would be trying to help us to understand. And this is what we have forgotten. We remember St. Thomas's Aristotle and his extraordinary loyalty to this man whom, along with his age, he called the Philosopher; we remember his Aristotelian language, methods, and procedures; we remember his willingness to find a remarkable harmony between revealed truth and Aristotelian philosophy, and therefore between philosophy as such and Aristotle as its spokesman. Unfortunately, in the process of remembering the externals of St. Thomas's historical engagement, we have forgotten the engagement itself, the character of the Thomistic theological synthesis, and especially how and to what end St. Thomas held that synthesis together.

It has proved a disservice to St. Thomas that he has been treated for so many centuries by his disciples as though he were both a theologian and a philosopher, and the main victim of that disservice is the very Thomistic philosophy traditionally constructed in isolation from, and outside, the theological world in which it was originally born. That St. Thomas had a philosophy within his theology, functioning as an intellectual instrument within a religious world that was beyond its grasp and perspective, is not in question. After all, this is what, in principle, any scholastic theology is: it is revelation, incarnated in a human intelligence, talking to men in the language of *being*. What is in question is the character of that philosophy, and the exact role it played in its theological engagement. If we are to believe St. Thomas himself, everything that he wrote in the *Summa Theologiae* is there *sub ratione Dei*.[1] This applies to

---

[1] See St. Thomas Aquinas, *Summa Theologiae,* I, q. 1, a. 7; II–II, q. 1, a. 1; for an interpretation, see A. C. Pegis, "Sub Ratione Dei," *The New Scholasticism,* 39, 2 (April, 1965), pp. 141–157.

such topics as the existence and perfection of God, creation, man, beatitude, freedom, and virtue. Of themselves, these topics can be philosophical subjects; but in the *Summa,* directed by the theologian's vision and purpose, which are the source of their existential status and condition, they are not and they cannot be treated as the product of a philosophical investigation philosophically conducted.

There have not been wanting voices among Thomists to defend the view that St. Thomas was a theologian and not a philosopher, and to argue that we can neither take his philosophy out of its theological context nor present it in a philosophical order that he himself never created. Etienne Gilson has been saying for years that St. Thomas was a theologian who had a philosophy in his theology, but that he was not a philosopher. On this basis, the eminent Thomist has refused, from the first to the sixth and latest edition of *Le Thomisme,* in other words, for a period of almost fifty years, to present Thomism in any but its theological form and order. As for Jacques Maritain, the self-styled old peasant of the Garonne, he said in 1960, with particular reference to "Thomistic philosophy," that a philosophy pieced together from theological excerpts and fragments was neither theology nor philosophy, but dead theology; and in his more recent and remarkably energetic *Le Paysan de la Garonne,* with reference to the same "Thomistic philosophy," he has accused Thomists of not recognizing that St. Thomas had a theologized philosophy, in other words, a philosophy that did not have an autonomous mode of existence in the work of its author. Enveloped by the theological purpose of St. Thomas himself, its role was to be the servant of its sacred mistress.[2]

There are many things that we owe to both Gilson and Maritain, but their meeting on the point that St. Thomas was a theologian and had a philosophy whose very form was dictated by its theological existence and employment, is certainly among our greater debts to them. If, as seems to be the case, the

[2] J. Maritain, *La Philosophie morale,* Paris, 1960, p. 8; *Le Paysan de la Garonne,* Paris, 1966, pp. 196–208, but the whole chapter (pp. 189–253) is eminently worth pondering by Thomists.

"Thomistic philosophy" that was made up of theological excerpts is dying in our day, the philosophy that continues to exist within the theological synthesis of St. Thomas remains intact. The question before us is the character of that philosophy in its own setting and its relevance to us in our world and in our day. Let us consider this question in relation to the problem that, in the opinion of M.-D. Chenu, dominated all others in the meeting between Christianity and Aristotelianism in the thirteenth century.[3] I refer to the problem of the nature and unity of the human person.

2.

It is scarcely necessary at this date to review all the well-known and much discussed positions that St. Thomas had the daring to create on the unity of the human person. In itself, the unity of soul and body was an old Christian doctrine, but in the thirteenth century it became associated with a new formula, namely, the Aristotelian doctrine of form and matter. Henceforth, the question of the unity of man and of his nature was not merely a question of saying that soul and body were essential parts of the human person. In a world dominated by the teaching, the method and the language of Aristotle, it was also necessary to explain human unity in technical metaphysical terms, and to say that, in his substance, man was an essential unity in that the soul was related to the body as form to matter. This is what St. Thomas did. Having done so, he faced two problems, namely, to defend his position as authentically Aristotelian and to justify it as a philosophical possibility. His defense is as well known as it is astonishing. Giving to Aristotle the benefit of his own metaphysics, St. Thomas created that most remarkable of philosophers, the Christian Aristotle, and unless you read him carefully you can easily conclude from him that Aristotle held the doctrine of an individual immortal soul informing the

[3] M.-D. Chenu, O.P., *La Parole de dieu, II: L'Evangile dans le temps,* Paris, 1964, pp. 428–429.

human body and constituting man himself by their unity. The Thomistic Aristotle evidently held such a doctrine, and it is also a fact that the doctrine exactly suited the nature of the Christian man as a being composed of an incorruptible soul and an organic body. But, in fact, it took a Thomistic grounding to make this doctrine possible, and St. Thomas not only created such a metaphysical foundation as the basis of his own teaching,[4] he was also generous enough to endow Aristotle's *De Anima* with it.[5] The foundation said that the human soul, having as a subsistent creature received its own act of existence, could and did share that act with the body. The body, in other words, existed in and by the existence that the soul had received from God and exercised in its own right. Clearly, such a doctrine was possible in a universe in which the religious name of God as He Who Is (Ex. 3, 14) was interpreted in metaphysical terms as the pure act of being.[6] This was the universe of St. Thomas Aquinas. In it the traditional Christian notion of a creature became, when seen in metaphysical terms, the notion of that which exists with a total, immediate, and unique dependence on God for its being.[7]

When St. Thomas came to present his conception of the nature of man in the *Summa Theologiae* he did so explicitly as a theologian.[8] This point of view required him, as he thought, to begin the study of man with the soul, on the ground that a theologian was interested in the human body only on the basis of his interest in the soul. St. Thomas therefore proved that the human soul was subsistent because intellectual, as well as immaterial and incorruptible,[9] before he went on to prove that

[4] See especially *Summa Contra Gentiles,* II, cc. 46–55.

[5] At the very beginning of his commentary on Aristotle's *De Anima* St. Thomas introduces an explanatory parenthesis whose effect is to make his own metaphysics of *esse* the foundation of the notion of the soul as form in Aristotle's text. See St. Thomas, *In Aristotelis Librum de Anima,* I, lect. 1–2, nos. 1–30, especially lect. 2, nos, 18–20.

[6] St. Thomas, *Summa Contra Gentiles,* I, cc. 22 and 28.

[7] *Ibid.,* II, cc. 15–21.

[8] *Summa Theologiae,* I, qq. 75, 78, 84.

[9] *Ibid.,* I, q. 75, aa. 2, 5, 6.

this human soul was (in the technical formula of Aristotle) the unique and immediate substantial form of the human composite.[10] The outcome of this procedure is not in doubt as far as St. Thomas's intentions are concerned. He intended, as a Christian theologian, to make Aristotle an acceptable spokesman for philosophy in the Christian world. He likewise intended to write a theology of man, that is to say, to present a religious interpretation of his existence as a creature, his pursuit of beatitude in the name of his intellectual nature, and his life as a pilgrim within the world of faith. But these Thomistic intentions seem to have been lost in the course of history.

It is obviously too late to argue about St. Thomas's Christian Aristotle. Since this Thomistic creation does not represent the Aristotle of history, it will always be possible to argue that St. Thomas was unfaithful to the historical Stagirite. And yet this is a little less than an adequate view of the matter. St. Thomas was not responsible for the coming of Aristotle into the Christian world of the thirteenth century, nor did he precipitate the new meeting between paganism and Christianity that the coming of Aristotelian philosophy represented. What he did create was a Christian theological answer to it. Believing as a theologian that nature and reason were so constituted by God that, if they followed their proper bent, they would gravitate towards God as to the source of their perfection and destiny, St. Thomas likewise believed that the proper way to represent philosophy within the world of the Christian revelation was to locate it as proceeding always towards the world of revealed truth. If grace perfected nature and faith perfected reason, what could Aristotle with all his great truths be but a spokesman for philosophy leading the human pilgrimage towards the Christian city? In principle, this is how things ought to be. At least, this is how St. Thomas decided the matter. The pagan shortcomings of Aristotle, of which he was aware but on which he did not always insist, stand in a purified light within the Thomistic theology. As a theological creation, St. Thomas's Aristotle is an ancient philosopher freed of his historical limitations and enjoying the

[10] *Ibid.,* I, q. 76, aa. 1, 3, 4, 6, 7.

daylight of a purer rationality in the world of revelation. If it is true that the theologian has the religious mission to save truth, rather than to argue with the philosophers at their own level of discussion, why is not the Thomistic Aristotle both an answer to a thirteenth-century problem and, what is more enduring, a monument to a theologian's vision of the role and the life of philosophy within the dispensation of faith?

But if we find it difficult to recapture St. Thomas's theological motives in recreating the philosophy of Aristotle, the reason is not merely that we have forgotten the far-away world of the thirteenth century and its problems. We have also forgotten something else, namely, the fact that even in philosophy St. Thomas aimed to be a theologian. The so-called treatise on man in the first part of the *Summa Theologiae,* far from being a philosophy of man, as many interpreters continue to suppose, is a theologian's first step in a religious vision of man whose proportions are so vast that we can scarcely see the theological edifice as a whole. Yet it remains that the whole second part of the *Summa* is devoted to man's life. It is devoted to his search for beatitude, his freedom, the passions that he must deal with in himself, the spiritual world of virtue and vice, the providential government of God that rules him in the depth of his mind, and the grace that he needs to stand erect before his creator. We are here face to face with all the mysteries of the human person living as a spiritual creature in the presence of a God who precedes and guides all his steps. But there is more. Having seen man in search of beatitude within the world of the divine providence, we go on to an even vaster journey in the world of faith. Now we meet the mysteries of the divine love openly present within human history; we meet God himself who, as St. Thomas has said, crossed from eternity to time in order that man might not despair in his journey from time to eternity.[11] The whole second part of the *Summa Theologiae* is St. Thomas's theology of the life of man, dominated by the needs of his intellectual nature responding to—and opening itself within—the transcendent invitation of God's love.

[11] St. Thomas, *Summa Contra Gentiles,* IV, c. 54, no. 2.

256

The treatise on man is not a philosophical prelude to St. Thomas's theology of man, it is an internal part of that theology. It is not as such a philosophy of man, except materially speaking; that is to say, it contains and uses notions drawn from philosophical sources, and chiefly from Aristotle. This procedure does not constitute a philosophy of man. Writing as a theologian, St. Thomas did not aim to make a philosophical synthesis out of his philosophical materials. He aimed, more than anything else, to construct what I can only call a metaphysical model of man, an ontological structure in which we can see man in his absolute location within reality rather than in the specificity of his nature. St. Thomas explains to us how man is one in his existence because the human composite exists wholly within the existence of the soul, and how it is possible for him to be composite in his powers and mode of operation. If man is intelligent and free, still he earns his intellectual bread and his moral freedom in and through the world of the senses and the passions. He lives on the borderline of two worlds, the spiritual and the material, and his intelligence descends by nature into the world of bodies in order that he may build there the transcendent edifice that he is as a human person. This is man, a creature somehow straddling the two worlds of spirit and matter within his own nature and even the worlds of eternity and time within his own life. What St. Thomas did with the metaphysical vision of man that he created was to go on and study it in purely religious terms within the world of the Christian revelation. He was interested in the Christian pilgrim; he was only indirectly interested in man as a philosopher, and only incidentally did he venture into philosophical explanations that went beyond his direct business as a theologian, namely, to elucidate in metaphysical terms how an intellectual and immortal soul could inform an organic body and constitute the reality that we call man.

If we read the treatise on man as a purely philosophical document we shall not only disfigure the purpose that St. Thomas had in mind. We shall do something more: we shall miss the explanation of human nature and human unity that St. Thomas goes on to give within the world of salvation. The meaning of human unity is there, as in a mirror, revealed in the religious world that contains man's destiny. True enough, the explanation that St. Thomas gives of man is that of a theologian, and in the world of revelation; it is therefore a religious account of the meaning of man. But if we follow this account on its own ground, we shall see that, by his participation in the world of faith to which he has been raised, man unfolds and so reveals his nature within the divine history to which he is struggling to respond. It is no secret that the Christian man, living with faith in the divine revelation and with hope in the divine promise, is a wayfarer in the world of time. Time, history, and the earth are a temporary dwelling place for him. But if we are to understand St. Thomas's view of man we must notice an astonishing phenomenon. Man is a pilgrim in the world of time and history not only because of his transcendent Christian calling, but also because of his own nature. His pilgrimage, as St. Thomas sees it, is twofold, namely, to God and to himself.

It is not always easy to see the philosophical implications of St. Thomas's notion of the unity of man. He did not bother to spell them out, and very often we have to content ourselves with a lapidary statement that he offers in reply to some objection. Yet the roots of human unity, as St. Thomas understands it, lie within the very essence of the soul, and in the soul they lie in its total intellectual poverty. The soul is not only barren of knowledge by nature, but experience and observation show that it is radically dependent on the senses, on the body, and on time for the intellectual and moral culture that it needs to acquire. To St. Thomas, discursiveness belongs to the human intellect by its very nature; it must externalize itself by slow steps in the world of bodies so that, through the passage of time, it may build an intellectual civilization within itself. And what we are here saying of the intellect must be said of the world of human liberty: it must be won by a life of deliberation and choice achieved through growth in moral virtue. The Thomistic man, then, is a temporal sort of being within the soul itself, and this temporality is the reason for his compositeness. The body is the instrument and the vehicle of man's spiritual temporality, and the world of time and space is his natural home —indeed, it is a part of him, as he is a part of it. He belongs in the universe of bodies not merely or primarily because he himself has a body, but, before anything else, because he has an intellectual nature that can exist only by creating itself in a personal history in the world of matter and time.

We shall not grasp St. Thomas's view of the unity of the human person unless we see and explore a phenomenon that St. Thomas, because he was a theologian, examined only within the world of faith and with the message of the Christian revelation as the ground on which he stood. If we are to find him at all, we must look for the Thomistic man in the world of faith, where St. Thomas examined his life as a pilgrimage to a supernatural beatitude; but if we observe man in that world we shall see not only his destiny but also the secret of his nature. That strange human composite of soul and body, which has been the despair of philosophers from Plato to Merleau-Ponty, was to St. Thomas a historical and temporal intelligence. Time is the measure of man's intellectual rhythm, and to say that man is a composite of soul and body and that he is a temporal intelligence are for St. Thomas one and the same thing. Temporality is of the essence of man, but it begins by being a spiritual temporality, and it is the source of human compositeness. Man belongs, in the name of the temporality of his intelligence, in the world of time, history, matter, and motion. He is part of what we call the world of nature, for nature both completes him and helps him to complete himself in the most intimate part of his being, his intellect and its internal life. Such is the vision of man's nature that St. Thomas the theologian, writing the religious history of man in the world of salvation, has included within his theology. It is this spiritual temporality with which St. Thomas clothed his metaphysical model of man.

3.

At the center of the Thomistic notion of the nature of human unity there lies a metaphysical perspective that it is easier to see in its origins than to measure in its consequences. Man is one in existence and nature because he exists in and through the existence of the soul and the soul contains the total explanation of his compositeness. His unity of nature hangs on this explanation, and St. Thomas is nothing if not consistent in arguing for a radical proportion between soul and body in the constitution of human unity. There is a proportion of the human body to the intellectual soul; the body is the instrument of the sensibility that the soul needs for its intellectual life. In turn, the intellectual soul is proportioned to the human body, so that its life finds its natural expression in the world of sensibility and its bodily organs. But we must go farther than merely to notice that such a doctrine is deeply indebted to Aristotle's theory of form and matter; to say the least, Aristotle, the author of the doctrine, had considerable difficulty in applying it to the case of man. Not so St. Thomas. The proportion of soul and body to one another in his teaching is there to prove that he saw within man's strange compositeness a unitary world made of spirit and matter, which was neither just the one nor the other, nor a sum of the two, but a new world—one in which matter is assumed into the world of spirit in order to complete it, and spirit lives through and within matter in order to achieve its completion. This is man, a spirit joining the world of matter—indeed, the world of nature—to himself in order to realize his nature and his destiny by that union. He is part of nature and nature is part of his life. He is a temporal and historical being, achieving in and through time the making of himself. But if we say these things of man, let us notice that, for St. Thomas, these characteristics belong to the soul before they belong to the body. Man is part of nature in the name of his intellectuality, and he is a historical and temporal being in the name of the same intellectuality. It is here that the consequences of the Thomistic notion

260

of the unity of human nature need to be considered carefully if they are to be understood and to function within the modern world.

To say that soul and body are proportioned to one another in man is to say, in principle, that the human soul has the nature to live in matter, to be part of the history of the world of matter and indeed to belong within that history as in its natural complement and environment. But to say that the human soul belongs in such a universe—let us even call it an evolving universe, one in which its history is part of its structure—and to say it in the name of the soul's own intellectual nature, is to say that the human soul is itself such that to be a part of an evolving universe of matter is the answering counterpart to the evolutionary history that is written in its own spiritual nature. I do not know what St. Thomas would have said to any theory of evolution or of man's place in an evolving universe. Nor am I here attributing to him an evolutionary theory of the human body or of the human soul. I say only that, if you accept St. Thomas's notion of the unity of human nature and try to think about it in its own terms but within the framework of the modern world, you must adopt not only an evolutionary view of the human body but also an evolutionary view of the intellectual nature of the human soul itself. There is, so to speak, a dual evolution in man, that of the soul and that of the body, and the second answers to the first and finds there its reason as a human phenomenon.

The Thomistic notion of man carries with it a decision of principle which is for this very reason a radical one but whose radicalness we are able to see much more clearly in the modern world than in the world of St. Thomas. The Aristotelian physics that St. Thomas knew was certainly dynamic, but it was just as certainly not evolutionary in its conception of nature or of the physical universe at large. Nature did not have a history and St. Thomas, even in thinking of man as part of nature, did not think of him as part of a history internal to nature. If man had a history and was himself a historical sort of being, this was true for St. Thomas eminently in the world of salvation, where, in being saved by God, man also achieved the perfection of his nature. But St. Thomas did not say that man was part of nature and its history in the sense in which such a notion has become familiar since the beginning of the nineteenth century. Even so, what he did say about the unity of human nature is such that not only is it open to including the notion of man within an evolving universe, it also grounds the place of man in such a universe in an intellectual soul that, of its own nature, is proportioned to living within the world of matter.

Thus, the *human* unity of man and nature is the first and most far-reaching consequence of the Thomistic conception of the oneness of soul and body in man. Man is part of the world's history because the world is part of his nature and history. In a sense unknown to St. Thomas, but not unknown to his principles, man is part of nature and nature is part of him. Its history is part of his own and, precisely, his history is part of the history of the universe. Within nature, but on spiritual grounds, man is a historical being. In order to be a man, he must become a man, and he becomes one by making himself into one. But he cannot become a man within himself unless he exteriorizes himself in the world of matter and time. He civilizes the face of the earth as the means of civilizing himself and coming thereby a little nearer to the dream and the mystery of his destiny beyond time. He cannot divorce himself from the world in which he becomes himself any more than he can divorce himself from himself. He must therefore think of his destiny as including both himself and the world in which he has become himself. In the kingdom of salvation he is not alone, since the earth is part of him and with him.

Such is the Thomistic doctrine of human unity if we make some effort to consider the philosophical implications of its principles. Here, it seems to me, we are standing at a crossroad where it is important to know both where we have come from and where we are going. We have come from the Thomistic theology, in which St. Thomas's philosophy reached its fruition in purely religious terms. Those who divorce the Thomistic explanation of the unity of man's existence and nature from the religious fulfillment of that explanation in the life of the Christian man as St. Thomas sees him, will have missed his account of the meaning of the human composite. Human nature is a historical and temporal reality in the very proportion of soul to body. It needs and has bodily exteriorization in the world of matter and time in order to achieve the spiritual and moral history that will be its nature. If God made man a spiritual wayfarer to a supernatural beatitude, he began by making him such a wayfarer in his very nature. He gave him a nature that was a pilgrimage to itself, but that could not reach its goal without also reaching God. God made man a mind with a brain and a body, so that he might think in matter and thus awake slowly to the spirituality of his composite nature. Human compositeness is for St. Thomas a spiritual phenomenon in man, matter is for man a necessary spiritual vehicle, and the human body itself is the instrument of man's visible but spiritual presence in the world of matter and time.

This Thomistic notion of man has many implications that are waiting to be explored, but perhaps on the present occasion the most appropriate one to consider is the spiritual union of man with nature. Not only is man part of nature in the world in which we are living, but, by his art and his technology, man is today helping to remake nature. Nature is becoming more and more the world of man himself, and his presence in nature is that of a maker and even a creator. Man's intelligence is mirrored and embodied in the instruments that are now modifying the world around us and giving to it human functions and human purposes. But in thus humanizing nature, man is also extending himself. He is filling nature with human structures and human purposes; he is filling nature with himself and with his life. Is not nature today beginning to be an extension of man's body, the technological organ through which he unfolds and creates his own humanity? And is not the Thomistic account of the unity of man's nature, especially the radical spiritualism of its metaphysical basis, expressive of this very spiritual union of man and nature as it is taking shape in the world in which we are living?

If the mystery of salvation, which is the object of the theo-

263

logian's meditation, is to reach man with the message of Christ and clothe him with its purpose, today it needs to reach him in the wholeness and fullness of his human world. No theology can speak of man or to man today unless it touches him in his unity with that world of nature which is more and more a part of his history and therefore a part of his own being, and which is reflecting more and more his own spiritual engagement within it. Surely, we are in search of a theology of man in which his spiritual union with matter, beginning with the matter of his own body and extending across the earth towards outer space, is the central and paramount reality. We need a theology of man in which, if I may use the language of a great but anguished modern thinker, there is a communion of man with God across the earth.[12] Such is the Thomistic theology of man as a spirit using hands to do a spiritual work, standing on the earth to build a spiritual presence in matter, and humanizing the world of nature with his intelligence in order to humanize himself. This is the theological vision that the Church needs if, in this ecumenical age, she is to open herself with a fullness that matches the desire of her heart, to the world of man and to man himself.

[12] Pierre Teilhard de Chardin, *Lettres à Léontine Zanta,* Paris, 1965, p. 99 (letter dated Peking, 15 April 1929).

13.

CONTEMPORARY RENEWAL AND THE JEWISH EXPERIENCE

STUART E. ROSENBERG

JUDAISM, for many centuries now, has been of little interest to those outside of the Jewish community. Its spiritual content had not been probed, nor even regarded with seriousness. Nor was much attention paid to the unique life-habits of its single bearers, the Jewish people. Indeed, both Judaism and the Jewish people were regarded as anachronistic relics of a surpassed time, not as a relevant part of a contemporary reality destined to inherit a future.

All this has changed. We live in a time when the world expects something from Judaism.

That Christians, foregathered to ponder the future shape of their own religious vitality, should be seeking out the Jewish historical experience for possible meanings and even guidelines, is nothing less than revolutionary. This, in the face of the last twenty centuries, is in itself a remarkable statement of their faith—that "Christian renewal" means to reopen questions whose older answers will not do, if they have brought hurt and not healing. It clearly and boldly suggests that classical positions which have long governed the world's attitude to Judaism and the Jewish people are no longer tenable.

What is at the heart of this major change? Is it principally the result of intramural scholarly and spiritual forces at work within the Church? Or is it, rather, a force at work from the outside towards the Church—the highly visible, if often enigmatic fact of contemporary Jewish renewal? Both questions, in fact, become one, and both are answerable as one. Christian renewal is related to Jewish renewal, and the former can be deepened by a sensitive awareness of the latter. Thus many Christians who wish to relate their faith to modern reality now feel called upon to demythologize older views of Judaism and Jews, and to seek instead new ways of facing the continuing contemporaneity of eternal Israel.

To begin with, let us pose the fundamental question. Which special hour, what dominant ideological elan and spiritual shape, which long-lived force in its millennial history, are most responsible for powering Judaism's recurring capacity for revitalization? Those Christians who now willingly and eagerly ask this question will come face to face with nothing less than the paradoxical nature of Jewish history when it is viewed with classical Christian eyes. Christianity grew up in the religious soil of Rabbinic Judaism. Yet from that time until the present, most Christians have regarded the Judaism of the Rabbis as unbiblical, arid, even sterile—the unmistakable hour and portent of the irreversible decline and fall of Judaism from the spiritually high place it had reached in the earlier biblical epoch. Nevertheless, it is precisely the spirit, teachings, and concepts of Rabbinic Judaism which in its time first made possible, and which in every succeeding age have continued to ensure the evolving, self-renewing religious civilization of the Jewish people. It thus becomes our special task to fathom something of this unique Jewish deep which became the major source of all waves of its future, to chart those of its unique institutions and insights which have consistently been the source of the ongoing vitality and the future-mindedness of Judaism and the Jewish people.

What did Rabbinic Judaism achieve? It guarded and saved biblical religion—for all men, and for all time. But to do this, it had also to preserve the Jewish people for all places and all times, as the special bearers of a renewable covenant. And it accomplished these monumental achievements by endowing three Jewish possessions with a double reinforcement that ensured their durability. The "Book," the "Sanctuary," and the "Land," were not only made holy, but portable as well. Wherever Jews went they could carry with them, in meaningful and fulfilling ways, their "Holy Bible," their "Holy Temple," and their "Holy Land."

By making it clear that Jews were given the divine vocation to bear these possessions with them wherever they might go, Rabbinic Judaism united the fate of the Jewish religion to the Jewish people. The new meanings and novel roles that were henceforth associated with each of these three religious patri-monies insistently required the existence of a living collectivity —the people of Israel—as a central and indispensable element of a vital Judaism.

What the Rabbis did with each of these supplies us with im-portant keys to the riddle of Jewish renewal. It not only explains the recurring adaptability of the religious life to the changing cultural and political environments of a variety of exiles, but most especially, sheds light on the crucial interrelation between Jews and Judaism. It explains the secret of the thriving survival of the Jewish people as a major minority, two millennia after the fall of the Temple, the loss of Palestine, and in a multitude of dispersions, as "God's witnesses" to the end of time.

THE BIBLE'S ROLE IN JEWISH RENEWAL

To preserve God's word—to fulfill it and to hearken to it— became the divine calling of the entire people the Rabbis taught. At Sinai the covenant God had once sealed with individuals— Abraham, Isaac, and Jacob—he made with all of their de-scendants, all of the people of Israel. At Sinai he gave all of Israel his Torah—his teaching and law—and thereby, all of Israel became the people of God. "You shall be unto me a kingdom of priests and a holy nation." Forever after, Israel stands in a special relation to God, for he took them out of Egypt and made them his people, when he gave—and they willingly received—his Torah.

267

Yet, "the Torah," the Rabbis took pains to explain, "speaks in the language of men." This was their way of transforming an ancient book into a holy one, and their way of making a holy book into a continuing source of self-renewal for the individual, and of Jewish renewal for the whole people. The word of God is revered as men seek its continuous unfolding in human life. The Bible depicts not only a movement of God to man, but also a movement of man to God. Thus, the covenant was regarded as bilateral: God chose Israel, but Israel collectively at Sinai, also chose God. To prolong and to deepen its group-awareness as the people of the covenant, Israel must grow in its knowledge of God. But for this to happen, the biblical words, too, must grow and deepen, as they speak to the heart-life of the person, and as they enliven and renew the hopes of the whole community.

A. The Personal Life

How did the Rabbis transform the Bible into a living source of personal renewal?

The Pharisee-Rabbis were ranged against the Sadducee-priests. What the priests had made into the cold and impersonal commands of Scripture, Rabbinic *halakah* clothed with the warmth of a new zeal: to build God's kingdom on earth by learning to do his will within the human situation. This meant that all 613 commandments of Scripture had to be carefully and lovingly restudied, from the point of view of human need. In the priestly tradition the commandments were regarded as means of sanctifying God. *Halakah* made more of the commandments: they were now required to yield up opportunities for the sanctification of human life. The *halakah* of the Rabbis reshaped prophetism and gave its lofty, humane concerns a concrete order and structure. Every commonplace, daily human habit could become sacred if it were seen—as the Rabbis insisted it should be seen—as an act of worship. The loving deed became more important than the cult of the Temple, and prepared the way

268

for a life style which could persist and grow, long after the destruction of the Temple.

The Rabbis proceeded apace to build new rituals, "rituals of interpersonal behavior." The commandments of the written Torah—the Pentateuch—were very specific and detailed when it came to rules and regulations relating to the sacrificial laws and priestly regulations. But what precisely did the Torah mean when it said: "Honour thy father and thy mother," or, "Love thy neighbour as thyself," or, "Remember that you were once slaves in the land of Egypt"? It was with questions such as these that the Rabbis deliberately concerned themselves, and the answers they gave made their oral Torah into much more than an ephemeral commentary or a passing fancy. They deepened, humanized, and universalized the older tradition. As the priests had been concerned with codifying the rituals of the cult, the Rabbis sought to codify love, loyalty, and human compassion, to transform these into inescapable religious duties of every Jew. How must one love his neighbor? What are the ways in which one must honour his parents? What must a man actually do to demonstrate to himself and others that he will not go back to slavery, but will seek to remain free?

The Rabbis answered such questions as these by giving the Pentateuchal commandments new meanings. What had been stated before as general propositions, they now spelled out as specific religious and moral duties, incumbent upon all. In effect, they renewed the Jewish religion by translating what had been prophetic sentiment into a personal religion built on "propositions-in-action." Hospitality to wayfarers, visiting the sick of all religious groups, dowering the indigent bride, giving charity anonymously, attending the dead to the grave, and helping to bring peace to those who lack it: these duties, for example, were never actually adumbrated in the Bible, although they are generally felt in spirit. The Rabbis fashioned them, and many others like them, into new commandments, or *mitzvot,* and thus made communion with God an act that could and should be experienced everywhere and at any time, with or without the Temple, the priests, or the sacrificial altar.

This strong emphasis which Rabbinic Judaism placed upon the life of the individual gave new meaning to personal ethics, highlighted the role of prayer over against sacrifice, and gave each person in Israel a priestly function. This significant contribution helped make the Hebrew Bible forever relevant personally, and it became a lively and continuing source for private study, meditation, and the renewal of personal and family covenants with God. It offered each soul an ever-renewing experience with the source of all life: the wonders of the word were as fresh, as new, and as inviting as our private experiences of nature's glories.

But while each person could now be seen to represent a whole world, it was not the desire of the Rabbis to privatize reality or to establish the single one as ultimate. They did not project the importance of the individual in order to erase that other world—the community of Israel—from the face of the future. Not *either-or: either* the individual is the centre of the universe and personal salvation must become the primary religious concern; *or* Judaism can be neither fulfilled or fulfilling. Rather, the Rabbis chose the way of *both-and: both* the individual *and* the community are conjoined. Without the one there can be no true meaning to the other, and both, in interaction, remain in a permanent state of bipolar tension that makes for continuing creative responses. All men are "persons-in-community," and to be a Jew requires that there be a Jewish people.

B. The Corporate Life

To help ensure the vitality of Israel as the people of God—as a holy nation and a kingdom of priests—the Rabbis turned to the Bible, and made Hebrew Scripture into the constitutional base for Jewish corporate life. But while the Law was regarded as divinely revealed, in the hands of the Rabbis, its interpretation was dynamic and expansive. The commandments were to be searched and re-searched in a continuing effort to find new significances that would keep the community alive to its role as God's witnesses. In virtually every generation since the Talmudic period, new features have been added to Jewish life by legislation or interpretation that were clearly the result of ingenious innovations undertaken in the spirit of the Law.

This major breakthrough prevented petrifaction of the spiritual life, and allowed for the periodic regeneration of Jewish religious attitudes and practices. It is directly traceable to the theological victory of the minority of Pharisee-Rabbis over their colleagues, the ruling Saducee-priests. The Rabbis were quick to agree that the priests had indeed been set aside as a consecrated class to administer the rituals of the Temple. But the Torah, the Pharisees argued, had granted them no other special religious authority. And as for the Sadduceean claim concerning the written Torah (Pentateuch), which they insisted had been entrusted to the priests alone, the Pharisees countered with the novel concept of a renewing tradition rooted in the group life. They contended that this tradition, which they called the oral Torah, went back to Sinai itself. There, the word of God— both the written Torah and its oral interpretations—was given by Moses to *the whole people,* not to any special religious order, group of believers, or priestly leaders. The oral Law is transmitted by the people, from generation to generation, and it grows as interpretations in the light of new problems and conditions are added to it. Out of the hands of the priests, the Rabbis took a fixed and unyielding tradition that had become congealed in words and cultic practice, and gave it over to the whole people. What is more, once and forever after, they ordained that all who would study and master that tradition might teach it, expound it, and ultimately, even amplify it.

This was a radical moment in the history of religion generally, and in the annals of Israel as well. To make a Scripture that had once been regarded as an unbending, revealed law capable of repeated innovation, and to do so by removing it from the sacred precincts of a ruling priesthood and virtually placing it in the public domain, depended upon a fundamental restructuring of the whole society. It called for universal higher

271

education. The Chinese were probably the first to establish formal schools for children; the Greeks were among the earliest to promote the highly selective, esoteric groups of philosophical students. But Rabbinic Judaism, if it was to achieve its goal of making the Torah and its interpretation the heritage of the whole people, had to develop an adult academy for higher learning as a popular institution.

Private insight into the Bible was in itself no longer considered sufficient, for the Law would now often be applied in ways remote from the apparent or literal meaning of the commandment or teaching. The schools for higher learning, or rabbinical academies, now served as centres of religious awakening, and lifelong study at these schools became a chief communal preoccupation. There, in these creative circles, brilliant students sought to explain to one another why each adhered to his own particular interpretation of Scripture, to different ancestral ways in great or small matters, in questions of rituals or doctrines, or in what each considered to be just and right for the individual or the nation. Many different schools vied with one another for a claim upon the people's allegiance. Their arguments, debates, and conclusions have all been recorded in the Talmud.

It can safely be assumed that few of the men who argued succeeded in convincing their learned antagonists. But what is of radical importance is that the views of all the disputants were always recorded in the Talmud—the minority together with the majority opinions. Even when the majority sincerely believed the minority to be wrong, the viewpoint of the minority was preserved.

Indeed, this was more than respect offered to rationality or homage paid to intellectual honesty, on the part of the Talmudic Rabbis. It was the cornerstone for future growth, maturation, and renewal of the collective Jewish spirit. For if a minority of Rabbis could realign and reshape a tradition long locked in the authoritative arms of the priestly powers, then, perhaps, a day might yet dawn when still another minority might need to be heard and followed. It is this special genius of Rabbinic

272

Judaism that made and kept Jews one people throughout the world and across the ages, despite the diverse and sometimes contradictory interpretations of its varied groups and parties.

The Rabbis taught that Israel was called into being for the sake of the Torah. But they also made it clear that the Torah could live only through its people. "You are my witnesses," the God of Scripture reminds Israel. To which the Rabbis of the Talmud added: "If you are my witnesses, I am God, but if you refuse to be my witnesses, then (so to speak) I am not God." In their paradoxical way, the Rabbis helped the community of Israel survive its own national destruction by serving the world—but always serving it as members of a distinctive people. Self-preservation came to be felt as preservation by God for his reasons—Israel was to be *in* the world, *for* the world, and yet not *of* the world. Here was a universal prophetic religion, which because of the Temple's destruction, the exile, and the dispersion—not to mention the unspeakable round of persecutions and banishments—became more and more bound up with the life and destiny of a single people.

The Rabbis knew, of course, that if the Jewish people no longer continued to exist, the Torah would disappear from the face of the earth. To be sure, the spiritual life gives to human existence its vital inner qualities, but without a community to support, strengthen, and enhance it, it is impossible for the spiritual life to exist. Thus, concern for Judaism required concern for Jews. Since the Torah was given to the whole people, and since all are equally responsible for witnessing to it and for handing it down to others, the collective life and destiny came to possess a sacred calling and significance of its own.

Thus, in Judaism, thanks to the teachings of the Rabbis, the place which the Church came to occupy in Christian thought is shared by the whole people of Israel—not by a small or large body of believers separated from the others, but by all Jews, the faithful and the unfaithful, the sacred-directed and the secular-minded. The whole people shares an irrevocable, divine vocation, *as a people,* and this explains why the Rabbinic legis-

273

lation of the Talmud concerns itself with much more than theology, but with all aspects of the corporate life—social, economic, and interpersonal.

As a result of being people-centred, Judaism became life-centred, and here again, the keys to its openness and the prospects for its ready renewal are easily discernible. This also explains why it was perfectly natural that the restoration of the people as a whole, and not the spiritual salvation or the physical redemption of the private person alone, should always have survived as the normative religious expectation of individual Jews. The people's Book had made it into the "people of the Book," and with that Book that people could transcend every exile.

THE SYNAGOGUE AND JEWISH RENEWAL

When the Torah and the Prophets became a Book, the day of the prophets was over, but this was not the end of Judaism. Now that God's word was committed to writing, a new type of religious leader came to the fore, neither prophet nor priest. First known as Scribe, later as Rabbi, he was seriously challenged and rebuffed by the priests, despite the fact that he never laid claim to their biblical prerogatives.

Then, in the year 70, when Jerusalem fell to the Romans, the day of the Temple and the priests was over, too. Nor was this the end of Judaism. Now, the Rabbi became the authoritative and unchallenged heir of both prophet and priest. Now, too, the synagogue came to flower as a radical religious center substituting prayer for sacrifice, and making biblical study and interpretation into an act of worship. Rabbinic Judaism did not consciously create the synagogue, but it did shape and adapt it as a portable vehicle for its ethical universalism and its faith in the unaltered spiritual vocation of the Jewish people, as the congregation, or community, of Israel.

From its very beginnings, the idea of a synagogue was centred in the congregation, or community, rather than in a

274

sacred place, a votive shrine, or a magnificent public building. Even when the exiles returned to their land to build the Second Temple, they carried attachments to this new and popular form of religious expression, which some scholars believe first began in the Babylonian dispersion. From that day, despite the fact that the Temple still existed, religious emphasis began to shift, although imperceptibly at first, from the sacramental office of the *priests* to the *people* themselves; from the holy *place* of worship to the *worshippers*—the whole people is regarded as a *holy congregation.*

This idea is represented in microcosm in the *edah,* which the Rabbis sanctioned as a formal religious congregation consisting of ten or more males. Wherever Jews would now assemble—in private homes, at the city's gates, in broad fields under open skies—it was their religious motivation as a "congregation *in* Israel" reflecting the reality of the "congregation *of* Israel" which came to dominate and invigorate Jewish thought. As a perennial reminder of the supreme sanctity of the Temple, the "orientation" of the synagogue prayer was, and remains, towards Mount Zion in Jerusalem. Indeed, the Rabbis awaited and prayed for the day when the Temple would be rebuilt. But, in effect, the synagogue transcended the Temple in the lives of the people because it became more than a "House of God"—it became the "house of the people" of God.

The synagogue became more than a "house of prayer," too. We have already mentioned the Rabbinic need to build a broad network of popular academies for higher learning. Since the Rabbis regarded the study of the Torah as an act of worship, it is easy to understand why, under their influence, the synagogue was to become a "house of study." The reading and teaching of Scripture became a central and crucial feature of Jewish public worship, and lectures and homilies given by recognized scholars was a regular instructional method which was built into the fabric of the service. But it was more than a mere pedagogical device. Worship, the Rabbis were thus saying, must be linked to ethical service, and without study and meditation, prayer without moral undergirding is insufficient for

275

fulfilling the biblical imperatives. Learning to do God's will requires constant study of the Torah, the prophets—and now, their newer interpretations, too—the Rabbis taught. This insistent claim became the theological catalyst they successfully employed in transforming every synagogue into an adult school for higher spiritual learning for the whole community of Israel.

Indeed, the synagogue soon became the house of the people, a place of communal assembly. Courts of law met in its rooms, heard testimony, administered oaths, and proclaimed judgments. Strangers to the community were welcomed into its hostel, the poor were invited there to receive alms, and community philanthropies were administered by its councils. In time, these broad communal and humane functions were to be so well integrated with its religious and educational programs, that the synagogue became the supreme focus of all Jewish life. Down to modern times, throughout the world, the Jewish community lived as a nation within nations: in that setting, the synagogue was nothing less than the "national centre" of a Jewish "religious-welfare state." Education, culture, religion, social welfare, the administration of justice, charity, betrothal collations, wedding parties, circumcision feasts—all of these human needs found their place in the synagogue so that nothing Jewish and nothing human was alien to it. The natural intermingling of the sacred and secular needs of men endowed the synagogue with a remarkable capacity for helping the congregation meet the changing horizons of new places and the challenging ideas of new times.

To most Jews, the synagogue and its adjoining "square"— with its abattoir for ritual slaughter, its dormitory for transient adult lodgers, its schoolrooms for children and adults, its library of manuscripts and religious treatises—was probably the closest thing they had to the lost and longed-for patrimony of the Holy Land. Indeed, although spiritually very much alive and integrated in many dispersions, the ultimate promise of the synagogue, and its most crucial spiritual gift, was the hope its continued vitality offered for Jewish renewal—through redemption from exile and restoration in the Land of Israel.

276

ZION AND JEWISH RENEWAL

The Land of Israel—Zion—has served the Jewish people as more than a national concept: it has been a continuing source of spiritual longing and anticipation, as both symbol and reality, of their capacity for regeneration under God, and as his people. The psalmist conceived of God as the King of Israel and he sang of Zion as the "city of the great King" (Ps. 48, 3). Ever since, Zion has retained this sacred significance: the Land of Israel is regarded not only as a holy land, but as *the* Holy Land. In all their prayers and religious devotions, the yearning and the mourning of the people in exile remained intimately bound up with it, and in Jewish mystical speculation Zion was often equated with an emanation of God himself. All of these associations with their land are still retained by the people of Israel; indeed, this not only makes their relationship to it unique, but explains why the idea of Zion has remained a remarkable force for Jewish renewal. Martin Buber has summarized it thus:

In other respects the people of Israel may be regarded as one of the many peoples on earth and the land of Israel as one land among other lands: but in their mutual relationship and in their common task they are unique and incomparable. And, in spite of all the names and historical events that have come down to us, what has come to pass, what is coming and shall come to pass between them, is and remains a mystery. From generation to generation the Jewish people have never ceased to meditate on this mystery . . . If Israel renounces the mystery, it renounces the heart of reality itself.

(Martin Buber, *Israel and Palestine: The History of an Idea* [London, 1952], pp. xii–xiii.)

This mystery of Israel's unfathomable being-drawn to its land is grounded in a fundamental theme of its *Heilsgeschichte*—its certain faith in a future Restoration, that it might witness to God out of Zion. Clearly, no other phenomenon in history

277

seems so extraordinary as that remarkable event represented by
the Restoration of Israel in the sixth and fifth centuries, B.C.
So far as we know, at no other time or place in world history,
has a people been destroyed, then exiled, and after a lapse of
time, come back to its home, to be re-established and renewed
as a people.

The personal drive towards *nóstos,* or homecoming, the
emotional and psychological need to return to the place of
ancestral roots, is a recurring theme in the literature of antiquity. The Tales of Sinuhe, the Shipwrecked Sailor of Middle
Kingdom Egypt, the epics of Gilgamesh of Mesopotamia and
Odysseus of Greece, all deal with episodic wandering that end
in *nóstos,* a happy homecoming. Similarly, the Genesis narratives dealing with the patriarchs also underline this human
need. Abraham wanders into Egypt but returns to the land of
promise. Jacob migrates to Egypt where he dies, but even after
death he is borne home: his burial in Canaan figures promi-
nently in the Genesis stories.

But more crucial and unique to Jewish thought is the way
the personal *nóstos* of antiquity was transformed into the collective heritage of a whole people. The restoration of Israel
to its land is no longer the emotional or psychological human
need of a *nóstos,* nor is it, as some have thought, a modern,
romantic irredentism. From the psalmist, and from the prophetic
teachings of Zion as a light unto the nations, the Rabbis forged
"Jewish homecoming" into an instrument of universal, messianic
fulfillment.

Some scholars, however, have devoted much effort trying to
disprove the biblical tradition of the exile, the captivity, and
the restoration. These critical researchers, far removed from
the essential mystery of Jewish history, have dutifully maintained that there was no real interruption in the life of Israel
as a result of the captivity, that the cities of Judah were either
not destroyed at all or were quickly and easily rebuilt, and that
life went on smoothly during the exile. Most important, their
critical hypotheses are marshalled as a prolegomenon to their

278

mighty counterthrust against essential biblical teaching: the restoration is pure myth, and never took place at all.

"Of course there was an Exile, a Captivity, and a Restoration," says archaeologist William F. Albright. "Year by year," he avers, "archaeologists make finds which have disproved the contentions of these (critical) scholars in detail. It is in fact the outstanding example," he goes on to say, "of complete refutation of historico-critical hypotheses by archaeologists."

For Israel, the Restoration was real because it was religiously true, and it could be religiously true only if it was also an event in history. History was not mythologized by the Jews; it was, rather, theologized. In their early past, in common with other ancient peoples of Canaan and Babylonia, their religious festivals were principally a record of the passing of the seasons in nature. The Rabbis, however, reshaped these festival days to reflect and to commemorate great events in the history of their people, while other peoples had continued to relate most of their celebrations to the enthralling rhythm of nature. The events of history are not eternally repeatable as are the processes of nature. They are unique. And the Rabbis regarded these events as religiously portentous because they enshrined God's activity among men and nations, as redeemer and liberator.

Perhaps the Rabbis would have regarded history less significantly had they considered their people's place in it like that of any other. But they believed Israel to be chosen by God to teach the world the meaning of his oneness. Therefore, they believed that what happened to Israel was important to everybody, because it was a demonstration of God's work in the world, through his people. Their own history became sacred history—*Heilsgeschichte*—indeed, it was to become, in the hands of the Rabbis, the very basis of their theology. Thus, the sacred calendar of the Jewish people, to this day, is essentially a re-enactment of the historical events in the life of Israel. Jewish celebrations of religious holidays are interpretations of the idea of God as the single redeemer in the living events of history.

279

In this way, even the Sabbath, which at first was celebrated as a reminder of the significance of the divine creation of the world, came to be seen as a weekly reminder of the power of God to enter human history as the creator who is also redeemer. The book of Deuteronomy recalls the extended meaning: "And you shall remember that you were a slave in the land of Egypt, and the Lord your God brought you out thence by a mighty hand and an outstretched arm; therefore the Lord your God commanded you to keep the Sabbath day." The redemption from Egypt, first exile of the children of Israel, would lead to the revelation of Sinai, and Sinai would point the way to their establishment as a people in the land promised to the Fathers. Forever after, these three historico-religious events— the exodus-redemption, the Sinai-revelation, and the Canaan-homecoming—were regarded as interrelated and interdependent.

It is little wonder that the restoration under Ezra should have become so significant a touchstone for future restoration, and no surprise that ever since the Roman exile, the theme of liberation, return, and renewal should have become a major reprise in Jewish life and thought. The return to Zion, not merely of individuals by personal choice, but of an assembly of Jews large enough to have representative value for "all Israel," became an integral part of Jewish messianism. Zion, and the return of Israel to it, was not seen as an escape from history to a purer, non-worldly sphere, but as the spiritual fulfillment of Jewish and universal history.

* * *

New winds blowing in the Christian world indicate that, in the main, Christian renewal is interested in and happy with Jewish renewal. There is an enlivened interest, generally, in Rabbinic thought and its contemporary meaning. Christian students of the Bible, for example, no longer bypass the Talmud, or for that matter, the medieval Rabbinical commentaries. On the contrary, more and more of them are seeking to renew their biblical and theological studies, not only by "fraternal dialogues" with contemporary Jewish teachers, but by serious study of the texts of Rabbinic Judaism.

In addition, for the first time in the life of many Christians, the synagogue has become a place to enter and to study, not as a relic of the past, but as a vital and relevant source of religious inspiration for our times.

The "Book" and the "Sanctuary" still speak to the world.

It is, however, with the last of the three vitalizing, regenerating gifts bequeathed by Rabbinic Judaism—Zion, the Holy Land —that a problematic has emerged. Recent events have once again disclosed the ambivalent views which Christians hold towards the re-establishment of Israel as a sovereign nation on its own land. To be sure, the almost unexpected proclamation of a State of Israel has created many problems as well as opportunities for Jews, as it has for Judaism. In many ways, Jews were not ready for it; surely, Judaism, as a religious system, has not yet been able to adjust completely to the new fact of corporate restoration to the land.

For Christians, however, it has brought into sharp focus the almost total theological unpreparedness for this new turn in Jewish history. In the first place, for many Christians, Jewish peoplehood did not even seem to exist after the Roman exile and the Temple's destruction. The dispersion of the Jews was regarded by many as a merited punishment for their rejection of Christianity. Wandering, dispersion, and exile—all of these were seen as normative for a people which had brought forth, but then rejected, the Saviour. Clearly, the restoration of a representative portion of the people of Israel to its land, as a sovereign state recognized by the international community, raises many theological problems for Christianity.

In reaction, some Christians have been tempted to regard the State of Israel as only a secular phenomenon, outside the scope of the promises made by God to Israel. Still others, like Yves Congar,* are willing to accept the new community in Israel,

* See Yves Congar, *Dialogue Between Christians,* Westminster, 1966, especially the chapter on "The Religious Significance of the Restoration of the Jewish State and Nation in the Holy Land," pp. 445 ff.

secular as it may seem, as a sign of Jewish renewal—but only as a renewal that will lead them to a new dispensation, the acceptance of the Christian Saviour as their own.

It would, of course, be presumptuous to urge Christians to structure their theology of renewal to take account of the dynamics of Jewish renewal. Nevertheless, if ours is truly to be the age of religious dialogue, those Christians who are interested in speaking seriously to Jews will also have to be prepared to listen carefully to them. They will have to face up to the ineluctable fact that Jews will simply not conform to the image projected for them by classical Christian theology, nor will they generally accept fraternal dialogues with those who can conceive of Christian renewal only on orthodox Christian terms.

Fortunately, however, the number of thoughtful Christians willing to see Israel's return to Zion as Jews themselves see it increases, day by day. Together, they regard it as an unmistakable sign of *Jewish* renewal.

These words, then, may conclude on a note of hope, of bold hope. Is it too daring to utter a prayer that the great and mysterious forces now moving the Church to seek its renewal may also seek the renewal of Jews and of Judaism, amidst the perilous world of non-faith that engulfs them both?

Is it too naïve a faith to proclaim that as Christians and Jews we are willing *to leave to God the work of his end-time,* while we move ahead together, staking our own lives on the possibility of living in the here and now, as Christians and as Jews, who accept each other's otherness, and who rejoice in each other's fulfillments?

14.

MODERN MYTH-MAKING AND THE POSSIBILITIES OF TWENTIETH-CENTURY THEOLOGY

LANGDON GILKEY

As its title indicates, this paper deals much more with myth and its modern forms than with modern theology. It is, therefore, to be taken as an essay in prolegomenon to theology rather than as a proposal in theology itself—for on that score it is sketchy indeed. The argument unfolds in three steps, which have a dialectical, almost paradoxical relation to one another. This does not, of course, guarantee the truth of the argument, but, nonetheless, the presence of paradoxes makes a writer on myth and theology feel much more sure of his ground! We shall *not* use the term myth in the pejorative sense of an ancient and so untrue fable. Rather it signifies to us a certain mode of language, whose elements are multivalent symbols, whose referent in some strange way is the transcendent or the sacred, and whose meanings concern the ultimate or existential issues of actual life and the questions of human and historical destiny. Myth is, in other words, to us the appropriate mode of first order religious discourse, and theology is involved yet disciplined reflection upon the mythical language of a historical community or tradition.

The three-fold thesis, then:

1. The secular mood of our time is such that in its eyes myth and its appropriate discourse are unintelligible, that is, explicitly

inadmissible, semantically meaningless, and experientially empty.

2. Nonetheless, mythical or symbolic language is necessary for the life of any culture, and consequently secularism contradicts itself and produces under the table, so to speak, its own important myths, but inevitably in distorted, abstract, and self-contradictory form.

3. Christian theology, as reflection upon the symbols and so the mythical language of the Christian community, provides the best basis for the self-understanding of secular culture—and in that role alone, namely as providing symbolic or mythical comprehension of ordinary, secular life, can it regain a sense both of identity and of relevance, of integrity in relation to its historic and traditional function, and yet of meaningfulness for a new secular age.

Probably few would disagree that the central contemporary problem of theology can be usefully described as the apparent emptiness or meaninglessness of its language, and that this sense of emptiness permeates the life and thought of the church itself, not just that of the unbelieving world. To some (such as Bultmann) this problem arises because the traditional biblical forms of orthodox theology are pre-scientific; to others (such as Dewart and the Whiteheadians) it arises because traditional theology has been set in a philosophical form—that of Aristotle —which does not fit the modern sense for becoming and process. In the one case the solution is, therefore, a purified or demythologized Word of God kerygma, in the other a theology based on a new, modernized metaphysics. To us the problem lies deeper: it springs from the conflict, not between modern secularism on the one hand and pre-scientific myth or even pre-modern metaphysics on the other—though these *are* real conflicts—but between the secular spirit and mythical language of all sorts, language which therefore includes *both* the purified kerygmatic language of Christian proclamation and those symbolic affirmations foundational to any speculative metaphysics, even a modern one. A demythologized Word of God theology and a modern process metaphysics are as strange to most of our

284

modern mentality as are the modes of theology they call out of date. To understand, therefore, the dilemma in our time of theological language across the board, we must try to understand why mythical discourse itself seems to be unintelligible to our age—and so why both theology and speculative metaphysics, which are reflective or rational explications of fundamental symbolic affirmations, are equally orphans and waifs in the modern world.

In order to comprehend our dialectic or paradox, how there can be modern myths in an age whose essential character is that it recognizes no possibility of intelligible mythical language, we must define myth. And to do this in an unmythical age we must go back before the modern critical period, and in fact before the rise of philosophy, which—in Greece, India, and China alike—I regard as essentially a noble rationalization of the mythical religious consciousness. Thus we turn, to understand mythical language in its pristine form, to the history of religions—my indebtedness here to my great colleague Mircea Eliade is deep and obvious.

Mythical language, as we find it in primitive and then in ancient cultures, has received many, often conflicting definitions. Since we are here concerned mainly with its contemporary difficulties, we shall characterize it primarily with that aim in mind.[1]

---

[1] The indebtedness of this discussion of traditional or ancient mythical discourse to my colleague, Mircea Eliade, is evident. The most important of his works in this connection are *Patterns in Comparative Religion, Cosmos and History,* and *The Sacred and the Profane.*

One of the most helpful definitions of myth, fully congruent with the themes of this paper, is Paul Ricoeur's: "Myth will here be taken to mean what the history of religions now finds in it: not a false explanation by means of images and fables, but a traditional narration which relates to events that happened at the beginning of time and which has the purpose of providing grounds for the ritual actions of men of today and, in a general sense, establishing all the forms of action and thought by which a man understands himself and his world. . . . But in losing its explanatory pretensions the myth reveals its explanatory significance and its contribution to understanding, which we shall later call its symbolic function—that is to say, its power of discovering and revealing the bond between man and what he considers sacred. Paradoxical as it may seem, the myth when it is thus demythologized through contact with scientific history and elevated to the dignity of

Archaic mythical language, the language of all pre-modern, ancient religious symbol systems, was a form or type of language expressive of a certain mode of human self-understanding, namely one achieved through an experienced relation to the fundamental sacral structures of man's cosmic environment. It proposed in all its forms an affirmation of intimacy with the most basic and therefore sacral structures of space, of time, of natural occurrence and of historical event. This intimacy and so this "knowing" had been experienced and were ever again to be re-experienced through special appearances of the sacred in and through certain symbols, and thus these mythical forms provided not only an explanation for the enigmas of life, but also redemptive exemplars or models for man's social and personal existence through which he could continually re-relate his being and his behavior to the ultimate sources of all. Three elements relative to our purposes were present within this archaic form of religious language.

1. The symbols which composed a mythical structure were multivalent and in a special manner. That is, they referred not only to a finite thing (sky, stone, animal, person) but at once also to the transcendent, the unconditioned, and the sacred that appeared in and through that thing and was, therefore, in a variety of ways, identified with it. Thus mythical language talked about *both* finite things and their relations, *and* the sacred or ultimate manifested in and through them; and, we might note, this strange intertwining of scientific and historical language about finite things and events with language about the ultimate has characterized religious discourse ever since.

2. Generally ancient mythical discourse referred to the cosmic origins of finite things. Archaic myths were cosmogonic, that is to say, the sacred manifesting itself in and through the present symbols was identified with the *originating* divine powers of things, of time, of space, and of natural and social forces. Thus the primary categories in which man understood himself were on the one hand cosmic and so ontological in form, and on the

a symbol, is a dimension of modern thought." *The Symbolism of Evil*, New York, 1967, p. 5.

286

other they referred to the originating structures and powers that founded the world. Through reunion with these structures, the chaos outside man became cosmos, and man's own existence was redeemed, for then each creature refound that order and that special place given it in the original creation.

3. It followed from the cosmogonic character of most ancient myths, that human existence was believed to escape dissolution and disorder by repeating the original and founding forms of things. Whenever, therefore, these originating forces repeated themselves cyclically in time, there renewal and freedom from disarray were found. Hence in ancient myth there was inevitably a backward look, a cyclical view of the sacred structure of time, and, finally, a sense that man's freedom was not fulfilled in creating the forms of existence but only when he re-enacted given, original forms posited into existence by the gods. We may sum this up by saying that the traditional language of religious myth referred to the transcendent within the finite, was attentive to the cosmic origin of creaturely existence, and sought to model man's life on these original cosmic structures and exemplars. While Christian theology, because of its emphasis on a linear history, on concrete revelatory events in history, on the power of the "new" in history, and the ultimate significance of the End, by no means followed this backward-looking cosmogonic pattern of ancient myth, nevertheless many other elements— especially with regard to the centrality of God and so of the categories of transcendence, of creation, and of the divine order —have reflected this traditional pattern. In any case our point is that it is precisely these traditional mythical elements, centering around the symbol God, in traditional metaphysical and theological language, which have been found apparently empty and meaningless by a secular age.

Our next question is, therefore, why are these characteristic elements of mythical language challenged in a secular age? Clearly this is a very complex question, involving almost every aspect of the intellectual development of modern man and so of the "secular spirit" which characterizes our age. For our

287

purpose three elements of that spirit are relevant to the gradual waning of the intelligibility of mythical language:

1. Characteristically the secular mind understands events in terms solely of their physical and historical causes, that is, insofar as scientific inquiry can speak of them. A "transcendent" or "sacred" factor or structure present and active in and through the finite is unknown and unreal to this mind. All that is real and effective are the contingent and relative factors succeeding one another on a finite level. There is no meaningful mystery about which we must speak beyond this level. Thus the multivalent character of religious symbolism is to this mind not a mark of the uniqueness and significance of this type of language, but rather of pre-scientific superstition, and so of the inevitable error, emptiness, and unreality of mythical speech.[2]

2. Characteristically, therefore, the sacred has vanished from the objective environment of man. The cosmos no longer provides a sacral setting for man's life, giving to that life its intelligibility and its potential meaning. A spiritual separation between man and his cosmic environment has occurred. That environment is for most of us characterized only by contingent, relative, and blind factors. Thus to many man is "on his own,"

[2] Of course, a good deal of the difficulty the modern mentality has had with myth is deserved. Because mythical language inevitably combines talk about the finite with talk about the sacred, much traditional theological or mythical language, in its pre-critical forms, has included many "scientific-type" assertions: about the age and geography of the universe, how it came to be, the characteristics of early history, and many of the events of the past. Here myth claims to supply information comparable to the kind a scientific or historical inquiry might produce. In those cases where science and history have found out what "was the case," such mythical science has turned out to be almost always wrong—and this was no accident, since such information is not included within the legitimate meanings of religious symbols and myths. After their long experience of seeing religious truths thus "disproved" by science, many modern men have reasonably concluded that myth was merely a form of pre-scientific information about the world, and therefore superstitious. That, however, they do not and frequently cannot see the *other* function and meaning of mythical discourse poses the much deeper problem for theology today (since most contemporary theology regards its language as post-critical and therefore its myths as "broken" symbols and not as scientific information), and so we have concentrated on this aspect of the problem of modern myth.

288

that is, utterly dependent on his own autonomous powers if
there is to be any order and value in his life. Insofar as myth
be comprehensible to most moderns at all, therefore, it represents the mistaken projection of the sacral potentialities of man's
creative powers onto a desacralized outward cosmos.[3] The factors causative of this development of the alienation of modern
man from his cosmos are many: the demise of all the "gods" of
nature through the biblical-Christian tradition; the radical continuation of this process in the eradication in science since
Galileo of teleology, valuation, and meaning from the processes
of nature; the spiritual or existential separation of man from
nature which technology and urbanization have effected; and,
finally, the gradual loss, culminating in the twentieth century,
of a sense of an ultimate order or directedness in the process
of things.[4]

3. Correspondingly the modern spirit emphasizes the creativity of human autonomy and so the possibility of the "new"
in historical existence. It is oriented not *backwards* to an essential order in which man's freedom must participate, but *forwards*
to a potential existence in the open future which man's freedom
may create.[5] For this reason the mythical seems to our age to
be not only pre-scientific and superstitious, not only empty or
non-referential and subjective, but also repressive and thus
destructive, imprisoning man's autonomous spirit in a prede-

[3] See especially the thought of Ludwig Feuerbach, *The Essence of
Christianity,* for the earliest expression of this understanding of the
mythical language of religion. In modern times possibly the best and
most appreciative expression of this anthropocentric interpretation of
myth has been that of George Santayana in *Reason and Religion, The
Realm of Essence,* and *Platonism and the Spiritual Life.*

[4] See the writer's article in *Christianity and Crisis.*

[5] It is this point that Karl Löwith makes central to the development
of the "contemporary spirit," namely that this spirit begins when man
ceases to understand himself in terms of an "essence" given him in the
total cosmic order, and instead understands himself in terms of his
freedom to create or enact his own being in existence. Thus for Löwith
existentialist thought, in denying an essence of man and asserting only
his existence in freedom, is the characteristic expression of the modern
attitude. See Karl Löwith, *Nature, History and Existentialism,* Evanston,
1966, esp. chs. 1, 2, and 3.

termined cosmic niche, and so setting essential limits to the freedom of man.[6] "God is dead" thus becomes a cry not only of rationality and maturity, but also of freedom and of openness to the future. Since in this phrase the symbol of God connotes the whole range of the traditional mythical consciousness, it is not surprising that into the grave of the cosmogonic creator descend as well all those other relics of the mythical consciousness that have traditionally structured the spiritual existence of the West, and so which have made its metaphysics, its moral philosophy, and its theology possible. These "relics" include the belief in the objective logos of existence that made metaphysical speculation possible, the sense of an "ought" standing over man's freedom which provided an inward locus for the experience of the sacred,[7] and the sense of a final goal towards which all process moves and which gave meaning to the symbol of the divine providence.

The opposition between the modern spirit, informed by a scientific view of the cosmos and by a corresponding faith in man's absolute autonomy, and the traditional mythical consciousness seems, therefore, to be absolute. We suggest that a certainty of this absolute opposition between modernity and myth is itself one of the fundamental characteristics of the modern spirit. Mythical language having to do with the transcendent and the sacred is to this mind superstitious, nonsensical, and repressive, and the supposed referents of this language are unreal and unneeded in today's world. It is of the essence of modernity to

[6] This concept, inspired of course by Nietzsche, has become the main thrust of the radical theology of Thomas J. J. Altizer: the transcendent "religious" search for origins and the worship of the transcendent is, he says, a cause of repression; the transcendent god must die if man is to be free, and with the loss of this crushing heteronomy, man's resentment, envy, and hostility will also vanish. See *The Gospel of Christian Atheism*, Westminster, 1966. For some of the same Nietzschian themes see Richard Rubenstein's *After Auschwitz*, Indianapolis, 1966.

[7] There is a long tradition that has taken conscience as the central and even initiating point of relationship between man and God. This is surely true of both Luther and Calvin; it becomes even more prominent in Kant, Ritschl, W. R. Sorley John Bailie, Emil Brunner, and, in our own day, Gerhard Ebeling. For the last, see *Word and Faith*, esp. pp. 349, 356, and 360.

290

believe that myth is part of the infancy of man, to be outgrown in the scientific and autonomous age of modernity.

We also suggest, however, that there is a split or a disjunction between modern man's *intellectual* comprehension of himself and his world—which we have called the modern spirit or mind—and his more *existential* self-understanding; that in fact the terms in which he explicitly thinks about himself are different from the terms by which he actually lives. There are many evidences of this split between the secular attitude or viewpoint on the one hand and secular existence on the other, but certainly one of them is the continuation, or better, the re-creation of myths within the modern consciousness itself. Strange as it sounds after the preceding discussion, there *are* modern secular myths as well as archaic and traditional myths. Naturally they take quite different forms than have the archaic cosmogonic myths or the mythical language of the theological tradition. Consequently our concern now is to see (a) in what way they are "myth" and function as such in modern culture, and (b) how in this secular setting the mythical consciousness expresses itself and some of the problems it encounters there.

Let us recall what we have said about the function and so meaning of myth in its traditional or archaic forms, and thus discover which of its elements are transferred, surreptitiously to be sure, into the modern setting. Myth or mythical language, we have said, expresses the fundamental self-understanding of man with regard to his origins and to his destiny; thus it conceptualizes his comprehension of the basic enigmas of his life and provides him with some ground for confidence in dealing with these enigmas; in so doing, it also provides him with the models by which to pattern his existence and to judge his behavior and that of his fellows. Myths are, then, on the most fundamental level, the way man structures his world and his own being within it. Thus they provide the foundations for all of his interactions with that world; that is, his modes of inquiring and knowledge, of art and activity, of communal relations and roles, and of personal life and death. Insofar as modern man asks questions about his origins and his destiny, about the mean-

291

ing of his life and that of his history, about what it is to be human in all of its facets, and what it is to be moral and to die, and insofar as he affirms or seeks foundations for all he does in terms of some ultimate horizon of meaning, then *these* issues will be answered in terms of mythical discourse.[8]

The near impossibility of explicating or even discussing such issues according to the canons of reasonableness, of intelligibility, and of meaning, recognized by a secular culture is, of course, well known, and need not be elaborated here. We will merely suggest that it is precisely these "mythical elements," unusual and unverifiable as they are, in traditional speculative philosophy —namely, an elaboration of the ultimate structure of things, of the felt character and obligations of man's being in the world and of man's relation to man, and of the ultimate meaning and destiny of process as a whole—which have been rejected as meaningless by most modern philosophy—at least in its empirical naturalistic, its predominant linguistic forms and much of its existentialism. But assuming that modern man, for a variety of reasons, does in fact wonder about these problems of the meaning and shape of his life in the world, we can ask what forms do these myths take, and how satisfactory are these forms as illustrative of the human condition?

We have characterized the modern view as suspicious of any multivalent symbolism, any intelligibility beyond the one-dimensional sequence of contingent and relative factors that, to an empirical investigation, bring things about. Thus is the cosmos out of which man comes desacralized of meaning, and man's obligations and prospects alike understood in terms solely of

[8] This understanding of religious discourse has been potently—but incompletely—formulated by the philosopher Stephen Toulmin through his concept of "limiting questions" that lie back of every special cultural activity, and so whose basis can only be expressed in what he calls "religious" language. See Stephen Toulmin, *Reason in Ethics,* London, 1964, esp. chs. 7 and 14. Thus in a most stimulating and important article, which inspired many of the thoughts of this paper, Toulmin discusses what he calls "the scientific myths" of our age, showing on the one hand how they "do" what ancient myths did, namely reassure us about total meaning, but on the other hand how they are based upon sophisticated scientific concepts rather than on anthropomorphic language. See Stephen Toulmin, *et al., Metaphysical Beliefs,* London, 1957, ch. 1, "Contemporary Scientific Mythology."

the development over time of man's own inherent powers. What sort of myths are possible in this atmosphere? First of all, one would expect that cosmogonic myths—myths referring to the sacred origins of things—would now be virtually unknown. Almost no modern understands himself or his world on this level in terms of its origins, or seeks to renew his life by returning to the original and divinely founded structures of space, time, nature, and human being. The question of "origins" has thus in fact moved quite out of the realm of sacral mystery and so of myth, and has become a series of "problems" for the inquiries of the special sciences, inquiries concerning the factors and processes on the finite level which have caused things to be as they are, whether we are talking of our galaxy, our solar system, organic life, man himself, or his significant institutions and mores. Such structures as are found at "the beginnings" have, therefore, no exemplar function for us;[9] it is not out of scientific views of original structures that our current scientific myths are fabricated.

Although there are, as we have noted, many reasons for this vast change of attitude towards the "beginning," the most fundamental, we believe, concern the concept of historicity, that is, of temporal development, of the centering, if you will, of the "world" in which man lives around the movement of *history* in time, rather than around the eternal order of natural and cosmic recurrence; and correlative to this emphasis on temporal or historical movement, a new understanding of human autonomy or freedom. Because of his view that he exists primarily in time rather than in space, and that time is a process developing towards a goal rather than a medium for the cyclical repetition of eternal structures, modern man finds his locus for meaning in the patterns of *development* in time and so ultimately is the

[9] One exception to this has been Robert Ardrey's interesting feeling that if modern political man knew that his first progenitor had been a predatory killer, this knowledge might shatter all our hopes for world peace today. Apparently Ardrey, though quite modern in his anthropological theory, shares the mythical feeling that the original form of man, did we but know that form, might exert a potent "exemplar" force on contemporary life. See Robert Ardrey, *African Genesis,* New York, 1961.

goal at the end of time, rather than in its originating structures. (As an aside, it is thus not strange that much of ultra-modern theology is oriented eschatologically, towards the End, and not towards either the sacral origins of being or its eternal order, and that it finds the focus of theology to be socio-historical rather than metaphysical, as the debate between Fathers Mascall and Metz indicated!) Modern man's models for his own existence thus typically arise out of a vision of *future* utopias rather than from a memory of *lost,* or originating, paradises. Correspondingly, the sense of the creative powers of his own freedom: his freedom over his natural environment, his social institutions, his moral norms and decisions, and even over his own physical being, make man feel that original structures are merely "given," and that to appeal to them and their authority is to appeal to the insignificant. All they provide is *material* for free, creative action, not forms to be copied by freedom. Insofar as these given structures do set patterns for his life, they seem now repressive rather than renewing, since the meaning of freedom, as modern man understands it, is that he faces an open future, and that he must create his own models for himself and not accept them passively from God, the cosmos, or even history.[10] (As an example, to make another aside, Father Lonergan significantly defined revelation *not* as a communication of eternal truth about man's eternal place and destiny, but "God's entry into man's making of man"—a clear recognition of this new modern emphasis on freedom or self-creativity in and for the future.)

[10] The sense that the "given" is merely material for man's creative remaking, that freedom is discovered or realized through giving new forms to traditional materials rather than through re-enacting the traditional, is expressed, of course, most potently in existentialist literature, especially that of Sartre and Heidegger. However, there can be little doubt that the same interpretation of the relation of the traditional "given" to freedom is present in the thought of John Dewey, for whom the central function of critical intelligence is that of testing and refashioning all traditional and given forms, social institutions, standards, and beliefs, and in the thought of Alfred North Whitehead, for whom the main function of freedom is to effect the ingression of original and creative possibilities into precedent actuality.

294

If cosmic origins and an eternal order are thus no longer relevant to man's self-understanding, does this mean that modern myths in no way express a union of man with the structures of the wider cosmic setting of his life? This by no means follows, and in fact the two primary modern myths, by which the majority of men in our present secular world probably still actually live and find meaning, can be called "cosmic myths." That is, they explicate a vision of the ultimate nature of process as a whole, and seek to understand man's nature, obligations, and destiny in the light of that vision—what is "modern" about these cosmic myths is that they understand life in terms of the *goal* of process rather than in terms of its origins. These are, first, the liberal view of cosmic and historical progress, well summed up in the great word evolution, and the allied but nonetheless significantly different vision of Marxism with its belief in a historical dialectic that is moving inexorably towards the Communist ideal. Both cosmic evolution and the Marxist materialistic dialectic represent myths in our threefold sense.

1. As applied to the whole of process, they do not represent limited hypotheses within the range of a particular science and its modes of explanation. Rather they deal with the universal structures and patterns of things, and can be neither verified nor falsified by any particular scientific investigation. They have, as Stephen Toulmin argues, "leaped out" of their original scientific base (in biology and in economic history respectively) to do universal service as visions of the total structure of things. They use multivalent language, speaking of universal and ultimate structures or powers within the observable interrelations of things.[11]

[11] In this discussion of the "myth" of evolution, we do not refer to the biological theory of that name which, of course, is a vastly respected theory in a particular science and so explanatory of a limited range of questions. We refer rather to the expansion of that concept into a law of universal process by means of which every sort of major natural or historical change is to be interpreted. Such a universal notion is not testable as are the hypotheses of a special science, and the concept itself clearly functions as a myth in our wider cultural life. See Toulmin's description of the "myth" of evolution in *Metaphysical Beliefs*, pp. 47–66.

2. They give an intelligible explanation of the evils and enigmas of historical life and contain a vision of an ultimate structure determining the character of events. Thus they provide "meaning" in life in that they are explanatory of its evils and reassuring about its prospects. As religions have always done, they relate our values and our hopes to the objective nature of things. It is significant that in both of them normative or "ought" language, what *should* be, becomes in the future tense identical with indicative and assertive language, what *will* be.

3. They provide models and norms for individual human existence, for social and political decisions, and for the patterns of education characteristic of the cultures which live by them. No system of *scientific* hypotheses functions in these three ways; thus the meanings of these visions are mythical and not scientific, and whatever validity they possess is to be assessed for them as myths and not as science.

Evolution and the Marxist dialectic are, then, myths in their linguistic form, in their intention, and in their usage; they "do" in our world what religious myths have always done. However, as our discussion has implied, necessarily they are in our society only surreptitious or incognito myths. That is to say, they cannot admit their status as myths, and thus they are forced to appear in another guise, as science. It is, as we have noted, one of the dogmas of a secular culture that all assertions about the world, all statements as to "what is the case," must be scientific statements, that is to say, verifiable or falsifiable by experience sharable communally among scientists.[12] Thus these two views of the ultimate structure of process, that it exhibits an evolving and progressive structure or a material dialectic, must interpret themselves as scientific generalizations, that is, derived by ob-

[12] The principle that all assertions about the world must be "scientific" assertions forms the basis for the philosophy of empirical naturalism and, of course, for positivism as well. In the case of the first, the defining principle of the school, that of the principle of the "continuity of analysis," specifies this point; and in the case of the second, the verification principle governing all assertions that are not tautologies, reiterates the same point. See Y. H. Krikorian, *Naturalism and the Human Spirit*, New York, 1944, especially chs. 2, 9, and 15, and A. J. Ayer, *Language, Truth and Logic*.

296

jective empirical inquiry and legitimatized solely by scientific testing. Since this is in fact *not* their linguistic form—they result surely from deep intuitions resulting in profound but untestable mythical visions—they are thereby weakened and distorted, since they are claiming a status whose requirements they do not, cannot, and should not fulfill. Presumably, unlike myths, scientific hypotheses are not revelations of hidden mysteries known only by faith and by religious or communal participation; rather ostensibly, as empirical generalizations, they can be objectively validated by anyone's inquiry, and falsified by any serious contrary evidence. A mythical assertion, on the other hand, is referent to a level of mystery in existence where structures are hidden as well as manifest. Thus it is based on a vision manifested to faith or assent in and through certain facts taken to be crucial, but is not established and objectively tested in relation to the totality of relevant facts. It represents, therefore, a vision affirmed and upheld by involved participation in the spiritual ethos and the ethical structures of the community formed by the myth. When such a vision has to pretend to be "science," it becomes vulnerable to requirements it cannot and should not meet; a "category mistake" has been made. In the case of these two cosmic myths, those scientists who do not participate in this vision as myth legitimately ridicule it as science; and those observable facts and sequences of events contrary to its intent as a theory are now as counter-instances relevant to its truth insofar as it claims the status of a scientific hypothesis. As myth a cosmic vision is not so vulnerable; its gods are admittedly *absconditus* as well as *revelatus*. Parading as science, such a total vision is in danger of becoming absurd in the face of the mystery of the total patterns of existence with which myths must perforce deal. Theology learned this in the nineteenth century when it claimed to be able to discourse on scientific subjects and thus was proved almost always wrong; Marxism and evolution have increasingly discovered this in an age when to many the observable facts have failed to fit the patterns apparently entailed by their explanatory categories.

The second problem for a cosmic myth in a secular age arises

297

from the same characteristic, namely that modern mythical language cannot be multivalent or analogical but must strive to represent the sequential, one-dimensional, and univocal language of science. Scientific language, to be sure, cannot accurately be called simply "causal." Nevertheless, its aim surely is to discover and so explicate invariable relations, sequences of events that, granted the conditions, "cannot fail to happen." In finding that set of invariable relations which exhibit how the sequence cannot fail to happen, a scientific hypothesis achieves itself as an explanation. Thus a modern cosmic myth tends, as Toulmin remarks,[13] not to be anthropomorphic but mechanomorphic, that is, to understand the determinative structure of things which makes them intelligible in terms of the invariable relations discovered by science, rather than in terms of personal wills and their intentions and acts. In the anthropomorphic language of most older mythology, the wills of the gods might, to be sure, be more potent than those of men, but implied in that language was the notion of an encounter of wills, a drama of divine and human actions so that the patterns of existence flowed *both* from the mysterious structures of the given and from the free, autonomous participation of man in and through those structures. When, however, such a vision of man's interaction with his world is set in scientific language, then inevitably this vision gathers to it the heavy sense of necessity rightly inherent in any scientific account, and consequently the participation of man's freedom in the patterns of events becomes more unintelligible and more precarious. More than their religious forebears, modern cosmic myths cannot handle the mystery of man's freedom, any more than they can express, as they must to be viable, the mystery of transcendence—and the result is that the enigma of cultural creativity as well as that of historical evil remains in most modern mythology superficially and so unsatisfactorily comprehended.

Although these two cosmic myths retain an important role among many of the most powerful elements of the modern secular scene, it seems to me that since the early part of the

13 Stephen Toulmin, *op. cit.,* p. 16.

century they have both tended to be replaced by anthropocentric ones,[14] and that the latter are in the end more characteristic of our present secular culture. What has happened apparently is that the questioning, empirical secular spirit has now begun to devour its own cosmic myths, to separate them as "myth" from their own scientific foundations, and to test them increasingly by the historical evidence at hand. For this reason evolution has more and more become a lower-case word, a theory in biology and the life sciences, and not regarded, as it surely was at the end of the nineteenth century, as a universal law of cosmic and historical progress. And the Marxist ideology has become increasingly regarded by its adherents in eastern Europe as a defensible theory applicable to economic and political life, but not an ultimate framework totally explanatory of man and his world. The results of this further development of secularity have been, as we noted, a deeper desacralizing of the cosmos and of historical process, a total separation of the great human questions of meaning and direction from questions about the nature of the universe and even of history, and thus a waning of what we have called cosmic mythology. In modern scientific naturalism, in positivism, in most language philosophy, and in existentialism alike only scientific assertions about the "nature of things" are possible or relevant. For this mood, religious and philosophical statements, whatever else they may do, cannot describe the ultimate structures of nature or of the course of history; there is no theological or philosophical "super-knowing" of an ultimate reality or order or pattern. Thus the cosmos is

[14] The movement from a cosmic mythology to an anthropocentric one is, in the lingo of evolutionary science, perhaps best visible in the tendency of contemporary evolutionists to distinguish, first, biological evolution from cultural evolution; and then to distinguish further the historical developments of the past, which were determined by uncomprehended genetic, social, and technical factors, from present and future possibilities of *deliberate* control over these factors through modern science. Thus in an age of science, man, so to speak, "takes over" from both cosmic and past historical processes the direction of his own destiny. For perhaps the clearest statement of this movement from cosmic determinism to human and so intentional control, see Julian Huxley, *Religion Without Revelation*.

299

merely nature as understood by science, and history *only* what historical research can uncover, namely systems of contingent, relative, and temporal factors illustrating no ultimate purpose or direction and so irrelevant to human questions of meaning and to human hopes for a better world. Man has here "come of age" in a directionless world, and nothing in the cosmos itself—God, evolution, progress, or the material dialectic—is concerned with his dreams or their realization. His "reassurance" and confidence about life and the models by which he structures his freedom are, therefore, reflective not of any ultimate cosmic or historical structure but of the capacities and achievements of his own autonomy. Most "post-modern" myths are thus myths about man and his powers. Whether these should be called religious or not is a minor matter; that they are myths, we have no doubt, and this we shall now seek to show.

When we speak of myths of human autonomy, we are speaking of images of man and his capacities which carry with them a sacral character and so can function in our culture as myths have in other cultures. More specifically, this means the language in which this image is described is multivalent or symbolic in form and thus involves assertions far transcendent to the level of empirical or scientific discourse; the narration of the image answers our ultimate questions of destiny and of meaning; and, finally, these images provide models or norms for important social behavior. Thus the lack of the cosmogonic or even of the cosmic and historical reference, characteristic of previous mythologies, does not vitiate their mythical character. It means merely that the sacred, that which is ultimate, healing, and normative, and that which gives meaning to the chaos of life, manifests itself in and through man and not in and through the environing world or its process. In such myths the "given" is meaningless; only what man can make of it can have meaning. It is, parenthetically, no surprise, therefore, but surely ironic, that these secular myths are generally gnostic in form: the sacred is spirit and not matter, manifesting itself in and through man's reason and will rather than through nature or historical process. We can now understand, moreover, why secularism believed it had

300

transcended myth: aware that it allowed only a scientific account of natural and even of historical process, and confident only in the autonomous human powers that made that scientific knowledge possible, it overlooked the fact that this confidence rested on a *mythical* image of modern, scientific man, and that because its confidence was in scientific intelligence and/or human freedom and not in God, this did not make it any less "mythical" or even "religious" in form. Scientific humanism, as well as theism or polytheism, must use mythical language in order to express itself.

There are in modern culture many such images of man whose linguistic form and existential function in some community qualify them as myths: there is the image, treasured by the professional and academic communities, of scientific man, the man of critical intelligence and therefore the man of scientific knowledge and of humanitarian principles[15]; there is the authentic man of existentialist philosophies; the unrepressed and so free and loving man of much philosophical psychology[16]; the liberal, democratic citizen of educational and humanist circles; the energetic, practical, efficient executive of the managerial class; the uncompromising and hard-headed rebel of the New Left; the "drop-out" man of much of the modern hippie generation; and finally the admired and famous man of public relations firms— and of us all! All of these have several factors in common. On the one hand they find little or no basis for meaning in a cosmic reference of any sort; and yet on the other they portray through this symbolic image of an ideal man, newly possible to modern

[15] Ernest Nagel gives a paradoxical formulation of what he regards as the essence of naturalism: the first principle of naturalism, he says, is "the existential and causal primacy of organized matter in the executive order of nature." On the other hand, human reason, continues Nagel (when speaking of our human hopes), "while not an omnipotent instrument for the achievement of human goals," is still "the only instrument we do possess" and it is "potent against remedial evils." Ernest Nagel, *Logic Without Metaphysics* (Glencoe, Ill., 1956), pp. 7 and 18.

[16] See the image of man as autonomous, self-aware, and so loving in the writings of Erich Fromm, especially *Man for Himself,* and the image of the new unrepressed, bodily, polymorphous man in Norman O. Brown's *Life Against Death.*

301

culture, a genuine confidence in and promise of a resolution of the enigmas and the terrors of past historical existence. And divergent as the content of these images of autonomy are, they do base their confidence in autonomy on two common assumptions:

1. Each assumes that for man to understand, to know about, or to be aware of something, is to be able in a quite new way to control it, to direct it, and to use it teleologically; that knowledge and awareness can turn what has been a blindly determining force *in* man and so a fate *over* man into a new instrument *of* man; or to use classical language, that knowledge is self-fulfillment or *arete*.

2. They also share the confidence that the realization of human freedom, however the latter may be defined, means freedom *from* evil rather than freedom *for* evil, and thus that in freeing man—from whatever is determining him against his will—awareness is at once resolving the problem of evil in his behavior and so the ambiguity of his history. Thus in these myths, evil is located outside of freedom, and therefore insofar as man is really free to be himself—insofar as he is entirely intelligent, authentic, unrepressed, liberal, or what have you—insofar is he free from the evil that has haunted him. Fate and sin arise from beyond the inward center of man: in ignorance, in repression, in the false objectification of things, in prejudice and false ideals. Consequently man may have confidence because the rapidly accumulating knowledge or awareness of man must lead to an increase of meaningful experience.

Surely one of the most important characteristics of a scientific, introverted, and specialized culture is its drive towards and faith in an almost total "awareness" of almost every conceivable factor influencing almost every conceivable situation. Total consciousness and self-consciousness is the characteristic goal of our secular culture; if we know or are aware of everything, we can control everything. This faith in the healing power of awareness leads in a culture in which knowledge accumulates at an accelerated pace to a tremendous optimism about a new day, an eschatology in which understanding of all the factors

302

outside us and self-consciousness about all those within will lead to healing control and enjoyment. In the typology of modern historic myths, therefore, anthropocentric myths are dualistic and gnostic accounts of destiny in which evil is a part of the chaos of the unorganized and so unintelligible "given"; but it is a "given" which the intelligence and freedom of the trained, the self-aware, or the critically intelligent man may, like Indra or Zeus of old, subdue into order through a sacral gnosis and autonomous freedom.

We cannot discuss in detail the problems of each one of these variations in the modern gnostic myths of autonomy, but we might spend a few moments summarizing the principal difficulties, as we see them, of that anthropocentric myth which, we feel, represents the dominant source of confidence, reassurance, and meaning in the West: the myth of the new scientific man. This is the image of the man in the white coat; the man who embodies the new methods of inquiry; who thus in modest actuality but also—and here is the mythical element—in infinite potentiality *knows* the secrets of things, what their effective structures are and so how they work; and consequently the man who can control these forces which he now understands and so bring them into the service of human purposes. This control over the blind forces of our natural environment—so the myth continues—has already been partly realized through technology; why cannot the same sort of knowing, directed now at man's own psychological, social, and historical problems—yes, even at the genetic structures which determine man's nature—lead to the same kind of control over human life, and thus lead at last to the directing of our own biological and historical destiny along the lines of human purposes? We are now beginning to see that man can literally create man, and thus can free him from his former bondage both to outside and to interior forces that have worked against his will. Let me quote, as one among many examples— Julian Huxley is the best known—from a recent speech by the distinguished scientist Dr. Glenn Seaborg. According to *The New York Times* of January 17, 1963, in a speech in Washington, Dr. Seaborg "expressed faith that man could, if he tried, solve all of today's agonizing problems—war, hunger, the population explosion, water shortages, pollution. 'Man may well have reached that point in history, that stage in his development . . . where he has not only been made master of his fate, but where his technology and his morality have come face to face,' . . . Science has given mankind an opportunity 'to control and direct our future, our creative evolution . . . I believe we can be masters of our fate.' "[17]

Modern academic and professional man *does* have confidence in the meaning and the vast possibilities of human life; that confidence is, he believes, reasonable. If one asks about the grounds for that confidence, something like the above will appear, we suggest: we now know how to know; we have unlocked the secret of critical intelligence. With that sacral tool we can change the character of the natural environment that surrounds us, of the socio-historical context in which we live, and even of our own recalcitrant nature; and thus can we master history itself.

Much might be said of this myth. The first relevant point

[17] This is a perfect likeness to the image we have sought here to describe: the sense of the unlimited potentiality of human freedom to use scientific knowledge creatively to control our destiny, the noticeable shift from cosmic, evolutionary symbols to anthropocentric autonomous symbols, and the direct relation of scientific inquiry to the control over our fate. These are the elements of the image which, we believe, is the foundation for most of the confidence and the hopes of the intellectual élite of our culture.

It is amusing and even ironic to note that many social scientists, who echo Seaborg's hopes, correctly scoffed at Senator Goldwater's emphasis on the control *economic* man has over his own destiny. Social science, said they, reveals that the economic possibilities or opportunities which certain classes enjoy are *not* created by their own wills and capabilities, as Goldwater claimed, but rather have been rigidly determined by their given or "fated" social positions, and thus that the conservative "myth" of the possibilities of freedom over destiny is really a rationalization for the freedom of the economic élite to gain and to retain their given economic privileges. And yet the same social scientists and engineers believe firmly that the social scientist, if not the business executive, can control many of these fates and so eradicate the power of the "irrational givens" in historical life. The conservative myth believes, perhaps, in the sacral autonomy of pragmatic, energetic executive man, the liberal one in the sacral autonomy of scientific man. Each alike assumes that the man who "understands" can control significant destiny by manipulating the logos of society for his own purposes.

is that like most myths it deals with the mystery of destiny and human freedom. Arising as it does within a scientific context, however, this secular myth sharpens this ancient paradox into what is almost a self-contradiction; and this self-contradiction, without the aid of the multivalent, symbolic language essential to myth, must remain unresolved. The image of the new scientific man able to understand and so able to control the determining forces of destiny is an image which promises a *more* extravagant freedom than has almost any previous mythical image. The irrational and purposeless forces of "fate," both natural and historical, both outside and inside man, are here felt to be, potentially at least, under the domination of man's rational and moral purposes; "decision" or intentional choice are thus in prospect given an almost unlimited range.

Paradoxically, however, the hope for this vast increment of freedom through scientific knowledge depends directly on the assumption that for scientific inquiry—in genetics, psychology, and the social sciences—man himself can exhaustively be understood as an *object* of inquiry, that is, as an object to be comprehended in terms of the determining universal factors or laws that operate in and through him, and thus comprehended precisely as a non-intentional creature, a part of nature's total system of determining factors. But if the man in the white coat is as free to control, and as intentionally motivated by creative purposes, as the image proclaims—and otherwise there is little hope in the image—then the man on the table, the object of his inquiry, must *also* be in part free. Thus he must in part be incomprehensible in terms of objective and universal laws, and so even creative outside the bounds of those laws and consequently destructive of them as well. Freedom in the object under control reduces inevitably the freedom of the controller to work his will. As Tillich once wisely remarked: man can always look back at his controller—and we might add, cheat on an objective test. And so, since in this case both controller and controlled represent instances of the same being, the myth tends to contradict itself. A myth which promises human freedom over destiny on the basis of man's complete subservience to outward determination is surely *less* intelligible than are even the most sharply paradoxical theological accounts of the puzzles of divine grace and human freedom! The simple deterministic language of scientific hypothesis, and the simple intentional language applicable to scientific inquirers in the laboratory and in engineering, are not capable together of producing a comprehensive myth on which our culture can live with confidence.

More important, the apprehension of the mystery of the enigmas of historical existence, and especially of human fallibility and fault (to use Professor Ricoeur's language),[18] one of the main functions of myth, is here too superficial to provide a secure base for creative self-understanding in these areas. Evil for the mono-dimensional secular mentality is a "problem," not a mystery; thus it has causes; objective explanation is possible did we but know these causes; and so the solution to evil is to find these causes through inquiry, to control them and thus to eradicate that form of evil. The model here is that of the engineer or the doctor; and the goal, as in these cases, is to control through knowledge the factors that cause evil. To know is to be able to control, and to control is to be able to overcome human problems.

Two difficulties, however, indiscernible in terms of these simple secular models, arise to challenge this optimistic identity of knowing with virtuous control: (1) Whether to control men as we control nature does not raise possibly more terrible potentialities for evil, and so problems for freedom. Control over men through knowledge may not in actuality so much *enact* human freedom as *imperil* it, as Father Mascall so clearly pointed out; (2) Whether the problem of the self-control of the controller (of the man in the white coat), when scientific technology enters the arena of social and political affairs, is not the deepest problem of all.[19] If knowledge is power, as this

[18] For the most stimulating and profound treatment of the paradox of the voluntary and the involuntary, its relations to fallibility and to actual evil, see the monumental volumes of Paul Ricoeur: *The Voluntary and the Involuntary, Fallible Man,* and *The Symbolism of Evil.*

[19] As is well known, Greek philosophy also tended to identify knowing with *arete* or virtue. Though this identification is also questionable (for

myth assumes, and if, as history surely indicates, the use of power in a social context is always ambiguous, then this picture of an unambiguous use of power by a scientific or intellectual elite is manifestly misleading. Historical evil is not merely a problem to be solved by an objective observer, as if it were caused by some discoverable objective cause as a flood or a disease is caused. It is a mystery which in concrete human experience infects human freedom, and therefore infects the enacted purposes of the observer, the expert, and the technologist as well. Thus the confidence in the virtue and rationality of the knower expressed in this myth of the new scientific man—potent in both West and East—is misplaced. When modern culture sees *this,* and realizes the utopian character of its mythos, then the extraordinary optimism of the secular community fades and is replaced by the deep pessimism of much of our present literature.

Perhaps the basic problem with this and other modern myths is that the insistence on mono-dimensional rather than multi-valent or symbolic language forces it into abstractions out of which the myth is then composed. When it speaks of the natural world, and of man as part of that world, it is confined to the abstractions of scientific language which, for the purposes of inquiry, presupposes a system of invariant relations. Thus is man seen as determined and the promise of control over his destiny made thereby intelligible. When it speaks of man as the

---

example, see St. Paul's remarks in Romans 7), nevertheless it should be noted that Greek thought presents a better case than does the modern version of the gnostic hope. Knowing, for Greek philosophy, was not *techne,* knowledge of how to do something; it was rather *wisdom,* knowledge of the self, of its structure or nature and its limits, and so knowledge of the eternal structures in which that nature of the self, in order to be itself, participates. It was, therefore, a knowledge not of objective interrelationships separated from the self, but precisely of the order inherent in the self; it thus led reasonably to self-direction and so to virtue. Modern knowing in science is objective knowledge of external structures unrelated to the self, or to the mystery of its freedom. It thus totally overlooks the deeper problem of the self-control of the expert or the technologist—and so, when it promises a modern version of the Republic's "ordered society," based on the wisdom of a scientific élite, it appears almost ludicrously unconvincing.

307

rational and free knower and the controller, it is confined to the relative abstraction of the experience of the scientist in the laboratory, where the concrete character and pervasive influence of our moral fallibility and our actual proneness to evil are in practice minimized and so in theory quite overlooked. In the concrete self-experience of man in his *Lebenswelt,* however, man is neither as determined as the first abstraction indicates nor as totally free and rational as the second assumes. He is bafflingly both determined and free, both good and evil, everlastingly compromised by a distortion that manifests itself in and through his freedom as much as it does in and through the forces that beset him from outside. To comprehend this concrete man, therefore, requires a multivalent language, a language which comprehends both the mystery of existence, that is, its depth or transcendence, and also comprehends the distortion of the essential structures of historical existence. All of this sounds irrational and meaningless to the secular mind; but it is far more faithful to our actual experience of the secular world than are the present myths by which that world lives. In the face of this mystery and ambiguity of man's freedom, we can see the ineradicable weakness of modern anthropocentric myths which locate the sacred and so healing power solely in the realization of man's freedom.

* * *

What is the relation of Christian theology to this discussion? We have in the above attempted to lay part of a foundation for understanding theological discourse so as to exhibit its relevance to the world, even the secular world. In this effort we have tried to show the following: (1) That secular existence, despite its heated denials, raises ultimate questions for which myth and symbolic language provide the only mode of conceptualization. (2) That mythical discourse is thus relevant to the life of secular culture, as evidenced by the significant reappearance of myths borne out of this culture. (3) That secular myths, however, suffer from the inability of the secular mind to think symbolically and so are unable to comprehend the enigmas as well as the blessings of life. Thus they provide an impoverished and unsure base for secular existence. (4) That what are lacking, in order to thematize the actual experience of a secular culture, are symbolic forms referent to mystery, to the transcendent and the sacred, and to the concrete experiences of dislocation and of fault. (5) In current secular mythology (with the exception of the cosmic myths of evolution and of Marxism), the meaningfulness and creativity of destiny, of the given, is too radically denied, and the ambiguity of autonomy too easily overlooked, and thus symbols pointing both to the creative mystery of the given and to the destructive tendencies of freedom are required. We have argued for the necessity in our cultural life of a mode of mythical discourse that is both "secular"—that is, relevant to the questions and perplexities of our contemporary culture—and yet "theological"—that is, capable of giving consistent symbolic expressions to the human experiences of the transcendent and the sacred.

Although it is surely a part of our argument, we shall not try to establish here that a secular theology based on Christian symbolic forms is thus implied—or even the best available. Rather we wish to conclude with some remarks about the form of Christian theology if it is to fulfill this worldly role of providing the myths by which a modern culture can live. In our discussion of the disjunction between the ancient mythical consciousness and the secular one, certain requirements emerged which, we feel, any relevant contemporary theology must meet.

1. A modern mythology must temper the cosmogonic emphasis of archaic myths, and thus relate its fundamental symbolic forms to process and to history rather than primarily to originating and so timeless structures. Thus will the legitimate modern emphasis on creativity, autonomy, and openness in historical existence be expressed. This is possible and even natural for Christian theology, since it was the biblical tradition that first brought history and its events into the center of the mythical consciousness. Thus we support post-Hegelian theologians like Tillich in his emphasis on the dynamic character of the divine life, process theologians in their emphasis on the funda-

mental categories of relatedness, of becoming, and of possibility as significant of the divine, and those elements of the writings of Father Rahner and Leslie Dewart that challenge an older static and supernaturalistic view of God.

2. The multivalent character of theological symbols, their referential intentionality towards *both* the finite and that which transcends the finite, must not be confused with scientific language about the finite and its interrelations. We have seen the disarray that results when scientific language seeks to do the job of mythical discourse. Historically, however, the fault has been the other way; theological language has sought to provide "scientific-type" information about the age of the world, the character of the first pair, the way events unfolded in natural and human history, and so forth. Mythical language *does* refer to the finite insofar as the latter is a medium of that which transcends it; it does not, however, inform us of the finite in and of itself. Revelation tells us of the God who manifests himself in nature and in the events of history, but not of the character of nature and what must have happened and when in that history. Thus we question both the wisdom and the theological validity of drawing implications about "matters of fact" from theological symbols or dogmas, as in the case of the theological assertion of monogenism.[20]

[20] Paul Ricoeur states this same point in the following: "What does it mean to 'understand' the Adamic myth? In the first place, it means accepting the fact that it is a myth. . . . It must be well understood from the *outset* that, for the modern man who has learned the distinction between myth and history, this chronicle of the first man and the first pair can no longer be coordinated with the time of history and the space of geography as these have been irreversibly constituted by critical awareness. It must be well understood that the question, where and when did Adam eat the forbidden fruit, no longer has meaning for us; every effort to save the letter of the story as true history is vain and hopeless." *Symbolism of Evil,* p. 235. "The disillusion of the myth as explanation is a necessary way to the restoration of the myth as symbol. Thus, the time of restoration is not a different time from that of criticism . . . a criticism that is no longer reduction but restoration. . . . It represents the advanced point of criticism, as an awareness of the myth as myth." *Ibid.,* p. 352. For a brilliant if, to us, misguided attempt to defend the monogenist theory on dogmatic grounds, see Karl Rahner's article "Monogenism" in *Theological Investigations,* Vol. I.

310

Finally, we think it very important that contemporary theology understand itself as providing symbolic forms within terms of which the deeper issues of ordinary, secular life are to be thematized, comprehended, and redeemed. Secular experience, as we have implied, is blind without mythical interpretation; but correspondingly, theological categories are empty if they are not related to secular experience. In that case, while their conceptual meanings may be clear enough in terms of the language of systematic theology, they lack felt or existential meanings. Thus, as in much contemporary church life, they can be known and even affirmed universally as true, but still they may *mean* nothing to the people who thus affirm them. Theological doctrines are not self-subsistent, as if they *meant* something all by themselves; they must be related to the stuff of life if they are to function as have significant symbolic forms. There are, we suggest further, no peculiarly "religious" or "churchly" problems to which theological doctrines or symbols are answers; there are only human and therefore secular problems, and in relation to these issues the theological doctrines are to be understood and elaborated.

The symbolic forms of a Christian understanding of secular life are, to be sure, traditional: they have been carried historically in the life of the covenant community, and for the theologian, it was *there,* in that community, that an understanding of life and a sense of its healing possibilities has arisen. Thus any "secular theology" must be tested first of all by the integrity of its comprehension of these symbolic forms, or "doctrines," as we have traditionally called them, as they have appeared in Scripture and in the history of the community. But, correspondingly, these symbolic forms express and communicate the manifestations of grace in *life,* and so in life as we all now live it. Thus they must be comprehended as mediating answers to the ultimate issues of our secular existence, and therefore as relevant to the questions and the problems of that existence. The most fundamental implications for theology of our understanding of myth have been: (1) the sacred appears mysteriously and yet creatively in the ordinary life of man, and thus in his cultural

311

existence of community, morals, artistic productivity, and inquiry; (2) that this experience of the transcendent mystery of common grace is interfused with the experience of the fault, of the tragic ambiguity and enigma of evil both outside and inside ourselves; (3) that no culture can understand itself without setting these experiences into symbolic forms. With its sense of transcendent mystery, of the creativity of the given in life, of the distortion of freedom, and yet of the presence of new grace, the Christian mythos is, I believe, able more powerfully than any other to comprehend these facets of secular experience. But that comprehension will remain inert and empty unless these doctrinal symbols are related at every point to the secular experience which they were, we believe, intended to redeem.

15.

CHRISTIAN CROSSROADS AND
ATHEIST *AGGIORNAMENTO*

ARTHUR GIBSON

THE Second Vatican Council was designated by Pope John XXIII as primarily pastoral.[1] Its scope and aim was to effect in the whole body of the faithful, a renewal of the original spirit of Christianity, the spirit of Christ, and to prepare the atmosphere in which that spirit and that inspiration could most effectively be brought to bear in the world of the twentieth century.[2] This aim was a direct expression of the missionary calling of Christians to preach the good news everywhere and, in the power of the spirit of Christ, to "renew the face of the earth."

Small wonder, then, that one of the acts to emerge from the conciliar event was the establishment of a Secretariat for Non-Believers. Two of the most populous nations of the twentieth-century world are officially committed to militant constructive atheism, although both equally solemnly proclaim the civic right of all citizens to freedom of conscience in all aspects of religious belief. Several smaller nations, committed, both by their own official world view and by fraternal ties with the Union of Soviet Republics and the People's Republic of China, to a similar line of action, must be classed as at least predominantly

[1] See the apostolic constitution *Humanae Salutis,* in *The Documents of Vatican II,* New York, 1966, pp. 703 ff., and Pope John's opening speech to the Council, *ibid.,* pp. 710 ff.
[2] See *ibid.,* especially p. 703.

atheistic. In many of the emerging nations there is a volatile atmosphere of religious crisis; and the unfortunate historical identification of religion, and more especially of Christianity, with colonial exploitation has tended to trigger a more or less violent revolt against religion in these nations. Finally, in the larger and smaller nations of what has come to be designated as the Western World, there is much uneasiness abroad, much questioning, much shaking of the foundations, in the whole area of religion.

Even where there is no official or organized progress of militant atheism, modern man, stumbling over the mystery of creaturely freedom, the technlogical explosion of the last three decades, the deadly menace of the atomic age and its simultaneous promise of a paradise on earth, is posing profound and radical questions concerning the very meaningfulness and relevance of religion, considered as man's relation to a Creator who transcends entirely the whole space-time continuum in which man lives out the little and tormented existence which he is coming to regard more and more insistently as the only, or at least the principal meaningful dimension for his action and his destiny.

By the very choice of its title, the most immediately pertinent document of Vatican II has endeavoured to stress the intimate identification of Christendom with the present crisis of humanity. For that document is entitled not *The Church and the Modern World,* nor yet *The Church to the Modern World,* but *The Church in the Modern World.*[3] To this end, the first step, as reflected in the first Secretariat (in point of time) to deal with "external affairs," has been an effort to achieve a functional and operative union of faith and purpose between the Catholic Church and all other ecclesial communities of the Christian confession. The next step, again reflected in the second Secretariat, the Secretariat for Non-Christian Religions, has been an effort to achieve an analogous rapprochement, a deepening of understanding and a common front of action, as far as possible,

---

[3] To this point Fr. Campion refers in "The Church Today," *ibid.,* pp. 183 ff., especially pp. 193 f., and Robert McAfee Brown in his Response, *ibid.,* pp. 309 ff., especially pp. 312 and 313.

314

with other theistic believers. The final step is precisely the effort, epitomized by the Secretariat for Non-Believers, to build bridges of understanding and cooperation with that enormous percentage of the present-day human race that is officially committed to militant constructive atheism, that is, to a rejection and denial of God as an indispensable preliminary to the construction of a better and happier and more fully human future for man.

In all three efforts, there is a real though distinctly peripheral and preliminary place for a clearing away of the underbrush of exaggerated propagandistic misunderstanding or incomprehension that always accumulates between human groups separated by painful historical circumstances. If this need is still felt acutely between fellow Christians, it is certainly and obviously all the more drastic between believers and atheists, especially between the Christian community and its hitherto most monolithic grouping, the Catholic Church, on the one hand, and, on the other, the Marxist atheists, the most monolithic grouping within the extremely heterogeneous class of modern atheists and, more pertinently, the only such atheistic group thus far to have become organized into a power structure. Such an effort at repairing the damage done by fanatical exaggerations on both sides is evident in the initial sections of Leslie Dewart's book *The Future of Belief*[4] (though the author quite specifically, and we feel, rightly, repudiates any intention of making this the main aim of his book) and in Roger Garaudy's *From Anathema to Dialogue,*[5] a contribution by a Marxist atheist.

There is solid evidence that this laudable effort has already borne much fruit: no longer is either side so ready to believe and publish the petty and infantile propaganda charges against the other which characterized the Stalin period in the Soviet Union and the McCarthy period in the Western World. But such removal of blameworthy distortions can, at best, do no more than clear the way for the serious confrontation, and I was very edified, in a recent colloquium held in Winnipeg between Christian and Communist representatives, to hear one of the Com-

[4] New York, 1966.
[5] New York, 1966.

munists say, after the mutually laudatory initial remarks of myself on the Christian side and a Communist leader for their side:
"I hope that, in this new atmosphere of sweetness and light, we
are not going to sweep under the carpet the very real differences
and radical disagreements existing between our two groups."

It transcends entirely the scope of this paper to enter into
detail on the dubious ecumenism inspiring much dialogue between Christian bodies and the equally dubious irenic spirit
animating the encounter between Christians and other religions
(notably the Jewish community, on which a rabbi recently had
harsh and thought-provoking things to say in an article in
Saturday Evening Post[6]).

I wish rather to attack head-on the very drastic differences
separating the Christian and the Marxist atheist, to consider
the problems posed by these differences and the present dynamic
of their discussion, both for Christian and for Marxist atheist.
I then wish to consider whether any meaningful collaboration
whatever can be envisaged between these groups. I shall answer
that question in the affirmative, but the answer will be profoundly influenced by my preliminary survey; in the light of that
answer, I wish finally to consider what form such cooperation
can take.

It has been several times remarked in recent years that the
Catholic Church (and indeed other Christian bodies as well)
can be said to be just emerging from a prolonged period of
practical Monophysitism. After the poignant definitions of
Chalcedon, the most important single ecumenical council in the
history of Christendom, it is alleged that the true and perfect
humanity of Christ, the theandric composite, has been practically neglected. This statement is, to put it mildly, somewhat
highhanded when one considers that almost three centuries
immediately following Chalcedon were devoted to the furious
battle on the part of orthodox Christendom against precisely
the Monophysite heresy which Chalcedon itself crystallized into
a formal heresy, and then against the last gasp of the Monophysite tendency, represented by Monothelitism, which, while

[6] December 1966.

alleging its readiness to accept two natures in Christ, resolutely refused to accept two wills. In fact, George Every in his stimulating work *The Byzantine Patriarchate*[7] makes the intriguing suggestion that Islam itself might be considered as the last-ditch stand of transcendentalist monotheism against the encroachments of what was considered by the Semitic mind exposed to the Christian witness to be an incipient radical heresy, attributing to the humanity of Christ a degree of reality inconsistent with pure religion.

Yet there is some justice to the charge of protracted practical Monophysitism as leveled against Christian tradition. In his excellent introduction to the English *Solovyev Anthology*, S. L. Frank has an illuminating commentary on this problem: "Two spiritual forces have been struggling against each other in the history of European peoples since the Renaissance: faith in God and faith in man. Speaking generally and therefore of course schematizing the manifold variety of the traditional Christian thought, one may say that its main tendency . . . was to magnify God at the expense of belittling man. Therefore when at the epoch of the Renaissance there sprang up the ardent faith in the great vocation and the creative power of man—a faith which, of course, was born of Christianity and could only find its justification in Christianity—it took the form of rebellion first against the ecclesiastical tradition and then against God. All the tragic history of modern Europe down to our own day is overshadowed by this fatal misconception. Faith in the freedom of the human spirit and its inalienable rights, a passionate appeal to secure to man conditions of life befitting his great dignity, become the inspiration of the unbelievers, their battle-cry in the struggle against Christian faith."[8]

Christians had, of course, not failed to grapple with this problem and to be troubled by it long before Marx came onto the scene. The Lutheran revolt against the almost Confucian stylization of creation was one such effort to take more meaningful account of the positive contribution of the individual

[7] London, 1947, pp. 82 f.
[8] London, 1950.

317

human soul to God, although the *sola fides* slogan of Lutheranism might be said to have depreciated this contribution to a total surrender. Nor can we evade the conclusion that the entire phenomenon of Protestantism was intimately linked with the great commercial, industrial, and incipient technological drive that was to breach entirely the smaller clusterings of the Middle Ages and pave the way for the titanism of the nineteenth and twentieth centuries. Jean Gottmann, in his admirable analysis of the dynamic of development of the United States of America and its economic hinge, *Megalopolis,* speaks repeatedly of the inspiration of the founding Fathers: their conviction that they had an "errand into the wilderness"[9] and that this witness to God would be authenticated by their financial and commercial success. Still the inspiration was firmly theistic but already man was taking upon himself the task of witnessing to God by productive and creative labor of truly drastic proportions, calculated to tether man's attention much more firmly to this earth.

In the wake of the philosophical, cultural, socio-political, and economic developments of the century between 1850 and 1950, many Christians of various denominations became acutely conscious of the necessity of total commitment to the City of Man; and the very essence of incarnationalism began to be interpreted in terms of this commitment. God became man in Christ in order to show man the challenge and the way of truly God-pleasing living in this world. In such genuinely Christian and Christ-centered visionaries as Teilhard de Chardin, the older short-range eschatology was expanded, in the light of a Christian evolutionism, into a very long-range vision indeed. Instead of individual and race being confined to the narrow compass of a pessimistically interpreted "little while between" wherein individuals must try to work out their own salvation with fear and tempestuous trembling, and the race was doomed to increasing alienation from God through growing pride until the end of time which would be an event violently triggered from outside, by the dramatic second coming of Christ, to be expected at any moment, there came into the Christian world view the notion of an

[9] Cambridge, 1961, pp. 76 ff., 773.

318

indefinitely long evolutionary process geared to the production of the perfect creature, who would indeed in the last days, incomparably more distant than traditional thought had placed them, be faced with a drastic choice between God and self, but who would evolve in an ever more solidary and ever more "interiorizing" centripetal drive. There emerged also the strong notion that mankind must more and more realize an absolutely basic community and even recognizable identity of being: man would be saved or doomed, at least in some sense of the word, *corporately.*

The combined force of modern circumstances and the dynamic of Christian response to those circumstances have recently tended to impart to Christianity a predominantly ethical bias, as Christians of all denominations plunge more and more energetically into practical witness at the civic level: civil rights (predominantly in the United States of America, South Africa, and Portuguese African possessions), the atomic test ban, world peace and disarmament, problems of illiteracy and general economic backwardness in the medievally organized emerging nations, the problem of world hunger, man's specifically secular neuroses and psychoses in the context of modern high-speed living—these are but a few of the civic and secular affairs that have absorbed Christians and brought Christianity to a dramatic crossroads.

Gradually the question is beginning to be asked: Is this Christian fact anything more than a secular ethical commitment? And if one can agree wholeheartedly with Father William DuBay that the Christian challenge, the challenge of Christ, *is* most definitely and unavoidably a moral challenge, one must assert with equal force that it is more, much more than that. Moreover, the true essence of Christianity resides not in that moral challenge, which is a secondary albeit inescapable consequence, but rather in the *ontological fact* that stands at the center of the Christian challenge. *And that fact is Christ, the incarnate God-Man.*

The Christian must assert categorically that it is hopelessly erroneous and phenomenologically unfair to pose the question

319

of the slide to atheism isolated from and in divorce from the question of the rejection of Christ. The Christian must assert equally categorically that no meaningfully Christian response can be given by man to his phenomenological situation which does not take account of *the historical fact of Christ* in all its implications, the most important of which is that the Creator-God has ingressed freely into the depths of his own creation, that ours is no longer a hidden God. In the wake of the Incarnation, it is no longer possible or licit to speak of some esoteric transcendental realm open to or existing for some citizens but irrelevant to the life of nations as a whole. Finally, the Christian must assert that any witness which would be a truly Christian witness must be a witness in the first instance *to Christ himself*. Vladimir Solovyev, at the end of the last century, expressed this cardinal truth in vivid form: "Christianity has its own content . . . and that content is singularly and exclusively Christ. In Christianity as such we find Christ and only Christ— here is a truth many times expressed but not very well assimilated. At the present time in the Christian world, especially in the Protestant world, one meets people who call themselves Christians but maintain that the substance of Christianity is not in the person of Christ, but rather in his teaching. They say: We are Christians because we accept the teaching of Christ. But in what does the teaching of Christ consist? If we take the moral teaching (and this is precisely what they have in mind in this case) developed in the Gospel and all reduced to the rule, 'love thy neighbor as thyself,' then it is necessary to admit that this moral rule does not represent the peculiarity of Christianity. Much earlier than Christianity, the Hindu religious teaching— love and compassion, and not only towards men, but towards everything living—was preached in Brahmanism and Buddhism. In the same way it is impossible to assume as the characteristic content of Christianity the teaching of Christ about God as Father, concerning God as being predominantly loving and gracious, for neither is this doctrine specifically Christian . . . If we consider the whole theoretical and the whole moral teaching of Christ, which we find in the Gospel, then the only new

320

doctrine specifically different from all other religions is the teaching of Christ about himself, the reference to himself as to the living, incarnate truth. 'I am the Way, the Truth and the Life: he who believeth in me shall have life eternal.' Thus, if one is to find the characteristic content of Christianity in the teachings of Christ, even here one must admit that this content means Christ himself."[10]

The crossroads at which Christianity stands today, the cross-roads to which Christianity has been brought by the radical swing of the pendulum in the direction of humanism, is a crossroads of *identity*. Shall and can Christians, individually and as a group, proceed to a collaboration with the world, in abstraction from the primordial and radical commitment to the person of Christ, the incarnate God-Man? Can we make a tactical compromise at least so as not to outrage an unbelieving world? Can we quietly endeavour to apply Christian principles in a collaboration with other men of good will who share these principles insofar as they are generically human principles? The answer is clear from Christ's own words: "Apart from me, you can do nothing!" It is simply erroneous and disloyal to onto-logical facts and theological dogmas to assert the Christ who came to satisfy man's deepest longings: for that Christ himself said that for *this* reason was he born and for *this* cause did he come into the world, *to bear witness to the truth*. And his other equally solemn declaration makes this proposition reflexive, for he said: "I am the Truth!"

This Truth clearly points man beyond himself, beyond even the incarnate Christ, to the great God who dwells beyond the whole dimension in which man now lives. Tragic in the extreme is the misguided pseudo-Christian humanism of a Paul van Buren who can assert: "Whatever men were looking for in looking for 'God' is to be found by finding Jesus of Nazareth"[11] and then go on to state "We do not know 'what' God is and we cannot understand how the word 'God' is being used."[12] Not

[10] *Lectures on Godmanhood,* London, 1948.
[11] *The Secular Meaning of the Gospel,* New York, 1966, p. 147.
[12] *Ibid.,* p. 84.

thus did Paul speak out on the Areopagus; rather did he say: "It is this God whom you are worshipping in ignorance that I am here to proclaim to you!"[13] On the day that Christendom betrays its interior commitment and its unremitting and uncompromising public witness to the incarnate God as the motive power of all history, it will lapse into a merely tolerated auxiliary of an impatiently secularized world. There may then indeed be cooperation between citizens of the world who style themselves Christians and other citizens of the world who deny the entire dimension of transcendence; but there could then be no collaboration between Christians and atheists, for there would be no Christians left.

*   *   *

The atheistic world, especially the part of that world organized into the political power structure of Marxist Communism, has in recent years itself been doing some serious rethinking, some updating and recasting of its own philosophy of man. A symptom of such re-evaluation is the recent book of Roger Garaudy, *Le Marxisme du XX° siècle*.[14] This book attempts a new look, as objective as a Marxist can take, at the phenomenon of religion. Garaudy dismisses as hopelessly simplistic the notion that religion is merely an elucubration of the power structure and opts rather for the possibility that religion may be an expression of the deepest aspirations of man, mistakenly externalized and personified into a transcendent deity. No convinced atheistic materialist could say fairer than that. Garaudy sees a valuable cultural heritage as having sprung from religion in general and, for the Western World, from Christianity in particular. He calls for a more educated and intelligent attitude by Marxists to this whole phenomenon and accurately and incisively points out that no real collaboration can be expected by any individual or group from another individual or group whose deepest convictions are not scrupulously respected by the would-be champion of collaboration. It would be sad indeed

13 Acts 17, 23.
14 Paris and Geneva, 1966.

322

to see Christians themselves disavowing or soft-pedaling those convictions they feel to be embarrassing to collaboration with the Marxist, at the very moment when a Marxist pioneer of collaboration is calling for a respect of those convictions.

Are we then left with a drastic head-on clash with no hope of meaningful collaboration? I am persuaded we are not; and I believe the key to the situation lies, on the Christian side, in a proper realization of the moral and world-wide socio-political consequences of the Incarnation, and a proper implementation of the code of ethics that Christ left, not merely as desirable for but as binding upon his followers.

I cannot entirely agree with Garaudy's contention, especially vividly presented in his first dialogue book, *From Anathema to Dialogue,* concerning the distinction between the Constantinian and the prophetic dimension in the Christian Church[15]; but I am entirely in agreement that Christians generally have, times without number, compromised shabbily with those Christian duties laid upon them by Christ. Indeed I believe that it was in very large measure this persistent and treacherous compromise that led, in 1917, to that metaphysical flash-point which fused two formerly demonstrably independent and separate streams of human endeavour: the needed drive for political and socio-economic reform, and doctrinaire philosophical atheism.

It is unjust to accuse the Popes of any dereliction of duty in this whole area. In scores of encyclicals, the latest of which, *Populorum Progressio,* of Pope Paul VI, caused quite a stir recently, the pontiffs have proclaimed Christ's teaching as concretely applied to the world of their day. The dereliction of duty has occurred at the generic Christian level of implementation.

The hard fact of the matter is that laissez-faire capitalism and liberal enlightenment are just as capable, have historically demonstrated themselves to be just as capable, of subtle distortion or brutal disregard of Christian principles and of Christ himself, as has Bolshevism at its worst! Specifically, too many Christians, individuals and groups, still are not firmly persuaded of certain basic truths that follow from the Incarnation, not

[15] See pp. 113 ff.

323

persuaded at the deep level where it begins to hurt personal or ethnic pride or begins to pinch individual or group interest: that all human beings have equal dignity, regardless of race or colour, because all are children of the same Father and members of the same Christ, all destined by him for the same eternal happiness; that ownership is not an ultimate right, devoid of all restrictive obligations; that war is an evil thing and thermonuclear war an utterly evil thing; that it is absolutely unjust for one individual or nation to exploit the chances of geography in order to pillage other peoples of the fruits of those few resources they do have; that it is gravely immoral for any nation to have millions of starvation deaths while surpluses rot in the graneries of other nations; that it is immoral and un-Christian in the extreme to contend that private gain or the profit motive is indispensable as an economic lever, or that no man can be expected to produce as zestfully for the good of his fellows as for his own; that some measure of public control, and to an increasing extent, of *international* control, over the complex machinery of the modern production line is indispensable to a just distribution of the world's wealth; that there is a crying need for a really effective international organization to manage the world's problems and mediate disputes *and* that the organization which currently exists for that purpose is deserving of all possible support.

Collaboration between theism and atheism is possible only if either or both betray or compromise the very principles which constitute their identity. Collaboration between theists and atheists, specifically between Christians and Marxist atheists, is possible because, as Pope John XXIII so intuitively saw, human beings always overflow their own conceptualizations of their world views, just as God overflows every created effort to articulate him. The universal power of appeal of Pope John came precisely from his ability to effect that mysterious phenomenon, usually described as the *existential encounter,* at least in the most recent technical jargon. I imagine Pope John would have smiled blandly at this term and referred it to his official theologians and philosophers for study while he went on effecting it. This statement is as little intended to be anti-intellectualist as was Pope John's whole life and action. But there is a whole vital dimension, especially today, that is preter-intellectual. Time is running out rapidly for our human race and it is of utmost importance in the circumstances of the uneasy equilibrium of terror presently prevailing that we do all indeed become as little children. Little children are generous, spotless, artless, and humbly obedient only in the disordered imagination of sentimental authors; but little children, as a subspecies, are *open and trusting realists*. Can we not emulate them there? This openness and mutual willingness to learn and to endeavour to understand is vital in every aspect and dimension of human relations but nowhere so urgent as in the theist-atheist and the Christian-Marxist dialogue.

This is no mere pious general platitude. As I insisted in a recent article kindly published in *The Marxist Quarterly*,[16] I believe there is today one major touchstone of human understanding and generosity, and that is the problem of the "agony and the ecstasy" of the People's Republic of China. The damnable thing is that we are all, Christian and Western Marxist alike, here repeating in unison the very error we each committed against the other in the grim days of the 1930's. We have far too little *information* and are exhibiting a blameworthy and, to me, utterly bemusing unwillingness to obtain more. The Chinese are an enormous people with a millenial cultural background, a people presently involved in a great transitional process; and we are judging them pusillanimously in terms of our own criteria. This is pushing them into ever greater isolation and stoking the fires of the very jingoistic exclusivist imperialism with which we reproach them.

It may be objected that there is little desire on their part for rapprochement and understanding; and to a dangerous extent, I think this is true. But how many voices have they heard from abroad calling for understanding? As I said in my *Marxist Quarterly* article, it may serve some small purpose for a Catholic priest to publish such an appeal and to be allowed to

16 *Horizons: The Marxist Quarterly*, no. 21 (Spring 1967), pp. 9 ff.

publish it in a Western Marxist periodical. By the same token, I wish that at this Congress at least one voice shall be raised unreservedly in a plea for understanding of the People's Republic of China, a plea with no hidden ulterior motives and no strings attached.

Again it may be objected: the difficulties in this particular case are staggering; we are but the pawns of high finance and power politics. This is a typical excuse for sloth. There are many periodicals and novels coming out of the People's Republic of China which are available in major Canadian and American cities. These at least can be perused. When I finally reach the People's Republic of China, as I firmly intend to do at some point within the next 24 months, I would like to be able to take with me specific requests for correspondence between young Chinese and young Canadians and Americans, between Chinese experts in various fields and their Canadian and American counterparts. This forum seemed a promising place to mention this desire.

The overriding secular concerns of our day, the chief immediate areas of concern of Marxist atheists are the concern of all Christians. And Christians can collaborate, nay, must collaborate, instantly with Marxist atheists in these areas. In this collaboration the Christian must never forget that his own contribution must and can be made efficacious only if it is made in the person of Christ. It is not that Christ is a well-loved mascot who must be protected by ritual declarations. It is that Christ is the only power, the only name in heaven and on earth in which mankind can be saved. The salvation of the world will come from the emerging recognition of that saving power of Christ and from a united world's response to that power that will not violate man's freedom. Did I not believe this, I would not stand here in a physical garb that openly proclaims me a priest of that Christ. No Marxist atheist (and I have spoken with many hundreds) has ever reproached me with this; only certain skittish Christians have wondered if a more prudent approach would be better. It would not! For insofar as we begin to converse simply as human beings with generic human

326

aims in common, I deny my innermost identity. One stronger than I, than all of us, must assist at the dialogue table. But it has never been his way to appear as a chieftain mighty in battle, at the head of an armed force, monochrome or motley! His gracious decision is to work through free human wills that have freely acknowledged him; and to inspire and assist those who know him not but are motivated in the dimension of nature by the unrealized desire to be instruments of his peace.

The Christian crossroads is the decision to proceed openly in Christ or to suppress him and the whole troubling dimension of transcendence. The atheist *aggiornamento* consists in taking another long look at man's history to see if that interpretation they have hitherto championed may not have mistaken the infamy of bad Christians for the impotence of Christ.

There is one key contribution Marxists can make to any Christian-Marxist confrontation, a contribution that I often feel persuaded Marxism was raised up to make, a contribution of the utmost importance to the operative effectiveness of Christianity. That contribution is Marxism's trenchant insistence on matter, on materialism. For if the besetting error of the Christian tradition on the practical level has been a failure of nerve or refusal to respond to the socioethical call of Christ, then the besetting error of that same Christian tradition on the theoretical level has been its tendency to angelism, pseudo-spiritualism, a haughty and irrational revulsion against matter. Although the most drastic form of anti-materialism, Manicheanism, was repudiated again and again by the teaching authority of the Church, Manicheanism nevertheless penetrated deep into the Christian tradition. Merging now as Puritanism, now as an exaggerated asceticism, now as quietism, and now as the Come-out-of-her-my-people complex, Manicheanism has cruelly hobbled Christian witness in the world. Manicheanism in any form is the exact antithesis of Incarnationalism and a flagrant repudiation of the Incarnation itself. After the personal ingress of God into the space-time dimension, after the assumption of the whole material world, in its highest form, to the divinity, there can be absolutely no more question of anti-materialism.

327

And the anti-materialism of Christianity is a stupid, pallid, neurasthenic thing at best. It has produced nothing but warped mentalities, incompetent to grapple with the true challenge of the Incarnation. It is the spirit of man that needs purifying, not the material universe. It is not the good earth with her beauty and abundance that creates the divisive problems of humanity, it is the nasty little soul of man. Souls are never to be trusted very far and pure spirits scarcely at all, for if they are not angels they are devils. Christians must have their noses rubbed firmly into matter. St. John seems deliberately to have chosen the most drastic articulation of the Incarnation fact to hammer this point home, the *Word was made flesh,* not *man* but *flesh, sarx,* with all the Semitic overtones of evanescence contained in that word, with all its evocations of the perishing grass set over against the eternal Creator. The Christian position rightly interpreted can give to matter dimensions of meaning and dignity entirely un- heard-of in the context of non-Christian materialism; but the Marxist can contribute substantially to a purification and clarification of the Christian notion of matter.

Christians must open their hearts to learn what Christ really means on the socio-political and moral level, so that Marxists may have an opportunity of realizing what he means on the ontological level. Then may they both unite forces to achieve that *temps des hommes,* that truly human age, which M. Garaudy invokes at the end of his *Marxisme du XX° siècle,* that age which is the expression of the achievement and maturity of the Mystical Body of him who called himself with predilec- tion the Son of Man.

16.

THEOLOGY IN THE CONTEXT OF
A PHILOSOPHY OF NOTHINGNESS

CORNELIO FABRO, C.S.S.

EVERY question concerning the true face of being is implicitly
an epistemological question, in that it poses the antecedent problem of a cogent identification or clarification of *the structure of
the very cognitive mechanism* that is putting principles into operation to reply to the ontological question. The God-problem,
thus posed, is and must always remain for man an inexhaustibly
open question. It is the dialectical question in its most drastic
form. It asks about the existence of God *before* there has been
any familiarization with his attributes which enable reason
to approach his essence. It is the thrust to penetrate what God
is and can be for man prior to any grasp of what man is and
ought to be *for* and *before* God! Two dimensions, the formal
and the existential, are here locked in mortal combat; and their
struggle permeates and nurtures the history of theology.

The same tension is mirrored in the divergence between the
two levels of the knowledge of God: the knowledge acquired
by the light of reason and the knowledge communicated by the
light of faith. Each of these levels has its own horizon; each of
these approaches has its own avenue of vision. The former
opens onto the existence of God and his attributes in the
realm of reason; the latter opens onto the transcendent economy
of the divine plan of salvation through the Incarnation in the
realm of faith. Here again we have two forms or dimensions of

329

meaning, essence and existence, reason and faith, both focusing on the same object, God, but each operating at a different level and hence under a different light and from a different angle of vision. Yet both seem to converge on the middle ground of theology, which is the extension of faith into and in the realm of reason and the effort of reason to carry the revealed message to the inner node of the existent, the historical human being, there to engage his freedom. Theological endeavour therefore has two focal points or poles of meaning: essence and correlative existence, reason and faith, God and man; and these two poles of meaning issue ultimately from the two sources of nature and grace. Between these two poles, theology endeavours to effect an operation of mediation and reconciliation.

Theology has meaning because reason can, upon contact with faith, receive enlightenment and itself give enlightenment. The locus of this meaning is the junction or rather the intersection of two principles, God and man, antipodal in the realm of being and capable of meaningful encounter only in the intentional realm of knowing and willing. Yet, in this encounter of two worlds, so infinitely mutually remote, man must treat with God of the infinitely proximate business of man's own salvation from death and sin, in the narrows of time. There is a dialectic operative in the problem of salvation which spills over onto the problem of the very possibility of theology: for man can comprehend the things of God only in human fashion; and yet, at the same time, God can address himself to man only in his status as man's Absolute and Saviour, and thus from the heights of the divine transcendence. Precisely, therefore, inasmuch as God *has* revealed himself, first "in the shadow of creation" and subsequently and above all "in the mercy of redemption," there has been set up a "transcendence of reference" centered upon man himself, in his simultaneous misery and grandeur. A "theological phenomenology" of the act of faith thus becomes an indispensable preliminary to the restoration in modern man of a contact with faith itself. Only such a preliminary will impel man in the direction of the act of faith and that "articulation of faith" which is theology, without which articulation faith and the act of faith can find no purchase on the existential level which is freedom in operation.

Indeed neither reason nor faith can effect the existential synthesis in isolation. Only as they meet and clarify each other in a mutual substantiation as the two poles of the human self can these two lights enter into a mutually fructifying confrontation within the field of consciousness and open up the ultimate horizon of freedom, as Kierkegaard remarks in the opening words of his *Journals:* "In order to make out a light, you always need another light. It is absolutely impossible to make out the origin of a point of light appearing in total darkness; for darkness precludes any determination of spatial relations. Only with the aid of another light will the position of the first point be able to be determined with reference to the second."[1] But today the classical definition of the "formal object" of any science (and of theology, as one such science) has been replaced by the Heideggerian "re-duction or re-turn to the ground or foundation," which amounts to a specification of the area of meaningfulness.[2] Now this specification involves a focusing of the situation from the angle of the object and of the subject. This focusing, in turn, amounts in the final analysis to a recognition of the relations the object can have, on the basis of its own ontological status, with the sum total of reality; and of the relations the subject itself can and does establish, as that subject operates out of the secret node of its freedom. A predominance of the former angle of focus over the latter will issue in that objective bias typical of classical objectivism; a predominance of the latter angle of focus over the former will give rise to the subjectivist bias typical of modern subjectivism. These two approaches present two antithetical pictures of man: man the knower (*homo sapiens*) and man the doer (*homo faber*). This antithesis specifies the crisis of our present age. Modern man has been said to experience only the absence of God, to be

[1] S. *Kierkegaards Papirer,* udgivne af P. A. Heilberg og V. Kuhr, Copenhagen, 1909, vol. I, p. 1.
[2] See M. Heidegger, *Was ist Metaphysik?*, Frankfurt a. M., 1949, pp. 7 ff.

incapable not only of "resolving" the God-problem but even of posing it. It is alleged that twentieth century man cannot even *see* the relevance or meaningfulness of the God-problem at all. This obvious total break with the entire classical theological tradition of our Western culture is rooted ultimately in a drastic shift of the axis of meaning within the human mind itself, a shift that has been accomplished over the past four centuries and occasioned by the whole drift and bias of modern science and philosophy. This shift has inverted the entire relation of the mind to being and radically altered the status of the mind itself in its transcendental potential.

A modern thinker, Bishop John Robinson, does not hesitate to speak of a "Copernican revolution" in the field of theology,[3] a revolution effected by the critique of the two crucial notions of classical religious thought and traditional theology: *the transcendence of God* and *the supernatural status of the Christian faith and its mysteries*. These two notions have been branded as incomprehensible and meaningless and consequently quite simply unacceptable.

The old way of conceiving the relations between man and God, between the sinner and divine grace, is part and parcel of an "outmoded view of the world," argues Robinson. The "new theology" must bear in mind that this entire world-view has been totally invalidated by modern criticism and is simply no longer acceptable or indeed even meaningful to modern man. Such an approach on the part of the new theology in no way involves a rejection of God, insists Robinson; rather it represents an effort to save him by rendering him truly mean-

---

[3] The most radical expression of this whole point of view is to be found in a work that is also a model of clarity: J. A. T. Robinson, *Honest to God,* Philadelphia, 1963, especially ch. 2, pp. 29 ff. Robinson has taken up the same topic again in his *The New Reformation?,* Philadelphia, 1965. Robinson and the death-of-God theologians generally have been influenced mainly by the "negative theology" of the two German theologians, Tillich and Bonhoeffer, both of whom have been in direct and substantial contact with the English-speaking world; a third influence has been the Heideggerian Bultmann with his *demythologization* drive.

ingful to modern man.[4] The old and already outmoded semantemes of traditional theology must be replaced by a whole new cast of conversation that will be on the same wavelength with the internal dynamic of the quest of modern man. This new theological approach accepts as a simple matter of historical fact that it has been the objectivist and metaphysical stance of classical theology which has eventually triggered that radical theological negation epitomized in the death of God, a negation whose long shadow has been loping over the whole field of Western culture for a century now, since Hegel's day. Intelligent theologians must therefore recognize that modern man can no longer make any sense of the traditional theological language which uses such terms as "nature," "substance," "cause," "relation," and the like, in speaking of God. And the reason is that all such terms are bound up with a particular sort of picture of the world which no longer serves nor indeed can serve any useful or positive purpose. Thus the "Death of God" is a profitable waystation on the road to the "rediscovery" of the Genuine God. A truly contemporary person, therefore, cannot help being an atheist; but at the same time he cannot remain permanently an atheist, because the Emmaus encounter constrains him to admit and accept the risen Christ.[5]

Theology must therefore operate dialectically in our day. And Robinson is most insistent that this dialectic must be pushed to the ultimate extreme: there must be a consequential elaboration of the negative moment integrally constitutive of all such theological relations as nature-grace, reason-faith, and so forth. Moreover, this very negative moment must be con-

[4] "Our concern is in no way to change the Christian doctrine of God but precisely to see that it does not disappear with this outmoded view," Robinson, *Honest to God*, p. 44.

[5] In his recent work, *The New Reformation?*, Robinson in fact poses the question: "Can a truly contemporary person *not* be an atheist?" His reply is: "There is no going back to the pre-secular view of the world, where God is always 'there' to be brought in, run to, or blamed. Yet, in another sense, he may find that he *cannot* be an atheist, however much he would like to be. For on the Emmaus road, on the way back from the tomb, the risen Christ comes up with him and he knows himself constrained" (p. 116).

333

verted into the indispensable motive power for the generation of the new theological articulation to the new man; atheism must be made the foundation of the new affirmation of God, of the new experience of God by the new man.

This new "Death of God" theology is the theology of defeatist capitulationism in the face of the negations inherent in modern thought from Feuerbach and Nietzsche down to Heidegger and Sartre. Robinson presents a very frank outline[6] of the dimensions of this capitulation.

1. *God is negligible on the intellectual level.* Neither science nor philosophy has any room for God these days. God has lost all meaning for man. The human intellect can get no hold on God and no one any longer feels the need of posing the God-problem (p. 108).

2. *God is expendable on the emotional level.* Not only does man no longer feel any need of God or religion. He is convinced that any such ties are positively harmful to him in a desacralized world, a world whose essence is, in Heidegger's phrase, to "worldify" (*Welt weltet*). This sort of world is a secularized world and "Secularization means that man must accept responsibility for his own destiny, neither trying to blame it on the gods nor expecting some providence to relieve him of it or see him through" (p. 110).

3. *God is intolerable on the moral level.* The operative factor in Robinson's thinking here seems to be the "scandal of evil," rather than the Kantian categorical imperative (as the theoretical context would require) or the extremity of Sartrian existential freedom. Thus Robinson asserts that "A God who 'causes' or 'allows' the suffering of a single child is morally intolerable" (p. 113). On the one hand, physical and moral evil is today spreading in forms and proportions hitherto unknown; on the other hand, sensitivity to pain and suffering has been and is being constantly increased by the progress of science and culture. The resulting tension has broken man's spirit and lamed his aspiration and he prefers to be left alone with his physical pain and his mental torment.

[6] J. A. T. Robinson, *The New Reformation?*, pp. 109 ff.

334

Sound theology must grasp the diversity and even disparity of origin of present-day atheism in order adequately to cope with that atheism. For instance, Anglo-American death-of-God theology confines itself to accepting not only the "death" but the total absence of God as a simple matter of fact; it virtually asserts that a Gallup-poll type inquiry into the state of mind of our world today would reveal a total lack of interest in God in every area of human life and culture.

It is obvious that we are here confronting that phenomenon that has been designed as "secularism" or "secularization": the very name of God has been voided of all meaning in culture, in daily life, in science, in philosophy, indeed even in theology itself; and God is now nothing but an empty name, a blank semanteme. "Secularism" is merely a euphemism designating this lack or absence of God in every area of the modern mind.

If theology wishes to be true to its vocation, it must get to the very deepest roots of this process of inversion which has effected a transition from the predominance of the "sacred" over the secular and profane to an initial recognition of the right of the profane to coexistence with the sacred and a terminal incursion of the profane into the realm of the sacred, an incursion which is presently resulting in a banishment of the sacred itself, of the Gospel, of religion generally.[7]

The negative theology of our own day blames man's loss of God on the traditional idea of God. This idea, it insists, has shown itself to be untenable; even though it may have fitted a former culture and may indeed have struck deep roots in our own training, it cannot, in the long run, be anything but "an idol." And the new theology concludes that what our contemporaries are repudiating may well be simply this idol and not

[7] A brief history of this concept and the stages in its evolution has been provided in H. Lübbe, *Säkularisierung*, (Freiburg and Munich, 1965). Lübbe agrees with Gogarten in proposing a distinction between "secularization" and "secularism." Secularization, argues Lübbe, is "condition" (*Bedingung*) and "consequence" (*Folge*) of the faith and consequently profitable to the Church in updating her visible form; secularism, on the contrary, is a symptom of an enfeeblement of the faith so drastic as to have issued in a world view leaving no more room for faith itself (pp. 119 ff.).

God as such. Therefore it maintains that the jettisoning of this traditional idea of God is the first step theology must take in its drive to bring God back into the world.

*   *   *

The "new theology," this negation of theology presented as the theology of renewal, pushes the negative moment to a degree of intensity never before attained in the tradition of the West. Two elements or stages can be discerned in this theological approach:

1. the stress on the *negative moment* as a cathartic process precipitating man into a genuine encounter with God; and

2. the absolutely and radically *positive character* of God himself as revealed in his immanent status of "ground" of the world and of man.

The *negative moment* is expressive of modern man's eventual liberation, after a protracted process initiated as early as the thirteenth century, from all hamstringing metaphysical exteriority. Man has finally attained the fullness of his own freedom. On this whole point, the pioneering pathfinder is Dietrich Bonhoeffer, whom Robinson cites at great length. Says Bonhoeffer: "Man has learned to cope with all questions of importance without recourse to God as a working hypothesis." And this Bonhoeffer holds to be true not only in the area of science, art, "and even ethics" but in the case of religious questions as well: ". . . it is becoming evident that everything gets along without 'God,' and just as well as before." The clinching proof of this is that the more a theologian insists on the proofs of the traditional apologetics, the farther he pushes modern man away from God. Modern man is poignantly aware that he has burst the bonds of his infancy and adolescence and has attained to adulthood, that he can now manage on his own. Says Bonhoeffer: "God is teaching us that we must live as men who can get along very well without him." And he continues, with evident relish for a progressively more paradoxical dialectical terminology: "The God Who makes us live in this world without using him as a working hypothesis is the God

336

before whom we are ever standing. Before God and with him
we live without God. God allows himself to be edged out of the
world, and that is exactly the way, the only way, in which he
can be with us and help us."[8] This Bonhoefferian dialectic is
less novel and revolutionary than it might appear to be at
first glance: it can easily be seen to remain faithful to the
Lutheran formula of "God, the hidden and revealed" (*Deus
absconditus et revelatus*), and to preserve the extreme tension
of the Lutheran notion of man as "at once righteous and a
sinner" (*simul justus et peccator*).

The *positive moment* of the new theology comes out in its
ontological definition of God as "depth" (*Tiefe*) or "ground of
being," a definition calculated to replace the purely spatial
symbolism of the pseudo-definitions of the transcendent in the
traditional terms of "up there" or "out there," that is, above or
beyond the world and man, by a more meaningful psychological
symbolism, intrinsic to that real existent who is man. Here the
pioneer is Tillich, who explains the import and the importance
of the new term: " 'Deep' in its spiritual use has two meanings:
it means either the opposite of 'shallow,' or the opposite of
'high.' Truth is deep and not shallow; suffering is depth and
not height. Both the light of truth and the darkness of suffering
are deep. There is a depth in God, and there is a depth out of
which the psalmist cries to God." The deepest level of this
meaning of the divine, considered as ground or foundation,
Tillich articulates in the shape of a drastic immanence, formulated in terms of his favorite dimension of depth: "The name
of this infinite and inexhaustible depth and ground of all being
is *God*. That depth is what the word *God* means. And if that
word has not much meaning for you, translate it, and speak
of the depths of your life, of the source of your being, of
your ultimate concern, of what you take seriously without any
reservation. Perhaps, in order to do so, you must forget everything traditional that you have learned about God, perhaps
even that word itself. For if you know that God means depth,
you know much about *Him*. You cannot then call yourself an

[8] Cited in Robinson, *Honest to God,* p. 39.

atheist or unbeliever. For you cannot think or say: Life has no depth! Life itself is shallow. Being itself is surface only. If you could say this in complete seriousness, you would be an atheist; but otherwise you are not. He who knows about depth knows about God."[9]

To Tillich's mind, therefore, depth is the "symbol" of the status of spirit, albeit itself a dimension of space. Hence the terminal transition, via the "depth" notion, from the negative way to the definitive *positive way.*

Tillich's theological dialectic of the negative moment demands an identification of God with "depth" and an all-out intensification of his immanence in the world, combined with an all-out repudiation of any idea of God as "above and beyond" all things. The antiquated idea of God as "above and beyond" is simply "an extension of the categories of finitude" and it "transforms the infinity of God into a finiteness." Theology therefore must break once and for all with dualistic articulations of God's transcendence and supernatural status: for such articulations, in their sheer exteriority, amount to an outright denial and restrictive negation of God.

Tillich is persuaded that there is a further advantage in conceiving of God as depth. It makes possible a meeting of minds with the "monistic naturalism" of man like Julian Huxley who contends that it is meaningless to explain the world by recourse to a principle above and beyond the world, that is to say, extraneous to the world. Tillich demands that theology accept "the antisupranatural criticism of naturalism" and he proceeds to specify what must be the bias of the new concept of God: "God is the name for the power and meaning of reality. He is not identified with the totality of things. No myth or philosophy has ever asserted such an absurdity. But he is a symbol of the unity, harmony, and power of being; he is the dynamic and creative center of reality. The phrase *deus sive natura,* used by people like Scotus Erigena and Spinoza, does not say that

---

[9] P. Tillich, *The Shaking of the Foundations* (New York, 1948), pp. 53 and 57. The passage cited is from a sermon of Tillich's, "The Depth of Existence," based on 1 Cor. 2, 1. and Ps. 130, 1.

God is identical with nature but that he is identical with the *natura naturans,* the creative nature, the creative ground of all natural objects. In modern naturalism, the religious quality of these affirmations has almost disappeared, especially among philosophizing scientists who understand nature in terms of materialism and mechanism."[10] Rather, an all-out effort must be undertaken to recover the deepest religious meaning inherent in naturalism, to return to the "experience of the sacral," to the religious *a priori* which safeguards "the infinite distance between the whole of finite things and their infinite ground." It has always been substantially an experience of this kind, contends Tillich, that has inspired and sustained the various types of classical theology: "Whether it is 'being-itself' (Scholastics) or the 'universal substance' (Spinoza), whether it is 'beyond subjectivity and objectivity' (James) or the 'identity of spirit and nature' (Schelling), whether it is 'universe' (Schleiermacher) or 'cosmic whole' (Hocking), whether it is 'value creating process' (Whitehead) or 'progressive integration' (Wieman), whether it is 'absolute spirit' (Hegel) or 'cosmic person' (Brightman)—each of these concepts is based on an immediate experience of something ultimate in value and being of which one can become intuitively aware."[11] And Tillich at this point adopts Heideggerian terminology to ascribe to this intuitive experience "transcending ordinary experience." "Ecstasy as a state of mind," says Tillich, "is the exact correlate to self-transcendence as the state of reality." We have here, then, a transcendence possessing at once a metaphysical and a sacral character. And it is into this pre-existent mystical matrix, common to naturalism and idealism alike, that the Christian message is subsequently interpolated. Both Bonhoeffer and Tillich, the chief sources of inspiration for the later death-of-God theologians, have certainly hit upon the real crux of the question concerning the tensions of affirmation-negation, reason-faith, nature-grace, and so forth, in their insistence on the vital element of human freedom and responsibility in the entire theological problematic. The intuitive

[10] Tillich, *Systematic Theology,* vol. II, Chicago, 1957, p. 6.
[11] *Ibid.,* vol. I, Chicago, 1951, p. 9.

contact with the sacral is effected, at least for Tillich, in terms of a reference to the human self in its status as a finite freedom, freedom being in fact a quality we experience directly only in ourselves. The idea of God as ground of being replaces the spatial depiction of transcendence by the concept of finite freedom. The creature is free to turn *to* God and likewise to turn *away from* God; and consequently the divine transcendence is identical with the freedom of creatures to turn away from the essential unity with the creative ground of their being. The reality of such finite freedom is a fact of human experience and it is the fact which makes pantheism untenable, since this freedom "presupposes" that the created "is substantially independent of the divine ground . . ."[12]

Unquestionably, Tillich's approach is a most impressive one. And it is readily understandable that his adherents should protest that they have not the slightest desire or intention of supporting or advancing atheism, but are rather entirely committed to showing the only way to overcome atheism, by using the "negative method," pushed to its ultimate extreme to issue into an affirmation of the Living God.

*   *   *

We must now consider whether this negative method can issue in a positive conclusion on the God-problem. Can the death-of-God theology metamorphose into an affirmation of the existence of God, an entirely new sort of affirmation, yet one that is solidly grounded and geared to modern man? The crux of the question lies in the mind-being relationship, in the interpretation placed on the meaning and generative dynamism of thought. For it should be carefully noted that *the meaning and issue of the problem itself is not primarily dependent on the tension between the negative and the positive moment.* That is a subsequent reflective specification of the mind-being relationship itself. *In its primordial form, this relation involves the*

12 *Ibid.,* vol. II, p. 8.

340

tension between the ground and the grounded. And it is only in terms of this primordial tension that the problematic posed by Tillich and his followers can be properly appreciated.

As we have already mentioned, these thinkers have accepted the disappearance and death of God in modern culture and everyday life as a matter of *fact.* They have blamed this event indiscriminately on the whole of the philosophy and theology of the preceding centuries; and they have even judged the wrecking operations carried out by modern thought, in this area, to be entirely justified. And we must here ask: Is this the right way to go about it? Is this a justifiable or even a safe approach? Will not those who call this tune eventually have to pay the piper? And will not the reckoning amount to an irremediable disaster for man in his search for the "ground" of truth and of justice? The following three brief but crucial observations are pertinent to a proper and adequate answer to these questions.

1. "Negative theology" is not a new discovery of the dialectical theologians. It has its roots in Platonic and Pythagorean thought. The notion of the "Unknown God" (ἄγνωστος θεός) is already implicit in Plato's tenet of the transcendence of the One and the Good; subsequently the term appears explicitly in Philo and is quite current in the Neoplatonic writings (Albinus, Numenius, Proclus, *et al.*).[13] In these latter writings, the notion burgeons forth into a plethora of terms such as "incomprehensible" (ἀκατάληπτος), "unutterable" (ἄρρητος), "ineffable" (ἄθατος), "inaccessible" (ἀδιήγητος), "unknowable" (ἀγνούμενος), and the like.[14] There is, to be sure, an "unknowing" (ἀγνωσία) of God, an "agnosticism" which is subjective and culpable, connected with the Fall. But there is also an objective "agnostic" dimension which is the metaphysical expression of God's perfection and

[13] See E. R. Dodds, *Proclus, The Elements of Theology,* Oxford, 1933, pp. 310 ff.

[14] See the brilliant study by A. E. Festugière, *La révélation d'Hermès Trimégiste,* vol. IV, Paris, 1954, pp. ix f., 1 ff., 92 ff., 130 f. Festugière takes exception to E. Norden's contention (see E. Norden, *Agnostos Theos,* Leipzig, 1913), that the formula ἄγνωστος θεός is entirely absent from Greek writings and would be totally at odds with the whole Greek spirit.

transcendence: to this dimension precisely corresponds that particular mode of knowledge that is *gnosis.* Neoplatonic theology can thus be called a "negative theology by excess," that is to say, a theology whose negative moment is based on the excess of intelligibility of the object (God) with respect to the finite capacity of the subject (man).

2. Unquestionably, this Neoplatonic line is followed by negative Christian theology based on St. Paul's sermon on the Areopagus (Acts 17, 22 ff.), in which the Apostle presents the gnosis and revelation of Christ as the perfect solution to the unknowability of God which the pagans had admitted in their cryptic inscription on that Athenian altar: ΑΓΝΩΣΤΩ ΘΕΩ ("To the Unknown God"). Neoplatonism certainly infiltrated the presentation of Christian doctrine and particularly the triadic dialectic of Proclus, to make the unknowability of God one of the pivotal expressions of the transcendence of his perfection. But in this whole tradition, the negative moment is no longer the constitutive moment. It is simply a transitional moment leading to the explicit assertion of the super-positive status of God's nature and his perfections. A symptom of this progress—and perhaps a particularly effective impulse to it—is provided by the interpretation of Exodus 3, 14, by the Greek Fathers, after Philo, as expressive of the fact that sheer existence is the constitutive metaphysical core and nucleus of God. Now our human intellect is built to know essences: that is the very simple reason why God as *Esse ipsum* proves to be unknowable to man. The supreme master of divine semantics is, in the patristic age, the enigmatic Dionysius the Areopagite: in his famous treatise *De divinis nominibus,* he draws out of the negative moment the positive moment of God's surpassing excellence, expressed by the prefix *super* (ὑπερ-) in a glittering constellation of neologisms such as *supersubstantialis essentia* (ὑπερούσιος ὕπαρξις), *superdea Divinitas* (ὑπέρθεος θεότης), *superbona bonitas* (ὑπεράγαθος ἀγαθότης), *quae est super omnia identitas* ("which Being-himself is above all things"), *omnium ablatio et super omnem positionem et ablationem* ("total remotion and beyond all postulation and remotion").[15] This approach might be called positive

---

[15] Dionysius Areopagita, *De divinis nominibus,* c. II, § 4 (PG III,

agnosticism and epiphanic negativism. Two revealing phrases of the Pseudo-Dionysius are that "negations are truer than assertions" in the case of God and that "God is at once He-Who-Has-No-Name ($\dot{\alpha}\nu\dot{\omega}\nu\upsilon\mu\upsilon\varsigma$) and He-Who-Has-Many-Names ($\pi\upsilon\lambda\dot{\upsilon}\nu\upsilon\mu\upsilon\varsigma$)." In the same neoplatonic atmosphere, the *De Causis* was to declare: "The First Cause is beyond all telling" (*Causa prima superior est omni narratione*),[16] in line with the tenet of the vertical descent or fall of the effect from the cause and of the transcendence of the former by the latter.

3. St. Thomas is certainly in the tradition of the Pseudo-Dionysius in accepting throughout the Proclan pattern of the Dionysian dialectic of the knowledge of God: *per causalitatem, per remotionem* (*negationem*), *per eminentiam*. And even in the third moment, which ought to be the positive moment of reflection or radical anteriority (Hegel's "second, reflected, essential . . . immediacy" [*zweite, reflektierte, wesentliche . . . Unmittelbarkeit*]), the negative element still predominates. St. Thomas writes: "This is the ultimate limit to which we can attain in the matter of the knowing of God in this life: that God is above and beyond everything that can be thought by us and therefore the denomination of God which proceeds by remotion is the most appropriate."[17] And hence St. Thomas' famous dictum: ". . . Because concerning God we cannot know what he is but what he is not: we cannot consider, in the case of God, how He is but rather how He is not."[18] And the reason is

---

col. 641 a). But the technical treatment comes in c. I, §§ 5–8, where we encounter the staggering formula *superbonitatis superessentia* ($\dot{\upsilon}\pi\epsilon\rho\alpha\gamma\alpha\theta\dot{\upsilon}\tau\upsilon\varsigma$ $\dot{\upsilon}\pi\epsilon\rho\dot{\upsilon}\pi\alpha\rho\xi\iota\varsigma$) (col. 595 c). In this chapter, Dionysius expressly cites Exodus 3, 14 ($\dot{\epsilon}\gamma\dot{\omega}$ $\epsilon\dot{\iota}\mu\iota$ $\dot{\upsilon}$ $\dot{\omega}\nu$) as the Name which is the ground of the *positive* unknowability of God (col. 596 a; the text is again cited in c. II, § 1, col. 637 a).

[16] See O. Bardenhewer, *Liber de Causis über das reine Gute,* Freiburg i. Br., 1882, pp. 69 f.

[17] "Hoc est ultimum ad quod pertingere possumus circa cognitionem divinam in hac vita, quod Deus est supra omne id quod a nobis cogitari potest et ideo nominatio Dei quae est per remotionem, est maxime proprie" (*In lib. Dionysii De div. nom.,* c. I, lect. 3, Turin, 1950, no. 83, p. 28 a).

[18] ". . . quia de Deo scire non possumus quid sit, sed quid non sit: non possumus considerare de Deo quomodo sit sed potius quomodo non sit" (*In I Sent.,* d. 2, q. I, a. 3 ad 2. See also *Summa Contra Gentiles,*

that the adequate object of the human intellect is *ens, a* being, the concrete transcendental, which is always, as such, a finite content; whereas God, being *Esse subsistens,* is sheer infinite Act, unfathomable and incomprehensible: from the finite beings participating in be-ing (*esse*), we cannot come to an understanding or knowledge of unparticipated be-ing (*esse*).[19] In his presentation of this doctrine. St. Thomas does not hesitate to use a startling and splendid formula of the Pseudo-Dionysius which is a fusion of Greco-Christian Neoplatonism and Arabic Neoplatonism: "Concerning the First Cause, that of which we can be supremely certain is that it exceeds all our knowledge and utterance. For that man is knowing God most perfectly who holds this concerning Him: that whatever can be thought or said concerning Him is less than what God is. Wherefore Dionysius says in ch. I of his *Mystical Theology* that man is *united* to God, *at best,* as to the entirely Unknown, *in that man knows nothing of Him,* knowing Him to be above and beyond every mind."[20] The metaphysics of Aquinas thus stresses the radical anteriority of being (*esse*) as constitutive of the very essence of God, who

---

III, 39, § 49 and passim. *Summa Theologica,* I, q. 3: ". . . quia de Deo non possumus scire quid sit, sed quid non sit.").

[19] "Ens finitum est objectum cognitionis finitae. Deus ergo cum sit infinitus, excedit omnem substantiam finitam, praehabens in se fines omnium; et, per consequens, est separatus ab omni cognitione, in quantum omnem cognitionem creaturae excedit, ut a nulla comprehendi potest" ("Finite being is the object of finite knowing. God, therefore, since he is infinite, exceeds every finite substance, holding beforehand in himself the ends of all such; and consequently all knowing of him is precluded, since he so exceeds the knowing-power of the creature that he cannot be grasped by any creature") (*In lib. Dion. de div. nom.,* c. I, lect. 2, no. 75, p. 22 b). See also *ibid.,* c. II, lect. 4, no. 180, and *In lib. De Causis,* lect. 6, nn. 174–175, pp. 46 f.

[20] "De Causa prima hoc est quod potissime scire possumus quod omnem scientiam et locutionem nostram excedit. Ille enim perfectissime Deum cognoscit qui hoc de Ipso tenet: quod quidquid cogitari vel dici de Eo potest, minus est eo quod Deus est. Unde Dionysius dicit in I *Mysticae Theologiae,* quod homo *secundum melius* suae cognitionis *unitur* Deo sicut *omnino ignoto, eo quod nihil* de Eo *cognoscit, cognoscens* ipsum esse *supra* omnem *mentem*" (*In lib. De Causis,* lect. 6, no. 160). See also *Summa Theologica,* I, 12, 13 ad 1. The Dionysius text in question is in all probability taken from *De mystica Theologia,* c. I, 3 (*PG* III, col. 1001a).

therefore has no essence. Such a metaphysic could never give rise to the presumptuous notion that God who is Life, Truth, Goodness, could be known "properly" by man. Only the essentialist bias of later Scholasticism and modern thought could father such an aberration.

* * *

The triggering impulse of the death-of-God theology came from Tillich's redirection of attention to the ground of being and his conception of God as this ground of being. The dialectical significance of the negative moment in man's knowing of God (the "Cloud of Unknowing" of the mystics) can best be clarified by an appeal to the metaphysics of St. Thomas Aquinas which ascribes to *esse* the primacy over *essentia*. Tillich himself vigorously criticizes the essentialism of nominalism, with its conception of *esse* (be-ing) as the "supreme abstraction" (*höchste Abstraktion*), as the all-embracing genus. Tillich holds that the concept of be-ing brings into play the opposition of being and non-being and that be-ing can therefore be described as the "power of being" (*Macht des Seins*), contrasting with the lapse into non-being or nothingness. Thus the word "being" if taken abstractly is the emptiest of all concepts; but if understood as the power of being in everything having being, then it is the fullest and most meaningful of all concepts. Tillich makes the admirable observation that no philosophy and no theology can surpass this notion of being, for God and being are inseparable, God is simply being-itself (*Sein-Selbst*), in the sense of the power of be-ing, or the power of conquering non-being. And Tillich is quite right in distrusting those theological pseudo-phenomenologies that are based on the I-Thou relation (*Ich-Du-Beziehung*) and presume to interpolate the man-God relationship in the context of a complete neglect of the ground of being.

But the same Tillich then proceeds to make the bemusing allegation that this being was lost and forgotten almost immediately after its discovery by Parmenides in the West and by the Hindu Shankara in the East, and was only rediscovered in

345

our own times by such existentialists as Heidegger and Marcel.[21] Like Bultmann and even Bonhoeffer in his own way,[22] Tillich is clearly a prisoner of the Heideggerian hegemony and therefore doomed to fall back into the toils of the negativism of the principle of immanentism. There is certainly a drastic return in Tillich's work as in that of Heidegger to the sense of and insistence on the primordial status of being and an appeal to the dialectic of being-non-being as the ground and structural matrix of truth. But what is this being, this power, this act, that is here in question? What is the epistemological bias of the ground of the relationship? There can be no room for doubt in the case of Heidegger or indeed of Tillich: the relationship is constituted and structured on the basis of the *transcendental status of the subject*.

This transcendental status is *Dasein* (there-being), which Heidegger articulates as a relation of the human subject to an indeterminate historical world and which Tillich sees as the relation of the same historical human subject to the historical world as determined by the revealed religious event. The difference between the Heideggerian and the Tillichian conceptions is this: for Heidegger, the relationship that is existence is always realized in finite designs; for Tillich and all the dialectical theologians taking their inspiration from him, the relation that is existence remains in taut suspension from the dialectic of being-non-being, of the whole and the void. It is in this very context that Tillich speaks of a "supra-personal God," of a "God above the God of theism," in the sense that the affirmation of this God arises out of that radical doubt that is at the basis of modern thought. "In such a state," writes Tillich, "the God of both religious and theological language disappears. But something remains, namely, the seriousness of that doubt in which meaning within meaninglessness is affirmed. The source of this affirmation of meaning within meaninglessness, of certitude within doubt, is not the God of traditional theism but the 'God above God,' the power of being, which works through those

21 See Tillich, *Systematic Theology,* vol. II, p. 11.
22 See D. Bonhoeffer, *Akt und Sein,* Munich, 1964, especially pp. 37 ff.

who have no name for it, not even the name God. This is the answer to those who ask for a message in the nothingness of their situation and at the end of their courage to be."[23] This dialectical theology patently represents the transposition into the realm of religious knowledge of the conception of existence as freedom to be balanced tremblingly over the void of nothingness.

This Tillichian conception certainly does provide a deep-thrusting and enthralling interpretation of the possible meaning of the religious experience and the theological question in the context of the Kantian modality of the modern *cogito* principle (the *Ich denke überhaupt*), as the native site of the self-revelation of non-being. It is against the ground of this non-being that the "leap into faith" is depicted and the "courage to be" is demanded. To say that this Tillichian "courage to be" corresponds to Heidegger's being (*Sein*) as the "thrustedness" (*Geworfenheit*) of being-in-the-world (*In-der-Welt-sein*) may indeed amount to a considerable oversimplification but it does trace Tillich's language back to its undeniable Hegelian and Heideggerian origins. For the Heideggerian notion in turn derives from Hegelian assertion of the identity of being and non-being. Heidegger specifically asserts that "Non-being is the not-thereness of beings and thus is Being as experienced from the point of view of the concrete individual being"; therefore non-being constitutes, for idealism, the ontological difference between being and beings.[24] Now this certainly leads to a position diametrically opposed to Parmenides' basic principle that "being is and non-being is not,"[25] whatever may be the case with Shankara's philosophy with which I am not familiar. The agreement between Heidegger and Hegel is to be sought not in the logical formula of identity, but rather in its ontological meaning: being

[23] Tillich, *Systematic Theology*, vol. II, p. 12. On this point, Tillich refers his readers to his other work, *The Courage to Be*, New Haven, 1953, in which he analyses the meaning of faith, against a background of anguish and despair, as the "courage to be."

[24] Heidegger, *Vom Wesen des Grundes*, Frankfurt a. M., 1949, p. 5. For Heidegger's agreement with Hegel, see *Was ist Metaphysik?*, Frankfurt a. M., 1949, p. 36.

[25] *Fragmenta* 28 B 6, Diels I, 232.

347

and non-being coincide not in virtue of their indeterminacy and immediacy, but because for Heidegger, being itself is essentially finite.[26] And why? For the simple reason that, after Kant, being cannot occur except against the background of space and time; meaningfulness coincides with our own situation in the world (*Welt*) which surrounds us as nature and history; the Hegelian Absolute is an unwarranted interpolation, a *deus ex machina*. This is the super-Hegelian, absolutely radical modality of modern immanentism, asserting the direct correspondence and mutual conjunction of being, non-being, truth, existence, and freedom. And Tillich's theology as a radical theology of immanentism and immanence fits exactly into this context and this immanentist conception.

From the principle of immanentism there inevitably derives the death of God, because the essence of modern immanentism consists in its constitutive negativism, understood as a negation of the truth of the immediacy of being and thus involving a mandatory mediation of being by the mind. And so the act or power of which Tillich is talking is an act of mind, an act of consciousness, an endeavour and a decision of freedom which is existence! And the God to whom this negativism and this decision is linked is simply the ultimate ground, without a name, a status, or even a structure.[27] This God is not personal but suprapersonal, the "God above the God of theism." This is the God that the death-of-God theology sees as being attained in the wake of the supersession of the henceforth outmoded theism-atheism antithesis. Tillich does indeed beg pardon for having had to have recourse to a terminology taking its inspiration from pantheism and mysticism. But our clarification

[26] Heidegger, *Vom Wesen des Grundes*, p. 50. See especially *Was ist Metaphysik?*, p. 36.

[27] J. Böhme likewise holds God to be an "ungrounded primordial ground" (*Ungrund-Urgrund*), but in an exactly opposite context. The notion indeed further goes back to the medieval mysticism of the *scintilla animae* of Eckhart and Tauler: it is in this *fundum animae* that there occurs the encounter between God and man and between the souls of the saints (See H. Hof, *Scintilla animae*, Lund-Bonn, 1952, especially pp. 161 ff.).

of the transcendent dimension of classical and Christian negative theology has shown us that this is not the real stumbling-block in the Tillichian approach. That stumbling-block is rather to be sought in the unquestioning acceptance of that negativism which is absolutely basic to the modern *cogito* principle and whose whole bias has inevitably led to the finitization of being[28] and thus to the positive atheism of the technocratic culture in which we live today.

* * *

We may thus conclude that Robinson and the death-of-God theologians generally are quite right in saying that the deepest reason for modern man's inability to grasp any longer the meaning of traditional theology or indeed to find any meaningfulness in it, for his denial of all meaning to transcendence and his adamant refusal to grant any status to the supernatural dimensions of faith and grace, must be sought in the simple fact that all these terms have indeed lost all meaning for him. But theology cannot content itself merely with stating and noting this fact; it must penetrate to the deepest inner cause of this catastrophe that has shifted the compass-needle of the human mind in recent times through an 180° angle: from the infinite to the finite, from God to the world, culminating in a definition of man's own reality as a "being-in-the-world," which is precisely the formula of all-out constructive atheism. This deep inner cause of our modern catastrophe lies in the primordial option, the primordial constitution of the relationship between being and thought, wherein is to be seen the restrictive reduction and clearing (*Lichtung*) of the ground. On this point, classical-Christian thought and modern philosophy are diametrically opposed: for the former, being is the ground of thought; for the latter, thought in general (*Bewusstsein, Ich denke überhaupt*) is the ground of being. For realism, it is being which actualizes and directs and impels the mind; for immanentism, it is the mind with its structures which makes possible the appearance of

[28] See C. Fabro, *Introduzione all' ateismo moderno, especially* c. VIII; ET *God in Exile*, vol. II, ch. 9, Glen Rock, 1968.

being and of its structures which can only be mental structures inasmuch as they are the result of that experience of the non-being of being which is called upon to serve as the ground for the new kind of transcendence, antipodal to the classical kind.

It is now clear that the death-of-God theology is a phenomenon proper to that Protestant theology which has twice lost contact with classical theology—and in two diametrically opposed ways: first, as a result of the Lutheran principles of *sola fides* (faith alone), a faith suspended in its own vacuum by a denial of all nexus with reason and leaving the mind utterly alone with the revealed word; and secondly, subsequently, as a result of the modern principle of consciousness which Hegel asserted to have brought to completion the work begun by Luther.[29] The first modality of immanentism led to the disengagement of man from visible historical authority in the realm of faith; the second modality of immanentism has fared forward still further, to the generic reduction of being to the spontaneity of the human subject. This has led to the loss of all theoretical tether and the *cogito,* as Heidegger has revealed in the wake of Fichte and Schelling, becomes the *volo,* the will-to-power (*Wille zur Macht*), whose only tether is itself.[30] In such a context, atheism is clearly inevitable and indeed the only consistent conclusion. The modern principle of immanentism is intrinsically

[29] "Was Luther als Glaube im Gefühl und im Zeugnis des Geistes begonnen, es ist dasselbe was der weiterhin gereifte Geist im *Begriffe* zu fassen, und so in der Gegenwart sich zu befreien, und dadurch in ihr sich zu finden bestrebt ist" ("What Luther began as faith, in the indistinct sentiment and witness of the spirit is the same thing that the still more mature Spirit is at pains to capture in *concept* and thus to free itself in the present and thereby to find itself in that present") (*Grundlagen der Philosophie des Rechts,* ed. J. Hoffmeister, Hamburg 1955, p. 17).

[30] "Wollen ist Urseyn, und auf dieses allein passen alle Prädikate desselben: Grundlosigkeit, Ewigkeit, Unabhängigkeit von dieser Zeit, Selbstbejahung. Die ganze Philosophie strebt nur dahin, diesen höchsten Ausdruck zu finden" ("Willing is primordial being and to willing alone correspond all the predicates of being: unfathomability, eternity, independence of this temporal cycle, self-affirmation. The whole of philosophy is but a striving to find this supreme expression") (Schelling, *Philosophische Untersuchungen uber das Wesen der menschlichen Freiheit,* collected Works, Part I, vol. VII, p. 350).

atheistic inasmuch as it amounts to the radical assertion that the human self is the ultimate ground of everything. Now the inevitable repercussion of such an assertion is the total banishment of God, a banishment rendered by the whole ontologico-epistemological status of the mind. In a more strictly metaphysical articulation, it can be said that the essence of the modern principle with its postulate of the radical and total immanence of being is and must be the denial of transcendence (in the classical understanding of that term!) of knowing, a transcendence which constitutes at once the bedrock of freedom and the first step of classical theism in the basic meaning of that term. The modern principle replaces the transcendence of God, understood as the radical anteriority of the *Esse Ipsum,* by the transcendence of *Dasein* (there-being) as a self-projection of the will into and in the world; to the negative moment involved in the inexhaustible, unfathomable, and inaccessible radical anteriority of the divine perfection (ἄγνωστος θεός), has succeeded the negativism of the ego, of the human self, which has returned to supreme power as the ground of non-being, after the interregnum of the idealist pseudo-Absolute, and has made non-being into the ground of being, in the light of the Heideggerian and Sartrian analyses of There-being (*Dasein*). Classical Christian theology is negative because the intellect, starting from the concrete being (*ens*), and plunging into the depths of be-ing (*esse*), observes that God appears as the perfection "beyond" every finite dimension or comprehension; modern dialectical theology is negative because the intellect, starting from the non-being of the concrete being, can only advance by plunging into the identity of being and non-being, of being and nothingness, inasmuch as the being of being (that is, the ultimate ontological power constituent of each and every concrete existent) is intrinsically finite. The phrase "the being of being" is meaningful only when referred to the world, because it is, in the wake of the great modern *cogito* principle, a being-conscious (*Bewusstsein*) of the world. The most drastic formulation of immanentism (which is simultaneously the sheerest expression of constitutive atheism) is a total semantic and ontological inver-

351

sion of the formula of traditional idealism. This traditional idealist formula read: "It is unthinkable that there could be anything beyond mind." The most drastic immanentist formula reads: "It is unthinkable that there could be anything beyond the world." And this immanentist formula, in effect, simply pushes to its extreme limit the internal logic of the idealist formula. Even the self has meaning only as a "relation to the world" for it is that void which is constantly crisscrossed by the pattern of lines or networks of this very relation.[31]

We can thus see that modern philosophy has run the entire gamut of its evolution with this revelation of active nothingness (*das nichtende Nichts*) as the essence of the *cogito* and of the freedom that is the radically constitutive element and dimension of that *cogito. This freedom, being essentially inclined to the finite and taking its very meaning from that finite cannot permit, under any circumstances, any transition to the infinite;* and consequently it cannot opt for the Absolute either: any effort in that direction is hopeless and meaningless from the outset, whether it be undertaken by Descartes, by Kant, by Hegel, or by anyone else down to and including Gabriel Marcel, Paul Tillich, and the death-of-God theologians. If non-being is the constitutive element of the very meaning and bias of consciousness (and consequently of freedom), then every act of consciousness is a transition from a finite to a finite, from a nothingness to a nothingness in the continual flow of time. And although it *is* intelligible that this transition from one finite to another should "hold to" non-being and consequently involve, from time to time, a "choice" and a "leap"—the individual finite having been reduced to non-being by non-being and therefore lying in a state of indifference—it is absolutely impossible to make any sense, on this basis, of that "leap" of freedom which is the option or

[31] Sartre is therefore entirely consistent when he writes: "The first procedure of a philosophy ought to be to expel things from consciousness and to re-establish its true connection with the world, to know that consciousness is a positional consciousness *of* the world. All consciousness is positional in that it transcends itself in order to reach an object, and exhausts itself in this same positing" (*Being and Nothingness,* New York, 1966, p. 1xi).

choice of the Absolute. Once freedom is itself the ground of meaning and purpose, that freedom can choose only itself, making of its own nothingness the truth calculated to let itself be in the world that keeps slipping back into the same nothingness that honeycombs it too.[32]

Theology, like philosophy, is the product rather of internal logic than of praiseworthy motives. Now the internal logic of the modern principle of immanentism favors atheism, and a very specific type of atheism at that, the atheism expressive of the brooding of the human spirit over that nothingness that lurks in the depths of the finite in its infinite flux.

* * *

The endeavour of the death-of-God theologians to rediscover God by an acceptance of the drastic and consequential denial of God by the modern world and by modern thought is an illusory and foredoomed undertaking.[33] It is a "counsel of

[32] Sartre is determined to banish even the apparently positive status of Hegelian *Sein* (Being): "Negation here springs from a consciousness which is turned back toward the beginning. . . . Thus reversing the statement of Spinoza, we could say that every negation is determination. This means that being is prior to nothingness and establishes the ground for it. But by this we must understand not only that being has a logical precedence over nothingness but also that it is from being that nothingness derives concretely its efficacy. This is what we mean when we say that *nothingness haunts being*" (*Being and Nothingness*, p. 19). This is the key to the understanding of Sartre's basic principle: "Human freedom precedes essence in man and makes it possible; the essence of the human being is suspended in his freedom" (*ibid.*, p. 30). And further, he says: "Now freedom has no essence. It is not subject to any logical necessity; we must say of it what Heidegger said of the *Dasein* in general: 'In it existence precedes and commands essence'" (*ibid.*, p. 535; see also p. 541: "If the will is to be freedom, then it is of necessity negativity and the power of nihilation"). This doctrine coincides with the Hegelian doctrine that "the Spirit is the negative" and with the principle on which Heidegger has founded his entire system of thought since *Sein und Zeit*: "Das *Wesen* des Daseins liegt in seiner Existenz" ("The *essence* of there-being lies in its existence") (*Was ist Metaphysik?*, p. 13).

[33] There is, however, a new "living God" current which is beginning to run strong in theological circles in the United States. The "living God" theologians foresee the supersession of the death-of-God theology.

despair," as witless as attempting to restore life by recourse to still larger doses of the lethal poison. It is a matter of taste and circumstances whether this kind of theology may perhaps be apologetically effective in rousing interest in religious problems in certain circles less sensitive to basic questions; but the method of the death-of-God theologians is vitiated by a total absence of any consistency or solidity, theological or speculative. The "death-of-God" is simply the logical conclusion of the principle of immanentism which is itself a quite meaningless principle: for the nothingness out of which consciousness is moulded must inevitably drag the mind back down into nothingness after each and every one of the mind's doughty upward sallies; indeed it is unintelligible how the mind could ever sally forth from such a bleak starting point as the vacuum of the *cogito-volo* to procure itself a "world" at all: the world appears rather as a foreign aggressor and even so it is unintelligible how that world could be snatched out of the starkly anterior void of nothingness.[34] For a mind that is a "being-unto-death" (*Sein zum Tode*), everything must necessarily evaporate into fortuitous and flimsy, futile relations, if there can even be any question of relations at all in such an outlook. The theology of Tillich, Bonhoeffer, and the new negativist theologians has irremediably lost, as the penalty of its own internal logic, all grasp of the transcendence of God; and this theology is all the less capable of giving any real meaning to the Nicene formulation of the doctrine of the Incarnation. Once the principle has been posited that the mind, consciousness, is a negative entity, the one inescapable consequence is the total inability to grapple with being, to relate to being: the ultimate issue must be a "sheer gazing" (Hegel's *rein zusehen*) and the act of be-ing can be nothing but an awaiting-of-death or a letting-oneself-die (as indicated in Heidegger's phrase *Sein zum Tode,* being-unto-death). But has

(See C. J. Curtis, " 'The Living God' Theology," in *The Ecumenist,* vol. 1, 1966, pp. 1 ff.).

[34] Sartre is therefore in error in here abandoning the Hegelian (purely logical) priority of being over non-being and claiming to ground nothingness in being, in the phrase: "Non-being exists only on the surface of being" (*op. cit.,* p. 19).

freedom any meaning when defined as "being-unto-death"? Can the Heideggerian theologians impart any genuine meaning to a "definition" of the being of man when that being is bounded by the horizons of the world?[35] What meaning can attach to the vast age from Adam to Christ if Fall and Redemption be alike restricted to the dimension of temporal immanence?

* * *

We have concentrated on the thought of Bonhoeffer and especially Tillich as the most direct sources of Robinson. But our diagnosis applies, without any substantial modification, to the other death-of-God theologians such as J. Hromavka of Prague, the CFK group[36] and the large and lively Anglo-American group whose sometimes fantastically titled works provide an impressive confirmation of our diagnosis. We might here mention Paul van Buren's *The Secular Meaning of the Gospel* (New York and London, 1966), Gabriel Vahanian, *The Death of God* (New York, 1966), Thomas Altizer, *The Gospel of Christian Atheism* (Philadelphia, 1966), Kenneth Hamilton, *Revolt Against Heaven* (Grand Rapids, 1965), William Hamilton, *The New Essence of Christianity* (New York, 1966).

I would like to express my thanks to Dr. A. Gibson for having provided me with the works of these American Death-of-God theologians and for having translated this paper into English for me.

---

[35] "If referred to myself alone, I lose my reality, and that means that I die. Heidegger's definition of existence in terms of a being (*Seiende*) operating with reference to Being (*Sein*) is applicable only to the broken man and only to the extent that that broken man has already squandered his existence. This sort of man may well be said to attain to his 'true being' in death and only in death. But this true being, this reality can with equal justice be said not to be the reality of his specifically human existence nor the true being of the creature fashioned in the image of God" (E. Resiner, *Der Dämon und sein Bild*).

[36] See R. Gerhardson, *Christen und Kommunisten,* Gütersloh, 1966, pp. 29 ff.

17.

SOME PHILOSOPHICAL CONTRIBUTIONS TO THEOLOGICAL RENEWAL

EUGENE R. FAIRWEATHER

1.

THE theme of this congress is the renewal of the Church. The theme of this essay is the renewal of theology. The professional theologian is tempted to view the two themes as one. The ordinary working Christian is more likely to wonder what connection there can be between them. Perhaps we can best begin our exploration by trying to set theological renewal in its place in the total renewal of the Church.

By way of a preliminary description, let us say that theology is the ordered endeavour to understand the world of grace as disclosed to faith. In other words, when the believer "does theology," he is trying to grasp intellectually the divine life and love which he first apprehends in a faithful listening to the Word of God.

It is surely as natural for faith to seek understanding as it is for hope to work towards realization, or for love to express itself in worship and service. Leslie Dewart has made the point effectively:

The appeal of the apostolic and early Christian Gospel pertained to the order of *praxis*, that is, existential engagement. . . . There-

356

fore, it called for a certain decision, namely, the decision of faith. But this meant the resolve to exist in the light of a certain understanding of the present situation. The Christian commitment, thus, unlike adherence to, say, a national religion, naturally inclined its practitioner to speculation. . . . For to exist in the light of any concept of existence is already to have entered into a process of conceptual development—and theorizing is but a mode of conceptual elaboration.[1]

In thus following the inherent tendency of his faith to pursue understanding, the believer benefits both himself and others. In the words of the most eminent of Canadian theologians, Bernard Lonergan:

The situation of one who understands is always better than that of one who does not understand, whether it is a matter of grasping truths, of teaching the truth to others, of the movement of his own inmost will, or of the giving of advice and direction to others. And thus, the more theological understanding extends to the whole of revelation, the more fully revelation itself is grasped and taught, and the more faithfully the whole of human life in all its aspects is directed to its final and supernatural end.[2]

But what is good for the believer is presumably good for the Church herself and will contribute to her renewal. Of course, neither theology nor any other Christian activity can by itself bring true renewal to the Church. Renewal springs from the gift of the Spirit, not from human enterprise. But one sign of the hidden Pentecostal stream which constantly enlivens the Church is surely the concern of theologians to renew their own special contribution to the Church's total life. The Spirit wills action, not inertia, and "*quietismus intellectualis*"—the phrase is Lonergan's[3]—is as far as any other form of quietism from genuine reliance on the Spirit's leading.

But just what kind of activity does theological renewal de-

---

[1] *The Future of Belief*, New York, 1966, pp. 135 f.
[2] *De Deo Trino*, part IIa, edit. 3a, Rome, 1964, pp. 12 f.
[3] *Ibid.*, p. 59.

mand? We may at once pose a double negative. On the one hand, renewal is not sheer innovation. On the other hand, renewal is not a mere substitution of new verbal formulations for old.

It is, I think, widely—if sometimes only tacitly—taken for granted that to renew theology is just to say something new and different. Some prophets of renewal do not seem to mind much what is said, provided only that it has not been said before—at any rate, by theologians. But to equate renewal with sheer innovation is to lose sight of the historical commitment inherent to Christian faith and life. If the word "Christianity" means anything definite at all, it means the acceptance of Jesus Christ as the key to the meaning of our existence. Christian theological renewal, then, must surely take the form of a renewed insight into the reality disclosed in Jesus Christ. To renew theology is to see him more clearly and to understand him more deeply, not to replace him by some other object of belief. Theology must indeed be "radical" in its effort to penetrate to the very roots of faith, but we should be wary of the kind of "radicalism" that makes a profession out of tearing up those roots and discarding them.

At the same time, it is not enough to view renewal as nothing more than an exercise in theological salesmanship—the dressing up of old theologies in new wrappings. If there is a true and deep continuity in Christian theology, there is also an element of novelty in all good theological work. Theology is more than a set of theses, established once for all and put into textbooks for students to memorize. Certainly, theology embodies its conclusions in propositions, and the theological propositions of the past are indispensable guides for the present and the future. But theology itself is nothing less than a sustained exploration of the reality given in revelation—a thinking through of God's self-disclosure with a view to the fullest possible understanding—and each theologian has to undertake that exploration for himself where he is, which cannot be precisely where theologians of past ages were. In at least one respect, the *Summa Theologiae* of Thomas Aquinas is surely

358

the acme of good theology—namely, in its skilful exploitation of the technique of the *quaestio* to display theology, not just as something we learn, but as something we do. (In passing, let me remark that there could hardly be a more conspicuous *corruptio optimi* than a *Synopsis totius Summae Theologicae* or, worse still, *A Tour of the Summa*![4] St. Thomas was evidently aware that theology is constantly renewed in the doing, in the theologian's personal effort to make the reality of revelation his own possession. But that effort involves much more than the designing of a new package.

In observing what theological renewal is not, I have found myself at least beginning to suggest what, in my view, it is. To sum up what I have been trying to say, I can hardly do better than to quote some pertinent words from Karl Rahner's appeal for a reform of theological teaching:

We must not suppose that the difference we are looking for need and can consist of a merely literary, verbal or rhetorical adaptation of an old theology to our time, in new "applications," "outlooks," or corollaries in the practical order. It is much more a matter here of a dogmatic theology, a genuinely scientific one (in the sense that it listens with exactness and seriousness, and reflects with exactness on what it hears), whose concern it is to be adequate to reality; for then it can allow itself to try to be adequate to its time—a preoccupation full of danger and generally quite unprofitable. For if it is in fact more intimately adequate to reality (than it has been), it spontaneously becomes adequate to its time: it makes the time its own and need not worry about suiting itself to the time, always after the event.[5]

We can now formulate the problem to which the body of this essay is to be addressed. Our purpose is to identify some significant contributions of philosophy to theological renewal. We have found some reason, however, to believe that the way

[4] I can certify that these works exist, but charity forbids any further identification.

[5] Karl Rahner, S.J., *Theological Investigations,* vol. I, London, 1961, p. 10.

to renewal lies through the more faithful and more intelligent doing of the ordinary tasks of theology, rather than through the planning and advertising of special programmes. Our question, then, is really this: What sort of contribution can philosophy be expected to make to the doing of theology? To find the answer to that question is already to know what philosophy can do for theological renewal.

Only one thing remains to be done before we get down to our main task: we must establish the sense in which the word "philosophy" is to be used. Let me make it clear that by "philosophy" I mean the ordered endeavour to reach a comprehensive, suprascientific or "metaphysical" understanding of man and his world through the exercise of human reason on the data of ordinary human experience. It is with the relation of philosophy in this sense to theology that I am concerned here. Thus the question which I am posing can be rephrased in this form: What sort of contribution can a metaphysical understanding of the world of nature be expected to make to theological understanding of the world of grace?

2.

In order to answer the question of the relation of philosophy to theology, we must first raise the larger question of the relation of human reason in general to faith. Is faith in any way dependent on the discoveries of human reason—as distinct from the processes of human reasoning, which even the most anti-rationalistic of theologians can hardly avoid altogether—either for its validation or for its clarification? For our present purpose, we need to give particular attention to two influential answers to this question, both of which exclude any conceivable contribution to theology from the side of metaphysical philosophy. One of these answers is based on an analysis of the content of faith and one on a particular conception of the unique role of faith in the Christian life.

According to the first answer, reason as such is not essentially alien to faith. The only form of reasoning, however, which is

360

recognized as relevant to Christianity as an historical faith is historical reasoning. The American theologian Carl Michalson put this view clearly when he wrote: "The logic of faith is a fully historical logic, which means that faith ought to be interpreted as history, with the kind of reasoning appropriate to historical reality."[6] Metaphysical reasoning is thus alleged to be ruled out by the nature of the object of faith.

According to the second answer, faith is wholly independent of reason. It requires neither historical reasoning to support it nor metaphysical reasoning to elucidate it. Indeed, to make any such suggestion is to cast doubt on the truth of justification by faith alone.[7] Metaphysical reasoning is thus alleged to be ruled out by the nature of faith itself as response to grace.

If we were satisfied with either of these answers, that would obviously put an end to our quest. We should have to concede that there was no room in theology for metaphysical reflection. But is it really clear that either answer is forced on us by the character of Christian faith? May it not be that, on the contrary, that faith has intellectual consequences which the advocates of these views have failed to appreciate?

Let us pursue the problem a little further by investigating the relation between faith and history. It is hard to deny that the exponents of theological historicism are right in calling attention to the place of historical affirmations in the Christian message. The Christian proclamation, like the prophetic proclamation which it brings to fulfilment, can fairly be described as the Gospel of divine action in human history. In it God is represented as dealing historically with man—as acting in particular human events and speaking through particular human words. Man is not somehow extracted from his historical setting in order to receive divine truth. Even before the

[6] "The Task of Systematic Theology Today," *The Centennial Review of Arts and Science,* 8 (1964), 189.

[7] Rudolf Bultmann exemplifies this thoroughgoing rejection of both historical demonstration and ontological speculation. (Whether his reliance on a Heideggerian doctrine of human existence in his hermeneutics is fully consistent with his rejection of speculative philosophy is another question.) Some illuminating comments on his attitude towards reason will be found in Basil Mitchell, "Theology and Metaphysics," *Union Seminary Quarterly Review,* 20 (1964–1965), 9 ff.

incarnation of the Word, biblical faith can fairly be called strongly "incarnational" in its sense of God's active presence in human life.

At the same time, we must not miss the point that the presence which the biblical faith apprehends in the midst of human history is the presence of one who transcends history. The Lord of Israel's faith and hope is no merely immanent power; on the contrary, his action encompasses history and penetrates it (so to speak) "from beyond." I simply cannot follow Harvey Cox's philosophical mentor, the Dutch scholar Cornelis van Peursen, when he writes:

The word "God" in the Bible has no meaning as such. But we too often give it a false, supernatural meaning. Then our interpretation stands between us and the Bible itself. . . . The story of the word "God" is that it has no given meaning, but acquires a meaning in history, as it is presented in the Bible in many ways. There are always people who are saying: "It is He again; it is the Name." And then history is made, humanity progresses, and the perspective of hope is revealed. . . . The Name is not a doctrine: it is a power overwhelming human reality, but within history, not as a metaphysical control. It is "God-with-us" (Immanu-El). "God-with-us" is a Name which manifests itself not in a supernatural but in a normal way, as a new meaning of daily events.[8]

We may agree that the word "God" acquires its familiar meaning in history—but that meaning is a metaphysical one. In Israel, Yahweh comes to be known as the one who has performed a uniquely divine deed, the act of creation itself. In other words, the God of Israel comes to be identified as the Creator of heaven and earth.[9] "All the gods of the peoples are idols; but the Lord made the heavens."[10]

The point may seem obvious enough, but it would be a serious error to underestimate the ingenuity of the antimeta-

[8] "Man and Reality—the History of Human Thought," *Student World,* 56 (1963), 20 f.

[9] A good account of the development of Hebrew belief in Yahweh will be found in Joseph Schreiner, "The Development of the Israelite 'Credo'," *Concilium,* 20 (New York, 1967), 29–40.

[10] Ps. 96, 5.

physical interpreters of the biblical faith. Thanks to their hermeneutical magic, they can readily show us how the biblical writers said one thing and meant another. Carl Michalson provides a good example of their technique:

A strictly historical hermeneutic allows a text to be treated as history. This does not mean judging the text by standards of plausibility imported from outside the text. It means letting the text supply the basis for its own interpretation. When this is done, one discovers that the Old Testament, when it speaks of creation, may not really be engaging in cosmology, as more technologically oriented ages seem to have inferred. It may rather be interpreting how the historical destiny of a minor people can be a mandate with a universal validity. . . . When the apostles talk about God, they may not be referring to his being, as metaphysical philosophies have conditioned us to suppose, piously drawing our attention to realms beyond our history.[11]

To deal adequately with these suggestions would require a thorough examination of all the pertinent biblical texts, sentence by sentence. Such an examination is, of course, beyond the scope of this essay. However, we should at least glance at one or two representative passages of Scripture. Take, for instance, the exclamation of the prophet: "Have you not known? Have you not heard? The Lord is the everlasting God, the Creator of the ends of the earth. He does not faint or grow weary, his understanding is unsearchable."[12] Does it make sense to treat these lines and the great religious poem to which they belong as nothing more than an indirect assertion of the historical destiny of Israel? Can we seriously claim that their author did not intend to make a significant affirmation about God and his world? Or take the Pauline confession: "Although there may be so-called gods in heaven or on earth—as indeed there are many 'gods' and many 'lords'—yet for us there is one God, the Father, from whom are all things and for whom we exist, and one Lord, Jesus Christ, through whom are all

[11] *Art. cit.,* 190.
[12] Is. 40, 28.

things and through whom we exist."[13] Can we plausibly argue that St. Paul was really talking about a purely historical experience of "God," with no metaphysical overtones whatsoever? Must we not read his words as a judgment on the ontological status of the "gods" of sinful man's imagination and a counterclaim for the God of Christian faith? Surely these considerations alone are sufficient to undermine Michalson's proposal of a "strictly historical hermeneutic."

We can now weigh the two views of the nature of theology which stem from the conflicting interpretations of the biblical faith just outlined. On the one hand, Michalson argues:

One of the significant points of arrival in contemporary theology is the almost general consensus that the reality of faith is historical. . . . The consequence for theology is that physicalistic concerns, hitherto included by theology in the discussion of such topics as creation, providence, miracle, and sacrament, ought to be eliminated in the interests of dominantly historical concerns. . . . The being of God-in-himself, his nature and attributes, the nature of the church, the nature of man, the pre-existent nature of Christ— all these conjectural topics which have drawn theology into a realm of either physical or metaphysical speculation remote from the habitation of living men should be abandoned.[14]

On the other hand, the English theologian F. R. Tennant writes:

I need scarcely remark . . . that theology and philosophy are largely identical in that theology is essentially metaphysics. Not a single theological statement of alleged fact—no statement that is really of theological interest—can be affirmed, that is not at the same time a metaphysical statement.[15]

We might well hesitate to subscribe *ex animo* to either expression of opinion exactly as it stands. I suggest, nonetheless, that the latter statement is much closer than the former to the deepest concerns of the biblical writers.

[13] 1 Cor. 8, 5 f.
[14] *Loc. cit.*
[15] "The Aim and Scope of Philosophy of Religion," *The Expositor*, 8th series, no. 32 (August, 1913), 142.

364

I move on now to a brief consideration of the relation between faith and reason. It is, of course, obvious that the Christian Gospel presents itself as based, not on human reason, but on the Word of God. It is from God's self-disclosure that man learns to recognize his hand in historical events and to discern his character and purpose. It may still be true, however, that reason has a significant part to play in man's apprehension of God's self-revelation.

I believe that in fact reason necessarily performs a twofold function in man's apprehension of revelation. If a man is to take firm hold of the message of faith, he must be able to see that message as something which is really addressed to him and as something which is meaningful to him as a human person. Admittedly, whatever "motives of credibility" may come into play in the genesis of man's response of faith to the Word of God, that response is ultimately the effect of the outward testimony of the Word and the inward testimony of the Spirit. But the outward testimony of the Word embodies historical affirmations, open to historical criticism, while the inward testimony of the Spirit can move a man to faith only insofar as he can recognize in the Word of faith a truth which is genuinely pertinent to his own being and life. In other words, the act of faith is inseparable from two acts of reason: on the one hand, the affirmation that the events of the Gospel have indeed happened and, on the other hand, the judgment that the message of God's gracious action is commensurate with what man can know of himself and of the outreach of his mind and heart.

If this view of faith is a sound one—and I do not see how we can reject it without making faith something less than a responsible and personal act on man's part—the consequences for theology are more or less obvious. From the two acts of reason which are bound up with the act of faith there stem two essential processes of theological thought. On the one hand, in what we may call the act of historical reason, we find the beginning of that process of historical exploration which is indispensable for establishing the subject-matter of theological reflection. On the other hand, in what we may call the act of philosophical reason, we find the beginning of that process of systematic explanation which is necessary if the subject matter of theology is to be made intelligible to the human mind. Clearly, a theology which is to be adequate to its role in the life of the believer and the life of the community of faith must embrace both processes within its range.

We now seem to be within reach of a preliminary statement, at any rate, of the sort of contribution that philosophy can be expected to make to theological understanding. That contribution will be found to lie within the area of systematic explanation of the content of faith. Philosophy does not create that content, which is given solely in God's self-revealing and self-communicating action. What philosophy can and must do is develop the picture of the world and man without which the Word of God must appear to be spoken into a void.

Given the view of the content of Christian faith which has at least begun to take shape in this essay, we can indicate further the way in which such a picture can be expected to function in the effective doing—that is to say, in the constant renewal—of theology. To put it in a single sentence, the essential content of Christian faith is the self-giving of the transcendent God to man in the history of salvation. From that content three questions immediately arise to which philosophical reflection is clearly pertinent: first, a theological question, then an anthropological question, and finally a soteriological question. In the final section of this discussion I shall try to indicate more precisely what sort of question I have in mind and to offer historical illustrations of the way in which philosophy can help the theologian formulate an answer to them.

3.

The primary concern of Christian theology is obviously the theological issue in the strict sense—namely, the doctrine of God. If everything else that theology touches upon is seen in relation to God, then nothing else in theology will make sense unless the doctrine of God finds intelligible expression. That cannot happen, however, apart from an at least inchoate philosophy.

The problem can be briefly stated. God does not present himself to us as one of the many objects of our common human experience. How then do we know what it means to speak of "God"? What is it that enables us to think of a particular event as an act of "God" or a particular utterance as a word of "God"? Can we expect the answer to emerge somehow from the Word of God itself?

What I take to be the right sort of answer to these questions is given by the English theologian Austin Farrer, when he writes:

Those who accept a revealed theology place among its articles the Creator of heaven and earth; this is the foundation upon which the rest is built. To know God as the absolute origin of all things is to know Him as God simply; the further revealed truths are concerned with what God, being such, has in particular done and said and, by these actions and words, shown or declared Himself to be. But these further revelations presuppose the first; nor is it easy to see how it itself can be a revelation in quite the same sense. . . . Unless I had some mental machinery for thinking the bare notion of God, could I recognize His revelatory action as that of God? That machinery might never have worked before. Let us suppose that it works now for the first time, when the revelation occurs. Still it does work now, and it is possible to study it and see how it works and what is the notion it produces. As we shall learn, to study this notion of God, of a supreme and original being, is to study what the mind can only see in and through the general nature of finite and dependent being. And this is to study rational theology.[16]

This answer seems to be consistent with the situation described in the Bible itself. At one stage in its history, Israel clearly identified Yahweh as one "god" among many, and

[16] For an illuminating discussion in the perspective of a particular theological programme of the second aspect of this question, see Karl Rahner, S.J., "Theology and Anthropology," in T. Patrick Burke (ed.), *The Word in History*, New York, 1966, pp. 1–23.

thus as something quite different from what we mean by "God." Eventually, however, the faith of Israel came to recognize the unique identity of Yahweh as Creator of all things. We may grant that this identification was reached by an inspired leap from the revelation of his purposeful power. It is, however, properly a philosophical notion—a recognition of the origin of contingent and finite beings—and for its adequate clarification it demands philosophical investigation of the meaning of necessary and contingent being.

It is not surprising, then, that the greatest of Christian theological syntheses should have embodied a metaphysic of Creator and creature—that is to say, of necessary and infinite Being and of contingent and finite beings. It is not always noted, however—despite the heroic labours of Etienne Gilson—that this metaphysic was developed under the influence of biblical faith, and more particularly in the Christian tradition itself, to meet the exigencies of theological understanding, and that, further, in its essential character it is significantly different from those Greek metaphysical systems from which it derived so many of its categories. To this development, of course, Augustine and Thomas Aquinas, in their different ways—just how different those ways were is a matter of current debate[17]—were the major Christian contributors. Thanks to this development, it became possible for Christian theologians to "place" God philosophically, and so to define the conditions of intelligible discourse about him.

I reiterate the point that the teaching of Augustine and Aquinas is significantly different from Greek ontologies—not in order to prove anything about Greek philosophers, but to show the significance of philosophy for theology. Augustine and Aquinas did not take over Greek metaphysics as an apologetic device or even because they were infatuated with Greek metaphysics. Rather, it must be said that in an important sense they did not take over Greek metaphysics at all. (A philosophy in which *ipsum esse* is the first principle is clearly

17 For an instructive account of these two processes, see Bernard Lonergan, *op. cit.*, pp. 33–41.

different from one based on the notion of the "One" or of the "Good" or of "Thought thinking itself.") What they did was construct a new metaphysics—to a considerable extent, be it granted, out of Greek materials—because Christian theology needed an ontology and they could not find a satisfactory one anywhere at hand.

Surely their instinct was right. Without at least the rudiments of a theistic metaphysic, there could be no clear, explicit faith in the reality of God and no worship of him unmarred by idolatry. Without the systematic elaboration of such a metaphysic, theology could not proceed with its task. In our own day, theologians have been learning or relearning this lesson the hard way, from the rather confused utterances of a John Robinson or the clear-cut arguments of a Paul van Buren. However we may assess the theological explorations of Leslie Dewart, Schubert Ogden, and other contemporary critics of "absolute" or "classical" theism, we must credit them with having seen clearly that no theology can function without a working philosophy of creation and its Creator. It is hardly too much to say that not only the renewal but the very survival of theology depends on an effective grappling with this question.

I turn now to what I believe to be the major anthropological question raised by the Christian faith. The Gospel of divine action in human history is essentially the message of God's self-communication to man in grace. If this gift, however, cannot be made intelligible to man, both as *gift* and as gift to *man,* the Gospel must fail to touch him. To make it intelligible, however, requires an at least inchoate philosophy.

Once again, the problem can be briefly put. Grace is offered to man as a gift which fulfils his being. In other words, it is at once gratuitous and pertinent to man. A twofold question immediately arises: How is its gratuitousness to be expressed without obscuring its meaning for man? Conversely, how is its significance for man to be expressed without obscuring its gratuitousness?

Both aspects of the problem appear more or less clearly in

369

Scripture itself. On the one hand, the Bible speaks of the sovereign freedom of God's dealings with men. Man can only attain to communion with the God of unapproachable majesty through God's own free act. On the other hand, both the Old and New Testaments take it for granted that the friendship of God is the ultimate good for man, and that without it he is lost and miserable. In sum, man is earthly and creaturely, not divine, and yet he finds his true life in communion with the divine Creator. Here again, we seem to have the elements of a philosophical question—an aspect of the problem of necessary and infinite Being and contingent and finite beings.

Since, in the concrete economy of salvation, grace is restoration of a communion broken by sin, it is tempting to seek the explanation of the gratuitousness of grace in man's sinfulness. In relatively modern times, this line has been taken by eminent exponents of what they at least took to be the Augustinian tradition. Its clear disadvantages, however, should make us pause. For one thing, it places the gulf between God and man in man's moral failure rather than in his very creatureliness, thus losing sight of a contrast which is crucial for biblical faith. Moreover, it tends to foster the notion that it is only in his failures that man needs God.

Augustine himself, for all his preoccupation with the dialectic of sin and grace, seems to have been wiser than his would-be disciples, distinguishing as he did between God's gift of being and his gift of sonship to himself.[18] It was Aquinas, however, who achieved a fuller clarification, through his exploitation of the Aristotelian notion of "nature."

I must emphasize the fact that this philosophical development was the response to a genuine need of theology, not an intrusive philosophical influence. Other medieval theologians dealt decisively with the problem of determinism as raised by Aristotelian views of nature without developing anything like

[18] This summary is intended to reflect the discussion of the one Christian mystery—Trinity, grace, incarnation—in Karl Rahner, S.J., *Theological Investigations,* Vol. IV, London, 1966, pp. 60–73. One might also point to the much debated threefold structure of the *Summa Theologica* of Aquinas.

the Thomist doctrine of nature and the supernatural. If Aquinas, on the contrary, worked out the kind of theory he did, the most plausible explanation is that he saw the need of it in theology. It is important, further, to note that the point of the theological doctrine of nature is not the fixity of specific creaturely natures but rather the drawing of the line between creature and Creator. What matters is to see that no created nature, whether contingent in existence alone or also in essence (to borrow Leslie Dewart's formula)[19] can enjoy communion with God apart from God's gift.

St. Thomas's way of developing the idea of nature and grace —at any rate, as I read it—is instructive. On the one hand, he stresses the gratuitousness of God's self-communication to the creature; on the other hand, he asserts man's natural desire for the vision of God. At the same time, he refuses to draw from that desire any stronger conclusion than that man is capable of the vision of God. Thus he leaves us with a paradox: nature desires grace, yet grace is not within the power of nature.[20]

This paradox was to prove too strong meat for most of his successors. No doubt they were concerned with a quite real danger—namely, that a natural desire for the vision of God might be interpreted as a claim on God.[21] But whatever excuses can be found, it must surely be said that Cajetan and Bañez and a host of others have seriously minimized Aquinas's own teaching on the desire of nature for communion with God. Perhaps it would not be unfair to detect in such a tendency a potential root of atheism, since God is made to seem something of an "optional extra" for man! Happily, in our time we find a number of theologians—in some cases at least under the

[19] See *The Future of Belief;* Schubert M. Ogden, *The Reality of God and Other Essays,* New York, 1966.

[20] Dewart's comments in *The Future of Belief,* pp. 207 ff., do not seem to me to bear on St. Thomas's actual doctrine. See p. 210: ". . . . nature ceases in every way to be opposed to grace: it is naturally apt to receive grace, because that is how it was in fact created." Surely that is one of Aquinas's own points.

[21] In other words, they were afraid of giving encouragement to Baianism.

influence of the notable Christian philosopher, Maurice Blondel—regaining St. Thomas's courage and squarely facing the paradox of nature and grace. It is, I suggest, through the kind of philosophy of the human creature which is involved in that paradox that theology can regain a full awareness of the existential pertinence of the Gospel.

I turn finally to the question of soteriology. The economy of salvation can properly be described as a continuing inter-action of divine grace and human response. If it is to be intel-ligible—not to say, credible—it must cohere with a rationally defensible view of God and man. To clarify that coherence, however, demands an at least inchoate philosophy.

The problem can be put in these terms. The biblical account of God's action in human history describes a number of events which, at any rate at first glance, seem to conflict with the demands of human conscience, of common sense, or of philoso-phical reason. Granted that at least some of these events are integral to the Christian Gospel, the question must then arise: How are they to be understood as at once appropriate to God and meaningful for man? Unless that question is answered, the biblical narratives are in danger of being dismissed as fanciful, or even immoral, myths.

The biblical writers themselves at least implicitly raise the problem we are considering. It is true that they emphasize the inscrutability of God's ways as inseparable from the tran-scendent mystery of his purpose. At the same time, their emphasis on the righteousness of God as the ultimate ground and highest sanction of human morality and their insistence on the wisdom of God as the highest wisdom would seem to make the question of the justice and rationality of God's alleged actions or commands a legitimate question. It is not surprising then to find that, through the centuries, Christian theologians should have proved sensitive to moral and rational criticism of the biblical history.

Some of these theologians, indeed, have in the end managed to take a high line against rational and humanitarian consider-ations. The English theologian Henry Mansel, for example, could try to undermine ethical criticism of the Old Testament by developing a theory of "moral miracles"—of divine breaches of the moral law, analogous to suspensions of physical laws—though we may note that even he (being at bottom a rationalistic Anglican!) sought a philosophical justification for his theory in the metaphysical agnosticism of Sir William Hamilton.[22] But his humanitarian critic, John Stuart Mill, is surely truer to the great tradition of Christian theology in his refusal to allow sheer unintelligibility, metaphysical or moral, to be overcome by blind faith.

Perhaps the most notable instance of an appeal to a philosophy of God and man to bring out the inherent intelligibility of the Gospel is to be found in Anselm's *Cur Deus Homo*. There he faces the criticism that the incarnation and passion of the Son of God are unworthy of the divine nature—in fact, that they are so incongruous as to appear mythological. He responds rather more constructively than some, at least, of our modern "demythologizers"; instead of denying the facts, he tries to put them in a perspective in which they can begin to make sense. His reply takes the form of an application of a metaphysic of cosmic order—Augustinian in inspiration—which he has already hinted at in his *Monologion* and worked out in considerable detail in three later dialogues.[23] Far from being unworthy of God, he argues, Bethlehem and Calvary are the expression of divine justice. By counterbalancing—in the only way in which it can be adequately counterbalanced—the injustice of men, the satisfaction of Christ restores the moral and rational order of the universe. Thus the divine economy of salvation is fully compatible with the nature of God and the essential principles of his dealings with his human creatures.

[22] There is a good account of Mansel's theory and of his controversies with J. S. Mill and F. D. Maurice in W. R. Matthews, *The Religious Philosophy of Dean Mansel*, London, 1956.

[23] On Anselm's philosophy of order, see R. D. Crouse, "The Augustinian Background of St. Anselm's Concept 'Justitia'," *Canadian Journal of Theology*, 4 (1958), 111–119; E. R. Fairweather, "Truth, Justice and Moral Responsibility in the Thought of St. Anselm," in *L'Homme et son destin*, Louvain, 1960, pp. 385–391.

Anselm's method of argument was to be criticized by later theologians, as at least apparently compromising the freedom of God in his acts of grace. Nonetheless, it must surely be admitted that he was impressively aware of one essential task of theology—namely, the elucidation of the economy of salvation, which all too often is left suspended in the air like angels in a Christmas "crib," by means of an intelligible doctrine of the Creator and the creature. Today, in Karl Rahner's call for a due "demythologizing" of Christology and eschatology, which I regard as one of his most important contributions to contemporary theology, we surely find a revival of the same concern. I suggest that along this line, as well as along the theological and anthropological lines which I have already discussed, there lies real hope of deepened theological understanding and genuine renewal.

4.

My three examples of the role of philosophy in theological understanding and renewal have been taken from the past. My choice was not altogether arbitrary. Not only were all three examples cases of epoch-making advance in the history of theology, but it is generally easier to evaluate intellectual achievements from a certain distance in time.

We cannot rest, however, on the memory of past theological achievements. However highly we value what our predecessors have done, we cannot evade our obligation to do in our day what they did in theirs—namely, to think through the issues of faith in the light of new questionings and fresh accessions of truth. This is not to say that truth cannot be carried from the past into the present, but it is to say that we cannot effectively assimilate it from any other standpoint in human history than our own. Furthermore, it must be admitted that—as pretty well any textbook of dogmatic theology will show us plainly enough—the philosophical development of theology in the past has been decidedly uneven. Thus there remain at least some significant areas of theology where we can hope to break new ground—perhaps with the help of hitherto unused philosophical tools.

As we set about these tasks, there is one supremely important lesson to be learned from that past which we have briefly considered. The history of the mutual relations of theology and philosophy suggests that philosophical contributions to theological understanding and renewal seldom (if ever) come ready-made. As the example of the two greatest constructive minds in the history of Latin theology goes to show, theologians have to wrestle hard and long to shape adequate philosophical implements for their task. It has been in genuine dialogue with philosophy, not in the submissive listening to a philosophical monologue, that theology has found a real source of deeper understanding. The history of the past nineteen centuries strongly suggests that it is an illusion for Christians to expect to make easy and immediate use of secular philosophies in the clarification and communication of the Christian revelation.

The moral for the present seems obvious. If theology is to derive further benefits from philosophy, theologians must take up the challenge to take part in the ongoing philosophical quest. They are not simply to sit at the feet of the philosophers. Rather, they are to become philosophers themselves, striving for that fuller and deeper understanding of man and his world which will make possible a clearer apprehension of the Gospel of God's self-revelation to man in that world. Above all, they should avoid letting apologetic concerns drive them to ill-considered speculation and statement. Theology is concerned, not with what any hearers may find immediately meaningful or attractive, but with what is true and intelligible. I am confident that, if theologians themselves focus their energies on apprehending the Gospel in all its truth and intelligibility, they will not long lack serious and responsive hearers.

NOTES ON CONTRIBUTORS

M.-D. Chenu, O.P., b. 1895, Soisy-sur-Seine, France; entered the Dominicans 1913, taking his lectorship and doctorate at the Angelicum, Rome; he taught theology at the Saulchoir (Tournai and Etoilles) 1920–1942 and was rector 1932–1942; he was for a time president of the Société thomiste, and was founder and for many years editor of the *Bulletin thomiste;* he is currently living at the Couvent de Saint-Jacques in Paris.

Yves M.-J. Congar, O.P., b. 1904, Sedan, France; ordained 1930, professor of fundamental theology and ecclesiology at the Saulchoir (Tournai, Belgium) 1931–1954; interned at Colditz and Lubeck 1939–1945; contributor on an enormous scale to important journals, bulletins, dictionaries and lexicons; competent and influential theologian of Vatican II now living in the Dominican house in Strasbourg.

Cornelio Fabro, C.S.S., b. 1911 in Talmasson (Udine), Italy; priest of the order of Stigmatines, professor at the University Institute of Education, and director of the Institute of the History of Atheism, Rome.

Eugene R. Fairweather, b. 1920 in Ottawa, Canada; advanced studies in the University of Toronto, Trinity College, Toronto, Union Theological Seminary, New York, where he took his doctorate in 1949; ordained 1944; associate professor of Dogmatic Theology and Ethics, Trinity College, 1949–1964; Keble Professor of Divinity since 1964.

Arthur Gibson, b. 1922 in Granton, Ontario, Canada; advanced studies in the University of Toronto, Princeton University, the Russicum, Rome, under Gustav Wetter, 1950–1956, The

Gregorian, and Catholic University of America where he took his S.T.D. under Johannes Quasten in 1965, presenting a thesis on "Liturgical Authorship in St. Basil," ordained for the Archdiocese of Winnipeg, 1963; translator of Russian for the State Department, Washington, 1959–1965; professor of Church History, Catholic University, 1960–1965; professor of patristics, Graduate School of Theology, University of St. Michael's College, Toronto, since 1966; peritus at Vatican II, 1965; consultor to the Secretariat for Non-Believers since 1966.

Langdon Gilkey, b. 1919, Chicago; Ph.D. Columbia University, 1959; has taught at Union Theological Seminary and Vanderbilt University; he has been professor of theology, the Divinity School, University of Chicago since 1963.

Etienne Gilson, b. 1884, Paris; student at the University of Paris taking his agrégé in philosophy, 1907 and his doctorat ès lettres, 1913; professor of the history of mediaeval philosophy at Lille, 1913, Strasbourg, 1919, Paris, 1921, Collège de France, 1932; founder of the Pontifical Institute of Mediaeval Studies, 1929 and its director of studies to the present; member of the French Academy since 1946.

Rabbi Abraham Heschel, b. 1907, Warsaw, Poland; Ph.D. University of Berlin and special studies in Jewish philosophy at the Hochschule für die Wissenschaft des Judentums, Berlin, 1934; founder of the Institute of Jewish Learning, London, 1940; professor of Jewish ethics and mysticism at the Jewish Theological Seminary of America since 1945 and visiting professor at Stanford, the University of Minnesota, and Union Theological Seminary.

Paul-Émile Cardinal Léger, b. 1904 near Valleyfield, Canada; educated in the Grand Seminary of Montreal and the Institut Catholique, Paris; professor of philosophy in the Sulpician seminaries of Issy and Valleyfield; pastor (1933–1939) of the cathedral parish and rector of the seminary, Fukuoka, Japan. In 1947 he became rector of the Canadian College in Rome, in 1950 Archbishop of Montreal, and in 1953 Cardinal of the Church. In

378

1967, following the congress, he resigned his See in favor of missionary work in an African leper colony.

Bernard Lonergan, S.J., b. 1904 in Buckingham, P.Q., Canada; studies at Heythrop College, University of London and the Gregorian, Rome; ordained 1936; professor of dogmatic theology in Montreal, Toronto, and from 1953–1965 in Rome; he is at present located at Regis College, Toronto.

Henri de Lubac, S.J., b. 1896, France's most distinguished Jesuit theologian, resides as a private scholar at 4 Montée de la Fourvière, Lyon, producing in rapid succession the writings which are the admiration and despair of professional theologians. He holds an honorary professorship in the faculty of theology of the neigbouring University of Lyon.

E. L. Mascall, b. 1905; emeritus student of Christ Church, Oxford; an Anglican priest of the Oratory of the Good Shepherd; professor of Historical Theology in the University of London.

Anton C. Pegis, b. 1905 Milwaukee; Ph.D. University of Toronto, 1931; taught in Marquette and Fordham Universities; professor of the history of philosophy, Pontifical Institute of Mediaeval Studies since 1944 and president of the Institute 1946 to 1954; fellow of the Royal Society of Canada and past president of the American Catholic Philosophical Association.

Karl Rahner, S.J., b. 1904, Freiburg im Breisgau; novitiate 1922; ordained 1932; D. Theol., Innsbruck, 1936. He has lectured in dogmatic Theology at Innsbruck and is now at the Institut für Christliche Weltanschauung in Munich.

Stuart E. Rosenberg, b. 1922 in New York City, is Rabbi of the Beth Tzedic Congregation in Toronto, the largest Jewish congregation in Canada and one of the largest in North America. He is widely known as an outstanding scholar and spiritual leader. He holds M.A. and Ph.D. degrees from Columbia University, and is a graduate of the Jewish Theological Seminary of America, holding the degree of M.H.L. from that institution where a "Dr. Stuart E. Rosenberg Professorship in Jewish History" has been established in his honour. He has himself taught comparative religion and the philosophy of religion in the University of Rochester.

Edward Schillebeeckx, O.P., b. 1914, Antwerp, Belgium; doctorate in theology from Le Saulchoir, Etoilles, France; professor of dogmatic theology in the Dominican House of Studies, Louvain, 1943–57; since 1958, professor of dogmatic theology, history of theology, and Christian anthropology at the Catholic University of Nijmegen, Holland. He is editor-in-chief of *Tijdschrift voor geestelijk Leven* and co-editor of *Tijdschrift voor Theologie.*

Michael Schmaus, b. 1897, Oberbaar, Austria; studied at the University of Munich; professor of the history of philosophy at the Philosophical and Theological Seminary of Freising; professor of theology at the Universities of Prague, Münster, and Munich, until his retirement in 1966; rector of the University of Munich 1951–52; director of Grabmann-Institut, Munich, until 1966; visiting professor at St. Xavier College, Chicago, 1966–67; editor of *Münchener Theologische Zeitschrift, Beiträge zur Geschichte der Philosophie und Theologie der Mittelalters.*

Max Thurian, b. 1921, Geneva, Switzerland; took vows, or as he prefers to put it, made *engagements* in the Taizé Community, Burgundy, France, in 1949. He was companion and first disciple of Roger Schutz, the founder. Brothers Roger and Max were observers at Vatican II as guests of Cardinal Bea.